Violent Offenders and Their Victims

Violent Offenders and Their Victims

Restorative Justice through Mediation

Chad C. Breckenridge

LEXINGTON BOOKS
Lanham • Boulder • New York • London

Published by Lexington Books
An imprint of The Rowman & Littlefield Publishing Group, Inc.
4501 Forbes Boulevard, Suite 200, Lanham, Maryland 20706
www.rowman.com

Unit A, Whitacre Mews, 26-34 Stannary Street, London SE11 4AB

British Library Cataloguing in Publication Information Available

Library of Congress Cataloging-in-Publication Data

ISBN 978-1-4985-5851-8 (cloth : alk. paper)
ISBN 978-1-4985-5852-5 (electronic)

∞™ The paper used in this publication meets the minimum requirements of American National Standard for Information Sciences—Permanence of Paper for Printed Library Materials, ANSI/NISO Z39.48-1992.

Printed in the United States of America

For Sally
As always

Contents

Preface

My own journey in this writing, like much writing, begins in autobiography. Certainly, childhood experiences and rich family dynamics inform many of our adult choices and interests.

Not the least of these experiences was serving as a correctional officer at San Quentin State Prison in California, to meet my obligation as a conscientious objector during the Vietnam War, from 1970 through late 1971. This turned out, ironically, to be the most violent period in the history of the prison, and ultimately, I myself was the victim of violent crime, barely escaping with my life.

Denzin suggests, "Interpretive research begins and ends with the biography and the self of the researcher" (Denzin 1989, p. 41). Clinicians are always aware of the importance of their own biographical history and the use of the self in relation to the patient. As Denzin states, interpretive interactionism "works outward from the biography of the person" (Denzin 2001).

Additionally, I have been involved in the creation of documentary and portrait photography throughout my adult life. The subjective sense I had in doing this type of photography was reminiscent of the sense I had while engaged with the people described in this book.

This subjective sense in photography is nicely defined by the documentary photographer Dorothea Lange who had a great influence on me in terms of her approach. Her definition bears a remarkable similarity to the methodological definition in this project:

For me documentary photography is less a matter of subject and more a matter of approach. The important thing is not what's photographed but how. … My own approach is based upon three considerations. First—hands off! Whatever I photograph, I do not molest or tamper with or arrange. Second—a sense of place. Whatever I photograph, I try to picture as part of its surroundings, as having roots. Third—a sense of time. Whatever I photograph, I try to show as having its position in the past or in the present. But beyond these three things, the only thing I keep in mind is [a quote by Francis Bacon that hangs on her darkroom wall]: "The contemplation of things as they are, without substitution or imposture, without error or confusion, is in itself a nobler thing than a whole harvest of invention." (Lange 1995, p. 46)This work began as a doctoral dissertation I completed at the Institute for Clinical Social Work in Chicago. The research model I chose to utilize is categorized as qualitative research. This is a distinctly different research model than that of quantitative research, which has historically been the model most favored for academic research projects. While there is a distinct bias toward the viability of quantitative research, largely due to its utilization of a statistical methodology and large sample sizes, I found the qualitative design more valid for this type of human subject research. I believe and hope that we are experiencing a new openness in academic research by embracing the validity of this model, especially for the study of human subjects.

In a variety of studies, Rosenthal convincingly showed that the human factor, even in laboratory experiments, is significant and can dramatically alter the outcomes of the most tightly controlled laboratory studies. Thus, the confidence that many in academia have placed on sample size and statistical analysis may not be as warranted as has been asserted. The "empathic factor," even if denied, continues to be involved (Rosenthal and Lawson 1964, Rosenthal 1966, Rosenthal and Jacobson 1968, Rosenthal 1989a, Rosenthal 1989b).

The research method employed in this study is *interpretive interactionism*. This methodology is defined by Norman Denzin in his book by the same name:

> a method involving the collection of thick descriptions and personal experience stories of problematic human interactions. The materials are then interpreted. The researcher listens to, and records, the stories subjects tell. The stories are supplemented by open-ended, creative interviewing. (Denzin 1989)

Using an interpretive approach emphasizes individuals' experiences and the meaning attached to them by those participating and directly involved. Thus, it is a particularly suitable research method for looking at the impact of a philosophy and social movement such as restorative justice on the lives of those directly affected.

A qualitative methodology is particularly interested in description, analysis, and the symbol of lived experience in human development. It is thus richly suited to social science, and, particularly, social work research efforts.

The issue for research, however, is whether this material can then be generalized and begin to represent a category or compilation of general human experience, where the reader can walk away feeling that what is read represents a larger reality and would apply to other, similar, experiences. This is where qualitative theory begins to overlap with literary theory, and even with journalism. It also speaks to the utilization by most clinicians of the case study method in learning about various diagnostic dilemmas and styles of therapy. The case study is a qualitative research methodology in itself. I am interested here, beyond the preservation of the voice of the subject in the larger meaning, in how these interviews inform the process and social movement of restorative justice.

This research model is the foundation of what is being referred to here as clinical ethnography. Each case is seen in both its unique as well as its universal form, with the language that is ultimately used to define the feeling experience, one that is held to be "true" in a larger perspective.

This entire narrative process moves between the offender and the victim initially experiencing the meeting; the participants then becoming the tellers, describing the experience to the listener (the researcher); and finally the reader producing what Brooks calls a "movement of reference." It is in this movement that Brooks suggests that change is produced: "the textual reader, like the psychoanalytic patient, finds himself modified by the work of interpretation and construction, by the transferential dynamics to which he has submitted himself. In the movement between text and reader, the tale told makes a difference" (Brooks 1994).

I am reminded here in relation to the struggle of putting feeling states into words of the original meaning of the word empathy in German, Einfühlung. The etymology of the word defined by Post suggests it was created in the nineteenth century by the German philosopher Lotze. Lotze created the word to define what is necessary to appreciate a work of art—namely, to project one's personality into the object of contemplation, to "feel oneself into it." This initial feeling of wordless profundity captures the experience of these narratives.

I will strive to understand not only individuals in this analysis, but also populations, which then go on to inform a social movement. The population is not a distinct or homogeneous population. It is a community made up of different actors. These actors are often divergent in terms of history, ethnicity, social standing, developmental issues, and psychological characteristics. Often, they are seen as being at odds with one another. The places where such divergent actors come together and support one another's account of an experience that is marked by emotionally charged and painful facts are of special interest here.

For this research, the actors are primarily the violent offenders. The rest of their community, which exists largely because of offender violence, is made up of victims or surviving victims' family members, police officers, mediators, therapists, prison staff, and finally, but also importantly, offenders' family members and loved ones.

In the case chapters, I will follow a brief and factual case history using bracketed excerpts from my interviews with the research subjects. The presentation of the quotes in every instance will follow the exact sequence of the interview. For the sake of readability, I will limit the use of interjections such as "uh" and "um," but beyond this, the words are exactly those of the interview subjects given in the exact sequence of the interview. If I make any observations, substitutions, or clarifying comments while presenting actual interview content, they will be enclosed in brackets [ ].

The initial research proposal was approved by the Institute for Clinical Social Work's IRB panel. All interview subjects signed permission documents. All names and other identifying information have been changed.

Introduction

The question at the heart of this book is this: Can an individual, because of the myriad of failures in early development that lead to the capacity to commit violence, develop, as a result of experience, a capacity for empathy? This development will also be described as a reflective self-function sufficient to create not only a capacity for empathy, but also a capacity for true reconciliation with those to whom they have done harm.

The burden of violence on this culture is profound. Most individuals in the United States report that they feel vulnerable to violence and are concerned about it in their daily lives. They buy security systems and a variety of weaponry. Some even obtain permission to carry a gun with them always, and recently two major fashion houses designed firearms in their colors for women (costing between five and ten thousand dollars).

It is doubtless a primal fear that most carry, this sense of a stranger violently infringing on the routine of our lives when we are not prepared for it, and hurting us or someone we love. Oddly, however, most violence is perpetrated by those familiar to us, our intimates or relatives. More than 15,000 murders occur yearly, and whether by known or unknown perpetrators, their aftermath to individuals and their communities is powerful.

The question of the cause of violence is richly debated. While there have been many theories proposed, in a pluralistic society, meaningful and focused efforts to address violence find little intensive support. This is especially true of primary prevention projects, and currently, also, for most credible rehabilitation efforts.

The emergence of my interest in the question of violence came following a period of work at a maximum-security prison, and was reawakened during a period of extensive involvement in the treatment of child abuse while at a community mental health center. My interest was enhanced by participating in a research project that looked at early intervention models toward the prevention of child abuse and neglect (Breckenridge and Anderson 1981).

While involved in this work, I became more interested in the questions of early attachment experiences and the genesis of failures in attachment with the anticipated developmental problems and their consequences. I struggled with these questions while attempting to treat parents, themselves victims of abuse and neglect, who perpetrated extreme violence toward their own children. I learned that much is known about both the intergenerational causes of child abuse, and the power exerted over the developing child caught in the experience.

I have always been interested in the obvious empathic failure of these abusive caregivers, and the meaning of the abuse or neglect on the development of empathy in the toddler, especially how this affects the development of the empathic ability toward prosocial behavior ideals in the growing child.

THE PROBLEM

In a career starting in corrections and later mental health, the sequelae of developmental failures on the individual and the costs to the individual and later to society seem unquestionable to me.

In addition to this are the ongoing public policy failures to address these issues. These failures continue to seem related to our culture's continuing resistance to promote and fund even minimal early intervention/primary prevention efforts, even though many of these undertakings have proven their effectiveness repeatedly. Even in states where advocates for funding have achieved major successes programmatically, a mere downward turn in the economy along with a change in power in state government often means the total withdrawal of funding for these innovative and useful programs.

With the number of violent crimes increasing, and their social sway becoming more and more profound, questions of causality and potential treatment become more significant.

In this book, the question of treatment and change is specifically focused on the perpetrators of violence. This question cannot, however, be easily separated from the victims of violence, as the meaning of violence has consequences first for the immediate family and friends, but also for the neighborhood, and, ultimately, the community as a whole (Peterson 2000).

As a clinician, I have been consistently impressed by the successful interventions of clinical treatment with populations that are often deemed undesirable or untreatable. These treatment efforts have proven, in many cases, more than effective and more than enough to generate true and lasting changes in these individuals. I have experienced this outcome in both child protection populations, as well as in correctional populations. I use the word "treatment" in its broadest definition here to include, in addition to psychotherapy, generic social work interventions, or a relationship with an effective probation officer or an active and effective child protection worker. I would also include, obviously, the clear effectiveness of chemical dependency treatment and the success of Alcoholics Anonymous in providing truly life changing opportunities.

In the child-abusing population, not only can the abuse cycle be disrupted, but caregivers with a profoundly disturbed early history can also benefit from psychotherapy. They can also be trained, coached, and deeply changed to provide the type of care that breaks this cycle in the next generation.

The experience that will frame this exploration is the coming together of victim and perpetrator in face-to-face meetings through the process of restorative justice mediation dialogues. These are victim-initiated meetings in which both parties are prepared by the mediator for their ultimate encounter with one another.

These encounters have proven to be enormously useful with lasting effects for both individuals. Thus, I will look at these meetings as the culmination of a variety of happenings in the life of the offender, which may serve as epiphanies or turning-point experiences, and explore the meaning of these experiences.

As has been seen with the child-abuser population, these individuals made use of therapeutic intervention to provide an empathic and nurturing environment for their infant, sufficient to enhance the infant's normative developmental needs. Efforts are also proving successful in certain populations to "teach" empathic skills and strengthen the individual's empathic ability to avoid conflict.

Similarly, this book will address whether a violent offender can achieve significant enough empathy to allow him to not only appreciate the nature of his acts, but also create sufficient change to address the violentization expressed toward others. ("Violentization" is a term used by Athens [1997] to denote the active induction of the individual into the performance of violent acts.)

The importance of these issues relates to questions of the cause of violence and whether these tendencies can be addressed in individuals who have already demonstrated a tendency toward violent acting out.

This question will be explicated in terms of the meaning to the individuals of their immediate experience, but will also focus on possibilities of prevention in a more global social movement.

It might be said in a broader view that my overall interest in this area relates to the efficacy of psychotherapy. Who better to consider in this regard than a population long thought to be beyond redemption? The discouraging belief that those considered psychopathic or sociopathic are beyond our efforts to treat them can be seen in both the psychologically informed among us, who disseminate strikingly pessimistic views of intervention, along with the general community, where the talionic impulse continues to be the dominant social response to crime. It will be important for me to knit together a variety of theories that lead to the development of violentization in society and the individuals that make up that society in the developmental and cultural theories. These theories are neither disparate nor opposing, but have been seen in some circles to be so.

My goal will be to bring together a variety of theories and concepts related to this issue, to provide a concise theoretical and practical formulation related to the development of empathy, to discuss the reasons and consequences of a failure of this development, and to describe the possibilities for the resolution or even restoration of this capacity.

Empathy, as I will ultimately be using the word in this journey, seems more than adequate to sum up the experiences discussed. This is seen in its loss, lack, absence and, ultimately, in its reintroduction to the scene in the lives of these participants.

RESTORATIVE JUSTICE

I will look at restorative justice as part of this project in two dimensions. First, it will be used as a method of intervention, providing victims and offenders a process for meeting and discussing the events that bring them so tragically together. Second, restorative justice will also be seen as a social movement and will be explored in this regard as well.

Restorative justice has been called the last vestige of liberal criminology practice since the "three strikes and you're out" notion that has been so prevalent in the United States since the presidential administration of Ronald Reagan.

The major focus of restorative justice has had its foundation in the philosophy that crime affects individuals and communities, not the state or the criminal justice system. Its major focus of practice has been victim/offender mediation dialogues. This practice brings together crime victims and perpetrators in mediated sessions.

Its philosophical base comes out of the Mennonite Central Committee, Native American tribal custom, and other native traditions (e.g., the Maori tradition in New Zealand). It is reported that there are currently more than 300 victim–offender mediation programs in the United States and 900 in Europe. While the major focus has been on juvenile and less serious property crimes, many programs have begun to use these principles in more serious violent crimes.

Mediation sessions in these violent crimes take place long after the trial. They are victim-initiated and the offender must agree to participate. Given the current correctional emphasis away from parole and toward determinate sentencing, there is little chance that the offender's participation will help his case in any way and, in some states, offender participation could hurt the opportunity for appeal, and this fact, remarkably, did not dissuade the offenders from participation.

Both parties go through a significant period of preparation with the mediator. Mediation can occur in one or a series of meetings over time with a mediator facilitating all the meetings that take place. Benefits that have been reported to occur for the victim or victim's families relate to the raising of the most difficult or highly emotional and spiritual issues that are central to recovery from violent crime. All who participate, along with a growing body of follow-up research, have spoken of a sense of "healing" and help in moving toward a greater sense of "closure" and ability to move toward some form of personal "resolution." That said, the experiences are very individualized. Some participants discuss coming close to issues related to compassion or forgiveness, which is currently a very controversial area in the field and will be discussed in this book.

These encounters seemed to me to be a clear opportunity for the exploration of whether empathy can be achieved in a person who has clearly demonstrated an empathic failure.

There will also be an opportunity to explore a process whereby empathy is compromised and to investigate whether and how it can be developed in such extreme situations within the victim of violent crime. The implications of the answers to these questions have a profound influence on both theory and practice.

To explore these issues, I will utilize case histories and in-depth interviews with a variety of participants with these experiences.

The case material utilized in this book was earlier part of a more formal research project. I have maintained some of this structure as I do, in fact, draw conclusions at the end of the book based on my experiences, and these conclusions need to be rooted in a formal way to evaluate the experience.

Given that these cases follow a narrative format and that they were referred to me as either cases in progress or "completed" cases that had a narrative organization, for the most part, I will present these findings in that form. This will allow me to present to the reader the case in much the same way that I experienced it in its development.

ATTACHMENT THEORY

I will pay attention to attachment theory. There is a great deal of developing support for this theoretical foundation coming out of current neuroscience research. This will be more fully described in upcoming chapters. As Lewis (2000) points out, the human brain is now being extensively prewired to experience attachment, and needs positive attachment experiences with others as much as it needs food and oxygen for healthy development.

It is through the subcortical or limbic system that we discern what other people are feeling or thinking, the ability to read social cues and connect emotionally with others. It is also in the limbic system that concepts such as "intuition" and empathy seem to reside. The limbic system is adapted at birth to connect with caregivers, and the limbic systems of caregivers are adapted to connect with newborns. This "limbic resonance" describes a biological dimension of the kinds of intersubjective responses that have long been described by theoreticians, and relates to our fundamental connection to others. In support of long-standing developmental theory, it now seems clear that when one is subjected to violence or rejection, neural pathways are developed and continually reinforced that become the pathological basis for later relationships.

The theoretical basis of this book is the belief that the nature of the phenomena that I am dealing with; the conceptual frame that violence enacted by one individual upon another, is at its basis a function of psychopathology. This psychopathology is a function of early experiences with primary caregivers, which have a direct influence on disordered or dysfunctional relationships across the life course.

I differentiate this from concepts such as "evil," which are also used to describe this behavior, and while concepts dealing with evil will be briefly explored, I will hold to the causality of violence as my frame of reference.

Further, the imparting of this psychopathology is strongly rooted in the psychosocial history of the caregiver and has a distinctly "genetic" origin in terms of these vulnerabilities being transmitted, both in an intergenerational as well as a social systemic fashion (Fonagy 1993).

One of the distinct consequences of these disturbed relationships, I will hold, is the failure of the development of empathic ability. This, on a broader level, is the development of a capacity for reflective self-assessment and an inability to draw accurate conclusions about the mental state of another (known by some writers as an accurate "theory of mind").

THE ILIAD OF HOMER

Ultimately, I utilize Homer as a foundational metaphor for this book. For this work, I have made use of two translations of *The Iliad*, one by Fagles (1990) and the other by Lattimore (1951). This was done for the sake of comparison. In most cases, I have utilized Fagles' translation, as it suits my text better.

Achilles was leading the armies of Greece against Troy in a long and destructive war. It has been suggested that *The Iliad* is really the story of the tragedy of Achilles. Achilles, a formidable leader of his armies, is betrayed by Agamemnon and, in a fury, abandons the war. During his absence, the Greeks suffer significant losses, and to redeem the situation, Achilles' closest friend Patroklos takes over the command. Hector, the son of Priam, the King of Troy, sees an opportunity to seek vengeance on Achilles and kills Patroklos.

When Achilles hears of Patroklos' death and feels the clear responsibility for it, he returns to the fight. Determined to avenge the death of his friend, he is clearly in what Jonathan Shay (1994) would define as a "berserk state," in which he goes about his assault with little regard for his own safety. Hector does not run and hide from Achilles, but rather stands his ground and is slain. Achilles, who is also angry that Patroklos has not been afforded a formal burial service, drags Hector's body around Troy at the back of his chariot. Priam, heartbroken at the death of his son, desires only to retrieve his body for burial, and to allow the Trojans a period of mourning. Achilles is not open to negotiation, and still in a rage, he refuses.

The gods at this point are alarmed by the situation and send Hermes to Priam to secure a meeting between the two. They also protect Hector's corpse from harm, even though Achilles continues to unceremoniously drag it around the city walls.

Hermes is successful in sneaking Priam into Achilles' encampment. When Achilles sees the old king, he is initially impressed by his courage. Priam kneels at Achilles' feet, and kisses his hand. The two sit together and, eventually, cry together at the losses they have both experienced during this long and devastating war. Priam appeals to Achilles to consider how Achilles' father Peleus would feel if he were in Priam's place. Eventually, Achilles shows "pity" on the old man, allows him to take Hector's body for a proper burial, and calls off the war for the requisite period of Trojan mourning.

In my early readings in trauma theory, and especially Jonathan Shay's work, *Achilles in Vietnam* (1994), Shay makes connections between this metaphor and general trauma theory, particularly as he links it to the experience of Vietnam veterans as both combatants and trauma survivors. The betrayal and disrespect experienced by Vietnam-era veterans, both during and after the war seems remarkably relevant to The Iliad.

The levels of betrayal felt especially by these soldiers from their command as well as their political leaders (related to defective rifles, for example) make a clear connection to The Iliad, as opposed to other wars that this nation has engaged in.

Most significant were the early writings of Daniel Van Ness (1997) and later the connections made by Dave Gustafson (2001) to *The Iliad*. Both men are key players in the restorative justice movement, and more will be said about their contributions later in this book. Van Ness all but says that the meeting in *The Iliad* between Achilles and Priam is the first restorative justice mediation dialogue. Gustafson later says that this meeting is the first example of reconciliation (for which Homer had no word in ancient Greek) and was so significant to Homer that he closes the epic with it, rather than continue to the more dramatic conclusion.

It could certainly be said that the mediator, in the act of taking the victim into the prison to meet with the offender, is acting in the same fashion as Hermes, who prepares and then takes Priam into the enemy camp to meet with Achilles. Through his act, Priam can regain his son's body, mourn his death appropriately, and regain his self-respect. Achilles regains his humanity and his ability to pity, and through this is also able to fulfill his mourning of not only the loss of his friend, but also his own betrayal by Agamemnon.

The meaning of this remarkable event will be further explained in the conclusion of this work, especially as it relates to the issues of "reconciliation," the restitution of pity, and one's humanity, and the facilitation of grief and mourning.

Simone Weil, who also used *The Iliad* as the foundation of important writing in her essay on the political outcome, found in the epic this significant meaning:

> *Might suffered at the hands of another is as much a tyranny over the soul as extreme hunger at the moment when food means life or death. And its empire is as cold, and as hard as though exercised by lifeless matter. The man who finds himself everywhere the most feeble of his fellows is as lonely in the heart of a city, or more lonely, than anyone can be who is lost in the midst of a desert. (Weil 1977)*

As Dietz suggests in relation to Weil's work, *The Iliad* contains the same spirit as does Weil's work in capturing a sense of "monotonous desolation" that weighs on the writing, "except for a few 'luminous moments' that make her vision possible for the soul to bear" (Dietz 1988, p. 96).

Victims of violent crime in the aftermath of the experience often describe this same sense of "monotonous desolation." As Dietz points out, Weil sees the moment of Achilles and Priam's meeting, which will be the key moment of my study, as a "moment of grace." In this meeting, Homer brings "mortal enemies together and erases their hostility" (Dietz 1988).

Chapter 1

Child Development Theory

No one theory accounts for the complexity of human behavior, especially violent behavior.

However, there is no better theory of child development than attachment theory. From a clinician's perspective, in dealing with the impacts of real life on real people, attachment theory is profound in its ability to describe both normal and pathological development in a manner that continues to hold to actual clinical experience.

In the case of infant development, even in John Bowlby's methodological model, development is neither as linear nor as dependent on the "critical period" hypothesis as we have been comfortable believing.

In terms of infant development, especially the development of empathy and prosocial behavior, this early achievement is particularly vulnerable to a host of possibilities existing in the genetic, social, psychological, and circumstantial risks to which the group focused on in this book is exposed. Further, failures in the early caretaking relationship account for predictable consequences in the development of a cohesive sense of self, which include problems related to the development of empathy, a sense of agency, and a relationship to one's own history, all of which seem present in this group.

ATTACHMENT THEORY

When John Bowlby's theory of attachment was initially published in a 1951 World Health Organization monograph, it was controversial. There are few, if any, concepts of human development that challenge the theory. Although it is sometimes underrepresented in graduate education, it is now accepted as an inherent component of human psychological development and has received widely recognized empirical support.

The human infant-mother pair seems hardwired for the dynamics of attachment to take place. It is now well understood that the infant is sensitized to its mother's rhythm from the uterus. It is also known that the human mother can, in a very short time, pick out her own infant's cry from a crowded nursery shortly after birth, and that the human infant can identify and turn toward the scent of its mother's milk, as well as almost immediately imitate facial expressions.

Bowlby's theory is one that starts from an explanation of normal development (as opposed to other contemporary psychoanalytic theories) and from this position attempts to explain abnormal development leading to pathology. This relates to the effects of the trauma of separation, either real or threatened, and excessive emotional distress. Parenting is looked at in relation to its real impact, its consistency over time, and the parents' sensitivity to the needs of the child (i.e., independence and autonomy).

> First attachments are ordinarily formed by seven months, and attachments develop with respect to only one or a few persons. It is understood to be the infant that selects its primary attachment figure(s), generally upon the basis of contingent social interactions … attachments emerge as the product of interactions with maltreating persons as readily as they do with sensitively responsive ones, and the biologically based proclivity to form attachments ensures that only in extremely anomalous circumstances will a child remain unattached. (Main 2000, p. 1060)

The two major ways that disrupted attachment has been categorized are related to parental abuse or neglect, or the effects of abandonment on institutional care. Much research, used to support the overall attachment theory, has followed and has been modeled around the work in these areas.

L. Alan Sroufe, who has conducted an impressive longitudinal study related to child development, has suggested that the development of self-organization out of a secure base of attachment has significance for behavior, adaptation to life in general, and social relationships in particular. He suggests that disruptions in self-organization are a direct reflection of disrupted dyadic organization and will contribute to subsequent problems in individual behavioral organization and adaptation to life, especially involving disrupted and distorted social relationships. He states simply that individual disorders cannot be separated from relationship disorders because individual personality is formed in a relationship: "Each personality, whether healthy or disordered, is a product of the history of vital relationships" (Sroufe 1989, p. 71).

Daniel Stern reminds us of the slowly specific way in which the infant's development evolves, in context with the parent, in an environment of mutual attunement. The learning and memory functions of the developing relationship and hence the developing sense of self are associated with a complex set of subjective experiences, which set down memory traces associated with distinct episodes of experience in what Stern refers to as "representations of interactions that have become generalized" (RIGs). RIGs become a set of repetitive episodes of memories of events. Stern uses the game peek-a-boo by way of example, stating that after the first game the child lays down a memory of a specific episode, but after the second, third, and twelfth experience of slightly different episodes, "the infant will have formed a RIG of peek-a-boo" (Stern 1985, p. 110). The significance of this becomes relevant if one considers a less than optimal environment with an emotionally ill-attuned caregiver, and especially a repetitive experience of neglect or trauma. In Stern's model, RIGs are far more ubiquitous than simply those related to the security of the attachment bond. Rather, they cover "any and all interactions that can result in mutually created alterations in self-experience, such as arousal, affect, mastery, physiological state, state of consciousness, and curiosity" (Stern 1985, p. 115). Thus, it is clear how sensitive and minutely tuned the interactions of this dyad become, as well as the consequences of potential disruption.

As the infant matures, the sense of subjective self becomes more defined by what Stern refers to as the "domain of intersubjective relatedness" with the caregiver. The evolution of this possibility is built on the foundation of "core relatedness," which has already been laid down in the interaction between the two as the fundamental bedrock of all future evolving development. Stern suggests that when the leap in the sense of self takes place, there is also an essential shift in the world of the child.

Along with this developmental shift, the infant develops out of its subjective experience a blossoming sense of agency through the relationship with the parents who take on the responsibility of the socialization of the infant's subjective experience. It is during this development of the subjective sense of self that the process of empathy begins to play an important role.

The successful development of an autonomous sense of self is correlated with the attunement of the caregiver, who will be sensitive to the child's arousal patterns, and will step in, when needed, to control and guide the expression of impulse and aggression. The well-attuned caregiver anticipates these times of frustration and intercedes when necessary, while at the same time allowing the child as much self-direction as possible. This makes possible for the toddler that ability to inhibit impulse, but under the watchful eye of an empathic caregiver. This sets the stage for the internalization of self-regulation and a sense of agency.

Many other authors (Fonagy 1991) discuss the importance of attachment as it relates to secure attachment's responsibility for the ability of self-reflection, a sense of history (past vs. present, real vs. unreal), as opposed to insecure attachment, which compromises these abilities. Relevant to how this concept of self-reflection and history is concerned is the belief that if an insecure attachment develops between an infant and caregiver, a pattern of self-protective defenses evolves to protect the infant as well as salvage any possible positive elements from the attachment relationship. Fonagy suggests that when the infant is not able to anticipate the caregiver's response, these defensive strategies evolve, which ultimately interferes with self-reflective capacity and finally with the achievement of a consolidated sense of self.

CATEGORIES OF ATTACHMENT AND ATTACHMENT RESEARCH

In revisiting Ainsworth's model (Main et al. 1985), Bowlby believed that attachment behavior was a biologically based tendency of the infant to seek proximity to a central caregiver, and that the responses of the caregiver are finite. If the caregiver permits and encourages access to the infant who seeks proximity, the result will be a secure organization; if the caregiver blocks access, the result will be an insecure-avoidant organization; and if the caregiver permits access unpredictably, the result will be an insecure-ambivalent organization.

In Ainsworth's extensive empirical validation of Bowlby's work, she developed the now universal "strange situation" experiment as a way of classifying the degree of attachment in the relationship between child and caregiver, but also to speak to the myriad of individual differences seen in these complex relationships. The categories in the infant strange situation response are: *secure*; *avoidant* (does not cry on separation, avoids or ignores parent on reunion, unemotional); *resistant-ambivalent* (preoccupied with parent, angry, seeking and resisting parent, passive, does not settle upon reunion); and *disorganized-disoriented* (disoriented in parent's presence, clinging while leaning away).

The unmistakable significance of the infant strange situation experiments was to validate, based on direct contact and study of the parent-child dyad, the development of attachment as a normal progression, and to also identify and codify disrupted or pathological attachment patterns.

Main, through the extensive study of parent-child pairs, developed the "disorganized-disoriented" classification, which was then included in Ainsworth's model, and is seen in cases of attachment loss (through death) or trauma (Main and Hesse 1990). The classification model was thus expanded in an attempt to explain why these children appeared fearful to the extent that the anxiety and fear could not be reduced through distraction or shift of attention, nor could it be helped by the approach of another attachment figure.

The disorganized adult attachment status has also been linked to the development of criminality, psychopathology, and violence (Hesse and Main 2000).

Fonagy reports that a child who experiences in the caregiver high levels of "negative affectivity, emotional outbursts, inattentiveness, and low frustration tolerance predict long-term peer relation problems and negative social outcomes." The outcome of the perception of these affects appears to be, "Because these children cannot inhibit negative arousal or suppress their negative reactivity, they cannot plan effective coping responses or control their attention to reduce exposure to disturbing stimuli" (Fonagy 2001, p. 42).

THE (LACK OF) RESOLUTION OF GRIEF AND MOURNING

Interesting here is the degree of focus Main and her colleagues devote to the issues of unresolved grief and mourning following loss and its contribution to the disorganized/disoriented attachment status.

It might be said that a similar process of grief and mourning exists with both an actual loss taking place (i.e., the death of a caregiver) and the loss of innocence that is experienced in childhood trauma. The efforts required to carry and attempt to resolve this predicament are often a significant draw on the individuals' psychic resources.

As proposed by Main and Hesse (1990, p. 168), the outcome of the resolution of mourning is significant in overall development. In their studies, it was found that unresolved loss is responsible for, among other things, lapses in reasoning and "extremely disorganized or disoriented behavioral responses to a death." If the outcome is a favorable one, "a reorganization of mental processes will take place, leading to renewed orientation to the present environment." In quoting Bowlby, this is the "successful effort of an individual to accept both that a change has occurred in his external world and that he is required to make corresponding changes in his internal, representational world and to reorganize, and perhaps to reorient, his attachment behavior accordingly" (Bowlby 1980, Main and Hesse 1990).

Main suggests that because of "frightening or frightened" behavior on the part of the caregiver (because of the caregiver's own unresolved loss or abuse), the child may well appear as disorganized/disoriented in later attachment. Thus, infants might appear disorganized not only as a result of their own, firsthand experienced trauma or loss, but also as a "second generation effect" of their parents' experience (Hesse and Main 2000, p. 1103).

In connecting this concept to trauma (defined in one article as loss of a close family member in an accident, loss of both parents, sexual abuse by a parent, or physical abuse by a parent), Main sees loss to be responsible for unresolved mourning (Main and Hesse 1990, p. 174) and is present in both the abused and the mourning populations.

It has been pointed out by some that Main seems in some respects to emphasize the impact of grief and loss issues over those of distinct traumatic events (such as direct abuse and neglect). To clarify this fact, I corresponded with June Sroufe to gain her insight into this issue. She responded to my question in an email reply as follows:

> Your question is intriguing … and I thought about it quite a bit, but am still not fully confident of an answer.
>
> I think the way to begin is to focus on the infant. If the infant is overwhelmed by frightening or frightened behavior, then it will become disorganized and ultimately vulnerable to a compromised development. A factor which is not specified at this point is how bad does it have to be to result in this condition, and relatedly, is there a continuum of severity of experience that is predictive of the degree of compromised development? Your question seems to be more relevant to the severity question because that is where abuse can be repeatedly traumatizing, whereas disorganization resulting from unresolved loss tends to be a discreet event.
>
> Ongoing abuse by a single parent (person) or abuse by a number of individuals in succession is not only disorganizing but damaging of psychic functions that would otherwise provide the victim with important coping responses.
>
> In theory, I believe that Mary (Main) would say these two sources of distortion are likely to lead to the same outcome—that is disorganization and unresolved loss, but that there are also other factors to take into consideration when appraising the psychological outcomes of these two very different experiences. (June Sroufe, Personal Communication, July 2001)

THE RELATIONSHIP WITH THE CAREGIVER

What seems notable in the development of this theoretical position is the significance of the interaction between the caregiver and the developing child. All major thinkers in child development currently believe that there is a necessary intersubjective process between infant and caregiver that is important to the process of development. Melanie Klein takes this concept further to develop a "one person" model, where the nature of object relationships, from the point of view of the infant, are largely, as Stern states, the "ontogeny of fantasy life, with no significant determining input from the behavior of the actual mother" (Stern 1989).

Emde suggests that this process be predicated based on the emotional availability of the caregiver, which then supports the security of attachment and the course of development:

> The mother's emotional availability has enabled the infant's continued emotional development within the relationship, so that the infant can cope with separation experiences, engage in positive reunion with the mother, and be confident enough to explore the environment in the mother's presence. (Emde 1989, p. 46)

D. W. Winnicott first described how such a process is related to how successfully the infant feels initially merged with the mother, how much the mother can allow herself to identify with the infant, then followed by a slow emotional separation, in which the mother maintains contact. Mutual understanding evolves, allowing the infant to develop an inner mental representation of himself (Winnicott 1956). Winnicott sums this concept up in his famous admonition that there is "no such thing as a baby," only a baby–mother pair.

Emde suggests that what is formative during infancy is not that an individualized pattern is established but that "infant-caregiver relationship patterns get set in an enduring way. Early relationship styles and patterns later become internalized by the individual in the progression from infancy to early childhood" or, as he later states, "relationship aspects become internalized by the individual, continue as strong influences in development throughout childhood, and are activated in similar relationship contexts throughout life" (Emde 1988, p. 28).

Out of this interaction, the development of prosocial behavior, morality, and empathy evolve. This process is thought to take place due to the obvious difference of intention between parent and child. It is seen through opposing forces within the child, which necessitates an interaction between the two around issues of discipline and the resolution of conflict., played out with the high stakes evident in the parent-infant interaction.

While the disruption in the relationship between child and caregiver is clear when gross failures, evidenced by violence or neglect, are present, much has also been understood regarding the impact on attachment if the child grows up with a depressed parent (Radke-Yarrow et al. 1985, Fraiberg 1980). Studies also point to the impact on the caregiver in a relationship with a child who is emotionally unavailable (Trevarthen and Aitken 1994).

Thus, destructive interactions between child and caregiver can be of a blatant nature, observable to all, or they can be far subtler. These interactions can be based on the personality deficits of the caregiver that may well be obscure to the untrained eye, but are communicated quite distressingly to the child. Examples of these interactions (in the nature of the semiotic exchange within the dyad) are the "double bind" concept of family systems theory or the concept of superego lacunae developed by Adelaide Johnson (1947).

Not only do the overtly depressed or mentally ill parents exact this toll on development, but the narcissistically organized parents, as discussed by Kohut (Kohut 1971), also impede the development of autonomy in their children. In the overt discouragement of the development of self and autonomy, these parents see their children as extensions of their fragile sense of self and treat their children as "territorial possessions" or as simple extensions of themselves.

THE INTERNAL WORKING MODEL

Bretherton discussed Bowlby's metaphor of the internal working model in an effort (significant to all psychoanalytic theory) to explain the relationship between a person's outer reality and their inner world. He devised this theory after work by Craik (1943), who defined the model in a way that was also important to Athens' (1997) later definition of phantom communities.

Thus, according to Bowlby and others, working models are developed in order to support survival in that they provide for both insightful and "foresightful" behavior that allows for planning and simulation as to what one expects in the world (Bretherton et al. 1990).

Bowlby believed that the individual develops internal working models that are constructed from the experience of interaction with the caregiver. These working models of the self and of the attachment partner are based on the joint relationship history between both parties. These internal working models importantly serve to structure the concept of the relationship, what can be anticipated from it, and what can be expected from it in the future. Secure attachment, then, is also associated with self-confidence and trust. The securely attached individual values relationships and, even during periods of high conflict or disagreement, can maintain a positive connection.

It is considered now that some form of internal working model is likely formed in the first months of life. It has been suggested that by the age of one, an infant demonstrates clearly observable individual differences with a particular parent, which is conceived as reflecting individual differences in the infant's internal working model of the internalized relationship with the caregiver (Main et al. 1985).

This construct was echoed in George Herbert Mead's theories on human development (Mead 1934). Mead felt that if an infant performed an act that was not picked up on by the parent, the infant would soon discard this action (e.g., holding up its arms to be picked up). As Bretherton states, however, attachment theory takes this concept one step further. Because human infants are prepared to expect caring responses to these signals, the caregiver's ignoring of these signals does not render the action meaningless, but rather suggests rejection, or conveys that "Your signals do not count." If these responses are pervasive and consistent, they are then incorporated into the internal working model and stated as "My needs are not important" (Bretherton and Munholland 1999).

Bowlby's concept of internal working models is important in that it comes closer to the emotional and motivational goals that become an integral part of internal representation and the development of a sense of self. In this way, as Bretherton points out, he shares a common theme with social psychologists Kurt Lewin and Fritz Heider, who wrote extensively about the making of personal and interpersonal meaning (Lewin 1933, Heider 1958). These theorists suggested that the individual develops internal working models based on the perception of how the behaviors of the other make. This takes place for both the child and the adult, with only the complexity of the attribution and meaning- making at issue.

One of the important aspects of the concept of internal working models is the belief that the emergence of a sense of self and the development of relationship representations converge with the concept of the working model. These working models are then seen to mediate the early relationship experienced by the child and the later ones that are created by the child. Children then behave in ways that confirm the existing and internalized working model. Working models, then, of secure attachments promote positive interactions that subsequently confirm the models. Working models of insecure or damaging attachments are later confirmed by the social rejection experienced on account of a child's negativity and aggressiveness: "Developmental competence is carried forward in the organization of self that has emerged from the parent-child negotiation of interactional issues" (Sameroff and Emde 1989, p. 221).

Emde earlier spoke of the sense of self in the community in relation to his concept of the development of the affective self. He suggests that in both clinical practice, as well as in daily life, we rely upon knowing other people by means of understanding their feelings: "Once we are in touch with another's emotional life, we are in touch with his or her humanity" (Emde 1983, p. 180).

Emde suggests that this is the basis for the appreciation of the other as a unique human being, and also allows us to enjoy, for example, a novel, movie, or play. He further suggests that there is a strikingly similar organization of emotional expression in infants, children, and adults, that is, we are all more human than otherwise.

As Bowlby suggested, internal working models are not passive pictures or passive introjections of the object and past experience, but are dynamic and active constructions. As such, they can be restructured, but as Bowlby pointed out, this is difficult, since the internal working model, once in place, functions outside conscious awareness, and, because of this, is resistant to change (Bowlby 1980).

THE POSSIBILITIES OF REPAIR

The consequences of these failures to the early developmental course are profound; the lasting nature of the damage, as well as how it can be changed, is polemical.

In dyads where the sort of disorganized/disoriented attachment exists, interactions can be of such an overwhelming and horrific nature that depression, despair, and significant mental illness are the result. The child is left in a state of distress with no comfort from the caregiver, who is, in fact, the source of the terror.

Bowlby, as cited in the work of Shane et al., also felt that "secure attachment with other than the primary caregivers can improve the attachment pattern of the insecurely attached individual toward a more secure attachment, and/or may make available a new, secure one" (Shane et al. 1997, p. 98). This, of course, speaks to the efficacy of psychotherapy, but also indicates the possibility of change and/or repair occurring in even the most severely damaged individuals.

Mayes (1999) suggests a model that questions the historically linear psychoanalytic model. This model suggests a process moving from a linear, stage-specific model to a nonlinear model where different areas of function proceed at different rates and their interactions at any point in time affect the child's adaptation and development in all other areas. Mayes sees this conceptualization to be in line with what we now know about brain development in that the amount and specificity of synaptic loss or connectivity is dependent on perceptual input from experience. This concept explains how the brain may become "hardwired." Mayes states, "While there is a general age-based regularity to patterns of adaptation, there is also the possibility for enormous individual variability in the specifics of capacities lost, reorganized, or maintained in order to maximize adaptation." The more adaptable the individual can be, the more this "increases the individual's chance to move to subsequent stages of development and to maximize gains from the environment based on a given endowment" (Mayes 1999, p. 180). Mayes sees this kind of adaptation continuing throughout the life span and offers the prospect, supported by other researchers, that even brain chemistry is alterable by external experience.

Chapter 2

Trauma Theory

I include trauma theory here given the high correlation in attachment theory between generalized trauma (especially abuse and neglect by a primary caregiver) and disrupted attachment relationships, with consequential toxicity to the developmental course. There is a plethora of studies that have linked this trauma (abuse and neglect) to the later commission of violent crime, some studies showing as much as a 100 percent correlation between these social factors and the later commission of violent acts (Lewis and Balla 1976, Lewis et al. 1979, Widom 1987, Lewis et al. 1989, Hickey 1991, Greenberg et al. 1993, Meyers et al. 1995, Lewis 1997, Lewis 1998).

In relation to attachment theory, trauma suffered by children is profound in its consequences. As Rene Spitz identified early in this field (Spitz 1945, Spitz and Wolf 1946), the loss of primary attachment figures represents the loss of virtually everything that the child embodies. This experience of loss can also be postulated when the child is traumatized by an attachment figure, although the consequences are more complicated for both parties.

As James states:

> The child abused by a primary attachment figure suffers in multiple and complex ways. There is the pain, confusion, and fear of the abuse itself; there is the mind-boggling experience of having the source of danger and the source of protection residing in one person. Most terrifying of all is the fear of loss of the attachment relationship, a loss children often believe is likely to happen if they try to protect themselves from being abused by a parent. (James 1994, p. 8)
>
> Children adapt to these situations by engaging in protective practices, such as dissociating, anesthetizing themselves physically, and muting sensory awareness. They commonly deal with the need to maintain a relationship with an abusive parent by blaming themselves for the abuse. This directs rage away from

the abuser and frees the child to seek love and protection from that person, thus preserving the essential attachment relationship (James, 1994).

For the research conducted for this book, while I am focusing primarily on the experience of the offender, the experience of the victim or the victim's family parallels, to a greater or lesser extent, the trauma experience. These two people, whose lives touch in such a dramatic manner, share the experience of trauma, emerging as it does at different times and in far different circumstances. As one victim told me in an interview, "We (she and the offender) will always be linked." My discussion of trauma, then, will be to some extent significant to both parties, and I will attempt to make distinctions where this seems informative, but I will primarily be focusing on the trauma associated with early childhood attachment disruptions and their sequelae.

Many writers have focused on the effects of trauma on the victims' sense of self, sense of meaning, and their relationship to other people (Herman 1992). Exposure to violence challenges and changes the individual's basic assumptions about personal invulnerability and self-worth. The perception of the world as an orderly, safe, and just place suffers greatly. As van der Kolk points out, how old a person is when the trauma takes place and what the individual's previous life experiences are like will have a dramatic effect on the interpretation and meaning of the traumatic experience (van der Kolk and Fisler 1994).

Fonagy (Fonagy 2001) suggests that trauma may interrupt developing functions related to "representation of feelings, thoughts, beliefs, and desires by creating a propensity for shifting into the mode of pretend." He supports the belief that traumatized children can grow up with a hypersensitivity to the mental states of others, with the goal being an immediate assessment of what those around them feel and think to anticipate and prevent further trauma. This creates "pseudo knowledge" of the mind that is selective and reactive, "scanning for danger signals" and not reflecting on deeper meanings.

This damage to the ability to mentalize is important to my project here, as it has a drastic impact on empathic ability and creates a repetitive function. As Fonagy states:

> mindless treatment, or neglect of the child, leads to the disavowal of reflection and rejection of mentalization. This should be understood not simply as a deficit but as an adaptation that has helped the child to attain some distance from a traumatizing situation.
>
> ... Conversely, mentalizing is an important component of the self-righting capacity of individuals who are able to withstand early adversity. Thus, there is a bi-directional developmental relationship between trauma and mentalizing; trauma may undermine the child's willingness to play with feelings and ideas

> (felt as too real) in relation to external events. At the same time, the lack of full mentalizing … will create a propensity for the continuous repetition of the trauma. (Fonagy 2001, pp. 176–177)

Shabad suggests that the impact of trauma relates to an incomplete mourning for the loss of one's childhood to the abuse. This loss, and the subsequent unresolved mourning of the loss, involves a need for repetition and assures the intergenerational transmission of the abuse theme (i.e., "That's how my parents raised me."). According to Shabad, "If we view mourning as a process whose aim is to become relatively free from the compulsions to repeat the past, then we can see how the disintegrating consequences of suffering chronic disillusionments work against the process" (Shabad 1993, p. 72).

Shabad discusses the more broadly defined concept of trauma, and suggests that actual trauma can be no more than a chronic pattern of frustrating experiences suffered in childhood with a significant attachment figure. When repeated daily over many years, this can accumulate into the "emotional significance of trauma."

Mary Main found that abused mothers who were able to find some perspective and forgiveness, rather than engage in denial, were less likely to abuse their own child (Main and Goldwyn 1984). This research also supports the idea that the key element and difference between abusive and non-abusive mothers is the quality of the internal working model that the mother carries of herself in relationship to the other. This seems to determine the likelihood of her repeating the intergenerational pattern of abuse. Ultimately, this all supports the importance of the early attachment relationship, but also underscores the ability of individuals to change in the context of a healthy and supportive relationship.

The concept of shame will be revisited throughout this book, and is a primary factor in the lives of these offenders. The role that shame plays in their development is thought to be a factor in the inability to "mentalize" or to create an internalized concept of the "other," so crucial to the perpetration of violence.

Attempting to block the knowing of the experience is common, and in adult life, primitive mechanisms of defense come into play (e.g., denial, splitting, amnesia, derealization, and depersonalization). The sense of self in traumatic memory becomes fragmented into "me" and "not me." As Laub describes the experience, it bears a marked similarity to Kohut's description of the vertical split, with a distinct separation between parts of the self, but also a knowledge (knowing and not knowing) that the self is fragmented (Goldberg 1999).

Lenore Terr has written extensively on the impact of trauma on children (Terr 1983, 1991). Often these children appear to their teachers or even clinicians as attention deficit hyperactivity disordered or conduct disordered, with anxiety disorders or affective disorders. High percentages (85%) of children who are seen with post-traumatic stress disorder (PTSD) are seen to have comorbid psychiatric diagnoses (Center for the Study of Childhood Trauma, Chicago.) The PTSD group showed a documented history of severe traumatic events, exacerbation of symptoms with a re-exposure to trauma-specific stimuli, and autonomic nervous system hyperarousal. These children also exhibited psychotic symptoms as well as anxiety and affective symptomatology, along with symptoms of conduct disorder.

SUBSTANCE ABUSE

As reported by van der Kolk, numerous studies of substance abusers show higher than expected histories of childhood abuse and neglect, along with obvious histories of parental substance abuse. There is also a higher than expected finding of substance abuse in traumatized adults. The specific "self-medication" qualities of both alcohol and other drugs of abuse (e.g., heroin, which has powerful effects in muting rage and aggression, and cocaine, which has a significant antidepressive quality) are well known, and it is seen that the treatment programs (e.g., AA's "Twelve Steps") tend to instinctively deal with effective post-traumatic treatment (van der Kolk 1996, p. 191).

DISSOCIATION

The quality of dissociation is also well known as a function of this degree of post-traumatic stress. Both children and adults who were traumatized as children often describe themselves as seeming to watch what is going on while feeling that they are at a distance, with the events not really happening to them.

It is thought that during the actual trauma, dissociation allows the person to distance themselves from the event, observe it as a spectator, and experience a limited amount of pain or distress. Such distancing protects the person from the full impact of what has happened (van der Kolk 1996).

van der Kolk also describes as "tertiary dissociation" the experience of learned dissociation in response to trauma in which the individual continues to dissociate in the face of any stress. This strategy not only tends to interfere with the conscious processing of new information, but also prevents the exploration of any forms of alternative ways of coping with stress, which interferes with active problem-solving strategies in new or threatening situations (van der Kolk, van der Hart et al. 1996). Dissociation may well account for the numerous reports made by my interview subjects of feeling, after the fact, a sense of wonder at the decisions and choices they made.

As experienced by the offenders in this book, and to the extent that trauma is associated with their orientation to their current life experience; the result of the trauma is understood as fundamentally a dissociative disorder.

There are developmental phases in which the individual is more vulnerable to traumatic stressors. Perry (1994) has found that the most vulnerable period occurs during the development of the complex stress-mediating central nervous system (in utero, during infancy and childhood).

> In rats exposed to perinatal handling stress major alterations in the ability of the rat to "learn" and to respond appropriately to stressors are seen later in life. The most interesting aspect of these studies is that exposure to unpredictable stress resulted in deficits while exposure to consistent, daily stress resulted in "improved" or superior behavior—these animals were "resilient." (Perry 1994)

This supports several theorists' beliefs regarding traumatic stress. In a discussion with James Grotstein, he suggested to me that his definition of trauma is a reality that happens before one can imagine it. Trauma then defines the self before the self can define it (Grotstein, personal communication). For the child, this may be the difference between a sense of controlling versus being out of control, or having a mother who will allow an optimal degree of frustration, but is also available when the degree of tension or anxiety becomes difficult to manage.

As stated by van der Kolk, trauma results in the "fundamental reorganization of the way mind and brain manage perceptions. It changes not only how we think and what we think about, but also our very capacity to think"(van der Kolk 2014). Because of this, he suggests that any recovery from trauma relates to both finding the words to describe it but also altering the automatic "physical and hormonal responses of bodies that remain hypervigilant, prepared to be assaulted or violated at any time."

The writing on trauma theory in the last decade has become far more assessible and elaborate than at any time in our preceding history. Trauma is more complex and pervasive in both definition and impact than was previously believed. The development of the theory stems from the fact that human beings are meaning-making creatures who are invested in a personal theory of reality that is both conscious and unconscious.

MEANING MAKING

Antonovsky describes the foundation of the making of personal meaning. Significant to the problems of victims, or adult trauma survivors, is the fact that as we develop a sense of personal meaning or sense of coherence, we also become increasingly resistant to change, having developed many "personal theories" that we become comfortable with. This makes us more rigid and less open to the unbiased interpretation of new information as it happens (Kuhn 1962, Popper 1963).

> In the immediate aftermath of traumatic events, victims experience the terror of their own vulnerability. The confrontation with real or potential injury or death breaks the barrier of complacency and resistance in our assumptive worlds, and a profound psychological crisis is induced. What generally begins as a threat to victims' physical integrity becomes an overwhelming threat to their psychological integrity as well. Suddenly survivors become dramatically aware that "bad things can happen to them." They are not protected, safe, and secure in a benign universe. (Janoff-Bulman 1992, p. 61)

In discussing a topic that is especially important to my work's population of victims, Janoff-Bulman quotes Bard and Sangrey (1979) in respect to the impact of becoming a victim of crime, stating that, because crime is an interpersonal event, the victim's feeling of security in the world of other people is seriously compromised. Another person has deliberately violated the crime victim. The victim's injury is not an accident; it is the direct result of the conscious, malicious intention of another human being: "Some people can't be trusted—again, we all know that, but the victim is confronted with human malevolence in a very graphic way" (Janoff-Bulman 1992).

Put another way, significant to both perpetrators' and victims' experiences of trauma is the ability to "remember the future," as described by Siegel. The inability to find resolution for trauma and grief creates in the mind a tendency to develop repeated patterns of disorganization, which happens often unconsciously. These tendencies are often precipitated by external events that are reminiscent of the trauma or can occur due to flashbacks from the intrusion of a mental model of the offending attachment figure.

Trauma theory is the lived experience of individuals who develop a set of defensive organizations that are seen as self-preservation, but later interfere with the development of empathic function. Trauma is not only seen as affecting the development of the infant and child, but also as a situation that is relevant to any life course phase, having monumental consequences on the individual.

Both attachment theory and trauma theory have meaning to the developing individual, which strongly supports much of the current research and understanding on how the infant and child brain develops, how the brain sets down patterns of learning, and how these patterns can change.

Chapter 3

Criminology, Violence, and Restorative Justice

Although it is necessary for me to address the enormous area of violence and criminal behavior, there continues to be no more complicated and controversial area of human existence. To further complicate these matters are the political ramifications of social policy structures in the United States.

Spending on criminal justice has become the largest sector of public spending in the nation, with little evidence that the problem is being successfully addressed. While the nation has, since the Reagan administration, embarked on a new "get tough" policy, the withdrawal of programs supporting rehabilitation seem clearly to have also contributed to increased rates of recidivism. States with the most extreme response to murder, the death penalty, also have the highest rates of murder.

The ever-growing numbers of prisoners in this country believe, cynical as this might be, that the removal of education, therapy, and other efforts at rehabilitation in the current prison environment is intended to increase recidivism. This increase simply ensures the job security of correctional employees in a rapidly growing sector of our economy. There is some indication that this is not altogether an incorrect hypothesis, given that recidivism rates have increased dramatically in the new environment. At the same time, prison construction and employment, often in areas of economic hardship such as rural economies, grows exponentially. The correctional officer's union is now the largest and most powerful in the state of California, having the power to swing state election results (Hallinan 2001).

Interestingly, psychiatry has acquired an increasingly dubious position in terms of its attempt to address criminal behavior. The psychiatric theory of this behavior has been questioned, and has in popular culture been equated more and more with the "liberal" and apologist ideology. This unfortunate politicization of the practice has led to the discounting of both psychiatric developmental theories accounting for the creation of the violent personality as well as efforts at psychiatric rehabilitation. This view is widely held to be an excuse rather than an explanation of the behavior. The insanity defense is now widely viewed as a technical, legalistic ploy to enable criminals to escape taking responsibility for their actions. This stance is not surprising in a culture where mental illness is continuously denied due to its stigma. It also speaks to the usurpation of a "process"-oriented theory base by the legal system (and the willingness of the psychiatric establishment to allow this).

The question of dealing with criminals in society is obviously not new to this era. There has been an ongoing debate, which has carried the same high level of feeling, since classical times. In a democracy, some form of jury system has existed since the Classical Greek era. For a comprehensive documentation of this development, I would refer the reader to Danielle Allen's interesting discussion of this history. As she states:

> To think about punishment is to think about the definitions of justice and fairness that are embodied in institutions, acted out in cultural practices, and explicitly expressed in normative discourses. It is to think about the definitions of desert that sustain the authority that supports the legitimate use of force in a political society. (Allen 2000, p. 10)

Concepts of justice and punishment are richly complicated, involving concepts related to a variety of fields of thought and encompassing issues related to political theory, psychology, and issues of gender and social control (Foucault 1991). The significance of these issues is torn between the dichotomies of "punishment" inflicted in a dispassionate way by society and "revenge," which bears more of a resemblance to kinship feuds and anger.

Most intriguing in the current direction of punishment in this society are continuing indications that the vast majority of the population, when queried directly and given a real choice, continue to favor responses to crime that are more focused on restitution, rehabilitation, and a sensitivity to the process of the victim (Van Ness and Strong 1997).

James Gilligan, a psychiatrist, takes a particularly social/cultural position in his deconstruction of violence in society. He suggests that our increasingly punitive attitude (the increasing use of segregation and the development of the super-secure prison, where inmates are totally isolated in cells for 23 hours per day) is serving to perpetuate the very violence we are attempting to control. Gilligan suggests that, "[Punishment] does not lower the rate or frequency of acts of violence. Punishment stimulates violence; punishment causes it. The more punitive our society has become, the higher our rate of violence (both criminal and non-criminal) has become" (Gilligan 1996, p. 184).

Suggesting that our prison system has become a lens through which to view society as a whole, Gilligan argues that the current system has established a classist stratification in which the "ruling class" creates a subjected and feared lower class, which holds the middle class in rapt attention, away from the exploits of the upper class. He suggests that this accounts for the phenomenon of people generally feeling more hostile toward welfare recipients than they do toward the overpaid corporate executive.

On a social/cultural level, Gilligan sees the ever-widening gap between rich and poor as being directly responsible for the increase in violence, the culture's response to it, and its ever-perpetuating cycle. On an individual level, Gilligan sees violence as being a product of shame, and shame being a product of the size of the gap between "aspiration and achievement" (Gilligan 1996, p. 290).

To explicate the "causality" of such a complex issue, there is no way to avoid a multiple causal explanation, which will have to encompass psychology, sociology, and biology. In a post-positivist world, there cannot be any other way to make such attempts at understanding.

PSYCHOANALYSIS AND GENERAL CLINICAL THEORY

Many psychoanalytic thinkers have attempted to make sense of violent crime. Some of the most interesting has been done around juvenile crime (Eissler 1947, Johnson 1947, Johnson and Szurek 1952).

Much of this early work, along with the most current, continues to be grounded in the theory that criminal behavior is rooted in the failure of the early dyadic relationship, which has a deleterious impact on early attachment and object constancy.

Early psychoanalytic theory had at its core two central hypotheses, which informed much of the theory up to the last twenty years. The first of these is psychic determinism, which asserts that nothing within the psyche happens by accident or chance and that each psychic event is determined by earlier psychic events. The second, and more profound for the modern era, is that of the unconscious, which suggests that linkages of causality or determinism in our psychic lives are not apparent because the most important psychic processes take place at a level below, or outside of, our conscious awareness (Halleck 1971, p. 57). Both hypotheses, to a greater or lesser extent, are at the base of psychological theories of violence, and provide the causal explanation for most confounding human behavior.

ADAPTATION THEORIES

Another trend in psychiatric thinking is related to concepts of adaptation. Fundamental to theories of adaptation are the theory of homeostasis which and concepts of emotional stress serving as a stimulus-and-response as well as connecting to other intervening phenomenological states.

Fundamental, of course, to the adaptation viewpoint is the notion of early troubled or failed interpersonal relationships leading to problems with object relationships and complicating unconscious motivation. The inevitable conflicts experienced in relationships, and the unconscious connections made during these encounters, create anxiety. Violent behavior is a way to either ward off, or lessen the uncomfortable experience of anxiety.

In these psychodynamic, adaptive theories, crime is an adaptation to the stress of life. The inherent question, related to the fact that the commission of crimes is also harmful to the criminal, is why would one develop an adaptation to stress that was ultimately also harmful to the self? The answer to this question resides in the very foundation of the Freudian paradigm, as later developed by Ferenczi and even later by Franz Alexander: "When confronted with stress, the organism may change itself (the internal environment), or it may attempt to change the situation (the external environment). The first type of behavior is called autoplastic and the second alloplastic. The criminal act is almost always an alloplastic adaptation" (Halleck 1971, p. 64).

Stresses come from a variety of sources, external or internal. They can be actual events between people or internalized perceptions. They are also seen as oppressive conditions of the social environment, making the person stressful because of a sense of helplessness or powerlessness through oppression.

> The subjective feeling of helplessness plays an important role in the genesis of criminal action. Unreasonable criminal behavior in particular can be viewed as a direct effort to combat the painful affect of helplessness or as an indirect effort to defend against the emergence of this painful emotional state. (Halleck 1971, p. 69)

Thus, the commission of the crime, even in the face of the possible consequences, is a way to regain a sense of power or agency. The violent criminal feels more in control of a hostile environment, more, as Halleck states, "the master of his own fate." Through the action, the criminal feels less helpless, since that action is being taken to change an uncomfortable or threatening aspect in the external environment. Thus, it is an assertion of autonomy. As Halleck points out, this is what sets the criminal "pathology" apart from neurotic adaptation, which is more of an "autoplastic" adaptation to inner forces.

Another driving force in crime becoming "ego syntonic" (consistent with one's ideal self-image) is the fact that it often survives in a culture, and thus creates an internal reinforcement that becomes very hard to relinquish.

Crime, in Halleck's view, becomes exciting and involves a level of risk that becomes stimulating and even addictive. This is based on the real dangers experienced in criminal behavior necessitating the development of a skill set and creative adaptation. Often this behavior takes on the feel of a game, where outwitting opponents is the goal, and becomes even more exciting when part of a group effort.

In the development of the psychiatric response to criminality, the evolution of this approach as a diagnostic formulation continues to be highly controversial. While the American Psychiatric Association, in DSM IV nomenclature, has maintained "antisocial personality disorder" as a cluster B personality disorder (which evolved from psychopathic and sociopathic personality), there continues to be debate about the role of such a diagnosis. This area has also become highly politicized, mostly due to the dubious role that psychiatry has played in the criminal justice system. The personality disorders have been designated on Axis II of this diagnostic formulary, making it necessary for a clinician to designate an individual as "mentally ill" only if they fit into the standard criteria of an Axis I disorder, which is now even more highly codified. This change was thought to be, I assume, a way to avoid the questionable and embarrassing use of opposing psychiatric testimony in the criminal courts (1994).

It was Pinel and then Prichard in the 1800s who suggested that a recurrent involvement in antisocial behavior must be a mental illness. It is understandable how psychiatrists, steeped in the positivism of the time, would desire to medicalize this behavior. It was an effort to make sense of it, but the diagnosis also made the "condition" available for treatment and a potential cure. However precipitated, the debate has raged from that point forward, largely because the general population, ever suspicious of behavioral science and scientists, has resisted aligning this behavior with "illness," seeing this definition as an attempt to excuse the behavior. The struggle continues whether this behavior, especially the most heinous and confusing behavior, is a sign of illness or simply evil.

Nevertheless, the notion of the psychopath continues to be popular. In its previous use in psychiatric literature, it was intended as an abstract state rather than a definite syndrome.

The psychopathic personality is a continuum of behavior and personality traits rather than a distinct given position. On this continuum, there are lesser, more approachable degrees of psychopathy, and at the extreme end exist a small percentage of criminals that are seen (and highly publicized) as unrepentant and dangerous individuals.

> "Certain individuals who are usually labeled psychopaths may sometimes approach this end point, but no one ever reaches it. The qualities that continue to define the psychopath are a distinct lack of a need for others, beyond their

> usefulness to him. A common understanding is that the psychopath lacks the ability to feel guilt, has a higher level of aggressiveness and impulsivity, and an inability to delay gratification. Psychopaths are seen as having a distinct lack of a sense of history. They are described as those with a lack of "commitment to people, causes, or ideas." (Halleck 1971, p. 107)

The psychodynamic theoretician sees these traits as defensive accommodations to subjective feelings of helplessness. Like many defensive structures in psychoanalytic theory, the ironic hidden desire is often counter to the stated goal. The psychopath, in striking out, soon ends up in a highly dependent state in an institutionalized setting, where his every movement is dictated and controlled.

James Gilligan, using the more negative definition of shame prevalent in psychodynamic theory, feels that the basic underlying element in the creation of a violent offender is the overriding sense of shame felt by the individual. He goes so far as to say that "The emotion of shame is the primary or ultimate cause of all violence" (Gilligan 1996, p. 110). This shame is usually connected to some sense of being disrespected or dishonored and then becomes linked with a sense of fatalism, seeing incarceration or death as preferable to living without pride, dignity, or self-respect. As Gilligan states, "the 'instinct of [psychological] self-preservation' does not hold when one approaches the point of being so overwhelmed by shame that one can only preserve one's self [as a psychological entity] by sacrificing one's body [or those of others]" (Gilligan 1996, p. 110).

Thus, Gilligan suggests that the goal of violence is to replace the sense of shame with a sense of pride. The other preconditions that Gilligan suggests relate to the individual who has no rewarding economic or social achievement to ward off the temptation to violence, and who lacks the "emotional capacities" such as love, guilt, and fear that for most people help ward off the sense of shame. (Shame is defined here as a "psychically life-threatening lack of love.")

John Bowlby himself attempted to deal with the issues of crime and delinquency. In an extensive quantitative study looking at forty-four delinquents, he suggests that at least one of five factors differentiate his sample from a control group: 1) genetic predisposition; 2) early and prolonged separation from the mother; 3) effects in the early years of an ambivalent, hostile, or anxious mother; 4) effects in the early years of a father who actively and openly dislikes the child; and 5) traumatic experiences of later years (Bowlby 1944). Bowlby saw the problems of crime and violence as basically problems of the attachment system.

Fonagy quotes the study by Greenberg et al. (1993, p. 203) in which he reports that insecurely attached children might develop internal working models "in which relationships are generally viewed as characterized by anger, mistrust, chaos and insecurity." Fonagy suggests that this accounts for attributional biases that have been reported in aggressive children, along with evidence that anxious, avoidant infant attachment is a predictor of a later tendency to attribute hostile intent to ambiguous social situations: "The avoidant child may have learned to expect hostility from early experience, and the persistence of the internal working model leads to preemptive aggression in later situations" (Fonagy et al. 1997, pp. 161–162).

The inability to "mentalize" makes it virtually impossible for individuals to have a capacity for empathy or have much of a sense, immediately, of the consequences of their actions for themselves or others. This lack might also contribute to the ability to dehumanize their victim, allowing victims to be treated like objects. Unacceptable conduct, then, might be rationalized as acceptable in certain, usually charged and stressful, situations.

While Fonagy believes aggression to be biologically rooted, he agrees with the more relational theorists (i.e., Mitchell) that aggression comes in response to perceived threats to the psychological self (through a sense of disrespect or humiliation and shame). Again, the reader will see the parallel in the sociological theory of Lonnie Athens discussed hereafter.

I maintain that there is a continuum of violence, and the character structure involved, from the sadistic/malicious to self-preservation types. As Fonagy also points out, the more sadistic types of violence are planned, purposeful, and emotionless, and are linked to the psychopathic character type usually associated with the serial murderer.

Most violent offenders fit on this continuum, at a position that Fonagy describes as characters who, "having sought proximity, then feel trapped by a persecutory object. The act of mindless aggression is characterized by an inexplicable build-up of uncontainable tension and rage just before the violence, the perception of the victim as a threat, and feelings of being out of control during the violent act. The act is aimed at reducing this threat and regaining intrapsychic equilibrium" (Fonagy and Target 1995, p. 488).

LONNIE ATHENS: PHANTOM COMMUNITIES, VIOLENTIZATION, AND SOLILOQUY

The writing and research of Lonnie Athens has made a tremendously important contribution to the understanding of the area of criminal theory (Athens 1992, 1994, 1995, 1997).

I will make use of a biographical account of Athens' life and work that has been very valuable to my understanding of his concepts (Rhodes 1999). Richard Rhodes' work has been helpful in its content, but also its form, as it is presented as a thick biographical sketch, suitable for narrative research, a good case history, or an ethnographic use of thick description.

Rhodes' exploration of Athens' history is informative for a variety of reasons. Athens himself grew up in a highly violent and abusive family. He clearly uses this as the foundation of both his understanding and theory of violent criminals, as well as for his style and way of connecting with his research subjects and conducting interviews. He states very clearly that his own life experiences were the beginnings of his "participant observation," much in the way that Clifford Geertz suggests that everything the researcher experiences in his life should be seen as "field work" (Geertz 2000). He did this work at a time when a qualitative methodology was not seen as acceptable in the academic world, and he experienced consequences to his professional career.

Athens' major mentor was Herbert Blumer at the University of California at Berkeley, who encouraged his efforts, seeing the value in his methodology (See especially Blumer [1969], which has also played a significant role in informing my thinking).

Rhodes quotes Athens' aim of seeking narratives as his research goal, rather than the more acceptable (at the time and probably still) quantitative approaches: "At the theater, reading a book, talking to another person, we all recognize narrative authenticity, whether factual or fictional. ... Athens's goal for his interviews 'was just to get beautiful narrative'" (Rhodes 1999, p. 62).

Athens constructed his theory based on saturated interviews with many violent offenders. He suggests that the violent person progresses through a series of interpretations. The first of these interpretations is to assess the victim's attitude and to assess the meaning of the victim's attitude. The violent person then engages in a self-dialogue, engaging and consulting with a "phantom community" whose attitudes he has internalized. This allows him to decide whether the attitude of the victim warrants violent action.

Athens points to four distinct types of interpretations that the violent person can make:

1. *Physically defensive*: He interprets the victim's attitude to mean that a physical attack is imminent or in progress. The predominant feeling of this interpretation is one of fear on the part of the offender, and, Athens reports, these violent people often see themselves as defending themselves or others.
2. *Frustrative*: He interprets the victim's attitude to mean that the victim is resisting or will resist what the offender's intent is (such as robbery or rape), or that the victim is attempting to initiate some form of control over the offender. The offender reacts with anger at this frustration.

3. *Malefic*: (From the Latin word for evil) Athens sees three steps that lead to this interpretation: a) the offender interprets the attitude of the victim to say that the victim is "scornful, belittling or otherwise contemptuous of him"; b) the offender interprets that the victim himself is evil or malicious; c) the offender determines to counter such evil malice with a violent plan of action. The offender's primary emotional charge here is hatred.
4. *Frustrative-malefic*: The offender makes the interpretation that the opposition that the victim is showing, causing the frustration in the offender, is coming from an evil or malicious place, and greets this interpretation with violence (Rhodes 1999).

THE PHANTOM COMMUNITY

Athens' concept of phantom communities is significant, and parallels many similar theories. For example, I suggest that this concept parallels and is equivalent to John Bowlby's notion of internal working models in child development theory. The phantom community, coming as it does from literal outside sources, does eventually become an internal process.

Athens basically replaces George Herbert Mead's concept of the "generalized other" with his concept of the phantom community (which also continued to put him at risk in the general sociological fraternity). Both concepts see the function of "interlocutors" with whom one consults as related to self-concept or making interpretations of the situations one finds oneself in. The important difference, for Athens, was Mead's notion that the "community" is the generalized community at large (not unlike the Greek chorus), whereas Athens' phantom community is a very specific group of significant past social experiences (Athens 1997, p. 139).

Athens contends that the human thought process is made up of an internal dialogue with ourselves that is quite literal: "We always converse with an interlocutor, even though it may deceivingly appear as if we are only speaking to ourselves" (Rhodes 1999, p. 82). This phantom community, because it is always with us, becomes a constant with more influence than actual people in daily life.

VIOLENTIZATION

Athens proposes a four-stage experiential process leading to the capacity to perpetrate violent acts. These are:

1. *Brutalization*: This refers to violent subjugation, personal horrification, and violent coaching. These all include acts of violence performed at the hands of others (attachment figures). Athens suggests that these very actors (or a substitute group) can later become a gang or family surrogate. Athens includes distinct physical abuse, in the form of punishment, by an authority figure. In personal horrification, Athens is suggesting that the person is not the direct recipient of violent acts, but witnesses (sees or hears) it happening to others (as in the case of a child witnessing spousal abuse). Athens suggests that the overwhelming sense of powerlessness and responsibility that takes place is ultimately turned against the self. Athens, in much the same way that van der Kolk describes the lasting impact of trauma, suggests that the individual is left to personally struggle and make meaning of these experiences, including "their larger general meaning for his future relationships with other human beings." He also states that "Violent subjugation generates relatively enduring emotionally charged thoughts that combine a barely repressed sense of rage with vague notions about physically attacking other people" (Rhodes 1999, p. 126). In violent coaching, Athens suggests that someone older is seen, literally, as responsible for the violent coaching of the "novice." This takes place through storytelling (personal anecdotes about violent acts); ridicule, belittling, and derision; coercion and physical intimidation; and haranguing.
2. *Belligerency*: Athens sees this phase as an attempt to externalize the feelings of worthlessness and powerlessness, which leads to a decision that, in certain cases, violence is warranted. This action is an attempt to focus outward the rage that is directed against the self.
3. *Violent Performances*: Athens suggests that crossing the line into violent acts is not easy. The violent person generally waits for an opportunity to become severely provoked. Once the line is crossed, however, a major shift of self-view takes place in both the individual and his community (assuming a "win" in the altercation). Often the system begins to treat the person as if he were dangerous or "crazy." This creates, in Rhodes' term, a "celebrity" status, and, while not without ambivalence, it creates a shift in the role and performance of the individual.
4. *Virulency*: The individual now is ready to "attack people physically with the serious intention of gravely harming or killing them with minimal or less than minimal provocation on their part" (Rhodes 1999, p. 133).

Athens sees the process of violentization to be developmental and sequential and necessary in all its phases to create a violent individual: "Violentization is an authentic developmental process, and unless someone has undergone it, Athens emphasizes, he will not become a dangerous violent criminal" (Rhodes 1999, p. 135).

Athens states that the "basic assumption behind my theory is that crime is a product of social retardation. Social retardation exists when people guide their actions toward themselves and others from the standpoint of an underdeveloped, primitive phantom community, an 'us' that hinders them from cooperating in the ongoing social activities of their corporal community or the larger society in which it is embedded" (Athens 1997, p. 144).

RESTORATIVE JUSTICE

I am proceeding with the supposition that restorative justice is a social movement that has significant ramifications for both individual meaning and community development. In this way, I see restorative justice as having the same potential ramifications on the individual and community—especially at a time of personal crisis or intensity—as does any other significant individual/social experience (e.g., psychoanalysis/psychotherapy; alcoholic intervention and treatment; religious conversion and commitment).

As such, I am suggesting that it holds the same potential for meaningful and sustained personal change as does any such form of personal growth and development.

The concept of restorative justice flows from the philosophy that crime affects individuals and communities, not the state or the criminal justice system. Its major focus of practice has been victim/offender mediation dialogues, community sentencing efforts, and community education.

As Van Ness points out:

> Restorative justice advocates view crime as more than simply lawbreaking, an offense against governmental authority; crime is understood also to cause multiple injuries to victims, the community and even the offender. Second, proponents argue that the criminal justice process should help repair those injuries. Third, they protest the government's apparent monopoly over society's response to crime. Victims, offenders and their communities also must be involved at the earliest point and to the fullest extent possible. (Van Ness and Strong 1997, p. 31)

Zehr suggests that restorative justice is not a "program" but rather a philosophy of justice that is grounded in the principle that crime is harm, and that all the real individuals impacted ("stakeholders" as Zehr declares) need to be involved in the response to a crime. A way to directly encounter each other, then, is the only way to apply these principles.

Dave Gustafson (2001) quotes Howard Zehr who originally defined the different paradigms of retributive justice and restorative justice. These include the fact that retributive justice is a single-focused process looking at one point (the crime) and one result (punishment). The primary focus of retributive justice is the state, which makes the laws, including the rules of evidence, which might lead to a dismissal of charges if these rules are not correctly followed. Also, these "rules" often support, even demand, the guilty party pleading "not guilty" to stay within the framework of the system. Zehr defines restorative justice as having a wider focus. (As a photographer, Zehr is using this metaphor deliberately.) The crime is not committed against the state, but against people engaged in relationships. The intent of restorative justice is accountability, healing, and closure.

Gustafson points out that the concept of "closure" is a difficult one, as it is unlikely that this is ever possible in the case of violent crime. It would, according to Gustafson, be more reasonable to look at this dilemma as degrees of closure measured by how much it consumes victims' lives (Gustafson 2001).

The most important and yet straightforward approach is what Van Ness (1994) terms the "encounter" between the parties. In most criminal procedures, the victim and perpetrator may never come face to face (apart from a relatively new and inconsistent practice of "victim impact statements" at the time of the imposition of a sentence). In the trial, the perpetrator is represented by counsel who speak for him to a judge. The victim sits in the gallery, facing the offender's back. In the legal process, there is often archaic language used, so the parties may not even understand the proceedings. In many jurisdictions, if victims are witnesses in the case, they are barred from sitting in the courtroom.

In the restorative justice model of the post-trial encounter, both parties go through a significant period of preparation with the mediator. In one of the states in which I did research, there is also an extensive number of written exercises that the participants are asked to do by way of aiding the mediator and the participants in the preparation.

This preparation period seems to be a vital part of the experience, both related to the mediator's ability to judge the preparedness and attitude of the participants. However, it also seems to serve as a healing process, in and of itself, for the parties.

The mediation session can be a single meeting or a series of meetings over time. The mediator, or in some of my cases a team of mediators, facilitates all the meetings that take place and often engages in debriefing sessions with the participants, or even with other family members who were not involved in the original meeting. In this way, there is a "ripple effect" of the original encounter that has an increasing impact on the larger system of the community or the offender population.

The benefits to the victim's families relate to the raising of the most difficult, highly emotional, and spiritual issues that are central to recovery from violent crime. All participants speak of a sense of healing and help in moving toward a greater sense of closure and resolution. Beyond this, the experiences are very individualized. Many discuss this to achieve a voice in the process and become "real" to the offender.

Peterson has covered in detail the impact on the survivors of violent crime (Peterson 2000). Not only do the survivors of violent crime undergo significant emotional sequelae, but this type of crime also impacts the victim's family, friends, and community. There are often reports of post-trauma symptoms in these "survivors," who express the same symptomatology described earlier.

The family of the offender, described by one participant as the "forgotten victims of crime," suffer similar experiences, along with their own stigma of shame and ostracism. These participants are now also seen as valuable and important "stakeholders" in the process.

Also characteristic of some victims of crime is a desire for retaliation. In this way, the current practice of criminal justice seems effective, as the retaliatory or talionic impulse is at the basis of the current criminal justice system in most cultures. The restorative justice effort has thrived, however, with those victims who, for a variety of reasons, have found this process insufficient to the resolution of their feelings. This seems to be supported in Peterson's study, as she found a negative correlation between vengefulness and a sense of personal coherence.

Relative to the impact of restorative justice on the offender, Van Ness states, "For the offender who has harmed another, the voluntary assumption of responsibility is an important step in not only helping others who were hurt by the crime but also in building a prosocial value system" (Van Ness and Strong 1997, p. 35).

In follow-up research currently being conducted by Umbreit, offenders who have participated in mediated dialogues with victims are reporting satisfaction with the preparation by the mediator and program. Almost all report the meeting to be helpful; most indicate a change in their "outlook on life," meaning that they felt more positive and content. All stated that their meeting with the victim greatly changed their understanding of how the crime affected others. Almost all stated some impact on their religious or spiritual orientation (Umbreit 2001, p. 266).

Chapter 4

Neuropsychiatry

We continue to learn that the human brain is an extremely complex and interesting system. What is thought to be significant about its structure is its organization, duplication of function, and resiliency. The brain is seen to have three distinctly evolved functions. The core of the brain, and the first to develop in utero, is what Lewis refers to as the "reptilian" brain, which is responsible for such key functions as heart function, body temperature, and respiration. The next layer is the "limbic" brain, which is the seat of emotion and feeling, including the experiences known as depression, anxiety, anger, rage, love, joy, and so on. The outer layer of the brain is the neocortical layer, which houses intellectual function, reason, logic, and episodic and explicit memory. While it has been interesting to view the brain in these distinct functional ways, the brain is far more complex in its structure. As Feldman Barrett states, "humans don't have an animal brain gift-wrapped in cognition" (Feldman Barrett 2017). Thus, it is far too simplistic to localize emotion as a "limbic" function alone, as it is clear that many areas of the brain deal with emotion.

In some research, however, it is seen that the limbic tissues have a more primitive cellular organization than do the neocortical systems. In animal studies, functions such as nurture, social communion, and play are clearly limbic functions. As Lewis reports, a hamster can have its entire neocortex removed but still perform her mothering function, while even a small amount of limbic damage deletes her maternal abilities (Lewis et al. 2000, p. 32).

NEURAL DEVELOPMENT AND LIMBIC RESONANCE

It is suggested that in infancy, in support of attachment theory, the mother provides a limbic resonance with the child in synchrony with the child's own neural rhythms. As the child develops and matures, the child's neurophysiology becomes more able to provide its own regulation, but only after this regulation has been provided by the caregiver "from the outside in," as the brain learns stability, consistency, and predictability.

THE IMPORTANCE OF RELATIONSHIP

There is much to indicate that the human brain is specifically set up in such a way as to be determined by relationship. Trevarthen suggests that "Fetuses in utero show coordinated activity, including differentiated movements adapted for perception-seeking and communication, before the cerebral cortex is functional" (Trevarthen and Aitken 1994).

These researchers believe in the adaptive plasticity of the brain, especially in newborns, but also highlight an elaborate and selective ability in the infant for engaging with the processes that motivate expressive behaviors in the caregivers, in the intersubjective sense. In this way, Trevarthen and his colleagues feel that attachment theory does not go far enough in defining the significance of neonatal development. They feel that interactions between infant and caregiver are more complex than only the control of tension and arousal. These early interactions are responsible for the development of a cognitive (in the sense of the development of the individual identity) and the intersubjective (related to the sense of a community). This is then seen as necessary to general learning and the development of culture, as well as the sense of community or "companionship" (Aitken and Trevarthen 1997, p. 655).

A BIOLOGICAL BASIS FOR ATTACHMENT THEORY

Allan Schore has been highly instrumental in connecting commonly held child developmental themes to psychoneurological development. He quotes a variety of studies that would indicate the biological basis for Bowlby's attachment theory, especially Bowlby's notion of internal working models.

In meaningful face-to-face interactions between infant and caregiver, there is a "synchrony or regulation" that takes place at the "organismic level," in which the "psychobiologically attuned" caregiver not only minimizes the infant's negative states, but also maximizes its positive, affective states. This "proximate interpersonal context of 'affect synchrony' and interpersonal resonance represents the external realm of attachment dynamics" (Schore 2000, p. 27).

Further, Shore discusses several studies which indicate that emotional experiences (in the infant) are stored or processed in the right hemisphere during the "formative stages of brain ontogeny." The infant then relies on these memory systems during the first years of life, using these areas of the right brain to store "autobiographical memory." He further states that "These findings suggest that early forming internal working models of the attachment relationship are processed and stored in implicit-procedural memory systems in the right cortex, the hemisphere dominant for implicit learning" (Schore 2000, p. 32).

Schore suggests that this area of the brain may well be the location of empathic ability, or, if impeded by either physical or developmental factors, may be the site of sociopathic behaviors: "Other research indicates that prefrontal damage acquired early in life provides the neurological substrate for a permanent impairment of empathic, moral, and social behavior, all of which were 'arrested at an immature stage'" (Schore 1994, p. 353).

THE BIO-PSYCHO-SOCIAL PERSPECTIVE: EMPATHY AND TRAUMA

It has been discovered that a variety of physiological effects take place when trauma occurs. These include a secretion of hormones, acceleration of heart rate, blood pressure changes due to vasoconstriction and rerouting of blood flow, contraction of muscles, immunologic responses, as well as alerting and arousal reactions. It has been well established that people with distinct trauma histories have a greater tendency to develop autoimmune disorders. In all of the responses to traumatic events, *catecholamines* become involved (Janoff-Bulman 1992).

Catecholamines are mobilizing chemicals (including norepinephrine, epinephrine or adrenaline, and dopamine) that are synthesized in the neuronal cells of the brain, adrenal medulla, and sympathetic nervous system.

Both Perry and Schore agree that the orbitofrontal area of the brain is the vital link between the physical and emotional development of the infant. Because of the vision center, expressions on the mother's face and her actions, and the connections between the two, are processed here. In the right hemisphere, the orbitofrontal area is most involved with the limbic brain, connecting it to positive and negative emotional expression, and extends into the lower limbic system and amygdala, hypothalamus, and autonomic centers in the brain stem, thus exerting control over both sympathetic and parasympathetic nervous systems. Here are created the bodily reactions to emotional situations. Here is the center of base anxiety which triggers the fight-or-flight response to external danger.

Perry believes that, as the brain develops, each of these areas is developing in response to the environment and are thus "use dependent," which means that they will be shaped by the individual's unique environmental circumstances. The more the system changes to reflect the pattern of activation, the more a "use dependent" development emerges. Every time a part of the brain is activated, it is also changed because of that activation; thus, Perry sees the brain as being highly plastic. However, this plasticity is not uniform across all brain areas. It takes less time, intensity, and repetition to organize the developing neural systems than to reorganize the developed neural systems.

When stressed or distressed, the brain releases endogenous opiates (which account for the experience of "tuning out" or dissociating). These brain chemicals stay longer in the body than even adrenalyn and create the repetitive-stress response patterning that ends up being built into the physical system. Inconsistent caregiving, for example, produces a constantly high state of arousal. These disorganized sensory experiences result in a disorganized brain organization.

Perry states that young children adapt to threat following one of two common response sets, which also account for biochemical reactions. In the "arousal continuum," the child is in a state of hyperarousal (leading to the fight-or-flight reaction), which increases norepinephrine, dopamine, gaba, and serotonin in the nervous system. The second is the "dissociative continuum," which leads to a defeated or giving-up set of behaviors, which increase opioid peptides, serotonin, and dopamine. He suggests that very young children, unable to easily fight or flee, will often manifest a predominant dissociative response which he refers to as the freeze or surrender pattern (Perry et al. 1995).

Significantly, Perry states that "Children in a state of fear store and retrieve information from the world differently than children who feel calm." Given that these children are experiencing a persistent sense of anxiety, accessing stored cortical information becomes impossible (Perry 1997).

This results in a disproportiante number of these children having "learning disabilities" (evidenced by pronounced verbal and performance IQ differences), attention deficit hyperactivity disorder, and so on, with teachers reporting that they are "smart" but do not seem to learn. Perry suggests that these symptoms are the result of a "use dependent" organization of the brainstem nuclei involved in the stress response apparatus generated by an adverse environment (Perry 1995, p. 137).

The result of this, as seen in child victims of severe trauma that Perry has studied, is distorted cognitive development because so much time is spent in a state of hyperarousal. The system that is most in play here is the limbic system, because it is the most hypervigilant to nonverbal cues, increasing the ability to "read" people and situations. These children have a resting heart rate far higher than the normal, are frequently seen with siezure disorders, and have frequent somatic complaints. They show affective lability, behavioral impulsivity, increased anxiety, increased startle response, and sleep abnormalities.

Schore states, "Any factors which increase the activity or reactivity of the brainstem (e.g., chronic stress) or decrease the moderating capacity of the limbic or cortical areas (e.g., neglect) will increase an individual's aggressivity, impulsivity and capacity to display violence" (Karr-Morse and Wiley 1997).

Dr. Perry is ultimately concerned about the current direction that society is heading in relation to the place of children in this culture and the breakdown of the family and community as a supportive unit with a commonly held value system. He quotes well-founded statistics that on an annual basis in the United States, over five million children are exposed to violence in the home, either through witnessing domestic violence or as direct victims of physical abuse. He makes a direct connection between this exposure and the increase in violence in society by youth in particular. This postulation directly supports Lonnie Athens' hypothesis regarding the making of violent criminals through his theory of violentization.

A frustrated three-year-old has a difficult time modulating his state of arousal, being driven by the lower brain functions, often throwing a tantrum. The older child when frustrated may feel like throwing a tantrum, but has the capacity to modulate the urge.

> The most dangerous children are created by a malignant combination of experiences. Developmental neglect and traumatic stress during childhood create violent, remorseless children. This is characterized by sensitized brainstem systems (e.g., serotonergic, noradrenergic and dopaminergic systems). Dysregulated brainstem functions (e.g., anxiety, impulsivity, poor affect regulation, motor hyperactivity) are then poorly modulated by poorly organized limbic and cortical neurophysiology and functions (e.g., empathy, problem solving skills) which are the result of chaotic, undersocialized development. This experience-based imbalance predisposes to a host of neuropsychiatric problems—and violent behavior. (Perry 1996)

In remarkable agreement with both Bowlby's theory of internal working models and Athens' theory of phantom communities, Perry suggests that, given the use-dependent fashion in which the brain develops, the neural systems that are activated repeatedly change and create "internal representations" or literal memories (Perry 1996). These memories range between cognitive memories, emotional memories, motor-vestibular memories, and state memories.

The child who is a victim of fear and threat has a brain physiology that is invested in these memory types in order to adapt to a world that is characterized by unpredictability and danger: "The brains of traumatized children develop to be hypervigilant and focused on non-verbal cues, potentially related to threat. These children are in a persisting state of arousal and, therefore, experience persisting anxiety" (Perry 1996).

Similar to the early reported history of many of the perpetrators studied here is the altered sense of time also experienced by Perry's children. According to him, they have a foreshortened sense of the future. They lack any real concept of what will happen in the months or certainly the years to come. Thus, immediate reward becomes the most reinforcing behavior, and delaying gratification is nearly impossible. They manifest no real sense of the consequences of their behavior, nor do they have an ability to reflect on this behavior. They act reflexively, impulsively, and aggressively to any perceived threat.

OPTIONS FOR CHANGE

Important to my overall interest in this topic, but also significant to the process of psychotherapy in general, is the fact that these authors are optimistic about the possibility of change in the individual—even as it relates to the structure of the brain.

One might argue that the major intent of psychodynamic psychotherapy in its most fundamental applications is to make connections between current memory and past experience that may be repressed or unconscious. This, through a positive "attachment" experience with the therapist, allows the client to make connections between dysregulated states, tolerate them, and learn of their origin and meaning.

Siegel believes that bringing conscious "reflection" to unresolved traumas allows them to be incorporated within an "autobiographical narrative" that serves to connect left hemisphere feeling states with right hemisphere autobiographical representations, allowing for the right hemisphere to "regulate primary emotional states."

> Such mentalizing reflective dialogue is also a fundamental component of secure attachments. Individuals with histories of disorganized attachments can thus become freed from the "prison of the present," in which they were repeatedly trapped when they had no words to reflect on their rapidly enveloping and terrifying states of mind. (Siegel 1999, pp. 297–298)

Schore quotes a number of studies (Schwartz et al. 1996) to indicate that there are demonstrable brain changes as a result of successful psychotherapy. Many of these indices, using PET scan and fMRI information, have indicated significant changes to metabolic activity in the right cortex and its subcortical connections as a result of successful psychological treatment (Schore 1997). These researchers point to the fact that even in the adult brain, the capacity for "experience dependent plastic changes in the nervous system" remains throughout the life span. Schore states, "In fact, there is now evidence that the prefrontal limbic cortex, more than any other part of the cerebral cortex, retains the plastic capacities of early development" (Schore 1997, p. 52).

In direct relevance to my current topic, Houser states:

> When an aggressor reconciles with its victim, there is some sense in which this interaction looks like a sympathetic or perhaps empathetic response ... For some empathy entails more than feeling the same way as someone else. It entails knowing or being aware of what it is like to be someone else. In its simplest formulation, empathy grows out of a mirror neuron-like system, where my perception of an event is mirrored by my enactment of the very same event. Once in place, however, this form of empathy is transformed—either in evolution or in capacity, individuals can think about what someone else feels, imagine how they would feel in the same situation, work out what would make them feel better, and from this deduce how to make the other person feel better. (Hauser 2006, p. 352)

Also important is the indication that these structures, previously seen as "hardwired" functions, can be altered throughout the life course. The brain, while complex, is now seen as eternally evolving, with the option possible for the reversal of previously considered intractable states (through what Linda Mayes has referred to as "dendritic arborization").

The significance to me of this information, beyond the obvious self-serving interest in the affirmation of the efficacy of psychotherapy, is the challenge to the long-held belief in popular and professional culture of the intractability of the personality of the psychopath.

Chapter 5

The Village

Johnny lived in a medium-sized city where he was born and raised. He had completed high school, but hadn't found something to do that was of much interest to him. Nevertheless, he felt that he was doing all right and that his life was going along pretty much as he had expected.

Even though he was a member of a gang, he hadn't gotten into serious trouble, as many of his friends had, and he saw himself as smarter than many his fellow gang members, whom he viewed as doing stupid, even self-destructive things. The only arrests he had on his record were for petty offenses or misdemeanors. He had come close to more serious problems, but was able to avoid trouble by using what he felt was a "sixth sense" of avoidance for bad or dangerous situations.

He did have a legal case pending, and while he felt he had sufficient money banked to hire a lawyer, he was not sure he had enough. He also had the responsibility of two children that he wished to support.

While sitting on his parent's front porch one day, a group of people he knew drove up and wanted to talk with him. His father was not happy about these people being in the yard, as he knew them to be problem kids from troubled families. Knowing this, Johnny sent them away, but caught up to them later, as they told him they had a plan that could not fail to enrich them all.

When he later talked to these friends, he was told that they had come across information that was reliable (coming from a relative of one of the group) of a drug dealer who lived in a rural area outside of the city and who had large stashes of both money and drugs in his home. The plan was to go to the house that night and rob the drug dealer of both his drugs and his money. The argument was that there could not be a more foolproof crime, as there was no way that the drug dealer would involve the police—for obvious reasons.

Johnny saw the logic in this argument and got into the car. He thought a little extra money would be useful. After a couple of hour's drive to the country, the map to the house was produced and, although it was rather crude and handwritten, the house was eventually found. One of the group went to the house and stated to the woman who answered the door that they were having car trouble and would like to use the phone. He was invited in, and the rest followed, wearing surgical masks.

Inside the house, a man, two women, and a four-year-old boy faced the group. The boy was sitting on the couch, and one of the women was reading a story to him. (The man and one of the women were parents of the child; the other woman was a friend of the family visiting from another town.)

One of the gang produced a gun and demanded the drugs and money. He was told that the family had no money and only a little bit of marijuana. The little boy, to this point, had felt that all of this was a game. He was not overly concerned until the gun was produced, and he felt the tension of the adults in the room. The man with the gun turned it on the little boy, and demanded of the mother, again, that she produce the money and drugs. She again pleaded with him, saying that there was no money in the house.

Johnny, at this point, went up the stairs to search the upstairs bedrooms. The boy's father and the family friend were ordered down to the basement. A short time later, Johnny heard a shot and ran downstairs. He had not found anything of interest upstairs and was beginning to think that there was a significant problem with the original plan.

While heading down the stairs he saw the body of the boy's mother lying at the bottom of the staircase, having been shot in the head by the gang member that still held the gun. At this point, an argument ensued between the gang members, which Johnny states he precipitated, about the course of this robbery. In the meantime, the gang member with the weapon had taken the little boy to the basement, along with the father and female friend.

In the basement, the little boy had been placed in a side room, and the perpetrator had demanded that the man and woman disrobe and that the woman perform oral sex on the man. Eventually, and, inexplicably, he eventually shot both in the head.

An argument then developed regarding what to do with the little boy. Two of the perpetrators, primarily Johnny, demanded that they do nothing to the little boy. Johnny argued that the little boy would not be able to identify them and would be of no use as a witness. The group eventually agreed, and Johnny erected a barrier of boxes, so the little boy could not see the bodies of the two adults. Then Johnny gave the little boy a push-up popsicle, which he found in the freezer, and the group left the home.

The next morning, a friend of the family dropped by and, getting no answer at the door, looked through the living room window. There, he saw the body of the mother on the floor at the foot of the stairs. He entered the house to see if she was alive, and called the police.

Deputy Smith, leaving for work that morning, received a call from his office saying that there had been a murder reported, and that his partner was already en route. Deputy Smith lived close to the home, and it was on his way to work anyway. He was familiar with this family, having grown up with the man of the house, and, later, having arrested him for a variety of petty offenses through the years.

When he arrived at the scene, his partner and the friend were standing outside of the house. The friend was sent away, as the two officers needed to search the home, not knowing the circumstances of the murder and considering that the perpetrator might still be there.

They drew their service revolvers and began a search of the main floor and upstairs. Then, they both heard "Daddy!" through a heater vent coming from the basement.

The two went down to the basement where they discovered the body of the family friend and then the body of the boy's father. When he checked, Deputy Smith discovered that the father was still living, and sent the partner up to call for an ambulance. He then holstered his gun and approached the little boy, whom he found still sitting behind his box barricade, still holding the plastic tube that had once held a popsicle. Deputy Smith picked up the child and held his hand over his eyes while leaving the basement, to prevent him from seeing the bodies.

Johnny had been dropped off by the group back at his home. They were all certain that no one would catch them, as they weren't known in that area. The group had thrown their guns in the river on the way back to the city.

As time went on, Deputy Smith was having a hard time with this case. None of the leads had panned out, and it was difficult to discover any motive for the crime. The little boy's father had been shot in the head and was left paralyzed by his injuries; he also had no memory of the events. The little boy, of course, was not a profound witness, given his age. None of his statements made much sense, and further, the boy hid under a desk when he saw Deputy Smith again. Deputy Smith felt he had a way with children, and it is likely that the little boy associated Deputy Smith with the event rather than as his rescuer, this feeling perhaps compounded by the fact that Deputy Smith had been wearing latex gloves that morning, just as the robbers had. Given the sheriff's office's difficulty in solving the crime, there was increasing pressure to turn the investigation over to the Bureau of Criminal Apprehension (BCA), a state agency. Crimes such as this were not, in fact, very common in this rural county. Given this fact and the lack of success he had with interviewing the only witness, Deputy Smith, somewhat grudgingly, eventually turned the case over to the state's BCA.

Eventually, a break came from an off-duty police officer in the city where Johnny lived. One of his snitches had heard the story of the crime from one of the perpetrators and was willing to exchange this information for future favors. Deputy Smith was called and, again, picked up the investigation, with the involvement of the BCA.

Once arrests began to happen and Johnny was questioned, he knew that things weren't going to go well. He left the city and traveled to relatives in a midwestern city and to friends in California, where he was eventually arrested. Deputy Smith, along with the county sheriff, flew to California to pick him up.

Deputy Smith was immediately impressed with Johnny for reasons that he was not quite sure of. It did not take Johnny long to decide to tell the truth about that night, as, in his absence, the other perpetrators were blaming him for everything.

In ongoing interviews with Deputy Smith, Johnny agreed to tell the truth about the events of that evening and agreed to testify against the others. Given this history, Deputy Smith was asked to transport Johnny to all the other trials, which he did. It was during these drives that Deputy Smith became more familiar with Johnny and his life, and continued to see him as an interesting individual.

In one of their discussions, it also became clear that the map that the group was carrying was being held upside down, as there was, apparently, a reputed drug dealer in this area, but he lived the opposite way of where the family was living. The group should have taken a left, and, instead, had taken a right.

The results of the trials were that one of the perpetrators was found not guilty, and the others received life sentences. Johnny also received a life sentence with the possibility of parole after ten years in prison.

Following these events, the little boy, Adam, was sent to live with his grandparents. He began having problems in school, and was seen by other family members as being overindulged by the grandparents, who were dealing with many other family problems. Because of this, Adam's aunt, his father's youngest sister, and uncle, argued with the grandparents that they could provide a better environment for Adam, and had the energy to deal with a now six-year-old boy, who was evidencing several problems.

The aunt and uncle reported that when Adam began to live with them, he was out of control. Diagnosed as having attention deficit hyperactivity disorder, he was prescribed the alerting medication, Ritalin, to little effect. Besides showing disrespect for his teachers, he would not comply with family rules unless there was a bribe involved (as he had come to expect when living with his grandparents). The new caregivers were heartened, however, by the fact that Adam seemed to be aware of his problems and was clearly uncomfortable with his life. He responded well, eventually, to firm parenting, consequences, and follow-through, and appeared to begin to flourish in their home. The couple made the obvious connection that Adam was struggling with the events of the evening two years ago where he had lost his mother and, ultimately, his father. (Adam's father continued with significant impairment from his injuries. He did make enough progress in rehabilitation to move to an assisted living situation. It was hoped that, with this progress, he would continue toward some greater form of assisted but independent living. A roommate, however, later murdered him in his assisted living situation after an argument following a night of drinking.)

Given Adam's progress, the aunt and uncle attempted to locate psychotherapy for him. Although Adam consulted with two therapists in his community, the aunt and uncle saw little progress in what continued to be a defiant and anxious presentation at school.

When the aunt and uncle met with Adam's therapists, they asked what Adam was saying about the murders and violence he witnessed in his home, and what feelings he was expressing at the loss of his parents. From both therapists, they were told that dwelling on such material by a child would not be of any use, and would, in fact, make matters far worse. It was the belief of both therapists that Adam should be encouraged to stay in the "here and now," and not go back into past events.

The aunt and uncle were discouraged. Adam, now nine, continued to make some progress, but also continued to struggle in school. Both parents strongly valued school performance. While they had long since removed him from the medication and felt that he continued to be responsive to their style of parenting, they were concerned about his overall welfare if he was not able to deal with the issues that they both felt, instinctively, were a major concern for him.

Deputy Smith was aware of these struggles, as in a small community such as his, he knew the family and lived not far from Adam, seeing him at community functions. The trials were long over, and he had been successful, given Johnny's cooperation, at keeping Adam isolated from the trials. When Deputy Smith and Adam met, they acknowledged one another, but they had no discussion about their history together.

The aunt was familiar with a "Victim Services" office located in the city and put in a call to them. A counselor was on staff that had experience in dealing with children and an appointment was made.

Adam, when given the opportunity, responded quickly to an environment where he was encouraged to tell his story. Using play therapy techniques, Adam began a course of therapy that was aimed at dealing with the aftermath of crisis and trauma that Adam surely continued to struggle with.

As Adam turned ten, his counselor, aunt, and uncle saw the immediate results of this work. Adam began to focus in school, and his grades, for the most part, showed improvement. However, one issue continued to bother his therapist. From almost the start of their work together, Adam was very interested in one of the perpetrators. He almost immediately said to the counselor that he would like to sit down and talk with the man who had "saved me." The counselor was sympathetic to his interest, and was intrigued, herself, by the events of the history. Adam's desire was tenacious, but she was clearly uncertain about his motivation or whether such a meeting would be safe or useful to her client. At the same time, in the work they had done together, she was impressed with Adam and his reasons for wanting such a meeting.

The counselor put in a call to a mediator, at the State Department of Corrections, who had conducted training for the office on Restorative Justice Mediation. She stated that she was dealing with an interesting case and wanted to tell the mediator about it.

After hearing the story, the mediator requested a meeting with Adam and was likewise impressed with his manner and the reasons he gave for wanting to meet with this man. He had all but written the rationale given for these meetings in his own way, as evidenced by his stated desire and reasons for wanting a meeting. The problem was that in no case, in which she was familiar, had a child been involved in such a meeting.

The mediator called a colleague, who was also involved in the restorative justice movement, and, coincidentally, was in the state where Johnny had been sent to be incarcerated, given that he had testified against the others and was thought to be unsafe in that state's prison system.

The two mediators began an extensive consultation with a variety of experts on child development and restorative justice so as to identify the possible problems in conducting a meeting between the offender and such a young person. They were gratified in that all the experts agreed that such a meeting might well be of great benefit to Adam, if his own vulnerability was not so great that the meeting would further expose him to trauma. At the same time, the feeling was that such a meeting might go a long way in helping Adam resolve his trauma. Both the local mediator and Adam's counselor felt that his desire was credible, and that he had the strength to at least begin the preparation for such a meeting.

During this preparation, Deputy Smith, with Adam's agreement, was invited into the counselor's office with Adam to tell him the story of that night and the resulting investigation. Adam was very thankful for the information, as it filled out either blanks in his memory or areas of his memory that were unclear.

In the meantime, the other mediator began to meet with Johnny. While somewhat skeptical initially, Johnny also held in his memory the vision of that four-year-old, and was concerned as to what had happened to him. Johnny was convinced when he was told the story of Adam's problems in school and other adjustment issues. Johnny's son was around Adam's age, which perhaps heightened Johnny's concern about the boy.

Preparation for the meeting took about a year. Adam's aunt and uncle were initially cautious about the idea, but were convinced by the professionals involved, and by Adam, who assured them that this was important to him. The aunt, a sister of Adam's dad, considered meeting with Johnny herself, and was encouraged to do so by everyone, but, ultimately, she opted not to do it. It had been thought, up until the last minute, that she would change her mind, and all involved, including her husband, felt that it would be meaningful and helpful for her to do this by way of her own recovery. Despite this, she decided that, for her, it would not be helpful to meet with the offender. She felt that she was still quite bitter, and was concerned that one of the motives for such a meeting would be to secure her forgiveness, which she was not prepared to give.

The preparation period went smoothly, which again indicated to the mediators that they were on the right track in proceeding with the meeting. Johnny, following a period of some hesitation, was now entirely convinced that he wanted to participate in the meeting. Adam continued to express some concern as to what would happen, how he would feel, and how Johnny would be, but was still determined to meet with him.

The meeting was eventually held in the warden's staff meeting room at the prison in which Johnny was housed. It had been approximately eight years since the murders.

In attendance at the meeting were Johnny, Adam, and the two mediators, both from different states, who had been involved in the preparation. Johnny's case manager was present, to provide Johnny with support if necessary. Adam's counselor was also at his side. Deputy Smith was invited to attend, and sat in the background. There was also a film crew of two videotaping the meeting, as is the tradition in these meetings. Members of the film crew were employees of the Department of Corrections in Adam's state. Adam's aunt and uncle waited outside of the room.

The meeting progressed well. Johnny's first gesture, not captured on the videotape, was to ask the group to stand and applaud Adam for having the courage to pursue the meeting.

THE INTERVIEWS

I will present the interviews with these individuals in the order in which they were completed. While the order of the interviews was usually determined only by the convenience and availability of the individuals, this presentation will allow the reader a view of how these narratives evolved for me as researcher.

Johnny's Mother and Father: Johnny's parents had been referred to me through the mediator, who had prepared Johnny for the meeting. The mediator had met with the family, at their request, and showed them the tape of the mediation. He had been impressed with their position in relation to their son and his involvement in the process. When I first called Johnny's parents to see if they would be willing to be interviewed, I, too, was impressed with Johnny's mother at once. She quickly connected with me on the phone, telling me instantaneously interesting information that I hadn't previously known about Johnny (i.e., that he had a son the same age as Adam, a factor that I found significant in other cases with offenders). She was also the first to alert me as to the position of the offender's family and how she felt that they were the "forgotten victims" in the process.

As the interview approached, Johnny's father began having second thoughts about participating, not knowing much about who I was, what I was interested in, or why. In my final phone discussion with the mother prior to my arrival, I reiterated my interest and my role, and told her that we would discuss this thoroughly, utilizing the informed consent documents I was using, when we met, prior to any interview questions. She told me that she had discussed this with Johnny (who also had not met me yet) and he had encouraged them to meet with me and see what they thought.

In each of these cases, I initially explained my role as that of a researcher, looking at many cases of these meetings and trying to determine, through interviews, the effects on the participants. While I told many of the participants that my occupation was psychotherapy, I was clear that my role in relation to them was to obtain data that would appear at least in my dissertation and possibly in other publications about the process.

Johnny's parents were interviewed in the main interview room at the Victim's Services office in the city in which Johnny had lived. It is a comfortable room with couches and chairs, decorated with typical types of posters with "sayings" that one finds in such offices. Many of my interviews for this group were conducted here because it was a comfortable place to conduct interviews. Moreover, the staff are friendly and inviting, and the office has a warm, safe, and secure feeling.

Johnny's parents are an attractive and obviously connected couple. Johnny's mother sits across from me on one of the chairs, and his father sits closer to me on the couch. They are dressed in casual, comfortable clothes. Johnny's parents have had a long and fulfilling marriage. Both are currently dealing with physical disabilities, which prevent them from continuing their careers. They had three children, two boys and a girl. Since Johnny's incarceration, they have been active in the lives of his son and a daughter, who was tragically killed in an accident while Johnny was in prison. Johnny's son continues to live with his mother, not far from his grandparents, and they have frequent involvement with him. They describe Johnny's son as a "typical teenager" and worry about his school performance. They also report many crises in their lives of late, including the deaths of several friends and family members. Johnny's younger brother committed suicide by gunshot a few years before the interview. It is thought that his motivation had some relationship to Johnny's incarceration.

Johnny's parents have also been active in their community and are well known as active community participants. This is a small African American community in a rather small city, so, not unlike Adam's little town, most people know each other. The family has lived in this city for all their lives, and the activities of "gangs" are thought to be more common in places like Chicago or New York. The family has not been touched by crime.

When I first contacted the family, as mentioned, they were eager to speak with me. The reason for their eagerness is their sense that the parents of offenders go through a remarkably similar crisis as do other involved parties, but are largely unseen.

The parents are also, as is common for this entire research community, incredibly impressed with the results of the mediation meeting and eager to participate in any way that will allow them to tell their story related to their feelings about the process.

They give me a beautiful narrative related to the cultural realities of being black in such an environment, and the ever-present racial issues dealt with in daily life.

I begin my interview by securing the history of their knowledge of Johnny's involvement in this crime and their experience of the investigation, arrest, and trial.

Mother: It was very, very puzzling to us. I think that's one reason why we understand, or we are still years later trying to understand what happened. Johnny was a very, I don't know, he wasn't a kid that was in trouble a lot with the law, and, he definitely had some problems, like most teenagers, but he just wasn't a disrespectful belligerent, hard to deal with type child, we told him to do something, and it was like, "OK," there just weren't any problems as far as raising him.

… never really been in jail, maybe had a minor traffic violation, but never knew what it was like to be locked up behind bars or anything like that. Then to find himself to be in the position he was in, he was just …

… my understanding, this was not something, it wasn't planned to come out the way it did. He knew that once things had transpired the way they did, he was just devastated.

Father: He wasn't even a drinker or a smoker. That night we had just got done cutting grass, and we were sitting on the patio, and this car just came riding by, riding by, and I told him, "Don't you get in that car" so, he waved um off a couple of times, 'cause we had the kids, and I guess they went and met somewhere else and the next we knew.

Mother: We just had a feeling. A lot of times as a parent, you will see one of your kid's friends or something, you'll just kind of get bad vibes, and a lot of times it would be a good thing to act on those vibes, because as a parent you may sense things that you hate to later find out could be true. These weren't acquaintances of his, or friends of his, I think it was just something where one person decided to "recruit" some people to do. And they evidently had been riding around looking for people to recruit, and they tried to make it sound like you know, "we're going to do this and nobody's going to get hurt" type thing.

Johnny later told me that he had an inkling, he had a really strong feeling, "no, no, no" and we sensed that something was wrong the days afterwards, because Johnny was very withdrawn, quiet, unavailable.

We would call his house, he was just asleep or whatever or he was just unavailable, and then we started to see things on the news, but at the time we saw newscasts about what had happened we didn't know anything. …

Well, so I think the way things transpired, Johnny quickly found himself in a situation that was 100 percent out of control. And yet he was in the middle of it and he didn't know how to come to me and his dad and tell us, "hey, I've made a mistake" or "somethin's happened."

… to get away, he ended up out in California, and I think he just didn't know how to deal with what he'd seen, what he'd been though, how to tell us. … He kept everything inside. And we found out on the news, and after that we had gotten a visit from a couple of gentlemen from the Department of Criminal Investigation, and that's when we knew. But we had been seeing reports, kind of what had transpired, on the local news, but didn't realize it had any impact on us, we had made comments about what ever had happened up there, and how stupid, you know, whoever this was, you know, and how senseless, but we didn't know how closely it was going to impact us.

because I seemed the most likely person to befriend him, try to assist him, but that wasn't the case. Johnny didn't want us to know, he never told us, and as a matter of fact, I don't really know how much useful information we can give you, because he wouldn't, didn't really didn't want us to know a lot about what had happened. He felt like that he had not only shamed himself, but he'd brought a lot of shame on his family, and he didn't want me or his dad involved in any way in what had happened.

He tried to protect us, and didn't really let me or his dad know his whereabouts, because, he later told me, "If you were asked where I was, I would never put you in a position where I would have to ask you to lie for me." So, he didn't let us know anything.

And he had a lot of he thought were friends that were trying to help him, they helped him get all the way to California, but you know, for a long time I was angry about that because no one would tell me anything, we knew something was going on, and when they did talk to us they didn't give us a lot of details either, just that they had to talk to him and did we know where he was and I felt like, they said they weren't following me, but every time I left the house I felt like they were following me. And I had a lot of anger about that, because I felt like I didn't do anything, I hadn't broken any laws, and I had a lot of doctors' appointments that I had to go to, I was scheduled for physical therapy and that, and one appointment was clear on the outskirts of town, and I looked behind me and there's this car, you know and then when I asked them and they said, "no, we're not following you" [laughing] and I was very suspicious of them.

Following Johnny's arrest and return to the community, the family was eager to talk with him. By this point, they knew that he had been involved in the murders, but weren't sure to what extent. At this point in the interview, they are beginning to feel more comfortable with me and are more open with their feelings.

They tell me that they couldn't talk with Johnny for a couple of weeks following his arrest and return to the community.

Mother: And at that time, we knew really more than we wanted to know when we did see him. I think that he felt like that we were going to turn our backs on him, or weren't going to be there for him, he was terrified, he was just terrified. And, you know, we asked him some questions, because we had many. [There was an affective shift in the mother at this point, becoming more sad and emotional at times in her story.] And he had talked to an attorney, and at that point he told his attorney that he didn't want us to know. He was still trying to keep us in this protective mode. And we were trying to tell him that we can't really help him unless you go ahead and tell us the truth. It's going to come out anyway, and it's better for us to know than to find it out from someone else. So, then he kind of opened up. He still doesn't talk about exactly what happened.

I ask the mother to tell me a little about the family and the family history:

Mother: And then Johnny's younger brother died about eight years ago now [she tears]. And since he's been incarcerated we've lost, I think we have a funeral tomorrow, which will make about number sixteen. And a lot of them have been closer, some a little more distant, but still an awfully large number of deaths, and, the thing about it is, you can tell people what's it's like to lose somebody, talk to people what it's like to have a baby, or to have a kid in trouble, but it always comes back to unless you've actually been through it you really can't say you know what that other person is feeling, you know, you can sympathize with them but you can't really say that you know what it feels like. You know it must be awful, but you really don't know.

The parents speak of the impact of the death of Johnny's daughter, and his decision to proceed with the meeting and what they believe are his motivations for this.

Mother: And for Johnny, when he lost his daughter, he wasn't able to come to her service, and that, I think, was really difficult for him, and that happened pretty shortly after he'd been gone, within a couple of years?

(Our granddaughter) was playing in the yard. There was no driver in the car, it slid on the ice, and that was it, you know.

But Johnny hadn't planned on, I'm not going to say that he was perfect, but he hadn't planned on getting involved in anything like that. And I think at one point rather than come back, he might have even contemplated suicide. Rather than have to … he did come back, and when we talked he said, "I need to undo, try to undo, the wrong that I've done." And I think that he has really set out, from that day, he says, "I'm going to turn my life completely around." And he's not really wavered from that as far as we can tell.

Father: Um huh. Because he'll cry, if you talk to him, because there are so many guys up there [at the prison] that can't read or write, and he's always telling us how sad it is.

One of my standard questions in each interview was to bring up the notion of what had been experienced as a "life-changing event" and asking how the individual felt the experience had changed them. When I ask the parents this question, they respond relative to the entire set of crises that had touched their lives in recent years.

Mother: Well, I'm surprised that we're not just covered in cobwebs, [all laughing] because [Father] and I both just shortly before this happened, we happened to become disabled, mine through a work-related injury, his through another illness. So, we've had a lot of time at home, we've been able to think. I think sometimes we are looking down the street, and we watch to see one of our kids come walking up the street, don't see them. We stepped in, at the time this happened, Johnny had two children, a little boy and a little girl, and we stepped in and not only tried to be a grandparent, I think we felt we had to make up for the fact that he was gone [tears]. We wanted them to grow up and not look back on life and say, well we didn't get to do this or have this because our dad was in jail. I wanted them to understand that their dad had made a mistake. He wasn't a bad person, but that he made a mistake and he had to pay for that. And they were pretty young, so it was very difficult. And also, I think by our names being, well they had Johnny's picture plastered up on the news. We're pretty well known in the community.

[Father] and I, we have a lot of excellent friends, and they stuck by us. … We had a lot of anger; we had a lot of confusion about what happened, we had a lot to deal with emotionally. Some people we would meet would kind of look at us kind of funny, "Oh, you're the parents of that kid that was involved in that trouble, you must be bad. …" You know, and it just made you feel real uneasy, and maybe people weren't, but you just felt that way, it made you kinda paranoid. And when people would ask how you were doin'? You didn't really know what to say. So that part was very, very difficult.

In terms of his own meaning making and epiphany, the father, who had been rather taciturn during the early part of the interview, but was eventually eager to offer his experience to me, reflected on his own change:

Father: I think the thing that helped me the most, I went to one of my friend's funerals, and there was this little white lady there, she didn't know me from Adam or Eve, but when they introduced me to her, she just jumped up and started screaming, grabbing and hugging me, started crying. She asked me, could she go outside and talk to me; well I thought she was crazy [laughs]. And I found out that all five of her sons had been in murders, and they're all doing life (the ones that are living) and crap, and she just said that she felt like she knew me all of her life.
Mother: One thing that I found, and I know [Father] and I talk about this a lot and I felt this happened to us, we were both raised here in [City], knew people in the community, went to school, our kids were born here, went to school, etc. And I found, that you know, with the crime now, used to be big cities like Chicago used to be someplace else, anyplace else, it was never right here, and it certainly was never you. And when we found ourselves in that position, I mean it had hit so close to home, I mean that people that knew us were like, "Gee, if this could happen to them …"

I mean, you know, wow … And we used to say, we would watch the news, and see Chicago's news, and we would say, "That's gotta be crazy living there," I mean to us that's scary. But then when you find yourself in the middle of something like this, then the whole small suburb, or segment of the community where everybody knows everybody, then you're just devastated, everybody's like, "Why?"

The mother, in talking about the experience, returns to the values that she feels her family has contained:

Mother: So, I don't know, we tried to teach Johnny, go to work, you know, raise your kids … the thing I felt the sorriest for were all the kids, and even, with Adam, I mean our … I cried, I cried nonstop, I could not stop. I hurt that bad for everybody involved, because I could see that this had touched so many people's lives. And it was really terrible, and it was like waking up, or like being in a nightmare and not being able to wake up, that's what it's like.

Johnny's mother can discuss eloquently the identification she is able to make with Adam.

Mother: But it was very, very traumatic, and then when I read that there was one little boy that was there, that to me was so hard to accept that all this transpired and this little boy saw it, but it wasn't until later that I realized that the little boy had been threatened. And I thought, he's four years old, and what happened that as bad as this was, they left a witness that could have identified them. And I don't, I don't know what it was he's just always, the little boy has always been on my mind.

I did know later from reading some of the transcript file that Johnny had given him a popsicle or something, there was some discussion that they were going to use the little boy as a bargaining chip, or something, "You do what we say or we're going to hurt him," and I think Johnny stopped that, and I don't know if that's why Adam wanted to see Johnny, to meet Johnny?

There were some things I guess that he could remember, and I can't even imagine from the things I read, I can't even imagine what it must have been like for him. You know, [Father] and I have been trying to spend the last number of years trying to understand, and yet this little guy witnessed all of this and saw this and how traumatic. …at that time, we were trying to deal with Johnny's two kids, one of them was about the same age and he didn't understand, he didn't even know his ABC's that well, you know, he didn't understand. … So, as far as trauma, as far as life being unfair and taking things from somebody, this little boy has definitely been through it.

Johnny's mother speaks poignantly about the reality of the family and loved ones of a person responsible for a violent crime.

In discussing Johnny's struggles with the initial request to meet with Adam, and her learning of Johnny's importance to Adam, the mother reports:

Mother: But I think Johnny was so thankful to get a chance to meet with Adam, but he was also terrified. I talked to him many times on the phone, he said, "Mom, I want to be sure, I want to do anything I can to help him" He said, "I feel so bad for what happened, if I can make up to him in any way for my part in what happened, I gotta do it." And at first, he must have called me to the tune of ten or twelve telephone calls. And wanted me to help him work through it. And I think that's what seems so hard for the perpetrator's family, is because you find yourself grieving for what happened, sorry; feeling like you would like to let somebody know that you are sorry for what happened, trying to play psychologist with your child over the phone, and you know, trying to help them straighten out what is already a messed-up situation, or they wouldn't be where they are. You know, and you find yourself doing all these different roles. And if there's kids you step in trying to be the parent that isn't there, the disciplinarian, and the grandparent, or whatever. And they're pretty hard shoes to fill. I feel sorry for any victim of crime, but I also feel sorry for the people on the other side, you know.

In relation to the meeting itself, the mother was very involved and moved by the event, both by what she heard from Johnny, as well as her experience on seeing the tape.

Mother: … and he had some very specific questions he wanted to ask Johnny, and I just don't think anybody would have been able to answer them but Johnny. Very specific. And from what I understand, and seeing the video, I cried. It seemed he needed to have answers in order to be able to move on. And I think it gave Johnny an opportunity to let Adam know how sorry he was for what happened, and I think they both need that in order to move on. But he doesn't want Johnny to get in any more trouble, he wants him, he wanted to thank Johnny, which, that part, from being a kid, I understand. He's able to forgive, where a lot of us, as adults, are not. That's just the innocence of being a child.

A theme emerges for the first time in this interview, related to knowing the "right words" to say and the importance of choosing the right words. The mother states:

Mother: But he was scared to talk to Adam … wasn't sure if he'd know how to deal with a young person, if he knew the right words to say, that would make sense to him, and wouldn't scare him and that. … (he said), "Mom, I didn't think I could do it. But if you ever get a chance to meet him you're going to meet the neatest kid in the world." And I told him,

"… children have a need to know the truth, and if you just be honest with him and talk to him" I said, "it will be alright because they'll know when you're not telling the truth and kids are like that." And he said he thought that helped him a lot. You know, he needed to have somebody be honest with him, and he needed Johnny to tell him.

The issue of grief and the impact of grief emerge for the first time in this research. The mother also defines another theme that will resurface throughout this research, related to individual experience and the capacity for empathy.

Mother: I tried to help Johnny with the grief of losing her [his daughter], and then I think he realized more what Adam must have gone through, because up to that point we hadn't really lost, maybe one or two family members, but after that it seemed like death was something that was, that we all got to learn more about than we really wanted to know, including Johnny. And I think that that had a lot to do with him wanting to see Adam. Yeah.

As often will be seen in these cases, Johnny's mother has developed a narrative theory for herself, to try to make sense of her son's involvement in this crime. She predicates it with the belief that Johnny had always been a good person, but momentarily lost track of that. This theory also goes to support the parents' belief that Johnny has now changed, and when he is released, he will maintain his determination and keep on the straight-and-narrow.

Mother: I think they [his positive values] were there all along, but as time has gone on those have been able to surface. They were there but he didn't really realize, he didn't realize, but now he realizes. ...but as a young man, because Johnny's short, he's grown since he got there because he doesn't smoke now, but he's a short person. I think he lacked the self-esteem. He didn't have confidence in himself, and I think a lot of that was due to his size, and running with a tougher group made him be like a bigger man and that, and that's when I referred to him you know, it's ok being who I am, and as a matter of fact I like who I am now. He kind of had a struggle with that, and I think that's kind of why he did get into this, he thought he had to be somebody or something that he wasn't. ... And now he realizes that he's fine, and he likes the person he's becoming now. So, and I guess being, like his dad said, where he's at he's had time, time to think, time to mature, time to grow, time to reflect.

Johnny's mother mentions numerous times throughout the interview that Johnny was "terrified," "afraid," and "scared" to do the meeting. These words are used frequently by offenders in my interviews. The mother also discusses a theme that is often mentioned by perpetrator's families: the desire to contact the victim's family and express regret. Again, mention is made of finding the right words.

Mother: ... but we had wanted so badly to let Adam's family know. ... and I don't know why, I had never been the victim of really any kind of crime, so I've been fortunate, but you know, that we just had this overwhelming need, or I did anyway, to let them know that we felt sorry. We were sorry for what happened, not just because our kid was involved in what happened, but just for what happened. We've run into a lot of people in, you know when my little granddaughter was killed, that would come up to me, and they just wanted me to know that they were sorry for what happened to us. But see, in a case like this, we can't do that. You understand, we can't do that, we can feel that, but we can't say, you know, "we're sorry." And sometimes those are the hardest words for a person to say, so you can imagine how frustrating it is when you want to say it and you can't.

And when we get approached [by people who come to them with problems, knowing that they have been through these issues], they are coming to us because they feel we've been there, they need somebody to show them some empathy, that they feel understands. You know we, I guess, we kind of can do that. And sometimes I think we've given people some good advice from some of the hard lessons we've learned from life. …

… if we had the opportunity to write a letter, even, if it was at their discretion if they wanted to read it or not. But I mean it is a terrible thing to want to apologize to someone in our society for something you know, feeling that you're not able to do that.

But this has impacted our lives so greatly, I wonder if it would help them to know that we're not monsters, that we were normal people before this happened to us too. And we've had a lot of grieving and a lot of healing to have to do and still will have to.

… after I saw the video with Adam, that I was really able to tell [Father], and my mother and other members of my family that I was close to that I have been able to let go of all the hatred that I had in my heart for anybody, because I found that hatred was destroying me. And I didn't want to hate anybody. And I didn't have any reason to hate anybody. I don't know when I saw that video, it helped me to a degree.

… But I'll tell you, it feels good not to hate … and I found that I was able to let that go, and I don't know if it was because I saw this little person be able to do that?

… it doesn't just impact one or two families, it's impacted our daughter and her family. My son, he had gone to see his brother shortly after his daughter had gotten killed, and Johnny had talked with him a lot about not ending up in the kind of place he was at, and within four weeks, our youngest son committed suicide … .

You know, it's just been a lot. But I didn't want the other family to think, "This happened and you people's lives have probably gone on, and you've been just fine, you know, and we've been going through hell," it's still and will always be like a living nightmare for us, always.

At the close of the interview, Johnny's mother becomes quite emotional as she tells me the story of having to tell Johnny about the death of his daughter, and the aftermath of the community rallying around the family. A local radio program helped raise enough money to pay for the funeral, and the school planted a tree in her honor. She closes the interview with this statement:

Mother: So I have to say in that way that Johnny going to prison was a good thing. So maybe when he comes out he will be a better person, and will be able to give something back when he gets out.

Deputy Smith: Deputy Smith was interviewed in his basement office in the sheriff's office in which he has worked his entire career in law enforcement.

His office is on one side of a two-way mirror, with a secured camera pointing into the adjoining interview area. Deputy Smith often conducts interviews with children, usually in child abuse or incest cases, and uses the mirror and camera for these interviews.

His office is decorated with cards, posters, and models of stock car racers. Stock car racing is a hobby for him. There is a golfing poster on one wall of a "Classic, 1999" in which he played. On his desk is a glass-enclosed model of "Inspector Gadget."

Deputy Smith is a soft-spoken and kind individual on first meeting. He is clearly a little nervous at anticipating the interview, and admits this. He is wearing "plain clothes," which has been his work attire for some time.

Deputy Smith initially gives me a long and complete narrative describing the events of the morning—what he was doing when he received the call, and what he saw when he arrived at the scene. This narrative was in the best form of a police narrative (just the facts), and has been largely recounted in my own description of the case and the scene.

Early in the interview, however, Deputy Smith, in recounting the story, tears when he recounts the part of the narrative where he hears Adam holler "Daddy!" from the basement of the house.

As he comes to the part in the narrative where he is coming down the stairs to the basement, he reports:

Deputy: And when I looked down the stairs and they were both lying there. This is one of the visions that I will always carry. They talk about "post-traumatic shock," I close my eyes and I can see it just as plain today as I did that day. (Adam's father) was down there, and they were both naked, and the girl was laying on her back with her eyes open, and I think my exclamation was, "Oh, shit." I told the deputy with me, … and by this time the sheriff had arrived, I told him that we better call BCI, and I told him I was going to go downstairs and get the child. I had brought my camera and had it hanging around my neck, I had my gun in my hand (I'm left handed), and when I got toward the bottom of the stairs I put my gun away, because I didn't want the child to see the gun, and I had rubber gloves on, but as I came down the stairs … .

When I stepped downstairs, I could see Adam, he was in a different room than the two victims; he was crying at this time, and hollering for his daddy, I mean he could see them. And so, I stepped across the woman, because I was in between them, and when I stepped across her, I heard a noise behind me that, I mean, scared me to death, because, you know, I had put my gun away trying to be a "nice guy" to the child, and all of a sudden I'm thinking, "maybe he's still here, maybe I shouldn't have done that." I turned around and I saw (the father) move, and I hollered; "now we need an ambulance." … I turned around and I talked to the child, I took my badge off my belt and showed him, and told him I was a police officer.

I may have even told him I knew his dad. (I had arrested his dad over the years, we had a history.)

In his further description of this scene, Deputy Smith is clearly still affected, as he tells me in the interview, by his memory of the scene itself. He gives a very good description of the experience of viewing such a horrific sight, and, as can often be seen in people who witness traumatic events, can simply close his eyes and have the scene return in its totality. His graphic, and at times emotional, description points to this.

Deputy: But anyway, I went to him, and I went into the room, and part of my situation was to observe, and I was trying to take some pictures at the same time, observing what the room was like. He had … whoever had left him there had left a blanket, and some of those frozen pops, that come in the plastic that you squeeze out, that was with him, and some other stuff, and either they had put up a board about six or eight inches high, across the door, and I'm not sure why that was there. But I went over to that area and went in, and bent down, and Adam grabbed me around the neck, and I mean he grabbed, and I told him he was going to be OK, and that I would get him out of there, and that everything would be alright. And we turned around and I think I told him to close his eyes, and I went through where his mother was, and went back to the top of the stairs, and out, and I gave Adam to the other deputy. He didn't want to go, but I gave him, and I told him I had to go back downstairs and take care of his dad.

In the interview, the deputy went on to describe in detail the investigation and the arrest of the perpetrators. He described the criminal history of each of the offenders, and described, as he understood it, that Johnny and one of the others were "adamant" about not hurting Adam.

He recounts the events leading to Johnny's flight and later arrest, and describes the first meeting they had and his sense of connection to Johnny:

Deputy: … we picked him up and we flew back. Actually, the sheriff [who is also African American] was giving him a hard time. Johnny had never flown before … he was giving him a bad time, talking about wings falling off airplanes. Johnny was kind of uptight, and I finally told the sheriff to stop, he was trying to be funny, but Johnny was getting uptight. So, we sat together and talked about everything but the crime. Johnny didn't have a lot to say. I started to explain to him when we hit air turbulence, telling him it was normal, because, you know, your first flight you hear things, don't know if it's normal or if something is going wrong. So, we talked. … And I don't know if it was then, but you know, I like Johnny. If it were under different circumstances, Johnny was my neighbor, we could be friends.

This developing sense of connection that Deputy Smith felt with Johnny continued throughout the course of the next period. The connection is hard for him to explain. He discusses feeling the growing trust between the two and, on their long car trips when Johnny testified, learning about Johnny's life. Johnny was honest with him about his criminal history and the street crimes that he participated in while growing up in the city. He admitted that he did not use chemicals but did sell them, and talked about his family, his children, and growing up in his neighborhood.

Deputy: You know, I guess it was one of the times that opened my eyes, because, you know, I went to (high school in the city), which was a racially mixed school, but I lived in a more affluent white neighborhood, was bused in, but things didn't dawn on me. Johnny and I were coming back from (city where he testified), where he had testified against D, and we were driving along, and we went by some sheep that were in a field, and Johnny was going kinda, "What are those?" and I said, "those are sheep." "I've never seen a sheep," he says, you know a live sheep. He grew up in the inner city of (city). It was then we started talking about whether he had ever been on a farm, things like that, and I guess I found out how isolated we can make the inner city, and how isolated the inner city can make itself. He was talking about his kids, and that he wanted them to experience more. So, we talked. Johnny was pretty open about these things. I guess the biggest thing about Johnny I felt was remorse. This kid had wished this thing had never happened.

I, too, found this a remarkable insight, both for the meaning it held to Deputy Smith, but also for the point he was making.

Deputy Smith goes on in the interview to discuss his first knowledge that the mediation was being suggested. He stated that he had questions about it until he was able to meet with Adam himself and talk with him about it. He saw that the questions he was raising were intended to:

Deputy: … kind of put closure on this, because apparently, he was having disciplinary problems at school, things were going on, some of this was really bugging him, that this might be a good thing. Knowing Johnny, and I was confident of this, knowing Johnny, Johnny wouldn't make it worse. He wouldn't make it worse. And from that standpoint it would probably help Adam. I was glad to be a part of it, glad to go up and observe.

In relation to the meeting itself, Deputy Smith observed that everyone, himself included, was nervous to begin with. He qualified Adam as being "apprehensive, but not scared." He said, "So, I sat and watched, and listened to the two of them. I thought maybe Adam would have had maybe more questions in some ways. However, Johnny was very truthful with him. I was impressed. I thought it was successful, it probably went as good or better than I thought it would."

Deputy: That was something I don't think that Johnny was asking for, forgiveness, he didn't talk about it. When I thought about it, I thought it was successful, and I guess I was happy with that, I thought it was good for me in a way, too, to see it, to be involved. I'm glad I was involved.

Deputy Smith related in the interview that in those years there was "a lot going on" in his life, including the loss of his wife to cancer two years prior.

I asked Deputy Smith if he felt that "empathy" played any role in the process. He gave the question a lot of thought (there was over a thirty-second pause on the tape) and, like numerous people to whom I posed this question, he struggled with the concept of empathy and whether that had a part to play. As often was seen, there was a struggle in these individuals to define its presence in the process:

Deputy: [Long pause; thirty seconds to think about question] I don't know, you mean for me? [Struggling with question. *Interviewer*: Well with you, or what you observed from them.] Yeah, I guess so. In the two of them, I remember walking out, we were still in the prison, I remember walking out Adam was, there was a sign of relief that it was over, too. I guess I feel for Johnny in some ways, like I say, he was really, it was one of those deals that if he had to do over again … but we can't do that, and he doesn't know what the future's going to hold when he got it started. He was kind of a bad guy, he had no qualms about going out and robbing a drug dealer. He didn't have any problem with that. So that's what the goal was, to rob a drug dealer. So, empathy for him, he made his own mess, and he's doing real well getting through it, or would seem to be.

I later ask the deputy a question that I ask all professionals in relation to "secondary post-traumatic stress" or "compassion fatigue." I am interested in whether they see this phenomenon, and how the take care of themselves in the face of it. Deputy Smith tells me an interesting anecdote, which is telling as to his own place in the narrative.

Deputy: I know my symptoms … I can't sleep … .

The other thing that struck me about this particular case and it happened in the first trial, I had done depositions about this, described what I had seen, but when I went to the first trial something that happened to me that I was really concerned about, and later found … I cried, when I was giving the testimony, I was talking about going down to the basement to get Adam, and this was being videotaped, by Court TV, and the news media actually played a clip of me, and I was, not breaking down or sobbing or whatever, but I can remember that, emotionally, that I was really concerned about what other police officers were going to think about me, seeing it on TV, I mean you would have to see it. Nobody said a word; it was mute, it didn't make any difference … I guess I didn't give my fellow officers enough credit. … my wife was a very good listener, she would know.

I'm still emotional about it.

The deputy reported that his view of the restorative justice process had changed because of participating in it, and that while he had heard of similar types of efforts, he had never formed a strong opinion one way or another. Because of seeing and being involved in this effort, he had hopes that the program would expand and that more people, if they did it willingly, would do it.

Adam's Aunt and Uncle: Adam's aunt and uncle, since the situation became untenable with his grandparents, have been his legal guardians. At the time of the interview, he had been living in the family home for approximately seven years. (The issues encountered by the family have been previously described in the case description.)

The interview with the aunt and uncle was conducted just short of one year following the mediation session. Adam, following the mediation, had a brief period of behavior problems, followed by a return of his better-than-average behavior, and his continuing involvement in a variety of activities that were both age appropriate and seen as further evidence of his continued good adjustment. The reasons for the brief regression following the mediation were in dispute among the people I interviewed. The aunt and uncle believed this was a reaction to the mediation itself. The mediators and therapist felt that it was due to the refusal on the part of the aunt and uncle to allow Adam to view the videotape following the mediation, saying that they wanted him to wait until he was an "adult" to see it.

As mentioned, the aunt and uncle from the beginning had been supportive of Adam's participation in the process. Their support was, for the most part, unwavering, although they were questioned by certain friends and relatives as to the wisdom of their decision to proceed with this plan. Much of their support was rooted in their initial observation that Adam had not dealt with, or been allowed to deal with, the meaning of these events in his life, and they were clear in their belief that this was necessary.

The major issues that came up for this couple, as the process evolved, were the aunt's participation in her own mediation meeting with Johnny, for her own issues. The other issue came following the aunt and uncle viewing the video of the mediation. At the close of the meeting, and as Johnny was exiting the room, Adam asked if he "could have a hug." This took place, and was, for all of those who witnessed it, a very moving moment. When the aunt and uncle saw this, however, the uncle had a very strong negative reaction. This will be seen in the transcript, and will be discussed further at the end of this interview, as, again, the reasons for his reaction and the resolution are in some dispute.

The aunt and uncle were interviewed in the conference room of the Victim's Services office already described. There was some question as to whether they would be interviewed separately or together, as they had some differing opinions as to the process. At the time of the interview, they decided that they would prefer to be interviewed together.

The couple is young, in their late thirties or early forties. Throughout their marriage, they have both worked.

They are supportive of my interview, but also express, at the beginning, the difficulty of "bringing all this up again." They state that they agreed to meet with me, and allowed Adam to talk with me only in the hopes that it would ultimately "help somebody else." They have had several crises in their lives of late. Following the death of the aunt's brother (Adam's father), the uncle was laid off from his job, and just prior to the interviews, the grandmother (her mother) died.

In the beginning of the interview, the aunt discusses her initial knowledge of the perpetrators. She describes them as "very scary looking people" and "pretty bad looking people" from their pictures in the news media. In discussing the course of the trial and her developing knowledge of the offenders, she states:

Aunt: Just to hear the details of what happened and what they did. Their story of what they were after and just hearing all the details of how they shot them and stuff, it was just something I hope I never have to go through again. That was not pleasant.

As far as the people, I don't know, you just don't care for these people because of what they've done. And I guess that's just it—it was just not a good experience.

Other than I just—I guess I just didn't care for them. Not too really—I wouldn't say hatred so much—these are people, for what they did and stuff, I just … .

The couple goes into detail with me as to the history of Adam's life following the murders. They state that he lived with the grandparents for five years prior to the decision to have him move in with them. They recount the problems of his living with the grandparents, his progressing behavioral and academic problems, and his starting Ritalin, a decision that this couple disagreed with from the beginning. They discuss the feeling that the grandparents indulged him too much, and that they felt the need to establish that they "were the boss," which took "five years of undoing" for them to accomplish.

They view that Adam had no "respect for adults or authority figures" when they had him move in, and by the fourth grade, he was threatening to kill himself. (The uncle felt that this was somewhat "manipulative," based on the efforts that the family was making to restore "order.") At one point, the aunt was called to pick him up at school, as he was threatening to kill both the teacher and himself. The school told her that she and Adam's uncle had to get him "counseling" within twenty-four hours.

Both report that the counselors they met were problematic:

Uncle: There's a world of "interesting" people.
Aunt: Lot of "different" counselors.

At this point, the uncle began to take more of an active role with Adam, which they both felt was a turning point. This is also the point where they began to question the helpfulness of the therapist's approach to the problem.

Aunt: And that's when you began to have your heart-to-heart talks with him. ...

Yeah, but we did take him, in fourth grade, we took him to see [counselor]. We didn't take him to a counselor that night. [Uncle] talked to him, trying to get some things under control. We did take him to a counselor, in fourth grade, I think we took him in fifth grade, and I told him—because we were dealing with problems—there was a period of time when we were taking him every week. And he was talking to him—the situations he got into and how he should handle them. And I told him once, finally, I said, "I think we need to get back to what happened. I don't know anything about counseling, but I think we need to go back to the beginning here." Well, he never did.

... well, I don't think he wanted to do it. So, then we got into fifth grade. Fifth grade, he had a male teacher, and he bonded with him. He did really good. At the end of fourth grade, we thought he had a good summer, we thought things were going pretty good. He gets into fifth grade, he has a male teacher, he's doing really good, and then we had two weeks before Christmas—[Uncle] had worked for [his company] for almost five years, they downsized, they let him go, and so we were having a lot of—our emotions have changed at home because of this. And then I think it was like in February, Adam starts acting up again.

At this point, the couple decides to try another approach. Adam was now in sixth grade, and the couple received the suggestion to try the Victim Services office from the school. They saw an almost immediate improvement in Adam's mood and behavior. They said, "she's [his current therapist] been excellent with him. They've done a tremendous job."

Within a year of starting this therapy, the process of the mediation began, and both were impressed with the concept. The uncle reports to me:

Uncle: I was pretty impressed. I thought it was pretty neat to break through and I could understand that closure that the victim needed at that point ... I told [Aunt] about it, and she saw the video [the couple were shown a video of another mediation session to give them the sense of the process], and she didn't want nothing to do with it.

Aunt: Well, I struggled with it for probably a month, month-and-a-half. It's like, I mean I could see—I probably cried the whole time I watched that video. And [Uncle] thought it would probably be a good thing for me, and [mediators] talking to me, and it's like "should I or shouldn't I." And finally, I just decided "I don't want anything to do with this." And it was just like such a weight off my shoulders, because I couldn't decide. I thought, well, maybe it will help. But I thought, I absolutely do not want to see these people … and I said, "If you really think it will help Adam, I'm all for it" but myself, I wanted nothing to do with it.

The uncle suggests partly why he was so immediately supportive of the idea. In the next exchange, the development of the relationship between Adam and the couple is understood with a great deal of insight as well.

Uncle: First off, Adam's pretty—he keeps everything inside himself because if he doesn't say anything to anybody, then he doesn't have to worry about anything. And so, the longer he's with us and goes on, the more he kind of comes out and is starting to trust people a little bit. Because there was absolutely no trust for nobody at all.
Aunt: The other side of that, too, is that with [his father], with my brother, we were not close at all. I mean, they kind of went their way. We had known that they had done a little bit in drugs and stuff. We don't do that, so we kind of split a long time ago. There was not the closeness. I mean, he did not know us that well, even though they lived close by. We'd see him once in a while. And it took a long time for him to get to know us, I suppose, and then to build that trust up.
Uncle: There was no consistency in his life, and no discipline.

Further, they both state that they were aware, through the developing trust with Adam, that this was important to him, and this was established through his communicating with them, which was a big step forward in their relationship together.

Aunt: Just because Adam—he was for it. He wanted to do it. I could see that he wanted to do that. And seeing that he—if I would have been—if I would have seen that he was having some doubts or anything, then I think that would have been harder for me. But seeing that he did want to do that ….
Uncle: This was a source for answers—deep answers. And he seen that.

Noteworthy in the interview with Johnny's parents is the desire for some form of contact with Adam's family in order to apologize, whereas the aunt and uncle are very clear that they want the impact of this meeting to be contained. They both speak about the worry of "humanizing" the offender in a way that will take away the meaning of the crime and the consequences. In the next sequence, they refer to a letter that one of the mediators brings down from Johnny, that he had asked him to write in preparation for the meeting.

Aunt: He [the mediator] brought the letter, he wanted us to read it and see if we thought it was OK for Adam to have it. And at that same time, [the local mediator] had clipped an article out of the paper. Evidently Johnny has a boy that's Adam's age, has a couple of kids, and she brought that. And at that time, we told her, no, we don't want this to be a personal thing at all. Don't want him to know anything about his family.
Uncle: And we don't want his family to know anything about Adam. We don't want any kind of relationships building up here at all. It's only just to be used for him to help him get past and be able to move on with his life. We don't want him to carry on a relationship afterwards. When he gets out of prison, we don't want anything to do with him.

... And when she brought that letter, and wanted us to read that, that was started in the back of my mind, this whole thing's going to get too personal. And what's going to get lost here is what they did. And that was kind of—yeah, the letter is nice. Yeah, he is a human being, but he did break the law. And that was where I kind of started—that was the seed; it festered and got worse.

Interestingly, I ask what they remember about the letter's content and the aunt responds as follows:

Aunt: They had told him that Adam was having problems in school, so he was trying to stress how important it was that he do well in school. So, I do remember that, and I thought that was very good. I think that was the most of what I remember out of the letter. And I think he talked about how he was educating himself in prison. I think the education part is the part I remember.

As the interview proceeds, the aunt becomes more comfortable and begins to show emotion related, again, to the question of whether involving herself in the process would be of any use to her. She discusses seeing in the video of the other mediation that there were many questions that the participant wanted answers to, and that she felt no need for answers. She returns often to the image of the night of the murders, the situation that her brother found himself in, and the victimization.

I ask the uncle to explain more why he felt it would have been of use to her to participate:

Uncle: Well, at the time, I was going off of how she was acting. It was quite a while after [her brother] had died, and she'd still sit like she was mourning his death and she'd just cry and things like that. There was still something going on that I thought maybe she wouldn't talk to me about or wouldn't tell me about—because I'm pretty good at getting information out of people. And I just couldn't get through to her because it was on a level that I didn't have any experience talking to people about. And the last thing I want to do is see her hurting. And so, I thought that's why it would help.

As the interview progressed, the issue of how the mediation went became more emotional for the uncle especially. The aforementioned "hug" continued to grate on the uncle, as it represented his fears about the orientation of the offender in relationship to Adam. He was also concerned that the idea of a hug at the close of the meeting was suggested to Adam during his preparation by the mediators, thus, he was concerned that the hug had been suggested to Adam, giving him no choice in the matter. He was also under the impression that Johnny initiated the hug.

Uncle: That, and just forgetting that he's a criminal. That he's in jail for killing people.
Aunt: And we are the ones that love him and care for him, but he's putting this guy— that was a lot of our problem.
Uncle: That just went way too far right there. When I watched the video, that just … . It went fine until it got down there towards the end. And then it started to become, all this, like it was a family reunion. And that was totally wrong to me! Absolutely totally wrong! And I got up and left. …I just couldn't … that just wasn't … . I remember very distinctly as we was watching that, boy, I couldn't talk, 'cause that made me mad.

… I guess if they do that again with a kid, let's not plant this seed of the hugging and things like that. If that's going to happen, the emotions are going to happen, and if that's the way them two people react together, then that's fine, but don't plant the seed in their minds about how it should end. That's the only thing that I ask that it be changed. Because we worked a long time to get Adam, just to trust us, that a hug meant that we cared about him [his voice cracks here with tears]. So that was a real personal time for me, whew.

Even with the strong feelings about the hug issue (and I will clarify the details of this in a moment), the couple remain strongly supportive of the experience for Adam, and remain remarkably able to differentiate their own feelings from his. In discussing the aftermath of the mediation, where Adam's behavior again became a problem, the couple reflects on Adam's behavior leading up to the mediation and his treatment at the counseling office:

Uncle: I think it stirred up a lot of memories and emotions and just took him back into that. And when he gets in the "zone" of doing that, he thinks everybody's picking on him, and everybody's just trying to mess with him. And I'm not kidding you, his eyes are black. He gets in that much rage. I went up there

one time to get him when he was in Mr. [Teacher's] class and there was four teachers out there. And he was running around the school yard and they were trying to get him back in, and they couldn't get him back in there. And I walked up there, and then he came over to me, and I was looking in his eyes, and they were just coal black. There was no color in his eyes whatsoever. He was that far enraged, and it took me about twenty minutes to talk to him and get him to settle down. That's how furious he gets about the whole thing. And it takes him a while to wind down from it. And that day up there stirred up a lot of emotions.
Uncle: I think it answered his questions for him and I figured it would stir things up like it did. I didn't realize it until about a month after we were into it, and I go, "Well, this is all a result of him going up there to see Johnny and stirred everything up again." But I think over the long run it helped, because that was the last incident we've had at school.
Aunt: Yeah, that was in sixth grade. Seventh grade, he hasn't had a problem at all. He had one incident which was just like a normal ....

Given that I had received a conflicting story from the therapist and the mediators as to the resolution of the uncle's feelings about the hug, and I was not hearing this from the uncle, I continued to bring him back to the incident to clarify the story:

Uncle: I got over it, because I just know it wasn't an intentional thing. Because Adam asked me on the way up there, he says, "Well, what if I don't want to give Johnny a hug?" When he said that, that's what made me think that the seed shouldn't have been planted about the hug at the end of the thing. And I says, "Well, Adam, your feelings will tell you what to do." And that was a good enough answer for him and he just left it at that.
Interviewer: That's an incredible response for you to make [given your feelings about the hug issue].
Aunt: This guy [her husband] needs to be a counselor. He is excellent.
Uncle: It's I never wanted to guide Adam. I always wanted him to be his own person because I feel that he'd been controlled enough by other people, and this world is too fantastic to not go into something with an open mind. And I just try to maintain an open mind on things and when it comes to Adam, he makes me do my best thinking.

And in his continuing ability to walk this emotional line between what Adam needed and his own sense of strong emotion, the uncle relates his perceptions about the meaning of the preparation, and his observations of the care taken during the experience. This continues to be remarkable given that he is hurt by what he feels was an implanted suggestion in Adam that caused him great pain.

Uncle: That's probably the reason why I was for it, as much as I was. Because I knew all the detail that went into make sure that everybody was going to be comfortable with what was going on, how the meeting was set up and structured, just the flat being safe, for all parties involved. You could just tell on their faces that there was a true sense of care there, with setting it up. And if there was any inkling that something wasn't right, that it would have just been ended. We could have ended it that day, right there, before we walked in the jail.

The issue of "forgiveness" comes up, and I ask the couple if they feel that forgiveness is somehow expected as an outcome of the mediation, or even if their feelings about Johnny had changed because of the process.

Uncle: Nope—he's still a criminal.
Aunt: I kind of had a hard time—I saw him and he looked totally different from what he had in the paper. I don't remember him that well at the trials. He was there to testify against these guys and I kind of remember him. He's not the one that made the impression, as much as those other guys did. Because you saw them every day, I guess. But he looked so different; I was kind of surprised at that. But then just to—I guess I had a hard time with my emotions as far as here's this guy, he's bettered himself, he's doing really good, he's talking to Adam, helping him out and stuff, but then it's just—I could never forgive him for what he did. He was part of it.
Uncle: "Thanks for helping Adam," but that's as far as it goes. I know [Local Mediator] always kept reminding us, well, he's a human being too. But that doesn't make up for the hurt that he's caused.
Interviewer: Does it feel, kind of as you went through this, that the issue of forgiveness is sort of expected or anticipated?
Uncle: Yeah, they kind of expect us to forgive him; kind of—that's a good thing to do. And there's no way we're going to forgive him for what he did.

And yet their ambivalence about the process and about Johnny continues to assert itself.

Aunt: You could see by watching it, he [Johnny] was actually touched. You could tell that it did—you could tell, at least in my opinion, you could tell that it was sincere, that he's not just doing this to make it look good so that he could try to get out. I felt that it was very sincere.

The divergent story that I heard about the hug was that when the uncle saw the tape and reacted so strongly to it, the group was together with both mediators. Adam was meeting with his therapist, given the couple's refusal to have him view it. When she and Adam heard about the uncle's reaction to the hug, the therapist suggested to Adam that she thought possibly that the uncle was confused as to Adam's feelings about him. With this, Adam went into the conference room and told the uncle, "I don't love Johnny, I only am happy that he met with me and that he saved me. I love you." With this, the uncle broke down and the two of them exchanged a long hug. The mediators and therapist felt very good about this exchange and reported to me that it had basically not only resolved the uncle's discomfort, but had shifted his position to a more positive stance.

During the interview, however, I continued to be vexed that the couple did not relate the story in the way that I had been told it by the others that reported it to me initially. I thus made a third attempt to elicit details from the couple in my interview:

Uncle: No, I just dealt with it because I had to realize it for what it really was. I had to evaluate it. I'm not a quick thinker and that's why I say I usually don't respond that way without thinking through something.
Aunt: I think there was a time too when we came in here afterwards, talking to [Therapist], and you expressed how you felt that Adam was putting Johnny up at the top and … but she talked to him, and Adam told her, he made her—I don't want to say that—that was not how he was feeling—he told [Therapist] that he loved [Uncle] very much and that was not … so, I think that helped you too, as far as understanding how Adam really felt. I think that was kind of helpful as far as a turning point.

Their memory of the event, despite coming closer to how it was reported to me initially, remained different regarding how the resolution was reached and in what manner. I asked the uncle if this in fact was a turning point for him, and he stated:

Uncle: Right at that moment it didn't, but after we'd left, it made a difference.

Throughout the course of the interview, the couple became more comfortable with the interview situation, and as this happened, they also became more informative and their answers became more of a narration. By the close of the interview, the aunt was revealing to me many issues in the family history that were significant areas of family dysfunction, which had been difficult for her to discuss. The sense was that in the discussion of the experience, the aunt was investing in her narrative to make meaning of her own crisis. This meant dealing with not only the violent death of her brother and sister-in-law, but other issues that remain unresolved for her about her family and family history.

Adam: At the time of my interview with Adam, he was thirteen years old. He presented like any thirteen-year-old in a meeting with a professional, and was reminiscent of any initial interview that I have had with an early adolescent client in my office.

He requested to have his therapist join us in the interview, and I had no problem granting this request. He admitted to me that he was initially worried about doing the interview and was even thinking about backing out of it. A few days before our meeting, I had called to firm up some details, and the aunt and uncle weren't at home, so Adam and I had a chance to talk. He said that he had liked the sound of my voice, so decided to go ahead with it.

Initially, Adam is a "man of few words." He gives brief and formal answers to my questions. Eventually, he warms up to me and is somewhat more spontaneous and informative, but the interview isn't easy for him, and he is clearly relieved to have it over with at its close.

Significant to his recent developmental course, he finds it much easier talking to me about his new job as the girls' basketball manager at his school.

Adam tells me about his experience immediately following the murders. He was placed in two different foster homes prior to moving in with his grandparents. One home he liked, as it was an Amish household, and they had kids his age. The other he does not remember kindly, as they made him eat tomatoes with sugar on them.

I reviewed with him the development of his problems in school. At this point, he begins to warm up a little and becomes more spontaneous and informative.

Adam: Well, it was in second grade, that was in 1994 when my dad was murdered, and then I started acting up, and I was just practically mad at anybody that got in my way and started throwing chairs and that kind of stuff.
Interviewer: And you think that was related to your dad's death?
Adam: Yeah. It happened until I got into seventh grade, and then I quit doing that. Because after sixth grade, I was starting to calm down, but in fifth grade, somebody got in a fight with me, and he didn't get in trouble but I did, and I got kicked out of class for the last two weeks of school, and then I started calming down in sixth grade and then in seventh grade, I was just fine.
Interviewer: What do you think happened, that things got better?
Adam: I really don't know. I just started getting better without me even knowing it.

In discussing the evolution of his notion that it would be helpful to meet with Johnny, he could not attribute the idea to anything beyond the fact that "I had always talked about doing something like that." When I asked him what he felt when he heard that it might be possible, he said, "I think I said something like, 'Cool!'"

To clarify further his reasoning, I asked about the questions he had for Johnny. He said, "Because I was always wanting to know why and how, and mostly why they did it. And when I got there, I just went from that, just asking questions."

When asked what was the most helpful thing that the people did to prepare him, he said, "Well, because I couldn't have done it on my own, because I wouldn't have been able to meet Deputy Smith on my own and talk to different people."

When asked how he was feeling right before meeting Johnny, Adam responded, "I was very nervous. I didn't know how he would react and I don't know how he would act. And so that just made me nervous because I didn't know what he would do or anything."

In light of what the uncle stated about Adam, I asked him what he was doing with the nervous feelings, how he dealt with them. "Well, I just kept them inside me and tried to act, look my best so nobody would find out the way I was feeling. But I was very nervous, and I think that the people could see it, because my hands were starting to shake, and I was starting to sweat."

I asked Adam what happened immediately. He stated, "He stood up and said to give me a round of applause for, I think, surviving this and being able to come." This caught Adam off guard: "I was just standing there like this ..." [adopts a comical, rigid posture].

In response to what he heard from Johnny about the crime, Adam reported that what he heard from Johnny was what he had heard before: "It was exactly the same thing as Deputy Smith told me."

New information for him was the story about the map being upside down:

Adam: He just said one thing new that he thought that they had accidentally turned around the map where they went backwards and went to the wrong house. He said that. Yeah, that he thinks they mistaked and went to the wrong house. And that they didn't plan on killing anybody at first.

In relation to how the mediators ran the meeting, Adam was supportive: "Well, if I'd get stalled up and then she would help me get unstalled. And then most of the time, she'd just sit back and let us speak." [This sentiment is universally stated as a positive aspect of the mediators: getting out of the way and letting the people talk.]

When asked about the first impression he had of Johnny, he stated, "He looked like a nice, caring person. Friendly."

When asked how he felt immediately after the meeting, he stated, "I felt better than what I did when I came. Because I got my questions answered, and I felt about the things because I know what happened and all that kind of stuff."

In terms of his feelings about Johnny, he said, "Well, I sort of like him now better than what I did. I really don't know why I changed my mind. It's just after the meeting, my mind just changed about him. And instead of not liking him, I liked him."

In relation to Johnny's feelings about him, he said, "I really can't tell, but they looked like they changed, to a good way. Well, because in the beginning it looked like he did not really think of me that much. And that at the end he was happy that he helped me and he liked me and he gave me a couple of hugs. He was crying and happy at the end when he gave me his hugs. And he was just—looked like he was happier." Regarding his tears, Adam said, "I thought that he really felt bad about what he did."

I asked Adam how he felt he could be certain that Johnny was being honest and genuine with him.

Adam: Because most of the time, if they don't look at you, sometimes like you can tell that they're lying if they're not really nervous—he wasn't really that nervous, and if he starts looking away from you, most of the time you can tell that he's lying because you'll—just a little bit smile when he looks away from you. And that's how you can tell if somebody's lying. Most of the time.

Adam's most impassioned answer came in response to the theories about his regression following the meeting. He discounted most of the theories that had anything to do with the meeting itself.

Adam: Yeah, and I know it wasn't because of going up to that prison. Because I went back and a teacher took me down to the weight room when I earned it. And he had picked up a bar from a kid because the kid just tried to hit me with it. And the teacher—I told him that I had to go to PE and I told my other teacher that I had to, and he said, no I didn't. And I kept on telling him and he raised the bar and started a motion like he was going to hit me so I grabbed him. And then pushed him away. And he went up to my PE teacher and asked him if I had PE and he told him yes and then he went and told his boss which is my teacher, and told her that I grabbed him, and he didn't tell her that it looked like he was going to hit me with the bar. And so, I got in trouble for it and he didn't get in any trouble. And then I went back and I asked him why he didn't tell about the bar, and then I got put back in school for it, and then when I finally got my time alone with him, when I could ask him—and I asked him why, and he said because he didn't really think that it mattered. And the point that mattered was that I grabbed him. That's why he didn't tell. And I don't get why he would say that because it does matter. So, I had about a couple months "in school" [detention] because I kept asking him why.

I asked Adam if he felt Johnny was like him or similar in any way. He responded, "Well, he's nice to people, which I am. He's nice, caring, loving, which I think match me, and I don't really know what else. I really do not know if we have anything in common."

I went back to his changes and asked how or if he felt he had changed because of meeting with Johnny.

"Well, I have been a lot nicer to people since I have done this. I've been a lot nicer and caring about people. Because I'm not being mean to anybody or beating anybody up. Stuff like that."

He then returned to his questions on the day of the meeting. He was particularly interested in the apparent confusion around which house was the "right one" and the appearance of their home.

Adam: Well, I asked him why they believed that the rumor about the ten thousand dollars and the drugs, because we don't have—we wouldn't be living in a junky house like that, with a car that's halfways torn apart, and falling apart—that we'd be living in a little nicer house, and have a nicer car.

I asked Adam at one point, if another kid was thinking of doing this and asked him his opinion, what would he tell him to do.

Adam: Yeah, because it's nice to get your answers and if you have a person that's nice to you, the feeling that you get from it is pretty good. And then you won't be really mad at anything anymore because if things happen like this to you, you gotta' turn to people asking you and bugging you and making fun of you for it. Then, after you get your questions answered, you can just tell them and they will quit saying stuff to you. And then you can feel happier.

When asked about the anticipation of meeting with me and whether he had any feelings about that, Adam stated:

Adam: Well, at first, I didn't want to do it, and then I kept changing my mind. Because first I didn't want to do it, and then I wanted to do it, and then I didn't want to do it, and then you called, and then I changed my mind again and wanted to do it.
Interviewer: What did I say?
Adam: I don't know, you just sounded like a very nice person on the phone.

With this, I was able to bring up questions about the day that the uncle saw the video and the reactions to the hug. I said that I had heard the story from a variety of people and that I was wondering what he thought about his uncle's reaction to seeing the videotape of the mediation, and asked was that hard for him.

Adam: Yeah, I think it was because I hugged him.

He discussed the incident with the therapist that day and remembered that she had told him about his uncle's feelings, and this made him aware of the dilemma that the uncle was facing. Both respondents remember that the therapist and Adam went into the room where the uncle and aunt were (the room where this interview was taking place), and that Adam said to the uncle, "Well, I do care about Johnny, but I love you." And with that, many in the room cried. Adam and the therapist also talked about his anger at his aunt and uncle deciding that he could not see the video until he was older. This became part of Adam's memory of the hug itself and how it took place.

Adam: Well, we were just at the end of the meeting and he asked me, just thinking, and then I just gave him a hug. Kind of shocked me when he did, but I decided to give him a hug.

[This is an interesting case of transmuted memory on everyone's part, as I was eventually able to view the tape myself. Clearly, it is Adam who first asks for a hug from Johnny. As the meeting is breaking up and it is asked if there is anything else, Adam states, "Yeah, one thing, can I have a hug?" This clearly takes Johnny by surprise. Then there is some talking, and just before Johnny leaves the room, Johnny initiates another hug.]

As my interview with Adam ends, I ask him the inevitable question as to what he is thinking about as a job. His response is, "A police officer or a tornado chaser."

Therapist and Mediators: I interview the therapist and the local mediator at the Victim's Services conference room. The therapist has been in the field for some time, with her major focus being work with victims and survivors of violent crime, abuse, and incest. The therapist shares with me that she herself is a survivor of childhood sexual abuse.

The therapist feels quite responsible for the outcome of the mediation as she feels responsible for initiating the meeting. When she began to hear her client discuss meeting with the offender, she initiated a call to the local mediator, who had the resources to make the meeting happen. Both were hesitant, given the age of the child and his history, but both relied on their "instinct" that this would be a positive experience for the child. They both express, during my interview, the depth of concern they had that it would "go well" for all involved in the process.

For the sake of imposing as much succinctness as I can without losing the voice of the experience, I will limit the quotes from these three people to the content that triangulates the experience of the other individuals involved.

The therapist led me through her involvement and treatment of Adam. This included how the idea of a meeting arose in the relationship, and how this became a reality. She discussed her therapeutic approach, which was to access him as if he were a four-year-old (his age at the time of the murders). Thus, play therapy was employed.

She finds it interesting that the clarity of Adam's memory for the events has diminished over the course of the therapy and following the mediation experience. She states, "I think it's because he turned loose of it."

In discussing her impressions of the meeting and Johnny, she stated:

Therapist: … thought that he was very genuine, and then when I saw him, he's so young, and he had these similar tragedies since he's been in prison, so if he didn't have it before, and he had a mother and father who loved him, and when she said she didn't raise him that way, I believed it. And he had—he'd lost a child while he was in prison. And it made me know—I mean I knew that this was real because he did—before he lost a child—intervene on Adam's behalf. It's like, when I heard him talk—I mean, I don't know … I'm just sitting over to the side and I mean, we are all bawling, it was just hard not to. I mean, I could not control—I mean I found myself crying through the thing because I thought this was meant to be.

Therapist: He [Johnny] was a beautiful young man, and that was—even though I know—I mean we do groups over at our local detention facility because we know that most of the kids who end up in trouble are abused, and victims themselves. I believed him. I'm not saying that he was a victim. I think that he was a teen who did what some teens do and didn't think very well and made a poor choice, and suffered greatly for it. I guess the biggest surprise was I believed him, too. Adam believed him. I believed him. And [Local Mediator] believed him. It's for sure that Deputy Smith did. I mean that's very unusual a detective is keeping an ongoing correspondence with a [criminal]—I believe him. I believe he felt bad about it. I believe that he made a stupid choice and paid dearly for it … It felt real to me.

Regarding the resolution of the uncle's feelings regarding the hug, the therapist stated:

Therapist: And then when he went in there, and of course, no practicing about it, he just sits down and says, "I like Johnny, but I love you." And so anyway, the only thing left from right after that was just I thought, "Oh, [Aunt], I wish you could have been here" [at the mediation]. And I don't think she would have participated, but I think she would have felt the dynamics and it could have been healing for her. I felt just this real incredible sense of "Wow!" Good, good feeling. A privilege to be there. Validated with Adam, and it was spiritual. It was spiritual. Whatever that is for different people, it was spiritual. It was like the people who see someone at a fountain or something, I mean, I don't have any doubt about what I just witnessed. So that's what it felt like.

Regarding the concept of empathy, she stated:

Therapist: It was palpable in the room. I mean it was, you could feel it all the way around. I felt like there wasn't a single person in there, including like his counselor, Johnny's counselor in the room—and I felt like—I mean, it was almost like everybody knew they were touching something very special.

… I felt joy that I was right about Adam [doing the mediation]. And I feel relief—relieved and validated. Relived that my decision—that initial decision to get involved with restorative justice continues to be validated.

The local mediator had been involved with victim services through the County Attorney's Office for many years. She is now working for the state's Department of Corrections as a coordinator of victim's issues.

She was also concerned but echoed the feelings of others that the preparation was "seamless" and that the feeling to proceed was always there, with no hitches or problems. She described her feelings during the meeting as "floating" and had distinct and clear memories of quotes from each of the participants.

She stated that her preparation and the decisions to proceed were made wholly intuitively, and not cognitively.

This mediator had a clear memory of the hug and its genesis, and the tape supported her memory of it. She stated that she was, "Profoundly moved by the experience, and I am always amazed by the power of the process."

The second mediator, who was involved in the preparation of Johnny, is a leader in the restorative justice movement. He was interviewed in a local restaurant.

Mediator 2: Because by the time he came into the mediation process, I think Adam was around eleven or twelve? But he was very very young when he experienced the multiple deaths. And you know there are many, many mediators and therapists who would say, "Don't go there," way too vulnerable a child. But I came into the process later, being asked to help with it, as a co-mediator, and I found out they had a therapist working with the child, they had a mediator, [Local Mediator], who I've done a lot of work with over the years, and I consulted with other people … people that know a lot more than me about childhood trauma, and was convinced that from what a number of people have said, a couple of other therapists too, that if done right this could be a very helpful kind of thing, so that he wouldn't have to live with the terror of that all of his life, at the full intensity.

So that preparation process was adapted there too, because it was one of the rare situations where one co-mediator had to do more prep with one person, and the other more with the other, and at later points we kind of crossed over to make sure there was human connection with both, and in doing "preparation" with that young of a child it's very different, we're on the floor, and we have a large stuffed animal, it's just very different, although the principles are in fact the same, which is to be very mindful to trying to connect to the world of the person you working with.

Johnny: Johnny is the last person interviewed in this group. I saw him on three separate occasions. The first interview took place at the maximum-security prison where he had been incarcerated for the ten years since the trials.

I arranged the interview with his case manager, who also serves as a counselor. As was most often the case when I visited an inmate, Johnny had no warning that I was coming, and on the day of the interview was told that he had a visitor. He presented in his prison blues, and had rows of braids in his hair, which was the current hair style. His size did not immediately strike me as it had others, but he is short of stature.

He was initially somewhat nervous as I explained my presence and had him read and sign the informed consent and releases.

He was interviewed in a lawyer's interview area, which is a semi-private area set up with six tables, which are somewhat separated from each other with partitions. There were one or two other meetings taking place between lawyers and inmates during our meeting, but the impression was that everyone else's business is intense enough that no one takes time to eavesdrop on other conversations, so the sense was one of relative privacy.

The room was situated right inside the main gate of the institution, so there was a great deal of human traffic and discussion going on outside. Since the rooms were separated only by bars, this conversation and activity is represented on the taped interview, inclusive of the large iron gate opening and closing numerous times. Happily, this kind of activity can be easily ignored and the conversation proceeded well.

Johnny impressed me as he had many other people. He presented as a very eager and engaged individual. He was still enthusiastic about the results of the meeting. He had been told that Adam had begun doing better in life almost immediately, and this continued to be very important to him.

Johnny showed a full range of affects during the interview, and appeared genuine and engaged in our discussion.

Johnny's course in the institution for the first ten years of his sentence had been without major conflict. He had received only one disciplinary infraction during this time. He had spent the bulk of his time, as reported by his father and mother, trying to better himself through education, and had learned a great deal about computers. He volunteered as a reading teacher for other inmates who were illiterate.

Happily, when I gave him my initial instruction (i.e., "I have some questions, but I am really interested in you telling me your story in your own way, etc."), Johnny said, "Oh, you mean you want me to give like a narrative?"

Johnny began by giving me a description of the events:

Johnny: Basically, I went with some gentlemen. They came up with an idea that they felt that they knew some drug dealers that had some money and they felt that it would be easy to get the money and that no one would really care because we were robbing some drug dealers and for some reason, I didn't really need the money, but I went along with them for some reason and that's what started this whole turn of events. We went out to this house. I was under the impression that it would be some drug dealers. We got out there and it was actually a real family, and we end up committing this crime and then it just kind of spiraled out of control. It ended up being a tragic event in my life and I'm sure for the family of the people that were involved too, the victims. But in my opinion, it should never have happened because we could have just easily just turned around and left after we didn't find any drugs, but they took it to another, they [his crime partners] chose to take it to another level.

In discussing his thinking regarding getting involved, he states that "people don't really care if a drug dealer is robbing another drug dealer. So, I thought the risk would be very minimal, and I figured the people we were robbing, they weren't going to call the police and say, 'we were just robbed by some other drug dealers for drugs,' so I thought it would be relatively safe, and would be a way to make some quick money."

Johnny: Because my mind was, like I was telling Adam, usually when it comes to making a decision between right and wrong, you generally know it in your mind. You know you usually say well this is right and this is wrong. Like I was telling Adam, it's like an angel on one shoulder saying no don't do it, and like the devil on the other shoulder saying oh go ahead, you can get away with it. If you listen to the bad side instead of the good side, that's when you get in trouble. You always listen to what the rationale thing that you know is right, and you'll stay out of trouble that way, but at that particular moment, I bent to temptation and I chose the wrong path that day. And I've been regretting it ever since.

Regarding the escalation of the crime to the extreme level of violence that took place, Johnny states that he was "in shock" when the shooting started. He did not believe that it would happen, and "would rather go to prison for robbery or something than go to jail for murder. If we get caught, so what. That's a lot better than murdering somebody … the guy that ended up shooting them, I never thought that he would even have the courage … ."

Johnny: We just sat in the car real quiet as we were driving back. They dropped me off, and I got back in my car, and I got on the freeway, and I was driving back home, and I just kept shaking my head. I was like "no not murder." I was like it can't be. Can't. I know he just. It was like a dream, but I couldn't wake up from it. So, when I got home, there was nobody there … . And I just sat in the house with the lights off, and I was just like, man I can't believe. This has got to be a dream. But every time I would think I'm waking up out of this it was right there at me. I couldn't get away from it. It was real. It was panic. It was sorrow. It was like everything mixed in one. It was like this went way out of control … And it just kept eating away at me, and I knew that, I wish I would have just followed. I got good common sense. If I would have just followed my common sense and didn't go along with these guys I would have been alright.

Johnny's internalization of Adam, both at the time of the murders and currently, is evident in his story.

Johnny: Four years old. I visualize all this in my head, and it's horrific. It should have never happened. It was carried on way beyond what it should have. There was no excuse for that. Like I said, my belief is that we could have just easily have left, and if they would have identified us, well what is worse going to jail for robbery or taking people's lives, what is worse? You're probably going to go to jail either way. You put these people's families through pain. What I try to do is put myself in the position of the families just to reverse it, just to see how painful and traumatic it would be, and when you think about it from those terms, it's real painful. The other guys that are involved they probably never tried to put themselves in the position of the family and seen the harm they've done. They're probably just thinking about themselves. There's always another side that hurt about this too. And I've had a lot of family member's die since I've been in here. I've lost a daughter to an accident in a car. I lost a brother. He shot himself in the head, and I don't know if it's because he seen me go to jail and he didn't want to go through it. He had just had a son that was one year old, so I'm going to have to look after him when I get out. Then I have my son.

Reminiscent of the interview with his mother, Johnny describes tearfully his values:

Johnny: It would be too much to bear. They say God doesn't give you more than you can bear, but I'm a strong individual as far as discipline. I've learned to discipline myself: I have a real strong desire to be successful, and for people to put trust in me not to let them down. That's what drives me, to prove that I wasn't the person that was out there that night. I just want people to think of me a little bit differently [crying].

In an extraordinary example of research triangulation, Johnny describes his impression of the therapist while in the mediation:

Johnny: I could tell she [the therapist] was real, when I was looking at, when we were in the meeting, I could just see that she was really enjoying how the meeting was going and how things were going fine, and it seemed like it was kind of like a relief to her. I could kind of see it in her face that this is going to do so much good. She was real emotional. She kind of got a little teary eyed. And I think it achieved the benefits that we wanted. The most important thing to me was not me, it was Adam.

… I try to display strength to my son too. It's not good. I used to just keep everything bottled up inside. And things would be bothering me in the back of my mind, but I wouldn't be thinking they are but they are, because stuff would happen, and I would be real stressful. I later found out from in here doing a lot of thinking, I've done a lot of maturing in here too though. I mean I'm not saying this is the best place to mature, but you get a chance to do a lot of thinking, and what good does it do to do all this time if you don't come out a better person. You have to come out a better person. You have to. I think before my heart was more hardened and I had a harder time showing people my emotions and stuff like that even though, kind of my dad was like that for a while too. He would never let you see him cry. But now he's even, I can see a difference in him now. He's done a 100 percent turnaround. I think that just rubbed off on us. Me and my brother, we just wouldn't show our emotion. We thought it was a sign of weakness. That's not the case.

I learned how to open up and I basically learned how to love people and show them that. You can still love somebody and keep it in there. My brother used to say, "you never want to talk about anything." And I didn't feel it was wrong that I wasn't talking. It just felt normal because our father was like that, and we shouldn't show signs of weakness. I guess maybe that was what we were thinking.

Regarding the aftermath of the meeting, this narrative reveals how it all settled with him.

Johnny: And I was proud of myself to have the courage to do it because a lot of people they just wouldn't do it for some reason or another. I was more happy that I had a positive impact than anything to do with me. I was more happy that it impacted him positively, and I was thrilled about the fact that it has the potential of helping get his grades and stuff straightened around too, because if he's not doing good in school now then there's only trouble later on down the road. Like a lot of these guys, they come in here and they don't learn any education and so when they get out they only know what they knew. If you were a bank robber when you came in and you don't pick up any skill, the only thing you know how to do is be a bank robber. You haven't learned anything. What are you going to do? So, either going to sell drugs or be a bank robber. There is nothing else you can do.

... I think it even humanized me more, and then it probably even strengthened the bond because now he [Adam] is talking to me and he knows me, and when you talk to someone, you can kind of get a sense of the person. So, a lot of the questions just by talking to somebody you can get a sense of that person. That's probably. Otherwise, he probably just seen a picture of me or something or whatever he could remember in his mind, but he never really talked to me and got to know my feelings and how this affected me as well as him. Because it affected me too because not only coming together, but my son, I've hurt my son too to a certain extent. Indirectly, because I'm gone from him, and he's got to see everything. Maybe if I was not in here maybe my daughter wouldn't have been living at that house, and then maybe she wouldn't have died. Because maybe my daughter's mother wouldn't have had to move out of the house she was in before to move to that house. There's all kinds of ramifications from me being in here. And one thing I want to convey to him is don't later on in life go off the deep end and get depressed and then you end up being in here. You know, throwing your hands up and getting frustrated, then you end up being in here. This is not the place to be.

I ask Johnny to tell me about his depression:

I'm not depressed (now). I was pretty depressed because just thinking of that I was with those guys. That's a big burden. When you take somebody's life, that's a big burden. That's not a walk through the park. I feel some relief now because I know in my mind that that kid was traumatized. He had to be. And then when he told me that when he found him there he had the popsicle in his hand, all this, you know when you view it that way it's real traumatic and frustrating, and I just wanted a chance to get my side out and to redeem myself and to let him know that, no it shouldn't have happened but let's go forward and let's not let you get into any trouble later on in life behind you. Because he could turn around and go the wrong way if he ain't careful.

When I left the meeting, it was like a burden had been lifted off my shoulders. I felt lighter. It was like at least this chapter is having some kind of conclusion. It's being brought to some kind of conclusion and it's being settled. It was a burden because I had things I wanted to get off my chest but I couldn't do it. I needed to address them to Adam, and until I got the chance to do it, it didn't do any good to tell any adults. Once I was able to tell him, I just felt lighter. It felt like any time you get good news. You know when you get good news you feel euphoria. I felt euphoric all day. And I still do because the worst thing that

> I wanted to have happen was to go around thinking that this kid hated me, and I don't care if he hates the other guys. I didn't want him to hate me because I didn't mean for anything to happen to his parents, and if it was up to me, nothing would have. I wanted to be able to get that off, and I was given that chance. I'm thankful to God. Like we said, it had to be God's intervention for it to happen. At least with us, and with him being so young. Everything just all fell together perfectly.

In describing his relationship with Adam after the meeting, I found it interesting that Johnny used the connection of being like a brother to him rather than a son.

Johnny: It seems kind of like we're as one because we've been down this endeavor together. You been down this, we'll always be linked through this. It's kind of like he's a little brother to a certain extent. When you want to see him do good, and you don't want to see nobody do anything that could hurt him or anything. You want to just keep an eye on him and make sure everything goes as smooth as possible from here on out. That's how I feel about it. As long as he's feeling good, I'm feeling good. And when he's feeling bad, I'm feeling bad.
I think what you see on the tape, you'll be able to see the benefits. Because he wanted to hug and everything. If he didn't feel good about it, he wouldn't do that.
Interviewer: Did that feel okay? The hug? Felt natural?
Johnny: Yes, that felt great. It was kind of like closure. It felt good and euphoric. It's special, man. Think about it. You have a kid go through something as traumatic as this and then you get a chance to make amends for it, and it works out and you end up being friends out of it, and you both get a chance to get this pain off your chest, and there's nothing like it.

My second interview with Johnny took place some weeks later. He had just been transferred to a medium security institution in the southern part of the state. The institution had, at one time, been a residential school for the deaf, and while it was clearly now a correctional institution, with fences and razor wire, the buildings were more like dorms and the feeling was much less intense than the previous maximum-security institution.

At the time of this interview, Johnny was clearly a little "unhinged" by his transfer. He had been working toward this and was clearly happy about it (since transfers to medium security units are usually done in anticipation of parole within a few years). At the same time, I had the feeling that he was knocked a little off center by the new surroundings.

I had seen the video of the mediation, and one of the rationales for this second meeting was to give me an opportunity to ask him some questions about the tape.

He talked about a section on the tape where he describes his understanding that they were in the wrong place. This had to do with the other perpetrator holding the gun on Adam to threaten the mother into telling him where the drugs and money were.

Johnny: Because I think that he felt that she was lying and if she was lying you would imagine that any parent, if you give an option of saving your child's life or holding out and hope or holding out on these drugs, you would take your child over these drugs so he figures, and I'm just speculating, I don't know what he was thinking, but he probably figured that well if I do this well she's going to take, if there are drugs here, she's going to take and give the drugs up because she wouldn't want anything to happen to the child.
… And when I analyze that and when I seen that he kept pushing and pushing and pushing, and she wasn't saying that there were any drugs out there, that immediately told me that there ain't no drugs out here because there ain't no mother in my thinking is going to jeopardize her child behind no drugs. So that right there was the first serious clue that we were sent out here on a bogus mission basically because there ain't no drugs out here.

In talking with me about the future, Johnny speculates about the threat he may feel having testified against the others when or if he returns to the community. He is clear that as a parolee, he will not be able to carry a gun, but I am interested in his thinking about his inner "voices" or the dialogue with his "phantom community" based on Athens' theory of "soliloquy." One can see by this passage the ambivalence he feels between the two worlds:

Johnny: Well, the main threat that I feel is I want to do everything I can for myself and for my son's sake to make sure that I don't get in trouble. It's not like I would go back there. I definitely wouldn't keep the same company, but there might be guys that like, well we hear that Johnny is out and they're bitter, and then they're like well other family members might approach me, and okay, visualize this, I'm a convicted felon now. I can't carry guns like I used to carry. So, say you're [one of the other perpetrators'] cousin or brother-in-law and you approach me about the situation, and you're mad. Maybe he sends to approach me and you're mad and you are packing and I'm not packing. So how much of a disadvantage are you now? You don't know what the intention of another person might be. If you can't feel comfortable and safe, it's not even worth being out. If you can't feel like, I would feel comfortable if I was able to carry a gun because I would have more than just my finger. And knowing the character of some of the guys.

[Later in the discussion] … We got a phrase in the hood called slipping. That's where you let your guards down and you get caught relaxed. It's always best to be aware of a potential problem so that when it comes it won't just catch you off guard. I'm not even saying that this will happen, but it's in my mind and I'll be aware of it, so it will be harder for someone to catch me relaxing or slipping with my guard down. Because there is a phrase, would you rather be caught without a gun or be alive and in jail. Think about it. When they say get caught without a gun, it's not like you're going to get caught without a gun and the guy is just going to stand there and look at you. When you weigh the pros and cons, that kind of like a little sacred deal that goes on in the neighborhood. Which scenario would you rather have? Would you rather go to jail for attempted murder or carrying a concealed weapon or would you rather be dead? Like I said, I can't do that anymore, because if I plan on staying out.

… Because I was living that lifestyle, but I always managed to, when something was real serious or something that would put you in jail, I managed always to stay away from it or, like one time, one of my friends we had got in an argument with some guys, and I'll tell you, I've never told anybody this, but one time some guy from another gang, I guess he liked my girlfriend or something, and then we got into an argument with him, and then me and him, we actually had a little shootout or something, right? And then, so I went to a bar to cool off with another one of my friends that was with me when we were shooting at this guy, and we went out to the parking lot, and I seen some more of my friends that were in the gang with me at that time, and they wanted to go to do something. They wanted to go do something. I was like well I'm going in here. Originally, I had my hand on the door. I was getting ready to get in the car, and I didn't. I said well I'm going to go do something else. I took my hand off the car door. I, actually, it was a two door Cougar and I actually almost pulled the door open and got in, and I said no I'm going to do something else. Because I knew that we're probably going to do something retaliatory. That's what I was thinking. But I wasn't for sure what they were talking about. So, I went in there. Later on, that night I'm in the bar and one of the guy's girlfriends come in there, well they shot so and so and killed him.

He again discusses the close of the meeting and the hug, and I ask him his impressions of it and how it developed.

Johnny: No, it was a total surprise. It was a surprise. And that right there, that speaks volumes if anyone watches that. If you think from the beginning of when this horrible day happened until now, to cap it off with that, that says that people are healing and moving on. We're learning about each other. He's learning about me, and he aware of my role and what I tried to do for him, and how he tried to open up for me and give me the opportunity to talk to him. That was the ending of it at that time, and that was kind of a powerful moment.

The third meeting I had with Johnny was a few weeks after the second. He had not seen the videotape himself, and I had arranged to have the second mediator accompany me to the institution and show it to him. His case manager at the medium security institution was very accommodating and helpful toward these arrangements, and provided us with an office and TV with a VCR to view the tape.

I record the entire session, and then ask them both questions at the close.

In watching himself on the tape, Johnny observes, "I'm nervous. I was real nervous. Now that I look back, I was real nervous."

During the early phase of the mediation, Johnny, at one point, apologizes to Adam, and during this sequence he breaks down. The language on the tape is, "I'm very, very sorry for my part. I'm embarrassed … I'm sorry." While watching this sequence, Johnny again tears up. While listening to Adam's description of the crime on the tape, he sighs deeply at one point. He remains emotional throughout the tape.

During the discussion about the tape at the end, Johnny states:

Johnny: The parts that really hit my heart when I was watching it was the part where he said where [the family friend who was also murdered] was reading the book to him. That part was real, real hard on me. And then the part about the wrong house. … those two parts right there was really, just [crying] … drove a spike through me.

Kinda like, I can't forgive myself for those two parts.

Something I would like to show [his son] the tape. They are trying to shield him from a lot of things. Saw his sister getting killed, and my brother … I asked him the other day if it was still bothering him, he said "yeah."

I started to calm down at the point we did the hugs and that. Then I started to get nervous again, that's why I was walking around like that, I couldn't leave. I was on an emotional high then, I think it was successful.

I felt a lot better afterwards. I went and did activities, went and played basketball. I called mom and told her how it went.

DISCUSSION

I present this case at the outset as it represents a landmark case in restorative justice history. It represents a successful mediation with a young child, the only one, at least at this time, known to have occurred with a minor. At the same time, it embodies a representative experience of the process, which is replicated in almost all my successive interviews. Thus, it is both unique and unexceptional at the same time.

It shows the systemic nature of the practice in the global sense, while giving a good example of the effect of mediation on individuals; thus, it offers an example of effects on both mega and meta levels.

One of the reasons I chose to broaden my interviews to include victims and mediators was the evidence I secured, in an earlier pilot study, that empathy seems to occur in these cases as a function of the system or community involved. If it can occur in the offender, it also seems to occur for the other participants. In some cases, they will deny that they achieved empathy (as was seen with Deputy Smith) and at the same time betray this in other parts of the interview, and in their words and actions toward the offender. This finding represents a key discovery of this project: empathy exists and is found as part of a social system.

The trauma experienced by Adam is undeniable, and its repercussions on his development throughout the following years of his life are evident. As is often the case with children, these repercussions are evidenced not in an obvious mood disturbance, but in behavioral manifestations that often elicit confused and confusing reactions in his community.

In attempting to deal with this behavior, his family encounters in the traditional arenas an often ambivalent if not avoidant reaction. It is an unfortunate fact that the family's experience with the therapeutic community is not at all uncommon. On countless occasions through my interview process, I am told of therapists who seem intent on avoiding the subject of the crime and its ramifications to the individual. This is done out of the rationalization, often, that it is better not to "dwell" on the past. It would be speculative to discuss the orientation of the therapists who so assiduously avoid this material in the clinical setting. Suffice it to say, however, that the clients consistently feel their needs are unmet, and that they have not been helped. The primary argument is that the material is too frightening and the feelings too intense. The facilitation of the mourning that these individuals are struggling with is the central component of their progress toward resolution. The telling of the story in all its detail is the vehicle for this mourning process. To avoid it serves only to imbue the feelings with shame and prolong and exacerbate the pain experienced by the individuals involved.

The reaction of Adam to meeting his final therapist, who naturally provides him with the support to put the obvious into words, shows clearly and graphically the need he felt to have this experience discussed openly, without evading the details of his life and crisis, in a safe and supportive holding environment. His behavior almost immediately improved, and the shift in his mood and attitude were clear to his family and his teachers.

My meeting with Johnny's mother and father was quite moving for me. It also opened a universe of other victims of violent crime that had not been evident: the family of the offender. The parallel emotions expressed by this group are strikingly similar to those of the victim's families, and are echoed in later interviews. While I was not able to conduct more interviews with offender families, I am confident that the similarities would be significant, based on information obtained in discussions with offenders and mediators about these families.

In discussing their sense that crime is something that happens to others, and only in big cities, Johnny's parents express a universal denial process that is common to all of us. They go on to describe the sense of shame brought on the family and on the self because of this, and describe how this, then, affects others in their circle. (i.e., "If it can happen to them, it can happen to anyone.")

One of Peterson's (2000) major topics in her study is how the trauma experience is like "a nightmare you never wake up from." Strikingly, both Johnny and his parents in my interviews use this phrase to describe the experience. Johnny's mother also suggests that Johnny is struggling to find the "right words" to express his feelings to Adam.

Significantly, Johnny's mother is also the first to connect the process of grief and loss to the experience. In this case, and borne out in my interview with Johnny, she surmises that his own grief and loss at the death of his daughter has allowed him to consider the experience from another's viewpoint, or to empathize. I would suggest that this experience of grief, at the loss of his own daughter as well as the death by suicide of his brother, was one of the many epiphanies that Johnny experienced in his growth.

Further meaning seems to be made from the occurrence of terror and fear, words that are constantly used in these and other interviews. Offenders frequently use these words to describe how they are feeling just prior to the meeting with the victim (e.g., terrified, afraid, scared).

Another example of a parallel with other families of offenders was Johnny's mother's desire to express her regret to the victim's family. Again, she describes the difficulty in finding the "right words" to do this. She states that the words, "I'm sorry" are the hardest words for a person to say: "How frustrating when you want to say it and can't." The universal reported to me in other cases is the desire to prove to the other family that "We are not monsters," and are just normal people. ("We were just normal people before this happened to us too.")

This sense, repeated throughout my time with the parents, supports a major finding of this project. It is embodied in Harry Stack Sullivan's "one-genus postulate," which eloquently states that "everyone is much more simply human than otherwise, and that anomalous interpersonal situations, insofar as they do not arise from differences in language or custom, are a function of differences in relative maturity of the persons concerned" (Sullivan 1953).

Johnny's mother's comment regarding her ability to let go of hatred nicely reflects Sullivan's postulate, which is reminiscent enough of my Homeric metaphor to be remarkable:

> After I saw the video with Adam, that I was really able to tell [Father], and my mother and other members of my family that I was close to that I have been able to let go of all the hatred that I had in my heart for anybody, because I found that hatred was destroying me. And I didn't want to hate anybody. And I didn't have any reason to hate anybody. I don't know, when I saw that video, it helped me to a degree.

She also describes the function of this meaning affecting the wider circle of her community, which is also significant.

The interview with Deputy Smith was also very significant. In many ways, Deputy Smith did not come across as a stereotypical law enforcement officer. This may be more common of law enforcement officers in smaller communities. He had a clear soft side, which he was not afraid to show me. Some of his attitude and worldview seemed to be because of his history in law enforcement, and some because of this and other life experiences. This crime, the investigation, the apprehension of the perpetrators, and the trial served as epiphanies for him as well.

His expression of the immediate connection he felt to Johnny was interesting and somewhat confusing to him. This connection was almost immediately established in his comment that he would like Johnny for a neighbor and would have him as a friend. His empathy for Johnny is evidenced in the example he gave of Johnny's fear of flying, and the sheriff's somewhat sadistic pleasure at taunting him.

His comments about the awakening in him of the realities of the racial gap in this society seemed to be another example of epiphany for him, as he claims this experience really "opened my eyes" to the meaning of growing up African American in this culture. One of the most poignant examples of this for him was Johnny asking what a live sheep was in a farm field while Deputy Smith was driving him to court. Although Johnny grew up in a city, the city is in the heart of an agricultural state, so the thought that he had neither been to a farm, nor seen a living animal was profound for the deputy: "I found out how isolated we can make the inner city."

The deputy's reaction to my question about "empathy" as part of the process was also interesting, as mentioned previously. I found, quite often, that people had a difficult time with this word. It is hard to know if the reaction he gave me was based on the perception of a role conflict, given his definition of the experience (i.e., possibly confusing sympathy with empathy), or whether he saw the word as somehow expressing forgiveness or compassion ("He was kind of a bad guy"). If so, this is intriguing, as he, himself, demonstrates compassion in his relationship to Johnny throughout their connection, and, as mentioned, betrays an obvious sense of empathy for this offender.

Another remarkable experience in this case was the reactions of the aunt and uncle. The aunt clearly continued to carry several unresolved personal issues related to her complicated family history, and the injury and subsequent death of her brother.

At the time of my interview with her, her husband continued to state his feeling that having her own meeting with Johnny would be useful for her, yet she continued to avoid this. The therapist, who had seen the aunt in a group session with other victim families, also felt that she carried many unresolved issues, and felt that eventually she would need to deal with these. Despite her strong negative opinion of meeting with Johnny herself, this did not get in the way of her allowing her young nephew to do it. The aunt is also evidence of issues of grief and loss, which can be encountered in this process.

The couple maintained continuing remarkable boundaries. The uncle's strong feelings about the hug incident, and fears that Johnny would somehow ingratiate himself to Adam, did not get in the way of his feeling that this was necessary for Adam. He based this opinion largely on Adam's stated desires and his own observations and instincts. This shows a remarkable Differentiation is a term used in family therapy to signify ability to see others as separate from one's self.

Adam, as mentioned, presents as any normal thirteen-year-old client. In addition, as is true with a thirteen-year-old client, much of the information gained is of a corollary nature, and must be confirmed or discussed in the encounter with the child.

Adam showed, as mentioned, his conflicts in behavioral terms—acting out in school, misbehaving with teachers, and performing poorly. He was, thus, defined as "hyperactive" by the school, referred for evaluation, and eventually prescribed Ritalin.

As was seen by the therapist in her work with him, he was not sufficiently developmentally advanced to describe his concerns verbally. She found it productive to use play therapy with him, and this was eventually the way that he could confirm his trauma and deal with it. Many of the events of that evening were not in his consciousness, and, as is often the case with children, once these elements attained consciousness, they were dealt with and forgotten. Adam confirmed this process for me in our interview.

The most obvious example of the meaning of the experience to him, however, is seen in his performance, and his moving toward normalization in his development. This transformation was seen, immediately, with the beginning of competent psychotherapy and culminated in the meeting with Johnny.

Another of my findings is that these offenders, relative to my research methodology, show a series of epiphanies that begin with the commission of the crime itself, progress through the arrest and trial, and come to fruition with the mediation experience, which includes the initial approach by the mediator, the preparation, and the eventual meeting with the victim.

Johnny gives evidence of this series of epiphanies in our interview. He clearly had a strong reaction to the commission of the crime. There is evidence from the informants, and given his early history, that Johnny had a capacity for empathy prior to this act. This may well have been related to his own process of fathering, which has been noted in other offenders.

Johnny gives phenomenal evidence of the gathering weight of the experience, which leads him to a strong empathic position toward Adam and others. ("What I try to do is put myself in the position of the families, just to reverse it, just to see how painful and traumatic it would be, and when you think about it from those terms, it's real painful.") It is at this point in the interview that Johnny shows the most undefended emotion.

Johnny confirms his mother's observation that his own grief and loss issues are significant to his discovering his own empathic abilities in describing his reactions to the death of his daughter and brother. Another important aspect of this reaction is his obvious sense of responsibility for both these deaths.

Johnny also shows a remarkable capacity for psychological mindedness in his understanding that his bottling up of his emotions, learned from his father, has been harmful for him. He now sees that showing emotion is a positive thing and is attempting to incorporate this into his life. The sense, of course, that showing emotion is a sign of weakness is often repeated by my offender population, heard in practically every interview. In this way, Johnny reports that engaging in the process of the meeting "humanized" him.

Finally, another finding, which will be discussed and is first described here by Johnny, is the sense that the victim and offender will, forevermore, be linked in some fashion. Johnny describes this as their being "like one" and later states that they will "always be linked." The hug graphically represents this to Johnny, symbolizing to him "closure," making "amends," and "letting go and moving on," as well as "learning about each other."

Chapter 6

The Exception and the Rule

LUCY AND HARRY

This case proved to be somewhat out of the ordinary as well, but is included because it provides interesting examples of the development of the process and the meaning of these mediations to the participants. This case is illuminating in terms of the participants' motivation to take part and what they hope to achieve when they enter, and then, what happens to these expectations. There is often much to learn in cases like this, which are exceptions to the rule (and may be exceptions that prove the rule).

This case also pushes the boundaries of the definition of these meetings for the mediators and therapists involved, and has the potential to turn out badly, but the meaning for the victim and offender remain important to explore.

I was also able in this case to meet with and interview the participants approximately one year before the meeting took place, during the preparation period, and then meet with them following the meeting and afterwards to view the videotape of the meeting. Thus, I have a "pre-" and "post-" experience with this case. I met with each of the participants once before the mediation session and then again following the meeting, and also viewed the tape with the victim participant.

In the fall of 1973, Lucy was a thirteen-year-old runaway who was hitchhiking in a medium-sized Midwestern city. Harry picked her up in his pick-up truck.

Harry seemed like a nice enough person to Lucy, about the age of her own father, and told her he would take her right where she wanted to go. When he got directions at a gas station, it sounded to Lucy that they weren't far from her destination, but Harry kept driving. She was not too worried, as she held her hand on a steak knife that she carried in her purse for protection.

Harry continued to drive, until the two were in a rural area. He picked up a hammer and told Lucy to move over by him in the truck.

Lucy was sexually assaulted and threatened. Harry told her that he would kill her with the hammer, or sell her to a gang. He took her out of the truck in a cornfield, and tried to get into the camper in his truck, but the lock jammed, and Harry became frustrated. He told Lucy to get dressed and get back in the truck.

Harry told Lucy that he would have to kill her, and told her he had done so to others. She attempted to keep talking to him, "like he was my friend," thinking that would be her only hope of survival. She told him her life story, and said that she was a runaway and was only thirteen and that if he killed her, she would never have a chance to patch things up with her mother, and that her mother would be so sad. This seemed to touch Harry, and he told her he would take her where she wanted to go.

Lucy was worried until she got into the house of her friend. Harry sat watching her until she got inside, as if he were waiting for her to be safe.

Lucy is convinced that this conversation did save her life, and, in fact, that something in her story touched Harry, making his demeanor change, and making him seem almost caring toward her. Harry told her that he "felt sorry for her" and "wished she were his daughter so he could take care of her." Lucy said, "He was a completely different person from when he first picked me up."

Lucy initially told the people in the place she was staying, but no one did anything or suggested that she do anything. She states that she was "real quiet, and took a lot of showers."

Lucy ended up in a juvenile center, and told someone there, but it was some time after the incident so there was no evidence, and not much seemed to be done about it. When she was in a residential program that Christmas, a man approached her at a Christmas service from behind, and touched her arm. He gave her a Christmas card with the words, "I wish you were my daughter," and a $5 bill. This event stimulated a flashback experience for Lucy, who ran out of the church and attempted to escape from the center. This near-escape brought more attention to her experience. Initially, she thought the man giving her the card was Harry, and identified him as the man who attacked her, but this was later determined not to be the case. The police, however, were struck by the resemblance of the man to another case that was getting a lot of press at the time. This person turned out to be Harry.

Harry was thought by the police to be a practicing serial murderer. He had been charged with the kidnapping and murder of a variety of women. At the time of these investigations, he was also charged with kidnapping and sexually assaulting Lucy in 1974; he was later ultimately at the trial he was convicted of the murders convicted of the murders of two women, and the kidnapping and assault of Lucy.

In terms of Harry's victims, Lucy and one other are the only survivors. Books have been written about Harry, suggesting that he is responsible for a host of unsolved murders in the West and Midwest of the United States.

The police officers that investigated the crime quickly became protective of Lucy, and took an interest in her life. The family of one of the investigators became her foster family, where she lived through her adolescence. Later, she married and had children, eventually moving back to her hometown, where she maintains a strained relationship with her mother.

Lucy has continued to struggle throughout her life with the consequences of her experience, which included Harry's arrest and her participation in his trial. She read a great deal about him, including the books in the popular press relating to the details of his suspected murders.

This reading has served to fill out a picture for her of her attacker, but also heightened her feelings of vulnerability and trauma resulting from her experience and close call with death.

She has had a great deal of psychotherapy since the event, and has been with her current therapist for some years. She feels that therapy has been a lifesaver for her, and that she has made a great deal of progress. At our first meeting, when she found out that I am a psychotherapist myself, she stated that she has been diagnosed with "borderline personality disorder, post-traumatic stress disorder and depression." She offered these diagnoses with a sort of pride that the diagnoses will define who she is in a way that I will appreciate. Lucy has continued to struggle with nightmares every night and feels that she harbors a great deal of anger.

The idea of meeting with Harry began to develop for her because of a variety of events that happened at the same time. She became aware of the restorative justice movement through the victim's community, and the notion of meeting with the offender was presented to her through the media, and through hearing about other cases. At this same time, Lucy approached a local Rape Crisis Center to volunteer. She felt that her experience as a survivor would be useful and had a strong desire to "give back" something to young women who were struggling with similar experiences. The director of this center, after speaking with Lucy for some time, in a very compassionate manner, suggested that Lucy still needed to do more of her "own work" before she could volunteer and be of use to others. The director suggested that she felt Lucy still had too much anger and too many unresolved issues. Lucy did not disagree with this, and was thankful to the director for her honesty. She began speaking to her therapist about her idea that it might be helpful to her to meet with Harry. The therapist was initially somewhat hesitant, but was ultimately convinced by Lucy, who felt that this might be the thing that would enable her to move on in her personal work and life in general.

Lucy called the mediator responsible for these mediations in her state. After hearing Lucy's story, he said he would initiate contact with Harry and let her know.

The mediator approached Harry at the maximum-security prison in which he is housed, telling him that Lucy had requested a mediated dialogue with him.

Harry gave a surprising and complicated response to the mediator. Harry, now in his early seventies, stated that he remembered Lucy from his trials. He stated to the mediator, however, that he did not do to Lucy what he was charged and convicted with. He stated that he believes Lucy's identification of the man in the church was no doubt the correct one, but that, at the time of the incident, the police were eager to find and place any unsolved cases on Harry. Because of this desire, he contended, they convinced the vulnerable child that Harry was the man who assaulted her.

Then, Harry made an unexpected statement to the mediator. He stated, "I'm not a good person. I have killed a number of people, and I admit that openly. I remember Lucy, and I felt sorry for her during my trial. If I can do something that will be helpful to her I would like to do what I can." Harry also stated that he had been diagnosed with cancer, and while it was not immediately life threatening, he was aware of his own mortality. Harry agreed to meet with Lucy if she wanted to, with the understanding that he could not admit to her the crime.

The mediator was puzzled by this response, but was also struck by Harry's sentiments and felt this to be a genuine and heartfelt offer. He contacted Lucy and told her of his experience.

Lucy said that she could accept this, and the preparation for the mediation began. One mediator met with Harry, and a local mediator (a psychologist) met with Lucy, also coordinating with her therapist and maintaining contact with the mediator who was meeting with Harry and who would be responsible for the meeting.

I first met with Lucy almost one year prior to the eventual mediation meeting. We met at a local restaurant. Lucy had no hesitation in agreeing to meet with me. I told her about my project and that I would simply like to meet with her to introduce myself and talk with her prior to the meeting, and then again after it. I did not tape this initial interview, but took written notes and then completed more notes following our meeting.

I came with some questions about my understanding of the case and the problems involved in it, questions about the meaning to her of Harry's denial, and questions about the process of the preparation. I was also interested in the risks of the mediation that she perceived, and whether she planned to get or already had her own support. I asked her about her greatest hopes and fears about the eventual meeting.

Lucy at the time of this meeting was a thirty-nine-year-old mother of two children. She stated in the interview that she had always felt that it would be a good thing to meet and speak with Harry, but she never thought that it was a possibility. She then began to hear more about restorative justice on television.

She was worried that he was agreeing to meet with her only for some benefit of his own, "To make it look like he's a nice guy."

She also expressed frustration at the mediator, who had said to her that he thought Harry's story was possibly true. Lucy is fully convinced that Harry was the perpetrator.

To deal with her expectations and his denial, Lucy had come up with what I felt was an ingenious solution: "I plan to not try to put him in a corner and make him defensive." Lucy decided to ask all her questions in a "third-person" manner, using Harry's other victims, or hypothetical cases, (e.g., "If you had done this to me, what would you have been thinking?").

This approach seemed positive in that Lucy would not place herself in a bad position by getting into a power struggle with Harry, and thereby have the situation become untenable.

I asked Lucy what her best outcome would be. She said, "Somebody takes responsibility for what's happened to me."

Significantly, then, it would be for Harry to admit, during the meeting, that he did, in fact, victimize Lucy. She also hoped that the meeting would allow her to "get over my nightmares" and move on in her own growth and resolution and to "help others." With this resolution, beyond her desire to work in counseling or with survivors' groups, Lucy admits to feeling some burden for the women that Harry has killed, and wants to be their voice. Her goal is a consequence of the research she did about Harry and his victims, and the information she collected during the trial.

Lucy also discussed her own family and the ongoing struggles she has with her mother. Her own father has been out of her life for a long time. Since the crime, she has also met Harry's brother and other relatives of his in the community, and stated that she felt there were similarities between them, which may have impressed Harry when they met, and may have even influenced his not killing her. She stated that his family history is like that of her own father, and stated at one point, "He's just like my dad!"

I next met with the mediator who was preparing Lucy for the meeting. He wanted to become more actively involved in the mediation process, is the father of a victim of violent crime, and had benefited from a mediation experience himself. He is also a mental health professional.

The mediator had many concerns about preparing Lucy for the meeting, and, ultimately thinking about the meeting itself.

Most pressing were the concerns regarding Lucy's mental health vulnerability, especially with her upcoming meeting with an offender who violated her so strikingly but refuses to admit to the act. The perpetrator's admission of the crime and taking some level of responsibility for it had been a primary expectation in previous mediations. Without this condition being present in this case, the mediator was worried that the offender was acting out apropos of his antisocial personality disorder, and that Lucy would be at risk. At the same time, he suggested that, at times, "surrogate" offenders or offender panels are used in other types of victim-resolution experiences, especially with victims of sexual assault, and that this format had been useful for victims.

This point opened for this mediator a discussion of the relative strengths and weaknesses of the restorative justice mediation model being employed in this case. He saw the strengths as "Facing evil and your fears. Allowing one to define and find humanity, and some common ground." The weaknesses, he felt, were related to the risk of harm to the victim. However, he also felt that too much reliance on one model was problematic and too limited.

When I met with the primary mediator, he continued to feel, on one level, that Harry was believable in his desire to help Lucy. At the same time, he was concerned. He too stated that, at times, "surrogates" were used in these meetings. He felt that this approach could be useful to the victim, and he saw this meeting as being along those lines.

At the same time, he too was concerned about Lucy's potential vulnerability, and was concerned that Harry was possibly getting some form of "secondary gain" out of meeting with Lucy. He stated that this concern would be the focus of his ongoing meetings with Harry. During this process, if he came to feel that the ultimate meeting would be unsafe for Lucy, he wouldn't proceed with it.

I arranged my first meeting with Harry through the psychologist at the prison in which he was housed. Harry had been participating in a group run by this professional, and, also, had been meeting with him individually. My first meeting with Harry was in the psychologist's office and was a private meeting. I presented the same preparatory statement to Harry that I had to Lucy, and stated, again, that I simply wanted to introduce myself to him and follow the process, interviewing him again, more formally, following the meeting.

Harry was dressed in prison "blues," and, even with his advanced age, is a large and intimidating man. While he hides his age well, one could see that, when he was younger, he was no doubt a forceful and frightening presence.

Harry immediately told me that he was innocent of the crime, and told me the same story he recounted to the mediator about the desire of the authorities to clear their cases. He stated, in roughly the same fashion that he did for the mediator, that he had had similar victims, so he thought that he understood her position. He also stated that his memory of her at the trial made him "feel sorry for her," thus, if he could be helpful, he was open to it.

I, too, experienced Harry's genuine desire to help Lucy in this discussion, and could appreciate the mediator's instinct. At the same time, I was aware that Harry is a serial murderer, the profile of which relates to individuals who are very adept at seeming genuine and taking in gullible people who, at some level, want to believe them, a quality of human nature that many serial murderers take advantage of. Perhaps Harry's realization of his own mortality, however, or his concern about his disease, gave him a genuine desire to help this victim. Ultimately, this is very hard to be sure of.

Harry, later in this interview, felt the need to tell me, in rather excruciating detail, the events of the three murders he admitted to, giving a distinct confirmation of his psychopathy in his enjoyment of telling the story, and his likely assumption of my reaction to it.

Given that I have had experience with such offenders, and have heard similar or worse stories, I had little reaction to Harry's stories. At the end of this narrative, Harry stated to me that he has been interviewed several times by a variety of people. He then stated, "You're OK, I can be straight with you," implying that, within a fairly short period of time he could judge whether he can be honest with a person or whether he can "snow" them, based on his initial judgment of them. I suggested that I assumed he was probably very good at this. He then deemed me "trustworthy."

Significantly, when I asked Harry what the "best outcome" would be for him, he stated that Lucy would realize, during the meeting, that it was, in fact, the other person she initially identified who was her attacker. This would give him, he stated, some sense of "vindication" in the system. He stated, however, "She probably believes that I am" [the person that assaulted her].

Following the mediation, I interviewed each of the participants in the same order. During these interviews, of course, they signed the standard informed consent forms and releases, and I gave them my standard instruction before taping the interviews. At the end of the interview process, I also viewed the videotape of the meeting.

Victim: Lucy was interviewed at the same restaurant. She appeared to be calmer and to have matured during the year since I first saw her. Lucy told me, in more detail, the events of the crime, and the impact it had on her life. She went into detail about the plague of nightmares she had had over the years. She discussed her family and the support she felt she had received from her husband over the years, a man she described as a quietly supportive individual, who could tolerate the story of her victimization.

Lucy went into some detail, describing how the identification was made of Harry originally, and why she is so confident that he was her attacker.

Lucy: Well, what happened is they took the picture of the man that I identified in [the center] and they showed it to the other girls and they said, "It looks a lot like him, but I don't think it's him." And so, they told me this, that they don't think it's him. And they brought me to [City] from [the center] then and we went through books of mug shots, and then I picked him out of the book. Yup, I picked him out in the book. And then they brought it to the others, and we all agreed, "That is him." I mean, I didn't even know the guy's name—I'd never heard of him—nobody else knew, and then I picked him out in a lineup too. I had no idea what this guy was like. I had no idea.

... There was no problem picking him out in a book or in person. He was a real scary man. I mean, this man had threatened to kill me. He was like a monster to me. And the fear I have in the back of mind is like being a little girl all over again and you're afraid of the boogey man getting you when you were little. That's what he was. He was my real live boogey man. He really was.

Lucy discussed, in the interview, the importance of her relationship with the police officers that were investigating her case, along with the impact on her of the crime, its investigation, and her evolving knowledge of the meaning to her of the events.

Lucy: ... I really didn't realize what I was doing. I was telling them what happened and helping in any way I could for them to find out the truth. I didn't fully understand the magnitude of it. It was almost like being in shock, having to tell my story to these people, which were really, really nice people. A nice group of detectives, real caring and sincere. But I had to tell them every little detail, so it was hard and it was hard to look them in the eye. Really hard to do that. Especially after I'd heard about the ones after me. I felt a lot of guilt and responsibility for them, and then there's what's called survivor guilt. I really didn't learn much about that for years later either.

In relation to the evolution of her relationship with these officers, Lucy stated:

Lucy: ... sometime after court, in 1975, when I was still in [the center], he [the police officer that became her foster father] came to visit me and asked me if I would like to move to his home when I got out of [the center]. He went and got his sponsor license and took me in, which, you know, they were all just really good.

And then living with [her foster father], I got to see all the detectives, all the time, whenever I wanted. Picnics, visits, camping trips, and stuff like that. We were all a close bunch of people.

[I commented that it sounded like she had quite an effect on this group of policemen.]

Lucy: Well, I guess I did. They all loved me, I know that. And I loved them, as much as I was allowed to love somebody. I couldn't look at them, and I couldn't trust them, really. And I always felt bad about that, because they were really good people. I just couldn't trust them, because they were men. But, really a good bunch of people. I was going to get married in 1981 and [foster father] was going to give me away at my wedding.

In discussing the evolution of her desire to meet with Harry, Lucy stated:

Lucy: But, yeah, I always wanted to for years because I wanted to see him, for one, where he didn't have any power, like behind bars, in shackles, and stuff. "Tell ya, I'm glad they got ya," and you know, I wanted to attack him more verbally, and at some times, too, I wanted to physically attack him, too, which is normal. But yeah, I always wanted to see him again.

… Oh, there was no question about it. It was just having the opportunity to do it. It was no second thoughts or anything. It was like I was so excited when I heard about [Mediator], and the opportunity—it was like, "Oh, I can't believe this!" That it's possible, I can really go do this. And ask him these questions. So, it was really something I looked forward to doing and it was really a relief to know I was going to go.

… And it was really nice because it's almost like a fantasy in the back of your mind: if I could only just tell him this or tell him that. And it was like a fantasy coming true, for me. It was—it was nice.

In relation to the preparation, and her feelings just before the meeting, Lucy stated:

Lucy: I was really nervous. I was kind of like, "I can't believe this is actually happening today. It's been a long, long time. I've wanted to do this for years, and now today is the day." I had a hard time sleeping the night before. We drove down, and I could just feel the pressure building, it was like I had a lump in my throat, breaking out in a sweat, just really nervous. But then I also got to the point where I was–knowing what I was going to go do, a lot of the old feelings came up of shame and guilt, and my husband and I, we sat in that little café before we went there, and I had a hard time looking out, I wanted to just look down and kind of hide my head. But I told myself that when I got in there with him, I was going to look him in the eye and try to give that back to him. And I was able to do that.

… but I walked around kind of in a daze for a few days before, thinking, "Something's going to happen." [Mediator] called that night before, or that morning, and I thought, "Oh, they're calling to tell me he died" that Harry died. And I thought, "That is just going to be so bad," this would be a missed opportunity for me. And so, I was real worried. I thought, "What if I get in a car accident on the way down?" I was real nervous.

… No, but like I said, I was really nervous, I kept breaking out in a sweat, and I couldn't believe I was there. After all this time, I was actually there. They kept apologizing about the delays and I'm thinking to myself, "That's really OK, I'm here, just as long as he don't die now. It's going to happen." And I was real excited and scared. And there was a room right past the check in—you have to check in there and they stamp your hand and there was the warden's meeting room or something right on the other side, so that's where we met. And they set it up and explained to us how the cameras would work and all that, and I told them I definitely wanted to sit with my back against the wall, not the door, because I have a lot of flashbacks and I could just kind of feel the hammer over my head. So, I didn't want him to be able to come up behind me. So, I made sure of that. That was really important to me. And sitting there, and [Mediator] says, "OK, I'll go get Harry." And that's when my heart really, really started going. I was really afraid I wouldn't be able to talk, even. I was really afraid I wouldn't be able to talk.

In relation to her initial experience of seeing Harry and her impressions, Lucy continued:

Lucy: … there was [Mediator] at the end of the table, I was to his right and Harry was to his left, and there was probably, I dunno, maybe four feet between us. He came in and it was like, I was so scared when he walked in the room. And then I seen him—he's still a big guy, but he's an old man now, he's in his seventies now. And I think he put on a lot of weight. And he looked old. He looked kind of shaky. And one of the first things I told him was that if I didn't know who he was, I would think he was just somebody's grandpa. And it wasn't really—at first—well, it was still scary seeing him, knowing the person that he is. But the way that he looked at that time, he didn't look as powerful as he did before. And as he had all these years in my mind. So, I was relieved about that.

… Then when I started talking to him and listening to him, I knew that he was just as dangerous as ever.

… And that's when I started talking, telling him why I was there. Like I said, I was so nervous (I didn't know if I could even talk), that I didn't even begin to describe what I've been through. A little bit, but it wasn't nowhere near what I go through.

... It felt good, but like I said, I was really nervous. I knew I wasn't telling everything that I wanted to say.

... He just sat there, quietly listening.

... Yeah. He just sat there and listened, and I would look him in the eye until I could feel myself wanting to fall apart, and when you see the video, you'll see that I start to look down, start fidgeting, and looking down. But I had to force myself just to look at him, I just wanted to look him in the eye and say these things to him. And I thought that it was really important for me to do that, because I couldn't at any other time. And I told him how, when we were in court, I was so afraid, that he was such a powerful person. Well, he turned around and told me that I was the one that had the power then. And it was like, well, I sure didn't feel like it, you know? Because he was still scary.

I reminded Lucy of our meeting a year ago, and said that I had been particularly impressed with her plan of how to approach Harry in order not to get into a power struggle with him. I asked her how that plan had gone.

Lucy: OK. First of all, I started out telling him that I wasn't going to get in an argument with him—I don't know if this was my exact words—but that we weren't going to get into whether or not it was him. I said, "You and I know the truth and we're going to leave it at that." And I tried to be firm on it, too, and he said that was fine. And so, I asked a lot of questions and hearing his answers, like I said, he wasn't really—I mean, he admitted to them, but they were for different reasons, or it was the wrong guy—with these other ones too. Or it was accidents. Or they brought it on, or something. So, I was a little thrown off by that, and it turned out that a lot of the questions I had, he couldn't even answer, because he wasn't really admitting to nothing. And so, I was a little disappointed on that.

But there was one question that really bothered me and that was why he had said that he wished I was his daughter. And I had to ask him in a way that it wouldn't give him time enough to think quick enough, but when he had said it—when we were in court, I had heard later that he did say he felt sorry for me, that even though he did the exact same thing to all these others, he didn't do this to me, and he felt sorry for me, that it should have never happened to me. So, I said to him, "When we were in court, you said you felt sorry for me, but why did you say you wished I was your daughter?" And he never said that in court. He never said he wished I was his daughter—in court. The only time he said it was the night that it happened. So, I blurted it out like that and he answered it.

And I would have loved to have just stood up and said, "Gotcha!" But I knew I couldn't do that, that I have no respect for him, but I had to have respect for the process of everything. And so, I was really glad to hear him answer that.

In a significant exchange between Lucy and Harry, she expressed to him her feeling that she was representing his dead victims.

Lucy: That I wasn't there just for me. That I was there for all of them. And I told him, "When you talk to me, don't just see me. You think of all of them." And I felt really strongly about that. And I told him, "It's not just *your* victims either ." Because each time there's a new case, I go through—I relive this all over again. And I wanted him to understand that. That was really important to me.

At this point, Harry attempted the same gambit he did with me. He attempted to tell Lucy the details of other murders. Lucy instinctively identified this maneuver and stopped him, in perhaps the most important moment for her of the meeting.

Lucy: He was going to tell me how he killed her. He was willing to say how. But I told him, "No, I don't need to hear that," because he was starting to almost get excited. And I thought, "I'm not going to let you sit here and talk to me and get excited about it." So, I told him, "No, I don't even want to hear about it, I don't need to know about that. All I know is she's dead." And he started, "Well, she was a prostitute …" and putting her down and stuff, and I thought, no, you're not going to do that. So, I stopped that there. Because that's the only time I saw him really react like he was getting excited.

… Harry started to answer, and at one point in the video, I put my hand up and I said, "No, that's enough." To anybody else, it's nothing. So what? You put your hand up? But my putting my hand up gave me power and it gave me the right to protect myself, and it was a big thing for me. Something so little, it was a big thing for me. And I didn't even realize that until after I watched the draft of the video. But it was really a big thing. I stopped him. I defended myself, and so that was good, you know.

In relation to her expectations and her follow-up feelings after the meeting, Lucy stated:

Lucy: Right, I still seen him like if I have a flashback or a nightmare, it's still him twenty years ago. So that was another important thing for me at this time, was to see to him—well it was always important to see him not in control. Where he couldn't hurt me or anything. But now I just got to see him as an old man. But even though he's an old man, he's still a pretty powerful man. But I thought to myself, I can take care of myself with you. That's what I thought. I thought, "You're in your seventies; granted I'm forty now" but I think I could get away a little faster than you now. So that was important for me too. To see him old like he is today, that would help with the flashbacks and the nightmares.

… Then that night [of the mediation], I had a nightmare. The very first night, I had a nightmare, but it was Harry as he was today. And when I woke up from my nightmare, I was able to pull myself out of it right away. But then within a few days to a week, I think—I might be wrong about the time frame right now, but soon after I had another normal nightmare where it left me depressed and for about three or four weeks after this I was depressed. To the point where I couldn't tell if I was physically sick, or if it was just from the depression … I've only had one other one since then, but that's pretty good. So, I mean, they've gotten less. I'm having less nightmares.

I asked Lucy how disappointed she was that Harry did not admit responsibility, and what that meant to her in terms of her expectations. Her response to this answer is significant as to the meaning for her:

Lucy: Well, I think it would have been good if he would have admitted to it. Part of changing, I believe—part of the process of changing, of course, is admitting to it and taking responsibility for it. And another thing is that, throughout my life, I had to take responsibility for me, my actions, things I've done. I've had to take the responsibility of it all, even though there's times that I feel like I've had to take responsibility for things that weren't really my fault, but I've still had to take it and pay for it. And it's like, for once, I'd like somebody else to do it for me, and I think the person who should have to do it more than anybody is him.

… I think if this could have been done twenty-five years [ago], it would have had more of an outcome, I mean, a better outcome even. Because I've had all these years—I mean, he's not just a part of one night or one or two years. I mean, he's been in my life for twenty-seven years now. And like my therapist says, I have to end this relationship with him. He's a household name around my house. I mean, I don't know if I'll ever get over him, but I hope I do. But it's been a long time. And, I think if somebody had the chance to do it sooner than I did, I think it would be better. They could maybe get that power back a lot sooner. And that's a lot of what I lost, the power to protect myself and be safe. And I think if it was done a lot sooner, they'd be able to get that power back.

Offender: I met again with Harry, following the mediation at the prison, where we had met the previous year. The interview was arranged through the normal channels at the prison. Since I desired a private interview with Harry, and could not be accompanied by a staff person, the rules required that I meet with him in the attorney's interview area, which was semi-private, an open space with six tables a few feet apart. When we met, there were only one or two other meetings taking place. The room is by the main-entrance gate of the institution, so everyone who comes and goes travels by this area; thus, the tape picks up the commotion of prison life, with conversations and doors banging open and closed.

Harry made mention that we weren't meeting again in his psychologist's office, and made an initial assumption that it was because he and the psychologist had had an argument, and are currently on the outs. I told Harry that this was not the case, but that I arranged the interview through another office, and was told that I could not see Harry privately without a staff member present. Harry accepted this explanation, and did not seem concerned about the space, but his voice was low enough that the transcriptionist had a hard time transcribing this interview, given Harry's low tone, accompanied by the cacophony of prison existence.

At the beginning of the interview, Harry made another bid for control, reading the informed consent form, but then setting it aside without signing it, saying that he would sign it at the end, "depending on how things go." The implication, of course, was that if I offended Harry in some way he would refuse to sign the consent, rendering his interview unusable. I noted this, internally, with fascination.

Harry hadn't changed over the year, physically or in affect, in the same way as my perception of Lucy. He was wearing his prison blues, and was, seemingly, relaxed and in charge. My own comfort level had increased, given that I had the advantage of a previous meeting with him, and knew more about what to expect.

Harry began by immediately telling me the story of the mediation. Interestingly, he started his narrative with a description, much like Lucy's, of where he felt she "tripped up" in her story, thus proving to him his innocence.

Harry: I went in without many expectations, and I think I went into it kind of—I had promised [Mediator] that I would not insist that things go my way, that I'd kind of let it be, kind of roll. And I did that. Actually, she gave the whole thing away, and I should have jumped on it but I had promised him I wouldn't. But she said, "the police showed me the pictures of the other people," and that's when she—see before that, the person she knew and that she was familiar with, and after they talked with her, she changes her mind. Well, it would have been different if it would have been a stranger, but it was somebody she knew.

... Yeah. And what her problem is, I don't know. Because I've been miserable at times. I've been [inaudible]. And I got a lot of pressure on me here because I won't admit this one.

The importance to both parties of the other changing their minds and owning up to their individual definitions of the history became a central theme of the rendition of the actual mediation they both told me. Within a few minutes of the start of the interview, Harry set out for me, in a few words, the multiple themes that dominated his experience.

Harry: I was kind of disappointed that she didn't change her mind but [and] I didn't feel that she was helped more. I thought maybe she'd leave feeling better. And I have a hunch she did, a little bit.

Harry outlined for me the events of the arrest and trial, where he said that he first developed his impression of Lucy. He also clearly stated his construction of the reasons for her story.

Harry: I felt sorry for her. By that time, I think she was convinced that she was doing what was right and she was probably convinced I was the right person, but if she wasn't, she was convinced that she was doing the right thing for the other girls. That's what I think—I think they convinced her, "lookie here, look at what he did to this person, we've got to get him off the street." And here she is, young and impressionable. And, in time she believes it.

The theme of Harry's feeling sorry for Lucy was again established, and it also remained a constant theme throughout the interviews. I ask Harry if he doesn't, given his belief, feel any animosity toward Lucy.

Harry: Oh, yeah, I felt sorry for her, absolutely. [*Interviewer*: Any animosity?] No. I wasn't happy. No, I wasn't angry at her, I was angry at the police. They're the ones that did it. Actually, I wasn't angry with them because I understood it. I was angry with the act—I was chagrined with it—I felt I had been wronged, whatever. That's the way I figured it. Well, whatever. This is life and this is the way my life has gone, so it's going to keep on going that way.

Lucy's therapist accompanied her in the mediation, and sat next to her. Typical of Harry's style, he developed an immediate and highly negative impression of the therapist, creating an elaborate narrative as to her thoughts and motivations. [The therapist said nothing to Harry, nor did she speak during the meeting.] Harry reports to me, "She's a real bitch." I challenged him and said, "How did you develop that theory of her?" Harry described his feeling that when he walked in, the therapist "was staring at me like I was evil, personified. I haven't seen Lucy for ages. I thought she was Lucy."

In his thinking about the situation, Harry had concluded that the conviction for Lucy's assault had only added "one day" on to his already long sentence. He was quick to point this out to me, and found a way to work this belief into the meeting with Lucy. This seemed to be his form of retaliation, although it seemed lost on Lucy when I interview her.

Harry continued in the interview to waver between this thinly disguised sadism, and his belief that he wanted to be helpful to Lucy.

Harry: … as I thought about it, after talking with me she remembers, you're really not the person, that would have been grand for me, would help my inner peace. But other than that, it wouldn't have done anything for me except helping her out. You know, I still like her, I really do. She started really bad in the meeting, and we stayed a long time … but I promised [Mediator] that I wouldn't get tough with her and I wouldn't be forceful with her, and I wouldn't make demands upon her and tell her, "Hey, you're wrong." I kept my part of the bargain. After all, it wasn't for me, it was for her.

In terms of the impression Harry formed of Lucy during the meeting, his assessment was interesting.

Harry: … Now Lucy was very clean and she was nice and she was tidy, and she had her hair done. She's got it done in an old woman's style of hair, and she shouldn't because she's younger and she's a little heavy, but she could be very beautiful if she wanted to be. And I sat there and kind of felt sorry for her again.

Throughout the course of the interview, Harry returned frequently to his obsession with Lucy's therapist. Each time, he projected the feeling onto her that he is "such an evil person." And, as Harry recounted the sense that Lucy also felt that he is evil, I asked how it felt for him to sense that feeling from these people. His answer again shows Harry wavering between his anger and his positive motivation.

Harry: Sure. But hey, it wasn't so hurtful that I was going to cry or anything, or jump up and be angry with her or something like that. It's just something inside of you just kind of pinches you up here, you know. And I tell you what [inaudible phrase] I changed my mind. I'm saying, "why am I feeling sorry for this person, when she feels this way?" And I just tell myself, well, she's deserving. And she was in bad shape … [in discussing what she might have gotten out of the original story]. And she's important. People are talking to her and looking up to her and treating her like an adult and they're telling her that what she's doing is so important. And that's a time of her life that she remembers. Probably the only time in her life that she's had anything like that. And I don't think she wants to let go of it. Can't say that I blame her. You know, everybody's got to have something.

This statement showed an incredible intuitive sensitivity on Harry's part, since Lucy intimates in her interview that this was an important time for her, and, in fact, given the relationship that she developed with the police because of this case, it was life changing. While Harry's interpretation was somewhat more characteristic of his personality, Lucy had never shared this feeling with him.

Harry felt that things got somewhat better as the interview progressed, but was frustrated that Lucy stopped it, feeling that more things could have been said.

Harry: … I thought she'd warmed up, not to me, but to the process … well, I was getting ready to get into it. I was getting ready. And I was going to tell her, "Look, I understand where you're comin' from. I understand your sorrow, I understand your pain, I understand what you're talking about." But then I would have had to say, "But you know, I didn't cause it." But then everything would have been undone. So, I was kind of searching for a way to get into it without having to go into it like that. But then she said, "well, that's all. That's all I have to say. We're done."

And regarding the outcome of the meeting, Harry was equivocal. He remained unhappy that he didn't get his needs met (by her recanting), and had a feeling that she herself was not as satisfied as she could have been (again intuitively correct on Harry's part).

Harry: Look, I don't want her to like me. I don't want her to do anything for me. The only thing I want her to do is have a little happiness in her life, and forget the past, which she's not going to do as long as she just has that one ultimate moment in her life when she was so important.

… I think she just needs to live. To let go of the past—all of her past not only this one night twenty-eight years ago, she has to let go of that and she has to become a person, she has to become her own person. Meet people, make friends, and forget about that. Make friends for the moment. Don't go back and say, "Well, I'm no good, you wouldn't want to be a friend with me." Because she is good.

Toward the end of the interview, Harry tried to seize another opportunity to tell the story of his crimes in a way Lucy describes as him "getting excited." Following Lucy's example, I stopped him and the result was interesting. I started by asking Harry how he had changed, and what he understands now about himself.

Harry: I guess you just change with age, you change with understanding. I'm learning things. The crimes that I committed weren't committed the way they were told in court … But they were committed. One was my girlfriend … I didn't mean to kill her but I did, I just couldn't let her run like that.

Interviewer: Yeah, you told me about that. [I stop him from telling the story and redirect him back to my original question.] What do you understand about that [How you got this way]?
Harry: It had to do with me. I was a person that was out of control. Anger would take me and I'd do anything. In another way, I was very sane and very composed and very sure of what I wanted.
Interviewer: How do you think you've changed?
Harry: I wouldn't say that I've changed. I'd say that the way I look at things, and I've mellowed. I don't go into rage—I know that's all gone ...

No, see, I was angry. I had very little in my life. And every time I'd get something, it seemed like it would be taken from me. Rather than to get so I could build on this thing, I'd have had nothing, when I got this, some son of a bitch took it, you know. After a while it becomes a pretty big thing. But now I look back and say, it was nothing. I had nothing before I got that, and I got along, what did I need it for? What bothered me the most—I had a job driving trucks when I was only sixteen years old, and this guy that I used to work for, he didn't like me. So, he was driving ahead of me, and slammed on his brakes, and he pretended like telling me to back off, and I went around him. I drove around him. And he speeded up and tried to pass me on the right side. Lucky, I was watching, so I slowed down and I let him go. He went and reported me and got my job taken away. And I don't know—that irritated me for years and years and years.

Compared to the pre-mediation interviews, both parties became more invested and hence more disappointed that the other did not shift their mutual story to coincide with their own meaning. While both were aware of this awkward problem, during the preparation for the meeting, despite both claiming to have it in check, it is interesting how they both left the meeting disappointed that the other did not satisfy their wish.

At the same time, in watching the video of the actual meeting, this power struggle is not a primary focus. Harry stated that the actual denial of his involvement comes in a more assertive fashion than either expected, but Lucy was effective in not letting this assertion become a focus or a power struggle between the two of them.

In watching the video, I made notes to myself of phrases and observations, and any interchanges that were interesting or striking to me:

Lucy: You really don't look like a monster.

You've been a part of my life for twenty-seven years.

Part of my family for twenty-seven years.

Harry: I've been involved in terrible things.

[I'm here] to help you in any way I could. I owe it to my victims. I owe it to everyone around me, I owe it to society. And if I can do anything to help you, to help you be happy, then I wouldn't have lost anything.

In watching the video of the mediation, I am struck by how communicative Lucy is with Harry about her feelings, even in the beginning of the meeting. She does not come across as restrained as she reported to me that she was.

Lucy: Our lives started out the same. Our paths have crossed. We know some of the same people. [Lucy had met and spoken to Harry's brother, and later a nephew.]

Why did you feel sorry for me?

Harry: Yeah, he's [his brother] a good person, a feeling person.

It shouldn't have happened to you.

Lucy: Even though it happened to you and your other victims? [It appears at this point that Lucy is "interviewing" Harry. She later reports this to have been her attempt to "trip him up" in his story, although it does seem to approximate her stated position when I first met her of not trying to push him into a corner.]

Harry: I always looked at everybody from my perspective … [in the prison therapy group] for the first time I'm really looking at the other people's side of things … I understand that it's what they feel and think, not what I feel or think.

[Lucy's effort to catch out Harry in his story is not as clearly represented in the actual meeting. When she makes her "daughter" statement to him he responds.] It was a long, long time ago.

It was clear at one point in the meeting that Harry made an effort to attack Lucy, as he mentioned the feeling that the thirty years he was sentenced for Lucy's attack was "meaningless." As he mentioned to me, he was under the impression that this will only add "one day" to his already lengthy overall sentence. Lucy's response to this was effective.

Lucy: Well, I'm serving every day of the twenty-seven years with no parole board.

Harry shared with Lucy some of his own history of being in orphanages and being sexually abused: "I think I have a little understanding of what you've been through."

As the meeting progressed, Lucy became frustrated with his denial.

Lucy: The questions I've always wanted to ask you make no sense to ask ….

Harry: Sitting across the table from you like this is like sitting across the world from you ….

Lucy: I'm done.

With this, the mediator tried to return Harry to a previous discussion looking for more on his feelings (remorse?) for the murders he had admitted to. It is at this point that Harry began to get into his stories (get "excited") and

Lucy put up her hand and said, "No, I'm done." Harry was genuinely surprised that the meeting was over, and seemed a little bewildered: "I wish it had gone better."

The videotape captured a debriefing that the mediator had with both parties immediately following the meeting. Lucy stated to the mediator, "I feel relieved. He's not as scary. He's an old man now. It doesn't bother me that he won't admit it to me."

In Harry's debriefing with the mediator, he reiterated the same sentiments he had to the mediator throughout the process:

Harry: I did enough in my life that I had a hard time living with myself too. It's from the other side of the fence, I'll grant you, but the feelings are very much the same. Feelings of unworthiness, self-loathing.

… I had a lot of empathy sitting across the table from her. I regret it didn't help her more.

Mediator: In my interview with the mediator, following the meeting, he was confident that it had been a useful experience for Lucy, although it was an unusual circumstance.

Mediator: The Harry/Lucy process is really quite phenomenal. It's absolutely pushing the boundary … Harry and Lucy, I don't know that there's ever been a case in which a victim desperately wanted to meet who she believed was the perpetrator of sexual assault and just terror in her life, and where she knew that person didn't believe it was him, he totally denied it. And it's particularly; it was so old it was after twenty-six or twenty-seven years. So, the circumstances of that case are really unusual, and that's why it took longer. We built in safety nets, to make sure that her therapist was totally supportive of it, and that the psychologist working with Harry was supportive of it, they were both present. Third, we actually had three therapists and an additional fourth PhD. We've never had so much support in that sense of the parties in one mediation. And frankly, after that mediation, which was fairly brief given these kinds of things, forty-five or fifty minutes, we saw some real value to Lucy, even though it didn't go like I thought, or the way these typically go. And I wasn't absolutely sure, and when I debriefed her, and I was real concerned, like "Oh, my God, have I violated one of my most important principles of do no harm" as much as you can. In the debriefing it was pretty clear, and validated by her therapist, that this was still of tremendous value. I can still remember her saying, "I wish I had done this fifteen years ago, how could I have let that blankity blank take that kind of power from me over all those years?"

So, in that case, there was major learning in that that could push this field in some new directions. Think of, cause we, I have always thought in my zeal to protect the victims that it would do no good to have an offender that doesn't own up to it meet with a victim who totally believes it's the person. Now the reason I did that, … if I err, I err in the direction of respecting the strength and wishes of crime victims. Sometimes that can backfire. But overwhelmingly it doesn't. And Lucy absolutely wanted to do this. We did enough checking with other people, and her preparation it was really ratcheting down her expectations. Making it clear that Harry didn't admit to it.

I asked the mediator about both parties going into a meeting with such clearly opposing expectations, both hoping the other would relent.

Mediator: In a way, this case validates exactly what I was saying before about respecting the strength and capacity of people to do what they need to do, particularly from the victim perspective. Because this, just the allowance of this case to get that far, into a dialogue, went totally against what we have always believed that people have to admit their guilty. The nature of what occurred could have been extremely frustrating. I mean, she was getting fairly agitated, she didn't believe what he was saying. She clearly made decisions not to self-disclose that much of her own pain. I mean, why should I waste kind of stuff of mine with this character. So, this, more than any case I have probably ever done, had the greatest potential for some level or levels of revictimization. And yet, by her own statements, it didn't happen. In fact, she may well have been more revictimized if I had intervened and tried to protect her and not allowed her to get what she needed.

DISCUSSION

The meeting with Harry clearly seems to have done for Lucy what she desired based on her statements to me of attempting to resolve her experience and move on. She appears to me to have changed physically and affectively since our first meeting. Most important, she reports a change in her inner psychic experience as it relates to the nightmares that she had experienced since the original trauma. She also recounts a reduction in her general depression and fearfulness.

While interesting, the issues related to whether Harry was the perpetrator or not ultimately seem less important to the overall outcome. This finding may confirm the mediator's suggestion that this experience is not unlike a surrogate experience.

While Lucy and Harry were clearly disappointed at not getting this part of their expectation fulfilled, the more important experience seems to be in Lucy meeting with the real Harry and finally seeing him face-to-face. In addition to simply seeing him and making him real is the incredible experience of putting up her hand, stopping Harry, and reclaiming her power. Strikingly, this is also experienced viscerally by Harry.

For Harry, there was an ongoing stated desire to be helpful, which was interpreted by both the mediator and me as a genuine expression. The origin of this motivation is impossible to specify. This meeting is the only opportunity Harry will ever have to express himself to a victim, so whether Lucy is a true victim for him, or a surrogate, is ultimately of little consequence.

In later thinking and writing about the experience in my first interview with Harry, where he told me the details of three of his murders, my assumption was that Harry's goal was twofold. One was to test me in terms of my credibility and stomach. The other was to assert power over me. Harry represents in personality and development one end of the continuum of psychopathy defined in my chapter on criminal development. He is clearly an unrepentant serial murderer. The establishment of power, in relationship, is significantly important to such personalities, and the effort made with me is about all that Harry has available, given his current circumstances.

It is also important for such individuals to test people and have them prove themselves. This need may no doubt be related to the fact that some individuals, while "attracted" to stories and personalities such as Harry's, have an incredibly difficult time containing their "countertransference" reactions in the face of such horrific tales. Thus, the experience represents a true test, by Harry's standards, while no doubt a somewhat sadistic attempt on his part to play with another victim.

Lucy's story is consistent with that of other victims with a notable addition. In Lucy's case, Harry is the perpetrator of the violence against her. While there are notable issues and concerns with the evolution of this meeting, most significantly Harry's denial of being the offender, Lucy clearly believes that he is; thus, the issue seems relatively unimportant in the overall preparation of this case. Whether one looks at it (as the mediator did) as a "surrogate" situation, or simply takes it at face value and proceeds, the meeting clearly had an important benefit for Lucy. The most obvious event was her gesture of putting her hand up and stopping Harry from "getting excited" at telling her the story of another of his murders. Lucy told me of the gesture and its importance to her in our interview, and the moment, when I viewed the videotape, was electric. Lucy took her power back.

Chapter 7

The Universe

I will present this data on a set of interviews that were conducted with offenders, and in some cases the mediators that worked with them. The cases presented represent a series of concurrent interviews that I conducted and represent a cross-section of cases. I will, for the sake of brevity, provide in some instances a more condensed version of the original crime, but will endeavor to provide enough material to give the reader context.

This set of interviews was done in a variety of cities at an assortment of different institutions.

All the interviews were requested to be "contact" interviews, meaning I would be able to have a direct discussion with the inmate, in private, rather than through a telephone or mesh screen.

Following these interviews, I viewed the videotapes of the mediation meetings between these offenders and their victims.

SPENCER

Spencer's interview took place in the open visiting room at a small table. He was wearing the requisite prison uniform and was a handsome man in his mid-twenties. He presented as open and interested in my project, and he was eager to tell his story.

Spencer, before this crime, had developed a reputation in his neighborhood as being somewhat of a leader. He had several adolescent and young adult admirers who looked up to him. While he did not consider himself to be a "gang leader," his neighborhood was his territory, and those that followed him were devoted to him. He had many felony crimes pending trial, and was most involved in drug dealing and other petty offenses.

When a group from another neighborhood came over to his, and especially because a young woman who was supposed to be going with one of Spencer's "boys" was in the back seat of this car "kissing up" on another guy, Spencer was offended. The young woman had asked the driver to stop to talk with Spencer, but insults were exchanged, and then threats, and finally, a gun was produced from within the car. Spencer's friends went to his house to get a gun, and the car drove off.

Beyond the biggest outrage—being "dissed" in one's own neighborhood—Spencer was also angry and hurt since the young woman involved, Suzi, had always been a favorite of his. He felt as if she were his own little sister.

It was known that Suzi was having a party that night, and it was decided that the group would go to the party to seek revenge.

That night, Spencer took a shotgun away from one of the younger guys, and, while the others went to look for the offenders, Spencer stayed in an alley out of sight. There was a commotion, and Spencer heard that the police had been called; as he began to walk back to the car that was parked up the street, he saw that his brother was in an argument with someone, and so Spencer approached. The person his brother was arguing with was an older man, and Spencer, who still had the gun at his side, told him to leave his brother alone and go home. The man, instead, approached Spencer, who said that he brought the gun out from his side; he says that he only intended to hit the man with the butt of the gun. As the man approached Spencer, he could hear the sirens coming fast, and, suddenly, the man was too close for Spencer to swing the gun and hit him. He lunged at Spencer, who then shot him.

The bullet traveled into his chest, through his lungs, and severed a major artery; he bled to death. The man that Spencer killed was Suzi's father.

Characteristically, Spencer's first concern was to protect his protégés, and he set about getting them out of town with some money. Spencer attempted to contact his lawyer, and the police came for him the next day. As he was leaving his house by the back door, a large contingent of police was coming up the back walk. Spencer reached for the shotgun, which he usually kept by the back door, but given that it had been used in the crime, Spencer had hidden it in the attic of the house. Had the gun been there, Spencer is convinced he would have been tempted to "shoot it out" with the police.

In discussing the initial reaction that he had to the crime, Spencer in the interview states:

> I can honestly say that I just didn't have any remorse. It didn't bother me at all. I sat down and ate and ate, and watched movies. It didn't affect me at all. I can say the only thing that affected me that night was when my mom called. Somebody had told her something happened or another, and she was asking about what happened to [the brother], and what did he do, and you know, that was about the

only thing that affected me was her phone call. Other than that, I did not have a conscience about this at all. Period.

Spencer was charged with first-degree murder, and, after a weeklong trial, the jury found him guilty and sentenced him to life in prison and a $10,000 fine.

Spencer reports that the trial itself was not hard for him, but when he saw his parents and his girlfriend (who was at the time pregnant with his child) in the courtroom, it was hard. He says, "The second I turned around and seen them sitting there, it just killed me … and just going back and seeing them every day, it hurt. Because I knew that I had did that to them."

Beyond this, Spencer stated that his attitude remained poor through his first months in prison. He kept to himself and was cynical. It was about this time that a variety of things began to happen for him. In a discussion with a group of inmates, he heard about the possibility of meeting with his victim's family members and talking about the crime. He thought that it would be "cool" to be able to meet with Suzi and her mother. He was told, however, that he could not initiate the meeting and that the initiation of mediation had to come from the victim.

Spencer: Well, up until February of 1997, I was a hardhead. I come down here and I didn't want to work for these people. I didn't want to do right. I felt that everybody was out to get me. I thought the system was out to get me. I thought they messed me over. We were out here in the fields one day, and there were some Christian guys standing next to me. And they were just talking about God and whatever, and then the dude standing directly next to me, he turned around and told me—he started asking about "can you get me some dope connections when I get out?" And it made me very mad, because you're gonna sit here and tell me about God over here, and then you're going to turn around and ask me for some dope connections. And I told him, I said, "Look. You don't play with God. You're either over there with God or you're over here. Don't go in between." I've always been a God-fearing man. I just wasn't a Bible thumper or nothing like that. And the guy that was standing on the other side of him caught on to this. We came here from the fields, we're standing here waiting to take showers, and he pulled me to the side. And he said, "Look… ." No, he told me about something about peace in your heart and joy in your life and all that stuff. I kind of blew it off. When we came in, he pulled me to the side, and he said, "Look. You can have that peace in your life." And anyways, I gave my life over to Christ.

So, there was a drastic—I quit cussing, I quit drinking, smoking, all that. I just gave it up, just like that. And that was where in my life, my drastic turnaround, where I found the peace—I found a conscience, I found out what I really wanted in life, what was true … I'm still not a Bible thumper, but I found meaning in my life, thanks to that.

We discussed, at some length, his changes, and the fact that this all seemed to happen to him based on a flood of insights. I wondered about this, and whether he had any hesitations regarding the meeting with the victim's wife. (During this period, he was approached by the victim's services office to see if he would be willing to meet with the victim's wife, who had initiated a call to them, an event he felt to be highly serendipitous.)

Spencer: It was kind of weird because I was like kind of rude to the guy who sat down and talked with me. He's one of my best friends to this day. And he helped me change my life around. I've still got a lot of character flaws and what have you, but I'm not the violent thug, for lack of a better word, that I used to be. I've found purpose in life. Things look good in life. Life is what you make out of it, not what other people make you think it is. So, this is a drastic turnaround. *[Interviewer:* Any hesitations about the meeting?] No. I think the only question that came to mind when I was talking to them and it didn't last very long, but the question was: whenever they came, they told me this could be used in a court of law. We're not sure—and for a minute I hesitated. But it doesn't matter. It doesn't matter anymore; it's over with. This is something to me that's greater than going back to court and fighting about this, that, and the other thing. This means more to me than giving back this life sentence. Because I feel that I owe very much an explanation, some words, something, to [the wife] and to Suzi. And so, the thought was just for a moment. But that was really the only question.

Spencer was the first in a series of interviews who highlighted the preparation process that this service engages in. I was struck (and will discuss this at a later point) by how, in the pilot studies that I conducted prior to this final research, I had heard very little about the preparation, but in this series of interviews, everyone I interviewed made mention of its importance. This preparation packet is no small effort. It demands a great deal of work and introspection from both the offender and the victim.

Spencer: I feel I was greatly prepared. Not necessarily because of the paperwork or what have you. A lot of that stuff was great. The impact essay was really good. Some of the essays they had in there was really good. But [Mediator] was the main; he's very good with people. He's an excellent mediator. A lot of the little questions and skits he put on were very emotional, very good. He gave me one of those psychological profile deals, a hundred questions right off the top of his head, without reading anything. He's very good.

Spencer's mediator used a fair amount of "psycho-drama" techniques in his preparation of Spencer. This included some dialogue with the victim (in an empty chair), which was quite emotional for Spencer. Because of this, he felt both profoundly impacted by the preparation, and, also, more nervous as to what might happen in the meeting.

Spencer: … kind of a lot of anxiety. Let's get it over with. Let's get it over with. A lot of fear of the unexpected. In a situation like that, you never know what's going to happen. You know, I might say something harmless to me, but it might upset her. You know, she might get up and slap me or she might walk out, or she might not be able to handle it. Or I might not be able to handle it. I didn't think about that. It's kind of funny, because the night before, [Mediator] came up here and gave me a couple of hours last rundown. And he told me, "when you go in there, just remember to breathe. If you need some time, we'll take some time. There'll be ice water, coffee, whatever, there." I said, "Yeah, yeah, yeah. Cool." *And I walked in that mediation, I couldn't breathe, I couldn't think. I couldn't—it was like I just wanted to get up and walk out. That's kind of—I expected that of her, and not of me. I kind of blew [Mediator] off in what he said, but he was right. In a situation like that, you just don't remember, or your body just doesn't—you're so full of emotion.*

This statement brought up, for Spencer, the fact that he is now preparing for a meeting with Suzi, who opted not to attend the one he had with her mother. This fact becomes very emotional for him in the interview.

Spencer: Yes, I'm going through the process again. This time, I can say it's a lot harder than the first. I know what's going to happen, what's to be expected, but the thing that's so hard about this is that she was a very close friend. Talking with [the mother] was talking to a stranger. And there was no ill feelings there, no—we started fresh, from not knowing each other. With Suzi, it's going to be a different story, because she trusted me. I was her friend. I was like a big brother to her, and I broke that friendship and that trust. And then you stack on what exactly happened—I took her father's life. All that together just makes for a bad situation. I know it's going to be a lot harder. She's not going to be as forgiving or understanding as her mom, because there's a lot more emotions there, a lot more involved. So, it's going to be very difficult [becomes more and more tearful].

Regarding the actual meeting with Suzi's mother, Spencer describes his initial feelings and the progression of the meeting.

Spencer: … She started by saying, "I want you to get to know [Husband]." And she had a big photo album; she talked about him for a long time, showed me pictures. She had crime scene pictures. She had cards from well-wishers, newspaper articles, all kinds of stuff. After about two or three hours, we kind of had a bond. We bonded really well. And it's funny because [Mediator], he wanted to break for lunch. And I guess neither one of us were really hungry; there's so much emotion, so much—we were in the middle of something and we didn't want to stop. So, we kept on until about 1:30 or 2:00 before we broke for lunch. And by that time, there was such a beautiful bond there between us. The most touching thing that happened was she wanted me to go to lunch with them. It didn't work out that way, but it was the thought that in just a few short hours, she had gained my respect. She had respect for me; I had respect for her. It was great.

I asked about the influence of the photo album on him, as well as the other materials. This question was especially significant, because Spencer, in my asking him about his "internal image" of his victim, had developed one during the trial of the father being a scoundrel, both because he thought Suzi had told him that her father was abusive, and he had also heard that the father was involved in some minor illegal activity. All of this was used during the trial period as a way for him to blame his victim and avoid guilt for the act. As Spencer stated, this internal image was "the image that I felt I wanted him to be—one that would look good in court, one that I could blame him for me shooting him. And I held strong to that image."

Spencer: Well, the first thing she told me was that she forgave me, that she never hated me. It was kind of a relief of pressure there. And as she went on and explained [Husband] to me, my thoughts were battling back and forth between the image I had built about him and the image she was giving me. And I finally, somewhere along the line, I decided to let go of the image that I had had, listening to everybody else, and decided to build a new image of how she was describing him, through his pictures, and the type of guy he was. And it was very relaxing. It was difficult when I got to the crime scene pictures. But after that it was pretty relaxing. I felt that in her saying that she wanted me to get to know [Husband], I felt that in her eyes, through her eyes, I knew what she was talking about. Even though I never knew him, I feel I have a better picture of him, the one that she wants me to see, anyways. So, it was really a good accomplishment.

Regarding his feelings immediately after the meeting, Spencer states:

I was kind of on an emotional high. I felt so much pressure had been lifted off me. So relieved that it went well, everything worked out. Grateful. Very grateful to [wife] and to [Mediator]. That the whole thing went through from beginning to end. That it didn't stall out anywhere. Grateful that I gave it my all, my hundred percent, because I didn't have to do everything that was involved. But I chose to do it. All the paperwork. Everything from front to back, I did it all. A couple of weeks ago, [Mediator] told me that I was probably the only one that ever did it all, because it's a lot of paperwork. But I was grateful, because it really did prepare me. It helped me to know that I did my best, and to know that [Wife], she did this, because I know it took a lot of courage. I know it did, regardless. And I was just very happy.

… A lot of—I felt real relieved. After a while I got tired, because everybody asked questions. Everybody wanted to know; five million people—they all just—they asked the same questions, tell the same story. So, I wanted to leave it to myself, for myself to meditate on for a while. And it didn't happen quite like that. Because I can't just blow everybody off and tell them "I don't want to talk about it." I never quite got the time to meditate right after the experience, but I shared it with everybody, which was a good feeling. Give them some hope. Give me a chance to talk to people about it. Listen. Maybe see what thoughts come to my mind. So, it was all right.

I ask many of these offenders the question I often get regarding the opportunity of the offender to "manipulate" or "con" those involved for either some personal benefit or for some sadistic enjoyment. His answer is insightful based on one of the principle tenets of the restorative justice movement. This central tenet relates to offenders, under the current system, who somehow see the victim and the system as the problem, and, ultimately, can blame the victims and the system in a way that allows them to feel victimized themselves.

Spencer: I would say that there's nothing you can say or do to the victim or victim's family or what have you that would cause them to think anything otherwise than they'll always have that doubt that there's going to be some kind of manipulation, or they're not serious, or what have you. But really, that lays on the mediator to be able to read, to know who he's speaking with, and what he's doing. And [Mediator] is very good at that. I know a couple of the other mediators, but that really—they have to put their trust in the mediator to know the person whom he's talking to. With [Mediator], that was really easy. But there's really nothing that you can tell a victim say or show them that would get them past that. No, they just have to sit down and take their chances.

I understand there's a lot of people, I would say 95 percent of the penitentiary, is the "system's out to get me," or "I can't trust nobody," or "My victim did this to me." They're all like that. With me, it was different. I was like that at one point in time. But at the same time, I know [Wife] saw that—she figured that's what was going on. I can't blame her. I had a preconceived knowledge about the penitentiary before I came here too. Everybody sees them on TV and it's nothing like what it is.

With all that raw emotion, I don't think anybody can come into a situation like this, unless they're just so hardened they don't want to do this, that that raw emotion won't just take over. You can push it down for so long, but the longer you sit there with that person, it's just going to come out naturally. I mean, there's just too much there. But if you're in that situation and you just don't want to participate or what have you, then things might be different. But that's up to the mediator to decide when everybody's ready. If they're still manipulative—somewhat manipulative—or what have you, you know—even if you go in there and you still are, somewhat, it's going to change. It's going to come out. You can't stop it.

Regarding his sense of being like or different to Suzi's father, following the meeting Spencer states:

Spencer: I see a lot of common ground there. I come to find out that [Husband], he's kind of like me. Very fun loving, outgoing guy that got along with everybody and everything. Liked to live life to its fullest. And we're kind of a lot alike. And I think that's part of the bond that came between us, that helped us out a lot. We also share the fact that both of our lives were destroyed by my actions. We're both overcoming great things here. It was a lot—I let her know—and I'm not making excuses and I'm not playing this down or anything, but my life was—I destroyed my own life, too. So, don't think that I'm not suffering—and not just because of the penitentiary. The penitentiary means nothing to me; it's the life that I destroyed that kills me. This is just a place, not being here with my daughter, my son, my family, all that. I let her know that I'm suffering too. It wasn't free. It wasn't just something that I just got away with.

I ask Spencer, in reflecting on it, how he thinks he ended up in this situation. His answer is supportive of Lonnie Athens' theory of the making of a violent offender.

Spencer: Trying to be somebody. Trying to run things. I decided at some point in time that I just had to be better than everybody else. And in so doing that, I went down the wrong direction. You know, I could have been a CEO or I would have been—not a doubt in mind, I could have been something great very fast. At twenty years of age, I was managing a department in a [convenience] store, one of the best in town. I know I could have done something with my life. But I chose to go the wrong direction with it. And instead of being a CEO with a great family and a great life, I ended up being a gang leader, running drugs, and losing my entire family and my life … and it would put fear in people's heart to think I'm a big macho type of guy. I just went in the wrong direction …
That's exactly what it was about. It wasn't—I felt I had to be somebody.

Spencer discusses the aftermath for him, and the meaning he tries to impart to other inmates who ask him about the experience.

Spencer: And it's great. I like to be able to talk to them, and let them know—you know, at some point in time, you have to let go of the fear of the consequences. You've got to accept the consequences. You've got to accept the consequences for what you did. Right or wrong, you have to accept it. And that's a hard thing for people to do. It's always hard to admit failure or mistake.

I viewed the videotaped mediation between Spencer and the wife. It was as Spencer had described, and, eventually, when he could find his breath, Spencer became quite emotional. In fact, he was quite tearful throughout much of the rather long meeting.

Much of what was seen in the video corresponded with Spencer's description to me, as excerpts from the meeting show. "V" is the wife and "O" is Spencer. Where common names are used in the dialogue, I have substituted initials:

V: When I got around the car there were two men standing there and I asked them, "Where'd you go?" I was looking for Suzi, and, then, I found [Husband]. When I got down, and he had this smile on his face, the smile I fell in love with, and he had beautiful eyes, you know, the street light was shining just on his face, and I hadn't seen his wounds until, he had one little trickle of blood, and the neighbor guy grabbed me by the arm and he said, "he's gone," I remember getting up, and I got up and up and up and up. And I can't tell you about the planning, nothing, 15 months. Suzi went off to college. We bought a car we sold a house, we went on, like a snow ball, and I have no clue what happened in that time.

I did know that I couldn't take it anymore, I couldn't live without [Husband], and I wanted to kill myself.

My daughter would have to get up and feed me and put me to bed. She had ....

O: (Looking at photographs) I have never seen a picture of him before, I had never seen him, hadn't met him. The memory I have is, when I shot him, his eyes just went blank. He was just looking elsewhere, somewhere else. [V: He was gone already, he was gone before he hit the ground.] The memory I have of him … [crying, offered water by V] It hurts, because I took a man's life for no reason. I try to rationalize it, and try to, I had no reason in the world to do what I did, and I don't have a reason, I have no reason at all.

I didn't know the man, had never seen him before, and I ruined a lot of people's lives. It's something that, no matter how much time goes by, you can't there's nothing you can do, you can't, you can't even make it feel better; you can't make any good thoughts of it, nothing. [V: We have to get beyond that too, you know?] No matter how far forward you move, no matter what steps you take, it's always there.

You come back and take a shower and everything.

And a guy came up to me after the shower and said, "do you really want to find that peace, do you really want that peace?" and there was just something that touched me in the way he said that, and I said, "Yeah, I really do" so we knelt down next to one of the vents underneath the window, and he said just follow me in this prayer and I will get you that peace. And right then and there I gave my life to Christ. There was no greater feeling ever than that moment, and everything was lifted off of my shoulders. All the burdens of life.

I was crying right there in the day room in front of everybody, and I didn't even care. All them hardheads, and I didn't even care anymore, that stuff didn't matter to me anymore.

And from that moment, I gave up the life that I lived. I gave up cussin', no foul words came out of my mouth. I quit fighting, drugs, I gave up all that right there. And since that time, three years ago, I can't stand violence, I can't stand hard music, that kind of stuff. When they go to fighting, I go to my house and pray, because it makes me sick to my stomach. My friends have left me. I guess I can't call them friends. My family, everybody left my life. They said that I preach too much. I wasn't the Spencer they knew.

When I agreed to this meeting, I thought it would be great. I wanted to sit down and let you know what happened without the lawyers. I wanted just to tell you what happened, first hand. This mediation has opened my eyes to a lot of things that I couldn't see. I've said a lot of things in this that I haven't ever told nobody. I don't talk about this very often. When I gave my life to Christ, I threw away all the newspaper articles, all of that, because this wasn't something to hold on to or be glorified.

My whole thing in this, is that I instigated it by calling J and J. There was a few things I didn't know that I should have known, but that didn't matter. I wired the whole situation up. I was the one that didn't react to what took place. [V: But you were in shock too.] I just, I didn't have a conscience, I didn't care. I went home and sat down and ate so much food, that I was out of control. I sat there and watched, "Forrest Gump" had just come out, I just watched "Forrest Gump" all night. Right after it happened. I just didn't have any clue, I didn't care, it didn't matter to me what happened.

[Later in meeting]

V: You said that when you shot him you turned away because you thought you were going to get splattered? When I saw him, he just had a little trickle of blood.

O: When I got back to S's I took my shirt off and threw it away because I thought it probably had blood on it. I just thought it. And I went in the bathroom and got this lotion and washed my face and body and put this lotion on it, because I knew the cops were coming. And I looked at my pants and I had three spots, and a drop on my tennis shoes. So, I got a pair of M's pants and washed mine, but the blood wouldn't come out.

I guess you could say that it's a pain, it's like stabbing your insides, you can't breathe, it takes your breath away. It clouds your mind.

I didn't think I had any more tears to cry.

What we've been down here for a couple of hours. I look at these pictures, and what I've done for the last few years is every day I think, "what is Mrs. X doing today? What is Suzi doing? Are they paying the bills? How are the friends and the neighbors doing? Are they alright?" Every year when Suzi's birthday rolls around, how does she deal with that? When your wedding anniversary rolls around, how do you deal with that? I think about this stuff a lot.

I've never had any answers to these things, they're just thoughts, you know.

I didn't know you before, so I didn't know what to make. These pictures and this letter, I guess I can see a little of your life. I know I'm never going to see everything. It's not possible. But at least I want to know what I can do to help, what can I do to help.

The whole situation was, in my mind, because they came over to my neighborhood and disrespected me and my friends. And that is why I did what I did, by calling them and saying, "Come on over, we've got to take care of this."

My pride and my ignorance and my control, what I felt I had to do was have control over all situations, was what led up to this.

I hope that adds a little insight as to why all of this happened.

[Offender reads letter written by Suzi]

[Daughter discusses her mother saying to her, "they should have killed you instead." Mother blames daughter for death of father as these were her friends, etc.]

V: She [Daughter] wants to know that when you say you're sorry, are you sorry about taking a man's life, or are you sorry about getting caught?

[O answers questions to daughter posed by mother. O plans to do a meeting now with the daughter]

O: Five years ago I would have said getting caught. But I wouldn't be here today if I wasn't sorry for taking your father's life, or destroying your life, or your moms or everyone else's. Part of my being here, I had to admit to doing what I did, and that's not hard for me to do. I totally accept that. I'm truly sorry for everything that has taken place, not just with your father but with you, your mom, the rest of your family.

I know them words don't mean a whole lot. All's I can say is that I will do whatever to help everybody move forward from here. It would be real easy for me to have left here this morning when the going got rough, but I didn't. We sat here and worked through this. And I hope that my actions and the leaning of your head will show you my sincerity.

When I shot your dad, I didn't have a conscience. I didn't feel at all.

*O:*The state is getting their punishment. But I wanted to let you know a little about what happened in my life. As you know, me and M had a little girl, L. L will be five years old the twenty-second. M got married to another gentleman, and they had another daughter. A year and a half ago, M came to visit, since that time we've had no contact.

In August of '96 my mom came to visit me and that was the first time I ever got to hold her, and the last time. As of now M won't have anything to do with me, and won't allow L to see me. It's possible that L doesn't even know I exist.

I later interviewed the mediator that worked with Spencer and the mother, and this mediator is now preparing the daughter for the mediation with Spencer and has asked him to reflect on the experience.

The mediator, a leader in the field, was interviewed in his office after I had interviewed Spencer.

Mediator: … And so, all that—and then here the father comes out and says, "What's going on?" And then from there … And so, Spencer was able to take each one of those events and take responsibility. How each event led to something more drastic in the sense that it made it closer to him committing the offense. In other words, it became high risk, high risk, high risk, of the chance of him doing what he did. And so, he began to see that. And at the mediation, he talked about that. And it was funny because the victims, or the wife, of [Husband], even though she was trying to tell him that really the blame was on other kid, the boyfriend of the daughter, "really it was his fault."

And Spencer was trying really hard to convince her that, yeah, he was there and all that, but it really was me. … So, he was owning his part and she was trying to hand him—"Yeah, I hear what you're saying, but also this other kid … ." But anyway, it got to a point there, the mediation, that I said to her, "Listen to what he's saying." Because the other kids came and there was the ones who did the fight and all that, but it was through his word—he's the one that enticed them, he's the one that motivates them. And these kids, they saw him as a model, I guess you could say, he was their leader. So, they were just kind of following what he had wanted them to do.

And one of the interesting things about—Spencer also—and that's what I like about this process—plus also the mediator has to really be in tune and to use all those skills to know where they are in the process and to trust it. Because one of the things that Spencer—almost all the way to the end—had not yet expressed to me were some of those emotions. And so, he did the talk very well and was very sincere in my opinion. But it was all in his—coming from head and not from the emotional. But I knew it was there. And I knew that it was OK, and I knew that even if we were to meet, that it still would have been fine, because I knew that it was there. And I knew that he would be able to deal with it and be OK with it, if it came out.

… the way I knew was through his work. So that was when I would read what he had given me, you know, it was there … he was sincere … .

In his effort to access Spencer's emotions, the mediator used the technique of having him talk to the husband in an empty chair.

Mediator: … And so, Spencer began to share just an incredible story of what happened and how he, he began to talk to the empty chair. And tears were just rolling out of his eyes. It was like his defenses were coming down. And to me, I don't think they were so much defenses that he was holding onto so that he could—but defenses in the sense that he was able to now let go, and really begin to talk about it, in a different level.

I did not interview the victim in this case, but the mediator recounted to me some of the issues related to her preparation and, in his view, the meaning to her of the meeting.

Mediator: With [Wife], her deal at the beginning was that she kept saying, "I want to go in there and I want to forgive him. I want to forgive him. I've gone through so much pain in my life that I've come to realize that my husband, if he could talk to him, he would forgive him for what he did. So, I want to do this, because I know my husband would want me to do this." And so, I just kind of listened and didn't push her. But as we began the process and she began to talk more and more and more, in one of those, she finally said it, and I knew—and she said, "I'm doing this for me." And I said, "Yes, you are. You're doing this for you." And she said, "Because I know my husband would forgive him. But I have to forgive him, through my own, not so much because he wants to forgive him, but I have to forgive him." And I said, "Well, good." But it came from her.

The mediator reported to me that the wife had also been in psychotherapy at a local clinic. The story of this experience, from the view of the mediator, was that numerous therapists that she was assigned to were apparently reluctant to discuss, in much detail, her experience. The therapist was also reluctant to get involved or endorse the mediation process. The wife was taking Prozac, prior to the mediation, and stopped it immediately afterward.

Mediator: And so, she did that, and a month after the mediation, she called me and said, "I'm not seeing the counselors any more. I'm not taking the medication anymore." And I said, "Well, [Wife], you know what you're doing. I will be visiting with you ..." And I mean, I wish you could just see her, a year later—and that's the way she's been after the mediation, an incredibly changed person. Back to socializing, back with her friends, getting a job, very confident. This is a person who was so—what's the word?—engulfed, I guess, or spent all her time talking about what happened, and her loss, that she said, "I'm not throwing away my memories, like the photo album, or all those things I have from my husband. But I'm putting them in a trunk, and I'm putting them in the attic." And she did.

Regarding the preparation and meaning that mediators make of the experience, this mediator echoes the process that I heard from most of the others interviewed:

Mediator: ... but I think mine has been through my own experience, I guess, and that is my own meditation, my own belief, my own faith, and so I do my prayers and I do my meditations, and I ask for guidance. So yeah, I prepare myself emotionally and mentally. And one of these things that is so incredible about this work is when we have to look at ourselves too. This is—this is my opinion—that if we get into our own ego, of saying "It was through my guidance, that I allowed it to happen"—it can get in the way. And so, what I like about this is that I go in there and I say, "This is their work. It's not my work. It's their work." And so, I constantly say, this is your work, Joan. This is your work, David. And so, go ahead, and take that opportunity to do that. And they're "oh, no, [Mediator], you did this and … ." And I say, "No, I didn't do anything. All I did was just kind of guide you through that, but you did the work."

And so, what I mean by the ego is allowing them to have that pain that they're experiencing and not taking that away from them. Allowing them to discern their own emotions or goals, of what they need for themselves. And then for me to just be there, in their presence, for whatever they may need. And that's what, to me, I like about that. And for me to even be aware of that, because I think that if we get into this thing of "well, it was through me that they were able to do that"—I think it does get [in the way]—in my opinion.

DISCUSSION

Spencer's case is representational of my offender interviews in many ways. Spencer is also a graphic example of Athens' theory of the creation of the violent criminal. Clearly, he was responding to the process of violentization described and a phantom community that supported the rationalization of his actions surrounded him, at the time of his crime. This also allowed him to justify and rationalize his feelings immediately following the shooting, which allowed him to successfully blame the victim.

The series of epiphanies that started to influence Spencer began, to a minor extent, at the time of the trial, when he saw his mother and his pregnant girlfriend, and had some understanding that he had "done something" to them. The beginnings of his epiphany took place when he heard about the possibility of meeting with his victims, which coincided with his being approached by the "Christian guy" who privately reassured Spencer that he could find the peace of mind he spoke of. This initial series of events all began a process of transforming Spencer from a "violent thug" into a man who found a different meaning in his life. He described this as a "drastic turnaround."

His comment about his hesitation, regarding the possibility of having his conviction turned over on appeal, and the fact that he gave up this notion is quite striking. He was quite clear that the taped material could be used as evidence in an appeal, and that the state's attorney had not agreed to make these meetings confidential. Spencer's belief that there was "something greater" and that he owed "an explanation, words, something" spoke to the significance of the act for him.

Characteristically, he described the attendant anxiety prior to and at the start of the meeting, where he forgot to breathe.

He also discussed the issue of the "bonding" that took place between him and the mother. This is also a common experience.

One of the major issues that I saw in this case, which I looked for as an example of empathy taking place in the offender, was the projection of a sense of similarity between Spencer and the victim of his crime.

> he's kind of like me. Very fun loving, outgoing guy that got along with everybody and everything. Liked to live life to its fullest. And we're kind of a lot alike.

Moreover, in this quote, Spencer found an incredible similarity between them in that "both of our lives were destroyed by my actions."

What was found, in this case as in others, was that the experience of viewing the videotape and interviewing the mediator provided not only a content triangulation of the data, but also a validation of affect congruency between the experience of the meeting and my interview with the individual.

The mediator's account of the wife's experience brought up another example of a failure in the professional community that seemed to be a combination of the failures of managed care, as well as a distinct avoidance of the material on the part of her numerous helpers. Here again was an example of a professional who was avoidant of the material, and thus did not provide a facilitation of the client's need to give a voice to, and mourn, her profound loss.

Significant, also, was the mediator's recounting of the changes he had observed in the wife, which included her stopping her antidepressant medication, her physical changes, and her beginning to socialize. The final change recounted was that she put her memories in a trunk and put them in the attic.

DENNIS

Dennis is a young man in his early twenties who was interviewed in the maximum-security prison where he had been housed for some time. Dennis was in "administrative segregation," which means that he was isolated from other offenders and was in his cell for twenty-two hours per day. He is brought out only to shower and briefly exercise, and for official visits.

The practice of using segregation has grown in the American correctional system. Entire institutions have been constructed with segregation in mind.

This practice has come under criticism in some circles by those who feel that this practice is only serving to enhance the qualities in these individuals that originally led to their violent tendencies.

Every time I interviewed an individual in administrative segregation, he was handcuffed. I routinely requested from the escorting officer that the handcuffs be placed with the individual's hands in front of him, rather than behind his back, to make him more comfortably seated during my interview. I began to make this request routinely in these cases, after having initially requested that the handcuffs be removed but having been told that that this would be impossible. In every case, the request to at least move the handcuffs to the front was granted. The escorting officer remained outside of the interview room, in sight of the offender.

In this case, the interview room was a sergeant's office, which is rather small. Coincidentally, this is the office where Dennis' mediation took place, which is remarkable given its size, thinking of three people and a camera operator being present.

Dennis' history clearly supports that he is struggling with ADHD. His school and behavior history certainly supports this observation, even without the luxury of a formal evaluation. He also struggles with a variety of other psychiatric diagnoses that are comorbid. During the interview, and significant to his neurological condition, Dennis showed a loose association pattern which frequently drew him away from his answer into other territories. He talked using a great deal of hand gesticulation, and I heard the handcuff chains ring frequently while listening to the interview.

It was difficult to ascertain how much of this pattern existed prior to his coming to prison, and how much was due to his imposed isolation. Dennis might well be an example of what old convicts call "stir crazy." In any event, with his neurology, the isolation has clearly exacerbated his presentation.

Dennis, upon coming to his first institution for this crime, was sexually assaulted almost immediately. Because of this assault, Dennis attempted to affiliate with a gang, to achieve some protection. He chose the "Aryan Brotherhood." Because of this choice, he had quickly developed a bad reputation with the administration, not helped by the addition of several violations, especially those incurred for making and carrying prison-made weapons.

Prior to this murder, Dennis had never participated in anything beyond petty crimes. He was not working, and was hanging around with a similarly inclined group of friends. One of these friends, a young woman, told Dennis and his friend that she knew of a drug dealer who had a large cache of money on hand, and that it would be easy to steal it. She stated that she was familiar with this individual, and that she could get them entrance into his apartment, and then they could simply tie him up and steal his money.

What both Dennis and his friend did not apparently know was that the young woman had recently been jilted by this individual and was eager for revenge. It is likely that her story of his having money and dealing drugs was a fabrication.

The trio went to the victim's apartment and, as promised, he let them in when he saw his old girlfriend at the door. The victim attempted, at one point, when their intent became obvious, to escape, running out of the apartment with his hands tied. Dennis rushed after him, hitting him and bringing him back inside. Another struggle ensued, and, eventually, the victim's throat was cut with a serrated knife from his kitchen. Dennis claimed, and still claims, that the other individual was the one who killed the victim.

They fled the state, but were shortly caught and tried, and all three were convicted of murder.

As I was frequently told by offenders in this group of interviews, when Dennis heard about the mediation program, he made contact, through the prison chaplain, with the Victim Services office. He was told that any meeting would need to be initiated by the victim's family, but that his name would be kept on file. Eventually, the victim's mother did contact the office, and the case began to be processed.

Dennis discussed with me about being on the run, and what he felt happened to him during that period.

Interviewer: How long were you on the run before you got arrested?
Dennis: I think they said a week. Six days or something like that. I thought it was about three weeks, but something like, you ain't got no track of time.
Interviewer: And were they looking for the three of you right away? Did they know right away that you …?
Dennis: Just two of us—they were looking for [the other two offenders]. And [Mother] said they didn't know nothing about me until they arrested us. And I think "damn," but I think, I don't know, I've been a real bad alcoholic, I can tell you that now. I was on my way to being one anyway, because I could drink a fifth of whiskey, Jack Daniels, and still walk a straight line. In one night. I did it before. I don't know how I did it, but I did it. But I don't think I could have lived with myself—I probably would have beat my girlfriend up and all that kind of crap. I mean that's the road I was headed for if I wouldn't have got caught.

[In relation to the decision to commit this crime] … but it was really mostly a spur of the moment thing. There wasn't no plan that involved that.

Quickly, Dennis told me that he generally kept to himself and did not talk with people much. He had, up to meeting the mediator, never told anyone the story of his crime, much less discussed his feelings about it. Dennis told me that this was the case because he worried that he would break down, and that crying was a weakness in prison.

Dennis: It was pretty easy [talking to mediator] because—it's just something—it felt like I could trust her enough not to judge me: "Oh, you piece of shit" and all that. And if that's what she thought, that's all right, because I am a piece of shit, to me.
Interviewer: That's how you were feeling?
Dennis: Took somebody's life for no reason. And so, I'm always going to think I'm that. Just like—I don't even trust some of these bosses [correctional officers] when they talk to—I know they think I'm a piece of shit. A lot of them don't even know what I'm in here for. Like one boss—the day we met, [Officer] was taking me and bring me—and he said, "what are you in here for?" And I said, "murder." I've gotten to a few words with some of these "laws" here, but pretty much I stick to myself. I stay up at night. I don't know if I told [Mediator] or [Mother], but I think that's the way I deal with what I call my demons. Because I can turn out the lights, sit in the dark, turn the radio all the way up and try to go to another world. But sometimes it don't work. Like I listen to that heavy metal group Metallica, my sister talked about wanting to play the drums, so a certain Metallica song or Guns N' Roses song, every time it would come on, I'd want to cry, right? But being in this place here where you're taught that's a form of weakness, it set up in here my mind that you can't do that. And it automatically stops it.

Dennis discussed his feelings at the time of the mediation. This passage is a good example of his process, but is also indicative of his observational abilities.

Dennis: See where these little bumps come up? [shows me what appear to be hives on his arm] Well, I get those when nerves start getting real bad. About two or three days before, some of them came up. I was nervous. Especially when I seen them when they came in—[Mediator] was pointing, she pointed right at SEG [the segregation unit], and I thought she was "there he is, right there!" I thought she was pointing at me. I don't think I told her that, either, about the pointing part. I mean, I was pretty nervous—very nervous. It was in this little office right here, they had it turned this way; [Mediator] was sitting over there, [Mother] was sitting here, and I was sitting here. They had paper all over the windows right there. I couldn't see. When I first come in, I had to sign a little piece of paper, get a notary public and all that—I thought, OK, here we go. I was like, "wait a minute. Stop! Stop! Stop!" That's what my mind was saying. But when [second mediator] came in here, and I seen it was just him and "whew!" Sign the thing and I went out and they put me in what they call legal booth, not the bathroom …

The first thing I thought: "She smokes" [the mother] because her voice, the way she sounds, her voice, which she does, because when she showed some pictures, I seen the cigarette in her hand. Which I wish I'd have had at that moment right then, because I really needed one … .

Dennis discussed the difficulty he had at hearing her initial statement about the impact on her of losing her son. Dennis reported that he had a hard time looking at her. This problem became an issue during the meeting, as the mother felt that his inability to make eye contact indicated his dishonesty or disrespect.

Dennis: Well, like I said, I had to force myself, because how can you look at somebody—you took something away from them—their son. How can you look at somebody like that? She was talking about sometimes when I ask him something, he looks away when he answers. She asked me why I do that and I said, "Well," I think I said, "Could you look at like my mom?" I can't remember how I phrased it, but could you look at somebody's mom and talk to them without wanting to look away—embarrassment or however you want to say it. It's pretty—you want to duck your head in your shoulders.

Dennis reported that he had been up all night the night before, and that the meeting itself was about six hours long. I asked Dennis what the hardest part of it had been for him.

Dennis: Actually, sitting there talking with her [the mother]. Because—well I take that back. The photo album that was on the table, right? You can see it in the video but you can't see the picture—right there, in a little square in the middle, it's a picture of [the victim]. And as I'm looking at her, I can see it, and I want to look down at it, but that's another thing I had to keep myself from doing. I didn't tell [Mediator] that either, I don't think. So, there's a few things you're hearing now, that [Mediator] probably don't know. I don't remember if I told her or not. Because usually once I say something, that's it. It's forgotten. To tell you the truth, I don't even remember what I told the cops the day we got arrested …

Yeah—[the photo album] it was like seeing a little small history of his life—pictures of his brothers, one of his friends when they went fishing, and this and that. So that was like—I like fishing, he liked some of the same music groups I like—Metallica, Guns N' Roses. I mean, I wasn't really into listening to really no rap music out there.

Dennis did not have any illusion that the victim's mother was influenced in her opinion of him because of their meeting. He was not at all romantic in his notion of how he thought she saw him.

Dennis: Well, that's when she found out exactly how he died, and maybe we could talk a little easier, if that's the way you want to put it or whatever. But as far as probably her opinion, I don't think her opinion of me has changed at all. Like I say, it might be easier for her to talk to me because I'm the source of information that she needs. I mean, my opinion of somebody that killed somebody I know wouldn't have changed. I told [Mediator] if somebody ever kills somebody in my family, and I get a chance to see them, I'm going to lie to you and tell you I ain't gonna do nothing. But first chance I get, I'm gonna bash your frickin' skull over the desk. I think—she looked at me like, yeah, I think you'd do that. Because I damn sure would.

Dennis shared a great deal in the interview about his family history and issues in his family of origin. He was not optimistic about his future in prison or, eventually, of getting out of segregation. He felt that he had benefited from the meeting in that he thought his temper was not as short and he was not as quick to "get aggravated." He had a difficult time seeing her position or extrapolating questions about how she might have seen him. This, he reported, was based on his inability to do what the mother did if someone hurt someone in his family.

He reported that his mother was not supportive of him doing this meeting.

Dennis: "What do you want to do that for?" I said, "Mom, wouldn't you want to if somebody killed me, wouldn't you want them to come and talk to you?" She just nodded her head. I don't think she could go through it though.

Dennis had a hard time dealing with my questions related to how, or if, he saw himself having changed because of the meeting, or if he felt that change was possible.

Dennis: Like I said, I think most of the time before I … I try to put myself in maybe her place. I already told you what I'd do to somebody and I don't even really like thinking like that. But that's just—I'd be so pissed off that there wouldn't be no talking, no nothing. Especially if it was one of my sisters. I got zero understanding when it comes to my mom and any of my sisters. None whatsoever. They say you did it, you better hope to God you did it. Because you're going to pay for it.
Interviewer: You kind of mentioned this a minute ago, but if somebody came up to you in here, when you get out SEG and said, "I know you did this, and they approached me to do it," would you suggest that they do it?
Dennis: Yeah. You walk around a little bit easier. It's not going to be easy, but I'd tell them, "that's something you need to do. You owe that person that." I kind of felt like I owed her to sit in front of her, feel like a big idiot, because I took her son. I used to deny it and all that, and say I didn't have nothing to do with it, but I had something to do with it. A lot to do with it.

MEDIATOR

The mediator who worked with Dennis and the victim's mother had been doing this work for four years. Regarding Dennis and his relationship with his crime partners, the mediator was clear.

Mediator: … All three got life sentences: the two males, for murder—the female for aggravated robbery. She had a better attorney. Dennis has this really weird sense of chivalry. He took the fall for her because she was pregnant. It wasn't even his kid. He was not the one she was telling was the father. But he did not think she should have to be pregnant in prison. Talk to him now, and he thinks she should burn in there.

Since I did not interview the victim, in this case, I relied on the mediator's view of her process of preparation, mediation, and follow up.

Mediator: A lot of information came out in that meeting. What was really interesting about that particular meeting—Dennis was the one [Mother] wanted to meet with, because he had taken responsibility from the beginning, and something in her knew that he would be the easiest one to work with …. [Mother] needed so badly to know what happened. She absolutely had to find out what happened that night. She needed so badly to know what happened, she developed this whole thing in her head. She just knew that [her son] was swearing at them and fighting them and blah, blah, and blah. And for two and a half years—and it took a little while to do that because of Dennis—they shift him from prison to prison—they `turf him, is what they do. And from isolation to isolation and so it took us a while.

And the interesting thing there is I would say to Dennis, "Your behavior has to be on this level in order for this to happen." And he would work on his behavior. He would do whatever it took … he was terrified [of the meeting].

…… But that level of shame, too. And he said that. "I'm ashamed. I don't know how I can sit across the table and look you in the eye, but this is what you're asking for." And you could see—maybe you had to be there to see the kid shaking, but [Mother] needed to know these things. And for two years I've been telling her what Dennis was telling me. It wasn't until she heard it from him that she could change the story in her mind. So, she got some surprises here that normally you wouldn't get, but it was because of her own inability to hear it from anybody but the horse's mouth.

Regarding her view of what the mother achieved from the meeting, she stated:

Mediator: She was able to say, "[Son] forgives you. I can't forgive you, but [Son] has forgiven you." And I went to see her maybe three weeks after the fact; I walked through the door, and her husband, who participated in almost every meeting I had with her, he even did some work. He said, "That little shit needs to know what I went through. I lost my wife, because she was nuts!" They had had a wedding anniversary, gone to [another city]; this man just jumped out of his chair and threw this big old hug on me and said, "I have my wife back. It's a hundred percent different."

And [Mother] was able to say that she had found some peace in talking to Dennis. She said, "I don't know how I found this peace, because I didn't forgive him." And I said, "Do you really want—you know, you're asking for my opinion here—do you want my opinion?" And she said, "Well, yeah, or I wouldn't ask." And I said, "You know, on some level, you have let him go. Whether you call that forgiving or not, you have put down that particular burden and you are now able to move on. I personally would call that forgiveness." …that this was the last thing she could do for her son. Just being a mother.

DISCUSSION

Dennis was an example of the type of case that exhibits a profound personal impact on the offender, and, by report, on the victim, but shows little outward evidence of change in terms of his daily life or relationship to others.

Dennis was clearly hampered, both by his psychological and neurological vulnerabilities, but also by his course in the institution, which, having been victimized himself, left him with a propensity for reactive violence.

Given all of this, as well as the frustrations in the interview process with Dennis, I was also struck by the way the experience with the victim's mother was bracketed by him, and served as a wholly important event in his life. Even as he recounted the most moving parts of the encounter for him, he told me that he could not cry because he saw it as a sign of weakness. Dennis restated this belief each time he was about to cry.

Dennis showed a capacity for engagement through the relationship he attained with the mediator, who, when I interviewed him, was the first person he had told his story to. Because of this connection, he continued to evidence an internalized and substantial relationship with her. He also showed a capacity for emotional availability by being affected by his facing of his victim's mother, and telling her the story and experiencing her reaction, much in the same way I experienced this reaction in all of these interviews.

Circumstantially, however, I am left with the question of whether the result of this experience may be squandered by Dennis' surroundings. He showed little capacity for insight, and continues with the reactive, violent fantasies that he must need as a defensive posture in the dangerous and hostile environment he dwells in.

DANNY

Danny and his wife had been together for many turbulent years. There were two young daughters in the marriage, but both Danny and his wife were alcoholics, and continued to drink and fight. Danny had been a drinker since the age of eight, when his father would drive the two of them out to the country in his truck and share a bottle of whiskey with Danny, while telling him stories of the family history and the places they would eventually visit together.

As an adolescent and young adult, there were not many chemicals that Danny hadn't tried. His wife was also the victim of a difficult family history, and because of a particularly violent and abusive father, had been placed in foster care. She had been the victim of abuse herself, and was witness to brutal beatings that her father would inflict upon her mother.

There had only been a few instances of actual physical violence between Danny and his wife in the past, usually when the two were drinking and fighting. On the night that Danny killed his wife, this was the case. On this night, the fight became especially heated. His wife told him that she was pregnant by another man, and Danny "snapped." The actual murder was horrific, but even during his alcoholic rage, Danny was aware of one of his daughters coming out of the bedroom to find out what was going on. He intercepted her and told her that "Mom and I are fighting, go back to bed." He tied a belt onto her bedroom doorknob, so she would not be able to come out again and see what had taken place.

Danny called the police himself, asking them to remove his children through their bedroom window so they wouldn't be able to see the awful scene in the kitchen and living room. He did not participate much in his defense, saying that he does not even much remember his trial, and he was given a life term.

His wife's younger sister, Annette, approached Danny for a meeting through the Victim Services office. The two sisters had not been close, given their gap in age and the family dysfunction, but the younger sister had long held out hope that they would reunite and that she would be able to reclaim a big sister.

Danny is a handsomely rugged looking, middle-aged man who is slight but sturdy. He wears the standard prison uniform. We meet in an office/interview room just off the corridor in a large, maximum-security institution. He has a ready smile and an immediately engaging affect. He is a natural storyteller, fitting with his interest in literature and writing.

Danny was perhaps one of my most emotional interviews. Due to many factors that emerged in this interview which speak directly to the essence of this study, Danny had done a great deal of thinking and soul-searching regarding his history and situation. The resulting interview is one of the most concise and moving of all those I did. Because of Danny's emotion and insight, I will represent a great deal of the text. His narrative, due to the feeling and honesty that he brought to our encounter, and the profound meaning that he had made of his history, violence, and future, was a reflective example of his personal journey.

Danny had agreed to be interviewed, but, as was always the case, was not aware that I would be at the institution that day, so he did not know who was there to visit him. Once we dealt with introductions and the informed consent forms, Danny wasted no time in telling me his story.

Danny: I tell you—for me, it's been pretty valuable too. To work on myself. It's helped me adjust and accept what I have and that's a lot, I think. You know, I can't describe that—it really doesn't make sense, because you have to understand where I'm at and how I feel now. It's—it doesn't match. The way I live and feel doesn't match the environment. All the anxiety and the worry and all that stuff, it's pretty much gone beside now. I really don't kind of stay caught up in my past, and I don't stay caught up in what's going on around here. I'm on a whole other level now.

… First of all, I've got a handle on my guilt now. I deal with that really well. I don't use it against myself. It's kind of like I'm handling that real well. I don't feel so negative. I feel kind of neutral. It's—sometimes it's hard to be positive, but I feel like if I can maintain that neutral, I'm doing good.

I ask Danny how long he has been interested and in touch with this feeling.

Danny: I was interested in it before but the concepts eluded me. I didn't have any idea what they were talking about. And as far as dealing with the guilt—my guilt—you know, guilt is compound, a compound type deal. It's not only from what you've done, the crime you committed, whatever that might be. But it's compounded on the effects that you had on other people as well, throughout your life. Your family, mother, brother, sisters, and just friends in general. The pain that you caused them. And it becomes accumulative; your atlas, your burden. And sometimes people, especially—I was like this—I took on that idea that I had all this guilt and this burden and I wouldn't bury it ever. It made me feel good. I wallowed in my miseries. And now, it's like it's not that huge. It's really as gravely important to me. See I made it a personal thing where it made me feel good. So, I could be miserable and feel good about myself being miserable, I deserve this, and all those kinds of things.

… so, I've learned a lot about me. Because I had to be honest, for one thing.

Danny described his history with his wife, and told me that they had been married for five years at the time of the murder, and had two children. The couple had grown up in the same community and had known each other for many years; they then went together off-and-on prior to marriage. He states, "It's like two people that had been through a lot of rejection in life, had come together, and then rejected each other. And that was a really tough thing for both of us."

Danny: … And I'd always had a problem drinking and becoming violent. Not that it happened a lot, but it was a problem. It happened enough—like three, four times in my life, I can show you what I've done. And those three or four times are enough to know that there's a problem, here's the connection—alcohol and anger and the violence. Of course, the anger was always there anyway.

… I either suppressed it or diffused it in different ways. Then when I drank alcohol, it seemed it made me want to act out, and sometimes that would be against other people in it. Not on numerous occasions, but the last time, that was the night I killed [Wife]—I had always drank to blackouts anyway, and I would consume way too much alcohol … but that wasn't the cause. The basic cause was rejection. What caused me to do what I did was being rejected. I felt betrayed and rejected and that's a really powerful thing for people. I'm sure that if you go through case histories that would be the cause of a lot of crimes.

… but it was really unhealthy [speaking of the relationship]. Really negative and unhealthy. And it was because of previous experiences in life. And then we came to a point where it was two people who had experienced much the same thing. She was a pretty angry person, too. Self-destructive. We shared a lot of the same traits.

Interviewer: So there had been physical violence between you in the past?
Danny: On three occasions—four occasions. But never anything like that. Never anything as horrible as that [breaks downs]. It's hard. It's still hard to talk about it. It's always going to be.

… speaking for myself, I had reached an emotional limit, where I didn't have any way out, of my world. This reality I had created, I had no way out of it. And I was stretched to the limit, and all the bands broke, all the bands broke [tears—long pause]. And honestly, when it comes down to it, the act was me saying, "Look, you're hurting me; I'm tired of being hurt. I'm going to show you how it feels to be hurt. I'm going to hurt somebody." That's it, right there. When I get right down to the bottom of it, that's it. It's—I don't know how that sounds, but that's the truth.
Interviewer: You felt that [Wife] wasn't aware of the pain …
Danny: No, I thought she was inflicting it, and that she was responsible for it. That's how I felt. And of course, I didn't know anything that I know now—that's kind of a sad thing. It seemed like you've reached that point in life where you've

already learned some valuable things—some people don't. I see them every day. I go to the day room and watch TV and I go to the chow hall and I see them.

… [while he was waiting for the police to arrive after he called them] And I had come to the realization then that for myself, pretty much, my life was over, as far as ever being free or having any contact with that world out there. That was—I knew that immediately. I realized that. And of course, then, I recognized all the other ramifications too. My children, and my wife's family, my family.

Danny discussed the meaning of the preparation material to his process which, again, he found quite helpful. [Two mediators worked jointly with Danny on the preparation of his meeting, and then facilitated it together.]

Danny: Yeah, there was quite a bit of it. I don't remember how many pages, but it was a lot. And a lot of it was repetitive, the same thing over and over again. They want you to try to answer it differently, express yourself differently—which is good. All that was really good. It helped. What it did—by the repetition, it made you tell the truth. Because you're not going to get anywhere if you're not honest with yourself.

… Well, initially, it seemed like it took forever. It was a slow, grueling kind of thing, you know. But it was really good. The best part about what we did in preparing for it was the role-playing. We did role-playing. And that helped me more than anything. They were really good at it. Of course, I didn't have to play, just had to be myself. And they helped me express myself. They helped me—because sometimes when you're dealing with feelings like that, you're dealing with a lot of pain and a lot of shame—especially the shame—when you're dealing with those things, the guilt and the shame, which are pretty heavy, they're hard to express. And then sometimes just saying things, saying the unspeakable, is very difficult. And they helped me do that. And then if I said something that was—how do I put it?—that was an excuse or justification, they call me down and point it out to me, so I could learn to recognize what those things are. And recognize them for what they are. And then after I got to—after they showed me what it was, well then, I could do it myself. And now I know automatically how when I'm justifying. This is self-interest, and this is justified, and—I can get it all. I know it before it's coming out. So, the best thing to do is just don't do it, just deal with it.

Interviewer: Did you have any concerns or hesitations of actually meeting with Annette?

Danny: A little bit. Like the more I thought of it, I thought, well, if anything, I at least owe her this. I owe her so much. If this is what she wants to do, I owe her this much. And that was the way I understood it to be. It was for her. And it helped me more to look at it that way—that it was for her. I didn't realize how much it was for me. I didn't realize how much I was going to get out of it. So, I worked on the basis that this was something she wanted, something that I could do. And I didn't—I'm not saying I felt obligated … yeah, I did.

That's the way I am. I felt that, yes, something she wanted, I'm obligated. She is doing something here that's out of the ordinary, it's not a common thing. And I said, yeah, I will.

Danny discussed his feelings prior to the meeting with his sister-in-law.

Danny: I was nervous. I was almost sick. I was almost sick, and I was about ready to not do it. And I was afraid. [*Interviewer*: What were you afraid of?] I was afraid of having to tell her what I did, to tell her what she wanted to know. That was what I was afraid of.

Interviewer: Why do you think you went ahead with it then?

Danny: Well, because it had to be done. If I'd have backed out then, there would never be anything resolved or any kind of reconciliation. And what specifically we resolved may have just been a few things. You know, this is what I think—I think that what we shared was important. That was almost as important as the points that we made as far as gaining an understanding.

In terms of the actual meeting, Danny felt that the presence of the mediators was important, and their role facilitating: "Yeah, they prompted us a few times. Because both of us were kind of timid people to start with, and so initiating something was difficult for both of us, and that kind of helped us through that."

The meeting lasted over six hours. I asked Danny how long the meeting seemed to him, if it seemed longer or shorter than the actual six hours:

Danny: It seemed like every bit of six hours. And myself, I was pretty much exhausted, when we were through. And I think I told Annette things that I never told anybody else before. And I'm just kind of like a loner—my private life is my private business. But that's not always the case, you know. Especially when you're doing something like this. So, I tried to tell her whatever she wanted to know. And the things she asked me about, I answered her to the best of my ability.

In our interview, Danny is articulate and moving as to his belief about the meaning of the experience to him and to others.

Danny: … See, I've got this idea that not only is it about the victim, it's about other victims, too, and other offenders.

… It's about the future. It's like a guy that goes and plants trees. You can go plant all the trees you want to, and it's a positive thing. You're doing some really good stuff by planting trees. And you won't really realize what that's worth till forty, fifty years down the road. And probably you're gone by then. And you won't enjoy any of it anyway. This is the same type thing. It's social problems we have. You know, mankind's been dealing with them from day one. And our technology has advanced to no end, but in most cases, our mind is still in the cave, in that primitive thing, and that causes a lot of problems. Well, anything we can do to change social dynamics that will make things better for people in the future, it's just like that guy planting trees. However small it may be, whatever contribution we can make, we've changed something. And things are going to change, we know that. And hopefully, we can give things—that's a quote unquote things—the impetus to change for the positive instead of the negative. That's why I like doing this. That's why I liked participating in this, because it's something that I can do. Otherwise, I'm a man in a concrete chamber. I live in a little six by nine crypt with some iron bars in the front of it. And I have no value for society at all, other than I'm just in my little tomb. But if I can do something that's positive, that affects people, maybe not today, maybe in the future, then I've done something. I've been of some worth, instead of a worthless thing.

I am, of course, while engaged in his discourse, both intrigued and moved by his insights. I am reminded, during our meeting, of Athens' theory of the internal soliloquy (1994), which seems very cogent to Danny's text, both spoken and internal. I asked Danny his thoughts about how these insights have developed for him, relative to the preparation and actual mediation with his sister-in-law.

Danny: This has come over time, over the past few months. I've come to realize certain things about life and existence and being here and what it's all about. And maybe in my case, every now and then I get down, I get depressed, because I'm a ghost. I'm talking about how I'm feeling, now, and I feel kind of like that's self-serving. But then I think I can feel all these negative things about myself, and my situation, but that's not what's important. I've learned—I've educated myself while I've been in here. I've read a truly tremendous amount already and I've learned from different writers. I'll tell you who I've learned from—I've learned from Jack London, Upton Sinclair, John Steinbeck. And I've learned from Herman Hesse. I've read tons of Hesse and I've learned that our whole purpose of being on the planet to start with is to change things for the better, to make things better for future generations; that's what our purpose is. And the problem is all the people who don't see that. But that's why I did this—that's why I signed those papers and I don't have any problem with [what] happens with the material. So, I'll tell it to anybody [Laughs].

I then asked Danny how he thought Annett's feelings possibly changed toward him, because of the mediation.

Danny: Well, … I got a letter from her, through [the mediators], they brought the letter. And it was really neat. She told me that she forgave me in a way. And that she thought that her mother felt the same way. I keep that letter. That's nice.

That lets me know that a lot happened. And a lot more happened there than what I saw. And it's kind of like I can't know how it is for her, but I know how it is for me. And I went in there and I didn't really expect anything to come out of this except that I'm going to cause her a lot of pain. But really, I come through it with a lot of self-realization. And a better understanding of myself. And that's worth a lot.

… I still feel like that there's probably nothing I can ever do for her that—there's nothing I can do to ever replace her relationship with her sister that she could have had. I'll never be able to do that. But I think that things that she didn't know or didn't understand, she has a better understanding now, of the relationship that [Wife] and I had and the things that were going on in our lives at that time. I think she has a lot better understanding of that. And I think that it would be important for her to be able to talk, to ask those questions. For her, that was the thing that she wanted. And she had some fears, she was afraid. And I think that helped calm that down.

Interviewer: What was she fearful of, do you think?

Danny: Well, you know she said that she couldn't sleep—she had to keep a nightlight on to sleep, and that she was afraid. And I think this helped that a lot. And the things that we think we're afraid of are not always the things that we really are afraid of. I know that from my own experiences, but the fear is still there. And so, if she's gained a little peace, that's—I have.

I discussed the concept of forgiveness with Danny, both in terms of how he felt about it from the sister-in-law, and its place in the entire experience.

Danny: I think that belongs to the victim. That's for the victim. If they feel that, then that's it—boy, that'll heal me. If they really truly have it, that'll do wonders for them. That'll change their life, because they're not just forgiving one specific thing. Forgiveness entails a lot of other things. The scope of this, the way it affects a person's life is that it goes beyond just the immediate victim and the offender, the specific incident that caused their need for the mediation. It goes way beyond that. It goes in the little dark corners of your life. And it goes way out there … .

I brought Danny back to the question of change, and his theory of the possibility of change in people.

Danny: I'm sure that, just like anything else, you're going to have people that try to use things to manipulate; they try to use things for themselves, some alternative gain. That's going to happen with anything. But by and large, if you've got somebody that wants to change and you work with a person long enough, you're going to figure out whether they want to change or not. Honesty and sincerity is going to come through. And truth. It's like—I go out here and sit in a day room, and I talk to a guy and we're talking along, and he's telling me all his goings-on in his life and his crime and stuff. And then from out of the blue, he tells me, "You know, I've never hit a woman." And I know right off he's lying. I told the same lie myself. And why does he want to try and tell me that? You know, it's for him. Doing it for himself. And I've told all those lies so I can recognize them. It's kind of like a good con man recognizes a good con game. And it's gonna come through.

… Of course. They're going to [change]. They gonna change regardless of whether they want to or not. They just don't realize it. And it's at what point in your life do you change? And you recognize what is—at what point in your life do you recognize what is valuable and what's not … .

… Like you have twelve-step programs for drugs or alcohol or whatever, sexual addictions, or whatever. You have these twelve-step programs, and they work if people want them to work. If they'll get in there and they'll do the work. You will change. And some people have religious experiences—they come to know some higher consciousness other than themselves and it changes their life. This is the same kind of vehicle. It can change you—I mean, it can help you change. … Well, for offenders, if we had this program here and there's something that I can do that will positively affect the future, to keep something like—what I'd be happy to give, or from being such a—it may never stop it from happening again, but it may make it become a rare occurrence, instead of a common thing.

In the interview, I asked Danny what changes he felt the experience might have caused in his general outlook on life.

Danny: … I'm learning—what it has done is help me to accept things the way they are. And if I can accept things the way they are, well then, I can live. I can have some kind of peace. And you can do that anywhere. There's people that are in the world that are a hell of a lot worse off than I am emotionally and physically. There are some people out there that are miserable. And I could be, if I wanted to. I'm where I am, my circumstances are probably not likely to change any time in the near—between now and when I sign off. But that's not the point. The point is that I'm here, and every now and then I have an opportunity to do something, like this.

… Well, I put things in better perspective. Where they belong. I don't have any anger. I have nothing to be angry about. I was angry at myself for a while, but that's not really doing any good. I'll let other people do that for me. They can be angry with me. But I'm not going to be angry with myself. And I've learned to accept that I can change. And what I did is I took the life of somebody. I took the life of a person who deserved to live and be loved as much as anybody else. As much as I do or anybody else on the planet, regardless of their situation or their personality or whatever. I did that; I can't change that. And I'll always be guilty of it, but for me to use that guilt to crucify myself daily is of no positive value. It really does no one any good. So, I'm not going to do that. I've changed that. I don't—the shame will always be there, too. But I don't have to live in the shadow of that. I don't have to grow it into a great oak and then live in the shadow of it. All those things I'll have, but I recognize them for what they are. And I've put them in their proper place. That's how I've changed. And I recognize that there are some positive things I can do, for me to survive.

... Right. I was still living under the precept that I feel and then I do. I didn't realize that I do and then I feel. I'm kind of a behaviorist now. I understand that a lot of things that I do, I do then and I feel later. It's not the other way around.

... All those things are changing for me. I've got some peace now. There's all kinds of old sayings and a lot of them are true. Like the "eye of the storm, the calm"—that's where I'm at right now. I'm in the eye of the storm. I don't have any guarantees that the storm won't get me, but I'm at peace.

In discussing Danny's family history and his (resulting) isolation, he states:

Danny: In my case, my family is—I know that they really love me and they're really good people, but they're really ashamed too. And they really have a hard time thinking about me and going on with their own life out there. So, they kind of—there's kind of a distance between us. My mother and I communicate pretty often, but I don't see them very often, so I didn't really get any feedback from them, how they felt. And then inmates, most of the inmates—I don't talk to most of them. I don't have many friends here. That's—in probably the eleven years I've been here, I've had one person I can call a friend. Because integrity is real thin. Occasionally you find people that have some. But it's a rare thing.

The mediation video of this meeting is strikingly sad. As Danny recounted, one of the impressions that came through in viewing it is the timidity of both individuals. Beyond this was the profound grief expressed by both. As the mediator discusses, however, during the six hours of the meeting, the timidity diminishes, and a rather dramatic and observable change takes place with both participants. Given that both mediators are facing the camera at their end of the table, their emotions are readily seen as well.

I will provide the reader with some excerpts from this meeting, to give a sense of how it flowed.

The two talked a great deal about his children, of whom the sister-in-law has brought in pictures for Danny to see. The children are living with the wife's father, who has custody of them with his second wife.

Annette: [Telling him about his daughters] They're in the choir. And they're both good students, A and B students. Very academic [Shows him recent pictures of them].

Danny: I grew up and learned history. My father lived in the past. He was one of those kind of people. I think he never left 1937. And he would ride around and drink, he would drink constantly. On the weekends when he didn't work he would ride around. And ever since I was a little bitty boy I rode with him and I would drink too. I drank when I was a little fella. And he would tell all these stories about different places and different people. And he would stop on the side of the road and we would go off into the woods and he would find an old house that was there, and he would tell me some story about it, and the people.

So, when I think about it I think about all those things too.

Danny: I just wondered if they [his daughters] had ever talked about it [the murder] to you or anybody?

Annette: Well, not so much H, but D since she was a little bit older she can remember parts of the night. She does remember … she asks, after the incident and everything, bringing her back to my dad's house in [City], apparently, she knew that her mother had died. She didn't go to the funeral, neither one of the kids went to the funeral. She would just mope around, and she would say, "I'm dying, I'm dying" [crying]. Maybe she overheard, or saw, I'm not quite sure. My father hasn't told me.

I had to go to the county to find out what happened.

They ask questions. They didn't show me the crime scene photos. They wouldn't show me any photos. I would have never looked at them, if I couldn't have brought them here to show you, because why look at something and have that image.

Danny: I knew that probably D had seen or heard something, because she woke up. And I've always worried about that, that that might have happened [crying]. But you know. Not just that. I think about you too, and your mother and your father. I do. I have thought about you all.

Annette: Well, we've thought about you too.

Danny: I know, well I don't know, I know how much I hurt. And I can't imagine. Maybe it's not comparable, you know. If I, all I have, all I can do is talk about it, you know. And all I have is words. And the pitiful words I have is to say that, "I'm sorry" and I know that's not enough. To me that will never be enough.

But I want to say that anyway.

Annette: Well I appreciate that. That means a lot.

Danny: When you said that you forgive me [breaks down], I admire that. That's strong. That's strength.

Annette: Well, the rest of the family thinks, I'm [laughs], I shouldn't be doing this, let's just put it that way. Especially my father. And I can see his point of view.

Danny: Well sure, but that's not you. You're not him.

Annette: D [his daughter] has gotten therapy and stuff for it. She still has problems. I think that she probably should have gone longer to therapy, that's just my opinion. Just from what she's told me that she still wakes up hearing you all fighting, her mother screaming and stuff like that. And that's real hard, its hard [crying]. Not so much H, she was smaller.

I guess I'll tell you what's happened to my family:

Me, I still, [Sister/Wife] and I weren't real close to begin with. Of course, we're sisters and everything. It, I'm thirty years old and I still sleep with a light on [crying]. And I guess the reason I do that, I've done that, is because you really messed her up [both sobbing]. And I have such an active imagination, that I'm just afraid that she'll be there. I don't know why I think that. But it's getting better. I'm getting better, you know. That's the reason that I keep the light on. It has helped me because, I've already told my husband to never lay a hand on me, because you're out of there, but we already put up with it from my father, our father. That's the reason [Sister] quit school, to get out of the house. She didn't want to be there and so that was her way to get out. My way to get out was I went to the children's home and lived. So, I wouldn't be around it.

Coming down to the domestic violence part, that's helped me to come to the decision that I'm not going to put up with it. [Danny: No, you don't have to.] I've stressed that. I'm sure that he's probably thought of that [laughs] you know, 'cause we all do. Anyway, I mean that's been the good part that's come out of it, you know.

I did go to therapy for a while.

Basically, I couldn't even stay by myself because I would freak out. [Danny: Afraid?] Yeah, afraid that I would see her, you know. I guess because I felt guilty, because I didn't come and see you all, instead I went to [City] to see my boyfriend. And like you said, we just never know what would have happened if I had dropped by [On the night of the murder].

Danny: You see; I don't think that would have changed anything. Maybe it would have changed it for that night.

Annette: Right. There's always "what ifs." You know. I think I was blaming myself, and I think that's why I had a little nervous breakdown, because I was feeling really guilty.

Danny: You know how we always drank, me and [Wife] always drank. And we had got to the point where that was just something that we did regular, you know. And we were always doing things to make each other angry. How I describe that, our whole relationship was one of us would have power over the other one for a little bit, and then we would trade it back and forth. Doing mean things to each other. That was a pretty regular deal. And the mean things I would always do, would be that I would hit her. That wasn't all the time, I don't want you to think that was an everyday thing. In the whole time we were married, I can tell you five instances where I hit her. It was always bad too, you remember . . . .

Annette: I remember her going to my dad's house, with the kids.

Danny: I wanted you to know it wasn't an everyday common thing, but it did happen. I learned that. I learned how to act that way I think. My father was

pretty abusive. So, I didn't think there was anything wrong. In my heart at that time, and my heart was pretty hard, that was just normal living.
Annette: I understand … .
Danny: What led up to that was that she was working, you know she was working in a nursing home. And I was working out at a place called [housing development]. I was doing a house slab for a guy out there, and I was working on the weekends and after I would get through, I was going to college during the day, and then I would stay the rest of the day while [Wife] was at work, and that Monday I had come back and we had like $35, and she had spent $25 with this guy next door and bought some speed. And of course, you know, I've never done that, I've tried it. But it always gave me something I could look down, being the alcoholic that I was it gave me something to be superior. I could look down on it and be angry about it. So, I was angry about that. So, I went somewhere and borrowed $20. And I went and bought some vodka and some beer, bought [Wife] some beer. And we drank. I've been angry see, things that had happened, she went out the week before and stayed out. And I found out where she had been, who she was with, and I was angry about that.
Annette: So, you went that night, you're talking about that night, right?
Danny: Yeah, and that week. That night, what had happened, I went out and borrowed that money, I was mad about the week before, when she left and I couldn't find her. Of course, I don't know why I thought I had a right to be mad because I would do the same stuff myself. Go to work and not come home until 3 o'clock in the morning, stuff like that. So, I don't know why I thought I had any right to be angry, but I was. Different set of rules.

So, I remember drinking the vodka. And I think [Wife] helped me drink it, and then we drank a bunch of beer. But after I drink enough alcohol I lose all control. What I'm saying is that I don't lose control, but it allows me to do things, horrible things.

And I remember being outside the apartment. After that I don't remember anything in a sequence. I can remember being outside the door. And apparently, she went in the apartment and locked the door. And I don't know if she let me in or I broke the door down.
Annette: I think she let you in. So, what were you all arguing about? Just something stupid … .
Danny: Yeah, it was some ignorant thing. It was the people she'd been with. I always hated the guy.

… she had told me that the baby she was carrying wasn't mine. Whether that was true. She probably just said that to hurt me. Then what I remember was just crazy [crying].

What I remember is hard to describe, because it happened real fast, it was fast. I don't know how the police write about it, but somehow everything happened in the kitchen. I remember, I had long hair, and I remember [Wife] had a hold of my hair. And we were just spinning around there in the kitchen. I don't remember consciously stabbing her.

When I came in the door, that's probably when I started hitting her.

I don't have a sequence for it. I dream about it sometimes, but the dreams are just like it happened, just a jumbled mess.

[Talking again about children]

Annette: And they don't have a mother or a father because of the situation.

Danny: And that's my fault. That's my fault.

Annette: I'm sorry that it came down to that. Because … .

Danny: I am too. But that was me. You know, that was me. It didn't have to be that way.

Annette: She could have stepped out too. I mean, but you all collided that night … .

Danny: You know it's not that easy. It's not that easy to just walk out, to get out. You know. And we loved each other, crazy as that sounds. That sounds like how could that be, but that's true. I know that sounds, I don't know what that sounds like. Unbelievable I guess, but it's true.

Annette: There's a fine line between love and hate, so … I guess that's who I feel sorry for, is the kids, all three of them [the two daughters and the unborn child]. But I mean, they have a good life. Probably a little bit more than you all could have provided. They live in a house that has a pool, they have their own rooms. They go to church. Sing in the choir. Which is good. And they love them, you know. They have a hard time getting to see my mother. [The parents are divorced, and the father has custody of the children.] Dad makes it difficult sometimes. He's overly protective. But that's their grandmother, but it's kind of sad. I have a hard time getting a hold of them sometimes.

Annette: The way I was brought up, you don't show any emotions.

Danny: Yeah, I usually don't, you know. But I can't help myself now. I wanted to, it's hard, but it seems that you are making it too easy for me. Can I say that? I wanted you to be angry with me. And I know you are. I know that's there. But I don't want you to be afraid either.

Of anything … .

Annette: I want you to be comfortable to be able to answer my questions. I guess that's why I'm not showing many emotions. I mean … [Danny breaks down]

That's what I mean, when I leave, I will probably cry all the way home. It's a three-hour drive. And my mother wanted to come up here, but I wanted to do this by myself. She would have been out in the lobby, so you could have seen her …

Danny: Yeah, I understand that. I understand that you had to do it.

MEDIATOR 1

Two mediators out of the Victim Services office, acting as a team, conducted this mediation. Their supervisor made this decision, as it was their first experience, and it was thought that they would serve as a support system for one another.

Both mediators were drawn to the work by their own experiences of trauma.

I met with this mediator in an office in the Victims Services Department. She was immediately open and eager to tell of this experience. She had conducted several subsequent mediations since this experience, but had maintained contact with both parties, which meant that she could update me on Danny's situation and progress.

Given the apparent fragility of the victim, and the fact that this was intended as her work, the pair spent more time in preparation. Danny was not hesitant and spent the expected time working on the preparation packet.

Early in the interview, the mediator told me of the impact of the process on the entire family system. Most important were Annette and her mother. Apparently, the brother is also eager to see the video of the meeting. The mediator also described other growth that took place for Annette in the meeting and preparation process.

Mediator: … But she has done some—a lot of growth from it, still. And her mother has come and viewed it. It was very good for her mother. One of the things that happened in the video is Annette actually admits out loud to Danny that she loved her sister.

And that's a very important point, because that was something Annette could not just say. She could not admit to that. She started this whole process with the thinking that it was her sister's fault that she got murdered, because her sister's morality was questionable to her. Some of the things she was into and the things that she did. And so, I think in order for Annette to feel safe herself, because she was in a marriage that's not all that great, and has been abusive a time or two, I think she wanted to feel that it was her sister's fault. But as the time progressed, we were able to help her see that it wasn't her sister's fault. And so, she could actually say to Danny in the mediation that she had loved her sister, while all the time proclaiming that "I'm very different from my sister." But that admitting that she loved her was a very crucial thing and the mother got a great deal out of that … because she said Annette never would say that to her, that she had really loved her sister.

The mediator admitted that Annette was not easy to prepare, as she was quite defensive and resistant. She also stated that she had some qualms about meeting Danny the first time.

Mediator: And then meeting Danny was kind of scary, because once I had read about the crime, and he being the first murderer that I knew of that I had met, it was pretty scary. Because we went in and he was not expecting us and he was very startled, easily startled in those days, and so it was good that there were two of us.

The mediator gave me a piece of important history that I had not known before related to the extent of Danny's mental illness and the early process of his incarceration.

Mediator: … But he's not an intimidating person and he was very interested right away. He loves to talk and although he was very frightened in that period of time, because he was living in a very dangerous kind of situation. I suppose you know all the history, that the first eight years he was in a psych unit. They diagnosed him with various things, schizophrenia, manic depression. And he definitely had hallucinations, and so they kept him there where he had a pretty protected environment for eight years. And there was a man who was very important in Danny's recovery, and his name was [CN]. I don't know if Danny told you about him. But he was the woodwork instructor at the prison, and he's the one who got Danny to tell him something about himself. Got him to tell all his childhood, the crime, everything. He just worked as though he were a therapist with Danny. So that was an immense help to Danny. And he looks back on that now and sees that.

And Danny was able to teach, to help his teacher, to do a lot of teaching on his own, and of course that made him feel better as a human being to be able to participate in something meaningful to himself. And then they decided, against psychiatric advice, to put him into the general population. And we met him shortly after they did that, and he was in a really bad unit, and he was very frightened for his safety. He didn't trust much of anybody or anything at that point. And so, he reacted—he became delusional again. And so, they sent him to [City] to [prison] unit which is another psychiatric unit. And so that's why it took us so long to do our mediation with Danny is we had to wait for him to go through various cycles of behaviors.

The mediation took place at the prison in which I interviewed Danny, and where he still resides. The mediator discussed the final phases of the preparation, and brought me up to date on Danny's current situation.

Mediator: And so, we went to [prison] to see him when he was in the unit there, and then they decided he was—they had him drugged and all that—they would send him back to general population in [prison]. And again, it was quite an adjustment for him, and he was frightened again. But he's now reached—I visited with him yesterday, and he's now reached a level of security where he's in the trustee camp, so now he has a cubicle instead of a cell, and he has—he feels a little safer, although there isn't really any safety in prison. But he's more safe than he was before. And so, he feels much better. He said he is at the height of

good feeling, of feeling good, that he's been all of his life that he can remember.
I asked the mediator if she believed that Danny was, in fact, mentally ill.
Mediator: I think Danny probably was mentally ill, but—I have my doubts as to whether he could function in the real world if he were free today. I don't know if he could. He seems very fragile to me in a way, his psyche is kind of fragile it seems to me. But of course, I'd love it if he could ever get to try that, especially if he could have some sort of mixture of security and freedom, would be ideal for him, in my thinking. He feels a lot better and he feels that now he understands his mental illness enough that he knows what to do if he ever sees something that isn't real, like a hallucination. He thinks, at least, that he can know when it's not real, enough to go and ask for help. And so, he has—yesterday he talked about whether or not mental illness is real, or don't we all have that to some degree and he feels like he's really healthy now, and that he's OK. But he's also aware that he has to take responsibility if he should begin to feel differently.

The mediator told me about some of the preparation of Annette, and the family history that she is aware of.

Mediator: … Because she is very withdrawn, and not very apt to express herself in any—stand up for herself. It's very easy to see that she grew up in a home where her mother was beaten regularly, and it was a family pattern. And of course, the daughter that Danny killed was a person who had been beaten regularly. And so, it's easy to see the family illness in all of them, the mother included. Her mother is very typical of battered women. And it's very sad actually. I think her mother suffers a great deal from depression. She has just a negative view of life, so—she's a very sweet woman and a very kind woman, and wise in some ways. But probably should be treated—she probably should have drug therapy for her depression. But she doesn't realize that, and doesn't do that. So, I'm making all sorts of judgments that I have no credentials for making, but I'm just giving you my opinion about it.

Echoing what Danny told me in our interview together, the mediator recalled that he benefited a great deal in the preparation from role-playing. In all, she felt the preparation of both parties was successful, even though Annette was more resistant.

Mediator: … one of the most important things we did was role-play, which I pretended to be Annette and I expressed anger and all this, to prepare him for the possibility of what she might say. And I read portions of the autopsy and told him he needed to explain all that.

So, I could see the shock in his face when I did that but it did help him. Because then when she did—and she was persistent—I was real proud of Annette that she kept persisting with her questions. She didn't give up just because Danny cried and was very upset. So that was one of the things that I was really proud of her about. And one of the things we had to teach her, because, you know, if you want to get your answers, here's what you have to do. You have to give him time to have his emotional reaction to your questions and regain his composure, and then he'll try to answer you. But if you come on like gang-busters and you try to browbeat him, he's not going to be able to respond. We were very afraid that Danny would become withdrawn, and just tune her out and not be able to be there emotionally, if she was too hard on him. Because of the fragile things that we see in him. So, we asked her, and taught her, and trained her and role played with her, to ask her questions and let him do his response emotionally, and then listen for the answer, and then come back and ask it again if you don't get what you need. And so, it was just kind of—we drilled them both, which I think was real helpful to them because then they were able to do that on that day.

The responsibility of the work is something that both mediators took very seriously, especially related to the possibility of unanticipated trauma for one or both people.

Mediator: The fears that we had were that Danny might—that it might have a negative effect upon him, that he might go back into his mental illness, into the previous state that he'd been in. It was also our fear that—you know, suicide is always something that we're always aware of. We're really aware of the seriousness of all these things and what a serious responsibility it is, to bring together when it might be very traumatic for them. So, we were concerned about it; and we talked to him about it and tried to prepare him to seek help if he needed it. We tried to provide help. He had a fairly good relationship with the chaplain and we got the chaplain lined up to see him afterwards, and to watch after him for a day or two.

In relation to her own feelings about the meeting during its process and successful outcome, she stated:

Mediator: I felt sad—I had some sad feelings because Danny was expressing so much grief. I mean, there was so much grief expressed, just real grief. And [D, another mediator who was filming the meeting], who's much more experienced with all that than I was, he was doing the camera work, and when we went out at noon, he just sat and cried for a few minutes. He said, that is just such a pure example of people expressing grief. And so, I felt that having some of that sadness for them, I felt a tremendous amount of pride, I guess it was, not pride in myself, but pride that they had come that far, that they could actually stand up and do this. And face up to how hard—knowing how hard it was for both of them to do it—I just felt so proud of them both, that they had worked that hard and that they were able to do that well with it.

The mediator then discussed the outcome and the changes seen in the participants during the actual meeting.

Mediator: ... We felt they both got a lot out of it. You could see, for me, we could see a lot of change in the two people, from the morning into the evening. Their faces were different. Annette is a very different person, and Danny is too. Danny is still a very private person, but his world is bigger. I said to him yesterday, "I just believe that you have a bigger world to live in now than you had before." And he agreed that that's true. He's made more friends. And he writes more people. He hasn't had visits; he doesn't have people who visit him, but he has—it seems like his mind has been stimulated. He's reading more. Since he's out of that depression, he's more active, so there's quite a change in him. He says—he told me yesterday that he now feels like he has become himself, and that he feels much more comfortable in his skin, than he's ever felt before. And he thinks a lot of that was the mediation. I think it gives the offender—I think he had a chance to be human again. A chance to feel his feelings again. A chance to make a contribution to others. And I think that that meant a very great deal to him, and continues to mean a lot to him.

... I think this helped Danny get past a lot of guilt and fear and I think for Annette, it let her get past a lot of feelings of being embarrassed, of being different because of this having happened in her family. About her shame about her family, and about the way they had lived their lives. About the beatings and the unhealthy mental stuff that was going on, the controlling, and all this. I see Annette as having worked through and accepted the fact that that's not her fault. That each of us is born into a family that's imperfect, and I think in the beginning there's a lot of shame there about that. How did I come to be in this place in my life where my sister is murdered and how did my family come to be here? And Annette has a lot of conflict in her family all the way around, with both parents. Her father is still very mean, and she still doesn't have his approval, and he was very much against the mediation. And he's a very difficult man. And Annette actually hasn't talked to him since she did that, because he was livid that she would go and visit Danny.

... I guess I was surprised that each of them was able to do as well as they did. I was surprised that Annette could be persistent, because Annette's a very submissive type person, and I think she said, "I'm sorry" about fifty times in there. And I was afraid—my fear for her was that she would not be persistent enough to get her questions answered, to get her needs met. That she would—once he started with his tears and his remorse showing and his feelings showing, because she's so uncomfortable with the showing of feelings, we were afraid that she would withdraw. And that she wouldn't persist, that she would just feel sorry for him, which is kind of what she always has wanted to do. But no, she was tough enough; she hung in there. She went in the face of her family, her husband, her dad, and her brother. She did it in spite of them.

Well, I think it's facing that most painful thing that there's a great freeing that comes from that. A great freedom in knowing that you've faced the worst thing you've ever done and now you can't ever top that. So, it just kind of relieves a need to offer pretenses, to cover up, I think that's what I see when people go through something like this, that it's OK now to just be me, it's OK to be real, that that was the hardest thing I'll ever do, and I've done it.

I asked the mediator to discuss what she feels happened in relation to the word, "closure":

Mediator: Yeah, that word—some people think there's not really such a word or such a thing as closure. But I don't know that I believe that. I think that we—in my own experience—that closure means that—certainly not that you get over or that you forget something—but that you have put it to rest. And I think we certainly do get to a place where we can do that. And so, I think for them, in a way, the mediations are a beginning, and in a way, they're endings. But I think for Danny it's certainly brought a lot of closure. A lot of renewed life, interest in life. I think for Annette, the closure that she got was that, well, I think it was self-esteem, I think it was—I think she felt really good about being brave enough to do what she did and I think it gave her a whole new self-confidence in who she is.

DISCUSSION

Danny's case presents a summary of my entire project in many ways. Danny shows, and discusses with eloquence, the development of a violent personality, with the attending family dysfunction that led to both his drug abuse as well as his mental illness.

Danny also supports the meaning of the concept being explored in this project of epiphanies and the role they play in supporting significant personal change.

He has developed a great deal of insight (which comes through clearly in my meeting with him, but is well supported in the interview with the mediator) related to his developmental history and the meaning of this to his actions. He states that these "concepts eluded me" for much of his life, even though he was aware of this material through his reading and college work. He describes this well in the section where he talks of his impact on others, and states that the pain he has caused has become his "atlas" and "burden."

He shows great insight into the evolution of his personal growth, especially as it relates to his character pathology, and its identification and confrontation in his discussion of his "wallowing in miseries," and feeling good about being miserable and feeling deserving of this. He also describes the psychodynamic understanding of male abusers in his description of his acts, "The cause wasn't alcohol but rejection ...," and suggests that this fear of abandonment and rejection may well underpin other violent acts.

His comment regarding "saying the unspeakable" speaks to the core of my effort here:

> ... They helped me—because sometimes when you're dealing with feelings like that, you're dealing with a lot of pain and a lot of shame—especially the shame—when you're dealing with those things, the guilt and the shame, which are pretty heavy, they're hard to express. And then sometimes just saying things, saying the unspeakable, is very difficult. And they helped me do that.

Danny sees the meaning of this meeting to be the culmination of this work, but also sees it now as a unifying and defining event in his life. He discusses it being "about other victims and other offenders," speaking to the ripple-effect impact that this process has, an effect that is well defined by many mediators in this field. He also sees this activity as relating to his future: I have cross checked the text and that is the accurate quote from the interview."

The writers that Danny is the most influenced by are also significant to his development. Hesse's treatment of dualism and the philosophical meaning of both Sinclair and Steinbeck have clearly supported the epiphanies that are spoken of when reading such literature.

Danny states, "The things that we think we are afraid of are not always the things that we really are afraid of."

His discussion of forgiveness is also very important. His statement that "forgiveness belongs to the victim," but the feeling that, when given, "boy, that will heal me," but also will do "wonders for them" and "change their life," shows a great deal of insight into the process of forgiveness.

Again showing a profound insight into his own process of change and the evolution of growth in psychotherapy, he discusses the resolution of his guilt and shame, which he connects to the resolution of his own depression. He speaks to "accepting that I can change" in his personal life, but being able to include and live with his actions in a more integrative and healthy manner. He states, "I'll always be guilty of it," but to "use it to crucify myself daily is of no possible value to anyone," and "the shame will always be there but I don't have to live in the shadow of that."

The information given to me by the mediator about Danny's history in the prison system also confirms this process. The meeting he had while in the psychiatric unit with the woodworking instructor, in which he told his story, was seen by the mediator as a "kind of therapist" for Danny. This likely served as another in a series of significant movements made by him toward his "resolution" and "reconciliation."

When I spoke with Danny, he was convinced that his hallucinations were connected to the large amounts of psychedelics that he had ingested in his life, especially LSD and hallucinogenic mushrooms. I did not have access to Danny's complete prison record, nor his psychiatric records that resulted. He has progressed, in any event, from a regular pattern of hallucinations, along with psychotropic medications for this, to taking no medications for some years, and feeling that he can maintain a more normal existence. As stated by the mediator, he claims to have never felt more together and happier than he does currently.

Significant also in this process is the role of grief and mourning in the meaning of these mediations. As expressed by all concerned, and certainly experienced by me, the overwhelming sense of grief expressed in this encounter is evident.

ERIC

Eric's case is the second of two criminal vehicular homicide cases that were interviewed for this project. As previously mentioned, while the deaths incurred in these cases were not necessarily "intentional" homicides, the apparent prevalence of driving while under the influence of chemicals in this country, and the wide amount of public attention this problem has received, creates a similar dynamic for the perpetrator of these crimes. This dynamic relates to the acceptance of personal responsibility, not only for the irresponsible, sometimes pathological use of mind and response-altering chemicals, but also the consequences of these actions.

Of equal interest in these cases is the process of the victims, especially as it relates to their own history of chemical use and history of driving while intoxicated. This provides a place of identification, which might lead to an empathic opportunity for these victims, which may be a way to facilitate their own process of reconciliation.

I met with Eric in the basement office of the chapel in an old and formidable maximum-security prison. He is a handsome, well-groomed young man in his mid-twenties, who, if one can say this about a standard prison uniform, appeared well dressed. He was initially nervous, but quickly became personable. My interview with Eric was one of my longest, lasting over two and a half hours.

Eric, as has been seen with several of these subjects, had given a great deal of thought to his situation, and he had definite and strong feelings about it. He was articulate and passionate about the insights he had achieved, many because of the preparation and ultimate mediation experience.

Eric had been living with his girlfriend for some time, and the two planned eventually to marry. Eric had been drinking heavily since high school, and had developed an increased tolerance to alcohol, which, if he had been evaluated at any point, would have indicated a serious alcohol dependency. Eric had tried other chemicals, but eventually settled on alcohol as his major chemical of choice. He had experienced blackouts in the past, and his alcohol consumption had created major consequences in his life and career, interrupting his goal of becoming an emergency medical technician. He was unable to consistently complete his coursework, and he eventually began missing shifts, resulting in his dismissal.

Five years prior to my meeting Eric, he experienced a crisis in his relationship with his girlfriend. She became pregnant, but did not feel that they were ready to parent a child. After a great deal of soul-searching and discussion, she elected to terminate the pregnancy, and while Eric did not comply with this decision, he did not object strongly, feeling that it was ultimately her choice. On the day of the abortion, Eric accompanied her to the clinic and drove her to their home afterward. He told her he was going over to his mothers to do some laundry, but instead went to a friend's house, where he drank for the rest of the day and into the night.

Eric began driving home in the early morning hours. Traveling at approximately sixty miles per hour, he hit a VW bug head on, likely traveling at the same rate of speed. Inside the VW was a young couple, both Eric's age, who were returning home from a dance. Both were killed instantly.

Eric broke his back in two places and some ribs. He got out of his car and went to the VW, which was on its side. He saw the young man, who was the driver, and felt that he would immediately get out of the car, and the two of them would exchange the usual information and call wreckers to deal with the cars. When this did not happen, and the young man did not move, he looked more closely. He could not see any blood on the young man, but quickly determined that he was dead. He did not get a clear view of the girl in the car, the young man's girlfriend, but she, too, was dead.

In our meeting together, after I gave my standard introduction, Eric quickly told me the history of his crime and its consequences, beginning with the initial scene of the head-on collision.

Eric: At first, I didn't want to admit that I was drunk and that's why it happened. I got real defensive and angry. And then after that, it kind of came crashing in. I realized that this was my fault, and it took me probably a month before I really even fully understood what it meant. That they were gone, and the effects that were going to begin happening in my life and other people's lives. I really was kind of mad that I had lived through it. I was kind of mad because they didn't live and I did. It was my fault … I was defensive.

In describing the VW, Eric told me the differences between the two cars, and said, that because the engine was in the back of the VW, "it didn't have any mercy on anything."

He described the police as being hard on him: "They were pretty angry. The animosity." But he was struck by how quickly he "felt normal" following the accident, saying that he assumed that the "adrenaline rush" had sobered him up immediately following the accident. His blood alcohol level, however, was a 2.2.

In telling me the story, Eric states that he had, at one time, met the young man, who worked for the same pizza delivery company that Eric did on the other side of town. While they had met, Eric did not consider them friends. He had not met the boy's girlfriend.

The reality of Eric's drinking had not been a mystery to him, or to his family and friends. He had been involved in one prior DUI incident and was referred to treatment, but he did not find much help there. On the day of the accident, Eric clearly identified depression as the feeling he was living with, principally because of the abortion. Eric discussed the immediate and long-range consequences:

Eric: The same day we had the abortion that morning was the same day the car wrecked. And after that, my wife [the two had married following his arrest and conviction] and I—I knew I had a drinking problem, but I didn't think it was anything bad. I thought, well, if this is what alcoholism is, it's not bad. And then everybody told me that I had a drinking problem. In fact, people told me that I needed a drink because when I wasn't drinking, I was a wreck. And after the wreck, I realized all the destruction I had caused, and everything I just—I didn't care about coming to prison, I didn't care about anything. I was mainly concerned with the other families and my family and the wake of destruction I had left. And I began to look at different things, and it was in that time that I became a Christian. I really just began praying and meditating and trying to ask for help with my family. And my wife and I—she forgave me and she began to put a little bit of faith in me and began to watch me and stuff. And I told her I was on my way to prison. She said, well, we'll just go one day at a time. She stuck with me. She's been here every weekend since I've been down. I've been here five years, going on five years, now. And she still drives from [City] every week, and we've been really close. Same goes with my mother and father and my little brother and sister. Those relationships have been restored and I'm thankful for that. … And after the wreck, all I knew was that I didn't want to drink any more ever again. I began to go to AA and I began to work the steps and I gave all the energy I had into that program.

It was with the parents of the girlfriend that Eric held the mediation. The two had divorced following the death of their daughter, so the mediations were held separately. The young man's parents had been intent on Eric receiving the harshest possible punishment, and have indicated no interest in meeting with him.

During the trial, Eric demanded that he plead guilty to the charges.

Eric: I was really sad that I had put these people through this. You know, to see them. I had to fire one attorney because he wanted to fight it and he didn't see any way around it. And I told him I wanted to plead guilty and that I just couldn't—pretty much my whole life I had run from taking responsibility for what I'd done. You know, I was only nineteen, but still I couldn't see any other way. So, I pled guilty and tried to make it—tried to give them some sense of justice being served.
Interviewer: And your feelings about that, and just about these two people ... .
Eric: Well, all of the families and stuff, I just didn't want them to hurt any more. And I wanted them to feel like, whatever it took for them to begin healing, is what I wanted. And I thought that if I pled guilty and they gave me the maximum time they could give me. It was my first offense. I had hoped even when it was over with—I was shocked but I also had hoped it would help them.

What shocked Eric was that the court gave him two twenty-year sentences back-to-back. Eric's feelings about this sentence became a significant focus for him in the mediation sessions. His reconciliation of this within himself became, as the meetings with the girl's parents progressed, a particularly significant piece of the meaning for him of the process.

As was seen with many of these subjects, Eric found the preparation process especially useful.

Eric: Yeah, but it [the preparation packet used] took me all the way through my childhood. I wrote over a hundred pages of notes just reading through the packet. And I found out things about myself and why I work the way I do and how other people—you know, it was probably the one thing that changed my life more than anything else so far. And it's been this program; that packet was really helpful. And I can see where if you didn't put much into it, then you wouldn't get anything out of it. It was very helpful to me and everything in there I applied with my beliefs in God and stuff, and I think that was what made it so worthwhile. Because it fit perfectly.

... And I eventually got away from everything and it was pretty cool. I began to find solutions instead of temporary fixes and like I said, by the end of '98 I was looking to start helping other people and using my story to talk to kids and stuff. The first thing I did, going through that packet, was write down my story and my testimony and everything. I wrote a real long story and sent it home, and Mom put it on the computer and sent it back to me. And I sent it out. That opened a lot of doors. It was published in the newspaper and stuff. It didn't make the newspaper until New Year's Eve 1999. But it was the right time. All the newspaper had in it was talking about drinking and partying. And right in the middle of all that was this big section about "here's what happens when you drink." And after that I got letters from Canada and other states and schools wanting me to write kids and stuff, and I've been full throttle since then. Now that happened after the mediation with [young woman's father] but during that time, I was trying to reach out and try to help people. That's been what changed me—what changed everything about me.

The role and relationship that developed with the mediator involved was also quite significant to Eric.

> We met probably every month for almost a year. And during those meetings, we would discuss what I had done in the packet and I really listened to her and put forth a lot of effort in that packet. I kind of saw it as a life and death thing more so than—and she helped me—she helped me—when I speak to the victims, not using the guess words: "and, uh, I guess, maybe." She taught me to be real clear. She taught me to convey what I'm feeling inside so it doesn't come out as something negative. She taught me a lot. By the time we mediated in October of 1999, I was very scared, but I also felt like I had been well prepared for this. And I felt confident. And it felt good to have [Mediator] there at the mediation, because she was—you can't share something like that with somebody and not become bonded with them in some way.

As was previously mentioned, the issue of Eric's sentence was significant to him, and in the mediation session with the girl's father, the sentence came up in a way that, ultimately, felt inappropriate to Eric. This also, then, became the vehicle for more insight for him.

> The only regret I have about the mediation itself was that we ended up on the subject of my time. And I told him—he had indicated that he wanted to change that and help me get out and naturally that sparked a lot of hope in me and it kind of conflicted with what we were trying to do. And I began to ask questions: "What is it you have in mind?" And looking back on it, it almost sounded manipulative, trying to get him to tell me what's he thinking, but it was just grasping out. And I was being honest with him. I really don't—I really wish I could change that, but it's not—what wasn't the time or the place for it.

Eric's insight about this after the fact allowed him to deal with it in a way that felt more honest to him when he later met with the mother of the girl. However, even with this one imperfection in his conduct at the meeting itself, the importance of the event was profound for him: "It's an awesome, powerful thing." He also developed an important connection with the father that was significant for him. The period at which the mediation took place coincided with Eric being placed at a newer institution that was populated with young and violent inmates. Eric referred to it in our meeting as a "gladiator farm." He felt little support or contact with anyone, and kept to himself. In preparing himself for the meeting, he discussed his feelings and how he dealt with his anxiety.

Eric: Over there [at the other institution] it was—you worry about your life half the time. I just poured myself into my work and stuff, around the unit that I had to do. I just concentrated on everything but that [the upcoming meeting]. I knew that I was ready and everything was in my heart. And all the preparation—you can't make yourself be something you're not. You've just got to go in and be yourself. And as soon as we began, it felt like—it was cool. It felt like we had—there was so much that was gained by just that first minute or two, just by sitting down in front of each other. There was so much said without saying anything. We mediated for nine hours and it felt like thirty minutes. I imagine he feels the same, but we were out there a long—it went by just—that whole day went by fast. It just washed over. It was an awesome thing. You get so complacent being in prison and there's so little hope. For the first time—I remember leaving that room and for the first time in a couple of years, I really wanted to go home. And I had learned to cut myself off from the feeling, because it's destructive. Kind of a child-like feeling of wanting to be home. I just felt like, well, I'm finally able to move on with my life and begin to do what I was meant to do in the first place. And you have all these hopes and ambitions and you want to start off on a new foot, and then instead of leaving, you go straight back to the prison. It's kind of a cold shot, but I guess it took probably a week or two before I really was able to—I was really volatile. I felt I'd given everything inside of me to someone and I felt vulnerable.

Regarding the beginning of the meeting itself, Eric stated:

He started, and then just—we talked. We sat down. He explained to me some things. And I did like a little—I wanted him to know that I was there for him, and that I was there to answer his questions. And whatever he needed, that's what I was there for. And from that point forward, we talked about everything from my childhood to his childhood to why I pled guilty at the trial. He was really concerned about that and that seemed to have helped him more than anything, when I took responsibility for it. It helped him more than anything else. And it made me feel good. It made me feel like I didn't get all this time for nothing.

Regarding the identification that Eric made with the father, he stated:

Mr. [Father] is very silent, very calculating. He's a computer engineer. So he's thinks very logically; he has to analyze everything. It's kind of like playing chess with him when you speak with him. But he's just a good dude. He's not—to me he's the epitome of why bad things happen to good people. He's just good people, he's honest, he's upright. He's not a conniving—not that would have made any difference—he's just—just seeing him made me feel sorry for—I really felt for him. Because these were good folks. They're just honest, hard-working people. He didn't drink. We talked about that. I asked him if he'd ever drank and drove before, because most people have that I've run across. People going through high school or college or something, it seems like a lot of people have done it. And I asked him, and he said, "No, I haven't." He said that he'd been tipsy one time in his life but other than that, he never drank, not at all. And that kind of shocked me, you know. He reminded me a lot of my father. My father doesn't drink, doesn't smoke. I think he's probably drank a six pack collectively, totally, since I've been born. And that was then we'd barbecue—he'd take a sip and then. Mr. [Father] reminded me a lot of Dad. He's real simple, a real simple man. I really respect him. I remember thinking during the mediation at some point, I wished we had met under different terms and I could have used him as like a mentor in my life. Maybe a boss, or a coworker, somebody I looked up to that would inspire me to do better.

Eric contrasted the experiences he had with the father and the mother in their individual meetings.

Eric: And her mom is a lot more like I am in the sense that she's more spiritual minded, she's more into the purpose behind all this and everything. She's very forgiving. She's probably one of the most—she's probably one of the few true Christians that I can look at and say, "This is the real deal." She's more what I would esteem to be. She doesn't just talk about it, she walks it. She forgives. And she loves unconditionally. And she told me—and we mediated in the chapel, so that was really conducive—and she said, "Eric, I forgave you. You gave your life to Christ as a result of my daughter dying. That makes it all worthwhile. My daughter died so that you could have life. My daughter was saved. And I know I'll be with her again someday."

She was—man, she was really powerful. She really blew me away. She shared some scriptures with me, and I told her point blank, "Mrs. [Mother], you know, I know that it's easy to want to go hide and be in the Bible as a crutch." And I asked her about that. I said, "If there's ever a point when you just break down and get mad, don't be mad at God. Be mad at me. I'm the one that did this." I told her, "I did this. God didn't do it." So she assured me that she wasn't just hiding. And I was concerned about that. We had a shorter mediation—it was four hours. But everything—we said everything we needed to say. It was pretty cool. [Father] and I prayed together at the end of the mediation, as a closing and so did [Mother] and I.

With Mrs. [Mother], I had a whole lot in common with her. She's been through depression, and she's drank and drove. She was pretty spirited when she was young. And I identified with her a whole lot. And so, we connected. And we talked like two people meeting for the first time. She was real nice.

Interviewer: In the beginning, when they … talked about the meaning of this to them and the impact on their life, what was that like for you?
Eric: It hurt. [Mother] had a photo album of [Daughter] when she was a child. She had her cat in one of the pictures. And other pictures were like prom, and school stuff. And it really hurt, bad, to know that I had taken—it's easy to let people become statistics or numbers or get mad at the system or whatever, but it was something that I deal with every day. Even now. And it really hurt. It kind of took my breath away to hear. But I had questions, too. I wanted to know when [Daughter's] birthday was and what she liked to do in life and what she was about.
Eric also felt that there was significance in letting the parents know him as a person.
Eric: Well, it's just like they have their idea of what kind of person I was and that's painted to them by the district attorney and it's all bad. And then when they meet me they realize that this is a real human being. It was important for both of us to realize that. And I told her, I told Mrs. [Mother], "Mrs. [Mother], you know I didn't mean to do it." I won't say it was an accident, because it could have been avoided. But I told her, "I didn't mean to do it. And I'm sorry. And if there is a way, or anything I could do, I would go back right now and change it. I'd trade places with them." And she said, "Eric, I wouldn't. There's been more good come out of this than I would have ever imagined." And man, that's really a strong thing for a mother to say when she's lost her daughter. To not wish for her daughter to be back. And even now, even today, I feel like I would do anything in the world to change it. Those people have been hurt beyond belief. It's one thing to be self-destructive, but then when you start involving other people, it's hard. I never intended to hurt anyone. I had a lot of friends. I was never in any fights or anything. I was real outgoing and everything. And I just can't imagine myself ever doing it to someone. It's kind of hard [tears].
Interviewer: How did you feel immediately after both of these meetings?
Eric: Like a giant. Like the earth had been lifted off my back. Man, it was an awesome feeling. I felt free, I really did. I felt like I was able to move on with my life. And might have a chance. It really helped me a lot.

… I've grown up a lot. I was nineteen when it happened and in my head, I was probably a thirteen-year-old. And I've had to grow up in this place a little bit. I've made a lot of progress. I can look back and see my progress. And I hope they can see that too. You know, one thing is I don't—a lot of guys in here want to get back out, and they miss home and they want to get back to their life. But me, I'm not looking for that because I didn't enjoy—I don't want that life any more.

… Well, for me, doing time is the easy part. What I go to sleep with at night is another issue. When me and Mr. [Father] met, I knew in my heart that for him to get anything, I had to give it to him. And for me to get anything, I had to give him everything. I had to give him my all and not hold anything back, and just offer my whole self, and say, "Here I am, Mr. [Father]." And I felt like that would be the only way that this would be able to be a genuine and positive thing. You now, I work in the chapel and I see a lot of guys that are in here for like child molesting and stuff like that, about homosexuality, and stuff that I don't understand. And I see a lot of guys that they proclaim themselves to be "I'm a good Christian" and this and that. And then I live with them, so they're not like that all the time, when I see them on the block.

And I explained this to Mrs. [Mother] and Mr. [Father], too, is that you've got jailhouse religion. And it's bad; there's a lot of it. Me, I don't claim to be anything special. I'm just trying to do the right thing and I believe that that's how God wants me to be is just to try to do the right thing and try to look to him for the answers, and man, 'cause I know what I'm capable of doing is not good. The best that I could do for myself is kill two teenagers and be a drunk. That's the best I could do. Obviously, I couldn't do any better or I would have done it. So anything that I have, I don't take credit for it, I don't ask for anything.

I asked Eric how he felt the victims of the accident live with him and his feelings about them, and if he felt they had anything in common with him.

Eric: I feel pretty close to her [the girl], like I knew her, in my heart. I feel like—you know, her spirit still lives on and I try to give [Boy] and [Girl] both credit. Anytime I'm able to do something to help somebody else. It's not me that's doing it, because me was out there drinking. They're the ones that changed my life, and so they're the ones that are changing other people's lives through me. And at first, I felt like was—for the first couple of years, I was a monster, and then I brutally, horribly did this. And I was a real piece of crap. And I still feel like that sometimes. But I know that what I did and who I am are two different things. I have to distinguish them. And I know that I didn't do it on purpose. Nevertheless, I feel bad for what happened to her. It's kind of a hard question. I believe that she's in heaven and I believe her spirit lives on, and I'll see her again when I die. She was a good girl, really smart, really loved animals. A real feisty personality. She was good people.

Well, we were all the same age. [Boy] smoked pot and partied too. His dad's—they're wealthy. And he was driving that Volkswagen and he was kind of like a hippie, kind of stoner type. Listened to hard rock, like I did. We had a lot in common. In fact, people have told me before, and the parents have never told me this, but my friends have told me that it could have just as easily been the other way around. Because [Boy] was a lot like me. [Girl] was a little bit younger. I guess she was seventeen. She was outgoing. Her mother uses the word "spirited" a lot, and I think that means kind of—she got in trouble a little bit. I think when people die and all the victims that I've been around, they always make it out to be like their child was something next to saintly, perfect in every way. Take away the human aspect of people and replace it—if you were to ask them, "Did your daughter or son ever get in trouble." "Oh, no. They were perfect. They never wet their diaper. They never did … ." I mean, come on, they were human, they were kids. We were all kids and I think I would have gotten along really well with [Boy] and [Girl]. I was a little far out there, though. I'd been—I don't think either one of them had done hard drugs like I had done. But I think they were just fun-loving kids. They weren't malicious. They weren't bullies. They were just good folks.

I have a lot of love for them both, in my heart. I only know them from what they were but I was the last one to see them, and it's a strange feeling, but I have a lot of love for them in my heart. I can't explain why. I just know that it's there. They're just like my brother and sister. If anybody were to say anything bad about them, I would try to stick up for them. I'm real protective of that. It's not a strange feeling, except in the sense that I'm the reason why they're not here anymore, and the reason why they're dead.

I mean, I was there. And such a traumatic event. And such a life-changing thing.

I asked Eric to discuss his theory of change in people:

Eric: The only way to change is to step forward, own up, take responsibility for my actions and to be a man about it, and say, "Yes, I did that." Not just use that as a ploy but to take the punishment and to make the best of it—to pick up and do the best you can from that point forward. And not until you face it and take a hold of it and own up for what I had done could I ever begin to change. Accountability is a major thing. And then from there, I had a real desire to make amends and to apologize and stuff. And rather than just say "I'm sorry,"—at the end of the mediation, we have an affirmation agreement, and there are things that I do—I mean, I believe actions speak louder than words. I live on that principle. If I'm a Christian, then I shouldn't have to tell you. It's going to be evident through the way I live my life. And if I've changed, for me to say I've changed is—that negates it anyways. That's just like saying you haven't changed. If I've changed, then it'll be evident. But in order for things to change is to take responsibility and say, "Yeah, I did this." And take all the grief and guilt that comes with it and begin to move forward.

And spiritually speaking, I believe in forgiveness and I believe that God wants me to be forgiving of other people. And I've been forgiven for so much. And Mrs. [Mother] said it, "And I forgive you." Well, I can't just take that and not do something with it. For me, in my daily—just—somebody—I get mad at the smallest things. Guys cutting line or be cussing or cutting up and talking about this and that. And I have to be forgiving. I have to take that and use it as an example, and lead my life that way. She solidified that, by being so forgiving. She showed me that God's forgiven me, she's forgiven me. Who am I not to forgive somebody or things.

But see, the attitude change has to come before the mediation begins. When they come to you and ask you, "do you want to be involved with this," you really don't know what you're getting into. If a person can go through the preparation packet and has a desire in their heart to make amends, the mediation is that—it's the medium, it's the vehicle by which that occurs. It's like that's the tools, that's how it's done. A lot of guys, they sit around and say, "I really want to make amends, and I'd love to speak with the guy's family that I killed" or whatever, and they never are able to actually do something tangible with that. And that's what mediation is for me. I've had a lot of guys asking me how can they get involved. And I tell them, you really can't. You can write them and be a surrogate maybe, but it's got to be initiated by the victim.

Aside of hearing about their life before I came along, the hardest part was anticipation. And in the preparation, I think some of the hard parts were looking at myself and seeing something so easily—I can see it plain as day now, and they hindsight's 20/20 and I think, man, this all could have been avoided if I would have just talked to somebody. Because obviously if I would have just—instead of go and try to solve it myself, try to be closed up about it, I would have found somebody that could have showed me—and all of this could have been avoided. The hard part is taking that cold hard look at yourself, and realizing despite of everything, you still want to move forward.

I can't really—I have a hard time—if a man had like broken into my house and I shot him, that would have been a conscious decision that I made. Or if a man had disrespected me or I would have beat him or anything like that would have happened, it would have been a decision that I made to get revenge or self-defense or whatever. And I don't know if I could have lived with that any—I think being that it was something that I didn't intend to do, my conscience seems like it weighs heavier than these guys that have just killed somebody because—you know, there's a lot of guys in here, if somebody breaks into their house, they shoot them, and then they're in prison. And they say, "Well, you know what? I'd do it again." Or say, "Well, the guy pulled a knife on me. I'd shoot him again if I could." For me, I think it's harder when I didn't intend to do it and they were just innocent folks, and if I had chosen to do it on purpose—and I told [Mediator] that one time. I told her that there's a difference between murder and killing someone. So, I can't imagine how it would be for any other type of mediation, but in this case, I had a strong desire to make amends. I think a man would have to really—I think it would take a lot for him to want to do the mediation if he had done something like this on purpose. It would take a lot more.

I saw videos of a mediation of a man that raped this woman's daughter, and killed her and dumped her in a creek. To face a victim like that after I had done something like that, I just can't imagine.

If you keep doing the same thing, you keep getting the same results. You're not going to change. And it hurts. Hell, yeah, it hurts. You've got to—it's like when you get hurt really bad. I got hit with a piece of pipe one time and it broke my lip open. And there's a scar there now, but it doesn't hurt any more, you know. It's not—I have the reminder of it. And I see the mediation a lot the same. It hurt a lot, it was painful. But I was able to do a lot of healing. And now there's a scar there, and I remember it, but I feel a lot different.

At the end of our lengthy interview, I asked Eric if there is anything he could think of that we had not touched on, or that he would like to add. In response to this, he gave me an incredible summation of the meaning to him of the process. He further remarkably speaks to the significance of the overall system that is the subject of this investigation:

Eric: Well, it changed my life. I can't really think of anything—the important thing about it from the inmate's side is the preparation. However much an inmate puts into it is what they're going to get out of it. And being accountable and being honest and taking responsibility for your crime, those are like prerequisites. You ask a lot of the guys in here, "Are you innocent?" Hell, yeah, I didn't do it, we're all innocent. But I'm not. I guess I can stand with maybe a handful of other guys like that. I can't really think of anything.

Yeah, there is one thing. Being in here, a lot of guys have a lot of animosity towards the system, and they're mad at the system, but when I started the mediation, it wasn't a system I was being held accountable to, it was a human being, a person that I'd made myself [accountable] to. And being held accountable to a system and getting mad at the state for giving you all this time is one thing, but when you're held accountable to a person, that's a whole other feeling. That is a major important thing about mediation, is that there's an actual person on the other end of the sentence that you're doing time for—not a machine. And that is important. It's very important to be held accountable to a person, and to realize that even when you get out of here, that person is still there. And this system is not why you're here. I'm the reason why I'm here, and I'm held accountable to [Mother], as a whole 'nother world from "man, you know, you sorry bastards, you gave me all this time for something I didn't even mean to do." That's a very real feeling sometimes. It's helpful. It's helpful when a person gets out, how they live their life after they get back. I think it's a key to reducing why so many people come back so much. You know how it is in Chicago … they came back in months. There's something missing. In the restoration packet, it explains how American Indian tribes were—they held a counsel and if you offended somebody, they held a counsel and you were accountable to a person, not a court system. And to me, that seems like the right way to live life. And I feel like mediation should be offered to people—maybe juvenile people, misdemeanor—it would be hard to offer that as some sort of—maybe a combination with punishment, but I think it should be offered.

As I was preparing to leave and packing up my materials, I told Eric that he could reach me if he had any questions or problems, and I asked if it would be alright with him, if a question came to me, if I contacted him again. Eric said "Yes," laughed, and said, "You know where I'm at."

The next day, I interviewed the mediator that worked with Eric and the mother and the father of the dead girl, preparing them for their meetings.

She gave me the history of how she first got involved in the case and the early history of the case.

Mediator: They were assigned to me. Eric was my very first case. Eric and [Father] were my very first case. And I got it because he was still in the county jail here and it was going to be real easy for me to run out—and actually, that one was referred—[Supervisor] and I had been out and done an in-service for the counselors out there, and three days later, one of them called and said, "I think I've got somebody for you here." And I said, "Well, he can't ask for it, the victim has to." And the next day, the victim called us. And that one took a while. Eric is an alcoholic. At nineteen, he was almost wet-brain alcoholic. When I went to meet him, he was circling the airport, but his landing wheels were not down. And when they moved him to [the intake institution], he wrote me a letter—or I went to see him, and he said, "I just can't do this right now. I have to get myself squared away here." And I backed right off. I am not going to push them; if they say they don't want to do it, I'm going to honor that.

About a year later, he wrote a letter saying, "OK, I'm ready to start again." And I ran right down there. He was a different kid. And entirely different—I mean, I am a licensed drug and alcohol counselor, and that kid had post-acute withdrawal syndrome like I have never seen before in somebody that young that wasn't a huffer [abuse of an inhalant, such as glue sniffing].

… I have met some heroin addicts that are that young, but rarely do I stumble across an alcoholic that's that kind of alcoholic, that far down the—that's that young. And it was a whole different kid that I met—and he wanted—he had done some of the paperwork, like the grief inventory and this, that, and the other. And he wanted to do it again, so he could compare to see what the difference was for himself. This is the kind of guy Eric is. He's always questioning everything. And working with him was so easy. … This particular kid has taken responsibility for his actions, with the exception of right there at the scene, where he said, "Are you the one that hit me?" He has taken responsibility for his actions. He fired his attorneys because they wouldn't plead him guilty. He pretty much served himself up on a platter, and got the sentence he got as a result. And while he would like very desperately to have a sentence reduction, which is not part of what I'm willing to help him do, he's still—we've mediated with Eric now twice, first with [Father] and then with [Mother]. And Eric has said both times, "If this is where you want me to be, then I'm happy to stay there." The [parents] would both probably go for the sentence reduction, but the other child's parents are never going to go for the sentence reduction. And Eric has to just get with the fact that he's going to be in there for at least twenty years.

Regarding her sense of working with the parents, the mediator reported to me:

Mediator: [Father] and [Mother] are both Christian. They have both forgiven Eric. [Mother], during the meeting, said, "I forgave you very early on." Interestingly enough, it wasn't until about three months before we actually mediated that [Mother]—I was speaking to her one night—and she said, "You know, I'm finally mourning [Daughter]. I didn't have the time to do that before. I had two other children, I had a husband what was leaving me. I had to go out and get two jobs so that I could support the two remaining children that I had. I'm struggling just to keep my head above water and a roof over our heads. And it wasn't until I really started doing the preparation work that directly involved [Daughter] that I was able to mourn her."

Regarding the actual mediation meetings, the mediator reported:

Eric and [Father] is nine butt-numbing hours in all. Who ever thought that two guys would find nine hours to talk—and it was so funny. Eric said, when we were doing the notary thing, he says, "Now, I'm not going to have to sit through nine hours of debriefing again, am I?" I said, "That's up to you, Eric." And [Mother] and Eric's is closer to four. A lot shorter. And it was just really interesting, because she's not angry at him. And I asked her, "[Mother], haven't you ever been angry? I mean, aren't you pissed? Your daughter was killed! I would be outraged." She said, "You know, I don't think so. I've never been angry. [Daughter's] gone home." I believe that her faith—do I believe she hides out in her faith? Oh, yeah. But I think—like sometimes drugs and alcohol keep people alive—I think faith can keep them alive too. Can it be a crutch? Yeah. As crutches go, you know, as long as you're not trying to force it down everybody else's throat and doing weird things to your kids because of it, it's your faith. And I think her whole life is faith-based. That's just how it is. And she gave this one to God when it happened. She was able to find two places in her journals where she might have been a little miffed. And I use the word miffed as opposed to pissed.

So, working with her was different for me than working even with [Father], who was able to talk about his anger. And he did have some anger. Eric's anger is all pointed at himself. I think he may be a little miffed at the way his trial turned out. I think he's probably very upset with the [boy's family], but he doesn't talk about it that way. I mean, he really has said, "this is what they must have needed for me to do to make up for"—Eric's biggest problem—I think his biggest problem will be self-guilt—guilting himself to death.

I asked the mediator her view of the period of the mediation between Eric and the father where the issue of the sentence reduction came up, and Eric was tempted by this possibility.

Mediator: Oh, yeah. And [Father] didn't have any trouble with that at all. He couldn't understand why I thought Eric was being manipulative at the end there. And I was. And were I in his place, I would have done the same thing. And I let it go on. I mean, I finally stopped it. And my deal is, it's not my work, it's theirs. I just didn't want—when it began to feel like [Father] was getting his back to a wall, it was time for me to stop it. [Father] has not done a damn thing about that sentence reduction, and he's not going to. He wouldn't even consider it unless the [boy's family] considered it first, and he knows there's no sense in doing it unless the [boy's family] consider it first. And he did not do it with [Mother].

This mediator has held a variety of positions related to counseling and mental health/chemical dependency treatment. She is clear that her role as a mediator in these cases is different, but as an interview subject, she brought a therapeutic frame to the process that included knowledge of the use of self and transference and countertransference themes.

We discussed the sentence that Eric got for these deaths, which exceeds guidelines for a case such as this. (For example, in another criminal vehicular homicide case interviewed for this project a fourteen-month sentence was imposed.)

> And she [the mother] did—she said, "I don't think you should be in here." She said, "If I could take you home with me, I would." And she would. She's got three kids not her own living in that house.
>
> My problem with Eric's sentence: Does he deserve to do prison—I mean, he did a crime, he needs the time. And I have no problem with that. I mean, every time I see Eric I think of my own son, my youngest son, who is so much like Eric. And I don't know which is going to be worse, if he kills somebody else or if he kills himself. And it just—I vacillate between having hope because I see what Eric's done—and total fear. And that's as much personal stuff as I can even let get in there.
>
> But do I think he deserves two stacked forty sentences? If you look at the other sentences that [his home] County hands out for the same thing, it is not equitable … [his home] County, two years later, a [local] High School student, … that this kid, drunk driving, killed a young lady, she was a nurse. And they agonized over was he going to get time or not. The jury agonized was he going to get time or not. They finally gave him two or three years. There was a young lady who hit a cop while he was directing traffic, and killed him. She finally got five years, and it took them seven or eight years to sentence her. Recently they gave somebody twenty years. Recently the law changed, too.

And I feel the same way about Eric's sentence. Do I think that his life is being wasted? To an extent, yes. To another extent, no. He is doing work where he is. I think he helps a lot of people in there. I think that he's the kind of person that they would come to for help. And he's smart enough to say, "This is what you need to do; this is what you need to do." He's working for the chaplain—what a place for Eric! [Mother's] mediation was the most laid-back mediation I have ever been to, as a mediator or as a camera—or whatever. We did it in the chapel. There was no officer. One would come in every once in a while, just to check, for count that he was there. There was no running Eric back, strip-searching him, bringing him back. There was none of that. And it was a very spiritual mediation. It really was. And I wish they all had that flavor.

DISCUSSION

My interview with Eric followed my interview with Danny by only a few days. It was incredible to have, in such succession, two such articulate informants.

Eric seemed able to internalize the image of his victims and had developed a highly personal relationship with both. As he expressed so eloquently in his narrative, he has also made an evolutionary step from blaming the "system" for his situation to coming to an internal acceptance of his responsibility for his actions, and inner peace with the consequences. At the same time, this may well be due to what appears to be the reality of the eventual time that Eric will spend in prison, and his work at accepting that reality philosophically.

In Eric's process, his first epiphany came because of the accident, and his first conscious awareness of its impact. This related to his internalization of his depression about the abortion that his girlfriend chose, and his acting out of this depression in his characteristic manner—drinking. There was, then, little effort needed for him to connect his depression with his responsibility for the deaths of these two young people. He pleads guilty. The next major step was finding himself in the "gladiator farm" and the crisis that this surely precipitated, no doubt with a return of his depression in full. His discovery of religion and AA during this time was significant. It was then that he also contacted the mediator to tell her that he was ready to proceed with the meeting.

Eric verbalizes a key component of the entire restorative justice philosophy in his statement, "So much is gained by just that first minute or two, just by sitting down in front of each other. ...so much is said without saying anything."

Also significant is the mediator's representation of the victim's mother, stating that, because of the mediation, she could proceed with her grief work for her daughter.

Perhaps the most profound statement from my interview with Eric came at the end, following up on a comment he had made early in the interview, "It's easy to let people become statistics or numbers or get mad at the system or whatever, but it was something that I deal with every day."

When he reports to me that "a lot of guys" have "animosity towards the system" based on the sentence they receive, he is speaking to the heart of the restorative justice model. He makes a clear distinction, which is important considering he did receive an admittedly excessive sentence for his crime given sentencing standards, between his anger at the system, feeling victimized by the court, and being held accountable to "a person." It is one thing, as he states, to be angry at the "system" for the sentence received, and quite another to be sitting across the table "looking into the eyes of the parent whose child you killed" and being held accountable to another human being.

Chapter 8

Pilot Study Cases

The following three cases are representative of cases that were seen in the pilot study. During the initial pilot study visit, two years prior to the final project interviews, I saw only the offenders.

Of the eight cases I interviewed in this earlier project, part of another research effort, I selected these three cases as representative, and interviewed the victims that had been involved in these cases as well as the mediators that facilitated the meetings. This gave me the opportunity to not only be familiar with the cases, but also to see and interview the offenders twice with a two-year time span between meetings.

These cases are interesting given the overall elapsed time between the crime and the mediation. Louis' case (Case 2), presented here, was the first victim/offender mediation dialogue (VMOD) to take place in the state in which it occurred, and was, when the first meeting happened, facilitated by HBO that was doing a story on restorative justice mediations. This first meeting was facilitated by a journalist/correspondent. Because of this, the state service, which was just beginning, was asked by the victim to facilitate another meeting that would not be as "produced" as the first; so the two met again.

Thus, many years have passed since the first meetings, giving all the parties a chance to reflect on the lasting meaning of the event to their lives. It also gives me a chance to see the offender and monitor his progress and the staying power of the experience. Thus, it is possible to ascertain, from these players, how the experience has been generalized, how it was "metabolized" over time, and its endurance in their sense of their own meaning. It will also be possible to see how the meetings organized and facilitated personal changes. This can not only be seen in the interviews themselves, but in the daily life evidence of the offender through his prison life (infractions and disciplinary actions) and plans (educational or vocational preparations) as well.

CASE 1: LESTER

I had been scheduled to interview Lester the second time after several interviews with other offenders. I was informed that Lester, at the last minute, had decided not to be interviewed. The mediator involved felt that this was likely a decision of the prison administration, feeling that Lester had received too much notoriety because of his involvement with the program. The prior year, Lester had been granted permission to appear with Anna Marie (his victim's mother) in a public forum discussing their process together.

Lester had also been moved to a new institution recently, and it was felt, by some, that this was also intended to isolate him from his progress to date and move him out of the "limelight."

Lester's case history reads like a pandect of the late adolescence of many African American males who end up in the legal system in the United States.

By the age of sixteen, Lester had dropped or been kicked out of his high school. His mother, already overwhelmed by her own life's demands and Lester's other siblings, and pregnant again, kicked him out of the home, or he simply left. Lester began living on the streets, sleeping at the homes of friends and other acquaintances, and making his way by engaging in petty crimes and drug sales.

By the age of seventeen, Lester had begun to develop a persuasive criminal record in the juvenile system, and had been arrested and released many times. He had two felony charges pending, and had spent a fair amount of time in jail already. Over this period, the seriousness of his offences began to increase, and with a few of his old high school friends, he began to involve himself in burglary.

Lester: I was … no way out, you know what I mean. I'm on the streets, my mother she's pregnant … it's just like you know, come back to prison or stay on the streets, you know. If any kids they ever experience the street they know what I'm talking about, you know, you can't survive on the streets, you gotta' do something, if it's crime you got to do crime, if its anything illegal, you got to do illegal. You ain't just gonna sleep on the streets. So, what I did I was selling drugs right before this crime—you know what I'm saying? And, like burglary—soon I got out [of a brief incarceration] I do two burglaries.

The other crime that Lester and his friends enjoyed was to "jump" people's cars by posing as valets at hotels, taking a tip and then joy-riding in the car until they abandoned it.

During this period, Lester was staying with a friend, and trying to pay the friend's mother as much money as he could for staying there. He paid her because he didn't want to "disrespect" her, and be taking advantage of her kindness, so he was able, through his drug sales, to give her $50 from time to time. He felt that she knew where he was getting the money, and she told him, "I'll help you, but just be careful."

Lester contacted his lawyer who told him that there was a warrant out for his arrest. Lester had failed to make a scheduled court appearance. The lawyer suggested that Lester just stay indoors until he had a chance to meet with the judge and get the warrant dropped. Lester told his lawyer that he could not do more jail time. He decided to try to scrape together enough money to leave the area. Lester stated that this was his lawyer's suggestion as well.

Two days later, in one of the burglaries, Lester and his friend found a pistol, and Lester took the weapon away from a younger companion, saying that he did this to keep this young man from further trouble, since he was still in school.

Lester: … but like two days later this little old Mexican guy, we broke in the house right down the road about two blocks down the road [there] was a TV, a color TV, and a portable TV and I took it. Now I got about two streets over he's behind me, he says, "Say man, turn around. I got somethin' for ya." I turn around and he's holdin' up a case. It was a .38 with three shells in it. He said, "This is mine, man"—you know. I just looked at him and said, "Man, you too young for that man."—He said, "What you wanna do man, you wanna go rob somebody?" I said, "Dang, I don't know, what can I do" You know what I'm sayin'. So, I went and sold the TV for like $100, right. You know. I took the gun out his hand, you know what I'm sayin', and he jumped up and down and cried and said, "You can't take that, it's mine, I found it." And he just went off you know… I say, don't you worry about no guns. You got a family, you got a mother, you got a home, big nice home. I said, "Man, I ain't got nothin'." I said, "don't mess your life up like this, don't get involved in this here."

So, Lester and his friend went over to try to "jump" a car, but someone became suspicious, so they went home. The next day, Lester continued to be disturbed by the prospect of going back to jail.

Lester: I'm just walkin' around my neighborhood with this .38 special and I'm just walkin' around the neighborhood thinkin'—I don't want to go back to jail, I just got out—I don't want to go back to jail, you know what I'm sayin'?

Lester decided, as he was walking around the neighborhood, that what he needed to do was to steal a car and make his escape to another town, to avoid being caught and going back to jail.

Lester went downtown and went into a video arcade in search of someone to sell some drugs to. It is there that he saw Anna Marie's son, Bob, who was playing a video game. Lester wasn't sure if Bob would be a good customer for drugs or if he might be someone whose car he could steal.

Lester: I asked him, "Say man, can I get a ride from you, I need a ride over here." You know what I'm sayin'. And he turn around and he said, "Yeah man—just let me finish playing this video game. I'll give you a ride, it's nothin, you know, don't worry about it." So, he finished playing the video game and he turned around and told me, "C'mon man," you know what I'm sayin' and I turn around and no one was lookin' and I go between two video games and I pulled out my gun and I put three shells in and picked it back up and put it back in my waist band, you know under my shirt.

Lester told Bob that his mom was sick and he had to get home to be with her. They got into Bob's car, and Lester gave him directions back to his neighborhood. Bob must have become suspicious, however, as he eventually became impatient with the convoluted course he was following and told Lester he had to get going. Lester said that he was close now, and to just take him to the end of the street, and he would get out. Lester directed Bob to the end of a street in a housing complex.

Lester reported, in the interview, that he had two or three joints with him, and that he and Bob shared them on the car ride. Lester attempted to get Bob to step out of the car, and told him to "chill out" for a minute while he went into one of the apartments to get some more drugs. Lester thought that he could entice Bob out of the car, lure him up a stairwell, produce the gun, and steal his car, leaving him in the project.

Bob, however, became nervous, and refused, saying, "I thought you said your mom was sick. I have to go. I said I would pick up my girlfriend at 11:00."

Lester was aware that the car was still in gear, and that Bob had his foot on the brake. He then attempted to get Bob to turn the motor off, as he knew it would be difficult to physically get Bob out of the driver's seat.

Bob demanded that Lester get out of the car, and Lester demanded that Bob cut the motor and wait for him while he went to get more drugs. At this point, Lester had retrieved the .38 from his waistband, and he stated that he saw Bob reach down to the side of his seat. Thinking that Bob was going for a "knife or a pistol," Lester shot Bob twice with the .38. "It just happened so fast, man." After being shot, Bob hit the gas and the car accelerated into a brick wall.

Lester: And when he go into the brick wall, I'm still in the car. It happened so fast, when I hit it, BANG, when I regained consciousness, I pushed the door open, I seen him and he was gunnin' the car [making noise of revving the engine in a car]. I rolled outta the car. I run down twenty or thirty yards, I run down the street like, and people start runnin' out everywhere, people just run out of apartments everywhere, "What's going on. . ." Hollering [imitates the people hollering].

I'm lookin'. I'm trying to hide 'cause I'm the one that shot this dude—and I know that if you shoot in these apartments it's gonna sound it's going to echo real, real loud.

So, I got away from the crime scene for about, I eventually got a ride from that area, you know, the police is surrounded the area maybe by about three minutes, police had that whole area surrounded. But I still got away from the scene of the crime.

And my mother just moved from her friends to [a new community]. Probably the same time I commit these crimes my mother had just finally got back on her feet. Had just got a house. But it was too late—I had already committed this crime, you know what I'm sayin'?

While running and hiding in the area, Lester took off his jacket, wrapped the .38 in it, and threw the bundle into a storm drain. Then, Lester moved back to live with his mother, and while she knew that he had been in trouble and had a warrant out for his arrest, he did not tell her of his recent crime.

Lester: But I just wasn't man enough to tell her, "Mom, I just shot somebody." You know what I'm sayin'. I don't know if he died, I don't know nothin', but I'm trying to get out of [State], you know what I'm sayin'?

Lester stayed with his mom for three days. At dawn, on the third day, the police kicked the door in and arrested Lester and his brother, who was asleep in another room. Lester and his brother were still in bed, and his mother was coming back from a trip to the store. They told his mother that they were arresting Lester, and read him his rights.

Lester: So, the minute I went into jail—I was standing up in an empty interrogation room and, one was a homicide officer walked up and down and throw a big plastic white bag to me. BOOM! A .38 pistol and this black leather jacket and I kept tryin' to deny that I murdered, that I shot this guy, but when they threw that big plastic in there, they said, "Who you think they're gonna believe?" You know, the jury.

You know what I'm sayin'? "Do you think they're going to believe you with all of this evidence in front of you? A gun with your hand prints on it, and your jacket. Do you think you're gonna walk up outta here? I'll give you a lie detector test right now, if you tell me you didn't do it."

And at the time, I still denied that I had shot the kid.

So, he did give me a lie detector test, with all these tapes on my fingers and my heart and stuff, and I failed it.

Lester was immediately charged. He felt that someone from the neighborhood must have seen him stuff his jacket in the storm drain, and pointed it out to the police.

The next day, his mother, sister, and brother visited him. His mother brought in a newspaper article detailing how a seventeen-year-old had been arrested in the murder of a twenty-one-year-old university student. Lester reported that his brother cried through the entire visit, unable to believe that Lester would be involved in a murder.

Lester was angry with his brother, because he had called him after the murder and told him about the crime, asking him to help him get out of the state. The brother refused, angry that Lester would involve himself in such a crime. Lester, angrily, said to his brother, "Man, it's too late to cry. It's just probably my whole life is over with. You come and got me like I asked you; I wouldn't be here right now. I don't know where I'd be, but I wouldn't be locked up here, I guarantee you."

Lester: "I asked you to come, I'd been gone." And he looked at me, kept lookin' like, he just couldn't say nothing, he just held his head down and went crying, you know, even to this day, man, that's been fourteen years man, I mean, right now, that's been fourteen years, even to this day that dude, my oldest brother, for fourteen years he come visit me … he gots a guilty conscious … he knows that I wouldn't have been locked up for this. So, he's kind of regretful, kinda remorseful about that.

While awaiting trial, Lester continued to deny guilt or responsibility for the act. He felt that, even with the evidence against him, he might luck out and get a light sentence, due to his youth.

What Lester soon became aware of was that Anna Marie, Bob's mother, had begun to lobby the county attorney to seek the death penalty in the crime. She was making a concerted effort, with a great deal of public awareness, to see that "justice was done," and avenge the death of her son.

Lester remained quite worried about this effort. It helped Lester, to some extent, when another, more experienced inmate informed him that given the nature of his crime, the state could not charge him with capital murder since he hadn't stolen anything from the victim. Instead, Lester plea-bargained for a sentence of forty years, and he accepted that.

Lester: I said, "I'm gonna take it man, I wanna go around and get this over with." So, the victim's mother, there wasn't nothin' else she could do … she was at the courtroom, she wouldn't even leave, she was so, she was so mad and so angry about me takin' her child away, which I don't, I don't disagree with that, I got no problem with that. What she did was try everything to try and get my life snatched up on me, but like I said, I don't blame her. Somebody kills my child and years past I wouldn't feel too much different … But she never said a word, she just looked at me with hate in her eyes the entire time, like she was going to go off, but she never, she never said a word to me.

The first number of years that Lester was in prison he attempted to go to school and get some vocational training as well. He had, however, a difficult time with this attempt. He had several minor, and not so minor, infractions of prison rules, which kept him at a low classification, and interfered with his efforts. Also, he was easily provoked by other inmates, and was frequently involved in fights, resulting in being stabbed on one or two occasions. On each of these infractions, he would lose his classification, and would be relegated to his cell, with no privileges, for up to a year.

Two graduate students at a local university, who were researching crime and sentencing, approached Lester. As part of this project, they proposed that they videotape an interview with him that they would show to Anna Marie, and then videotape an interview with her, that they would show to Lester. Lester agreed to be a part of this project.

What Lester remembered from Anna Marie's videotape was that she was "really pissed off." "And she just explained how she felt, just feelings mostly. Ms. [Mother] is real, real emotional."

Lester also remembered the story she told on the videotaped interview of having the coroner call to tell her that they thought her son had been killed. She said she could not believe that, but added that her son had a birthmark on his ankle. The coroner put the phone down, and Anna Marie heard his footsteps walk over to her son, look, and heard his footsteps return to the phone, where he blandly told her that he had located the birthmark.

Lester said, with this, Anna Marie "just went off, you know what I'm sayin'? She almost lost it. You know, it's not real easy, I seen it [the tape], it was just real emotional …"

At this point, coincidentally, Lester was also approached by the state mediation service, which had been approached by Anna Marie to see if Lester would agree to mediation.

The preparation took many months.

Lester: It was a long process. It took practically seven months … Preparation, yeah. Healing process. And it was like therapy. And [Mediator] showed me films where he'd been in prison and other victims would sit down with their offenders … I seen several videos of other people sit down across from their offenders and

I seen how they showed anger and frustration and let out their emotions, and it got me kind of prepared for mine, you know what I'm sayin'?

I tried to determine, in my first interview with Lester, what would account for his willingness to do this. I wondered what benefits he thought he would achieve by participating. He remembered being asked by one of the graduate students if he would ever consider sitting down, face-to-face, with the victim's mother. He said, at the time, that he would not consider it, because he did not think it would do anyone any good.

He said, "No, I don't have nothin' to say to the victim's mother, nothin'. All I want to do is my time and get out of here. I'm ready to go home, that's all I want." The graduate student said to Lester, "Well, you could at least tell her that you're sorry for it." Lester responded, "Man, tell her I'm sorry!? That's not gonna change what happened to her child! That's not going to bring him back, that ain't gonna change nothin'." The student said, "Well, I know it won't bring him back, but you could at least be remorseful for what you did." I said, "Well, you know, I'm remorseful for what I did. I mean, I wished I never had done it and I would never do all this time." The student suggested that he could express his feelings to the mother and that she "might forgive you, you never know."

At the time, although he was agreeing to be involved with these students, he still saw himself as an angry person: "I was still angry at the time. I just wanted to go home. I'd been locked up practically all of my life. I didn't want to be bothered with it." But the suggestion stayed with Lester. He began thinking about Anna Marie every day: "If this lady dies tonight in her sleep, she would benefit from this here, these questions she has." It felt to Lester that the thought had "completely taken over my mind."

Lester: Well, there's really no benefits—I didn't—I feel it was me—I hurt her just as much as I hurt myself because I never have a chance to go out and be with my family you know what I'm saying? But the only thing between me and him is she can't see him no more, my mother can still see me—I've grown to learn that—that's the only thing different his mother will never see him or talk to him again—my mother will probably never see me walk the streets again even today because my mother she might die—that's the only thing I … my suffering—but benefits it's to me—there's no benefits you know what I'm sayin' and the least—the only thing I could give that woman [Anna Marie] is answers to why her son was murdered—she thought for years and years it was a hate crime … there's a lot of questions, mysteries that was hauntin' her all these years …

Lester, when approached, was also quite concerned about what might happen when the two were face-to-face. He remembered her stares, while in the courtroom, and her anger from the videotaped interview he had seen. He asked the mediator about this.

Lester: Yeah, I also got a personal feeling of judgment and how she might take actions too and might just go off on anything—but then [Mediator] over and over again, he was constantly saying, "Man, I been doin' this quite a while, and so far, we never had no one attack their victim, I mean offender." You know what I'm sayin', so he just put it in my hands …"I can assure you she won't go off and I can assure you that I will be right there just in case something was to happen—so give me, give me a chance to follow up on my procedure—I promise you even if she does go off it won't be nothin' violent it's not like she's gonna kill you or stab you, because she's gotta go through a routine preparation—just like you do."

Lester and Anna Marie finally met. It had been almost fourteen years since Bob's murder. The meeting did not proceed without initial problems. When Lester came into the room, as the mediator was setting it up, he saw the video equipment and operators, and got scared.

Lester: I ain't gonna do it, you know what I'm sayin'. It messed him up [the mediator]. He begged me like an hour straight. Blah, blah, blah [laughs]. "Man, I got all this stuff here …," and I said, "Man, you don't need all this television and all this shit … I ain't never seen these people, I ain't gonna stand in front of all these people, I ain't gonna do it" and he said, "Man, just do it for her man, you know, that's all she asks you, just give it a chance."

In Lester's view, the thing that was the most helpful to Anna Marie was to learn that the act was, in fact, a senseless act of violence that was a result of Bob being in the wrong place at the wrong time. She had feared that Lester had specifically chosen Bob, or that Bob had been singled out for some reason. This fear was not helped by the fact that Bob's apartment was burglarized on the day of his funeral.

Lester kept himself rather contained during the meeting, until Anna Marie became more and more emotional. At that point, Lester himself began to feel feelings that he hadn't anticipated.

Lester: I'm gonna say it like this here—yeah, it was more emotional than I thought it would be—at that time—it was so emotional man. I damned near—I thought of committing suicide because I seen all—there was so much crying up in that thing man. I hate that she was crying—I grabbed some Kleenex from her and I was wipin' the tears from her face, like it was just so emotional—I got tired of seeing her cry so much right. She just said, "I can't help it man, you just don't know man. That's all I have—don't no nothin' else matter to me." You know what I'm sayin'—that's all she ever had you know what I'm sayin', was that boy you know, she kept over and over and over again kept saying that I took the only thing she cared about. Yeah, that's the whole thing that was really, really hard for me—sittin' across from somebody that I damned near took her life too, she tried a couple times time too you know [to commit suicide]?

In viewing the videotape of this meeting later, this scene was quite remarkable, and did, as Lester said, mark a significant shift in the tone and course of the meeting. Anna Marie had cried for some time, and, eventually, Lester, crying himself now, reached over and took some Kleenex that she was holding and wiped her tears from her face.

Later, when the mediator showed Lester the complete video of their meeting, he also saw the debriefing with Anna Marie. In viewing this video, he learned that she had expected Lester to be more frightening than he was: "All beat up, looking like Charles Manson, or Jason, or something." He also learned that she was showing concern for him: "Like her child, you know, and she asked, 'do you think he's going to be all right?'"

Anna Marie also confronted Lester about his prison record: "Why do you have all these cases!? You have almost one hundred cases here, how did you do that?" Lester said, "And I just explained over and over again … that I didn't care, when I came to prison, I didn't care about dying."

Lester was also impressed with the fact that Anna Marie, a middle-class Caucasian woman, made an effort to educate herself about the realities of Lester's life. She told him that she had read *Black Rage*. She also read, and gave him a copy of, *Out of the Madness*, which Lester had read before. She honestly and innocently told Lester, during the mediation, that she had been totally unaware of the challenges of his life, or much of anything about the black experience in America.

Anna Marie told Lester that she wanted to help him: "What do you mean you want to help me?" She told him that she expected him to finish his GED, get his classification returned, learn a trade, and stop getting into trouble in the institution.

"Lester, I could go off filled with hatred. I just don't hate you no more." Lester states that Anna Marie asked him to tell her his life story, how he was raised and his experiences, which he did.

Lester: I could sit here and try to describe the feeling but there's no way I can describe that because it was—it was real emotion—it was so emotional—I thought I could come in here and sit down and talk to her right. During all the time—in just ten minutes I sat down and looked into her eyes and I couldn't say nothing—I just dropped my head. Couldn't say nothin'—I mean, I sat down and looked at her and she looked at me and I looked in her eyes and I just couldn't find any words to say to her for about ten minutes and I looked over at [Mediator] and the victim and he said, "Man, it's gonna be all right, just …" "I just, I just don't know what to tell her, what to say." So, she looked at me she said, she's real nice, "Lester, would you like me to call you Lester?" … it's something, it's real different. Real different.

And she said, "I know you can't bring my son back alive, but I'm askin' you please, do all that—two things—it's all I ask you for." I said, "What's that?" "Get your education and your right class back—can you do that?" I told her, "I will."

Right. And I only caught one beef. And it really don't affect me, it was like three months ago and, if it wasn't for that woman. I'm gonna tell you like this—you might not understand this here but this is the way it is in my life—I just got a three-year set off [the next time he will be eligible for a parole hearing] for my record—I got all these cases—if I do two years in 2000 they might send me home—there's no more cases between now and then. But, if I never would have done this meeting with that woman who knows where I'd be. Because she said I changed her life—I took effect on her life—she took effect on my life because I made a commitment—I'm not gonna mess up—I'm gonna do what she told me—and get my class back. There's been time with the officers … I almost got in a fight on the basketball court—I shoot basketball everyday—where I almost got into a fight and I say, "You promised," and I don't. If I hadn't done this meeting I wouldn't care, man. I wouldn't care.

… it changed toward her because again like I said, she looked at me like I was just a demon—just a murderer—stone blooded—I'd a had no feelings toward society in general you understand—you know I was just a thrown child on the streets—I didn't care … but she found that I do got a heart—I do got something—I do—I have feelings—I'm not just a cold-blooded killer . . .

While disclaiming becoming a "Christian," Lester did credit the meeting with a change in his spiritual life. He said he doesn't miss a Sunday in the chapel.

Lester: I wouldn't miss a Sunday—I ain't no Christian or none of that—since that incident happened with [Anna Marie]—I turned my life around—me and the chaplain—we are like brothers—I'm there all the time—a lot of things I don't fight no more because I'm trying to change my life around—I'm not perfect but ah, I pray to my God in heaven because he's the one who blessed me through these matters, but without him alone I wouldn't have made nobody, you know what I'm sayin'?

Lester was quite conscious of the emotional bond that occurred between him and Anna Marie.

Lester: She's, she's real concerned about me man. She's as a matter of fact, more concerned about me than my mother—she calls up here every week—my mom's got other kids and babies to look out for—she don't have time to sit here lookin' just after me . . .

In my interview with Lester, I asked him about his sense of Bob, if he felt that he and Bob were "alike or different" from each other.

Lester: The only thing that's different between me and that guy is he's white, not black—color—that's the only difference between, that is, the only thing between that is this right here—he went to the university, I dropped out when I was a sophomore [in high school]. He was going to graduate from, he was out of school. He had more book sense than anyone you'd probably want to meet. He just didn't have any street … he just didn't know how dangerous the street were at all. As far as I'm concerned, I don't have no book sense right now, you know what I'm sayin'. I'd took the [section test of the GED], I got "literacy skills" but I ain't got the GED yet. And I don't have any college thing. I'm in the process of getting my GED but other than that—that's her goal [Anna Marie]—that's my goal but that's her goal just because she wants me to change.

I had the sense in my first meeting with Lester that he was committed but nervous about the agreements he had made with Anna Marie. These promises were written down in an "affirmation agreement," which both parties agreed to and signed. This exercise is a common part of some system's mediation process, and probably bears the most resemblance to a standard mediation meeting. As Lester mentioned earlier, the agreement included that he not get into any more trouble in the institution, get his classification upgraded, and complete his GED and do some work on gaining a trade.

Lester: So, I've got several months left, four or five months, on getting my line back [classification]. Everything, I should have another trade by then. [Lester is looking at late 1999 at this point. The interview was done in 1998.] I should have a GED, I should get ready to graduate. I should have my everything—my mind is set on that, you understand? But I don't know what they're expecting on a day-to-day basis. We get locked down sometimes. There are strains or fights, but you gotta go do it, but if you're in the wrong place at the wrong time and they're fightin', or whatever, you got to be prepared for that. You gonna suffer too.

At the close of the first interview, Lester continued to be almost surprised at the outcome of this meeting on his life. He is also still quite moved by it.

Lester: … it's kind of weird at the same time, you know, things change. Like she said one time [Anna Marie], she was prayin' that I would get killed down here—you know what I'm sayin'—she was just hopin' that somebody killed me or I got AIDS, and her life changed and she found out how I was and it just messed her up. She kinda wished she wouldn't have felt that way, about all them years, but after knowing me she said I'm a different person …

I wanna share this with you before we close. Ms. [Mother] made the statement to me, in the face-to-face meeting, she said, "After someone done something like this to me and my child, you would think I'd be on a committee in [State] trying to pass laws to keep violent offenders away from … I'm trying to help you all, man, because some people in violent crime, they make laws, you'd think I'd be on one of those committees to get those laws on murderers, I'm not. I go around and try to help you so you all won't do the same thing. I dedicated my life. I did it on my own free time. I don't get nothing for it. I just dedicated my life."

Some people donated certain things … she is the strongest woman I've ever met, you know what I'm sayin'. My mother ain't got none of that woman, she's strong! She's not sitting on committees trying to keep everybody down. She's real articulate. The way she feels about us [inmates] she's not trying to keep everybody in prison because [of] what happened in her own personal life—she not looking at that—she tryin' to stop some of the violence—she don't wanna hurt nobody. [She don't want to] have another mother do what she did, standing over [her] child looking [down] at it [in a coffin]—don't wanna do it.

INTERVIEW WITH ANNA MARIE

My interview with Anna Marie was one of the last I did for the project. She is, as everyone I had previously spoken to prepared me for, an incredible person. At the time of Bob's murder, she had become a very successful small businessperson, running her own company. She had raised Bob, as a single mother, when his father abandoned the family after their divorce.

Anna Marie's father was a rigid fundamentalist preacher, with his own church, and I got the sense, in the interview with her, that she had a relatively rough life with this man. He was also a staunch segregationist, and preached this position from the pulpit, so Anna Marie was in no way prepared to deal with the nuance of the racial issue in Bob's murder. With her history, Anna Marie felt unsupported by her family in dealing with the crisis of Bob's death. To add to it, both of her parents became ill and died in the year following Bob's death, so she had to deal with an excess of grief.

For the first years after Bob's murder she was angry and reactive. She woke up daily hoping that Lester had died that day. During the trial, she became active in advocating the death penalty for him, but, apparently, the details of the crime did not allow such a sentence. She then spent a great deal of energy writing to the parole officials attempting to forestall any consideration of parole for Lester.

Since the murder, Anna Marie has become active in the victim's movement. She is currently the assistant director for a small victim services office, where she does victim advocate work. She has also received training in mediation, and has served as a volunteer mediator, in cases of violent crime. When not involved in this work, she is a successful, and often requested, motivational speaker in the prison community, having just spoken before an audience of 1700 inmates at an institution the week before I interviewed her.

Anna Marie could best be described as a "gentlewoman," a trait that she was aware of and utilized when she needed to. She had become very aware of the gendered nature of criminal justice, especially in her part of the country, and had become an increasingly effective voice in the victim's community.

As well as having seen parts of the mediation videotape, I had interviewed all the other players in this case before I was able to arrange the interview with Anna Marie. Because of this sequence, I was aware of the details of the crime.

Perhaps the most striking part of the history, unfortunately replicated in many of these case histories, was the brutal and unthinking manner that she was told of Bob's death. The story of this telling was an important key to Lester's emotions in this case as well, since it had a profound impact on him.

Anna Marie: I was asleep and got a phone call and it was ten minutes to one and the man said—I answered the phone because Bob called all times of the day or night—you know how kids are—and he said, "Do you know Bob Jones?" And I said, "Yes, I do." And he said, "Somebody shot him a couple of hours ago. You'll need to come pick up his body." And I said, "Who is this?" And he said, "Oh, my name is [X] with the medical examiner's office in [City]. Are you related to him?" And I said, "Yes, I'm his mother." And then he said, "Who is with you?" And I said, "Nobody's with me." And at that point, he said, "Oh, I'm so sorry." And you remember these things vividly, and I said, "I am too." I don't know what he was referring to—he was sorry that someone wasn't with me, or he was sorry that Bob was murdered. But we both said, "I'm sorry."

In her sense of disbelief, Anna Marie insisted that there were a lot of people with names like Bob's, and asked was the coroner sure that it was him. She insisted that he go and check Bob's body for scars and a birthmark that Bob had. In a particularly gripping piece of the story, she heard the man's footsteps walking over to Bob's body, checking it, and then walking back to report that, yes, it was in fact Bob.

Anna Marie: But it could be that somebody stole his billfold and Bob had a scar right here between his eyebrows. He had a scar here and a birthmark on the right side of his chest. And he had a scar up the back of his leg. So, I asked him to go and check, and he went, "Oh … well, he had ID" and I said, but would you please go and look. And he took eight steps, I counted … And he came back and said, "Yeah, it's him." And I said he had blue eyes. So, I gave him several things to check for.

This experience, even at the moment it was happening, convinced Anna Marie that there was something drastically wrong with the system:

> So that was the first thing that I knew I had to change in the system. After the fact, I went to the medical examiner's office, and I said, "Don't ever do this again." So that one phone call right there, "Anna Marie—get the big picture, and don't let anybody else do this."

Lester was arrested in relatively short order, and quickly confessed to the crime. When Anna Marie was called and told that he had been arrested, and a little of his history, she began, immediately, to deal with the issues of "why" such a thing should happen.

Anna Marie: … But why do you walk the streets with a pistol when you're only seventeen? You ought to be chasing girls and playing basketball and have a job. So, my concept, if you will, that part, that element of society was so far from my reality that I had a hard time grasping how someone got to be seventeen, angry, violent, a murderer. And he didn't look like a murderer. When you see them on TV, they're always the bad guys. And he didn't look like a bad guy. So that was my—I was afraid of him. He was handcuffed and shackled and kept away from me. I felt a great deal of fear just looking at him and connecting him with what he had done.

At the same time, even at this early phase of the process, she got in touch with some feeling for Lester that she immediately connected to a mothering instinct.

Anna Marie: I actually felt sorry for him. Because there was no one in court with him at all. No family member came. I didn't have anyone with me. But I was forty-four years old and I'd raised Bob as a single parent from the time I was twenty-three. … So, I was mother, I was daddy, I was breadwinner, custodian of everything. Disciplinarian. I did everything, which made me very strong, and I'm looking at this seventeen-year-old kid, and I'm going, "Where's his family?" And through all of these things, knowing that no matter what Bob did—not that I would have condoned it or approved—but I would have been there for my son. And his mother said she just didn't think she could stand it. Well, you're the mother. You are the parent. You are there. You're part of that child's life. So, I don't cut them any slack for not being there. See, I can be a hard-nosed person.

Anna Marie's first knowledge of the mediation program, through Victim Services, generated a very negative response from her. In discussing this with me, she made a significant connection between her negative response and her own unresolved anger and grief at Bob's death.

Anna Marie: No. As a matter of fact, when they put the program in place in [State], I went, "No, no, no." I'm on the State Victim Assistance Advisory Council, the only person that's been on there since its inception years ago. And they started talking about this program and I felt the legalities, the changes we would make, with the legal system would not be worth what one would receive from it. My own personal experience with it—I was extremely suicidal. I was extremely suicidal, and bought a one-way ticket to go get rid of myself because you cannot handle the pain, day after day … . But the pain is more than you can understand because in our society we are trained that they're always going to find a cure for it; we don't accept death in our world.

but I would wake up every morning thinking "I hope he [Lester] dies today"—only I put some more adjectives in there. Every six months, I came to [City]. I personally went to protest his parole. Not up for parole. His file's about this thick. I wrote a letter every month. I wrote a letter every other month. I put Bob's pictures there. I did everything because I had no other way to vent, if you will. And I didn't want to—he shouldn't take up oxygen on the planet. Oh, no! And when they put this program in, I was the one that fought it. I said, "No, they shouldn't ever be allowed to apologize. Just get rid of them." Well, it helps him. I don't care. So, we've come full circle.

Anna Marie experienced many changes throughout this process. In addition to becoming more involved and active in the victim's world, she also began to explore her own spiritual life to try and make sense of her situation, her suicidal feelings, and her anger.

In asking what she felt was responsible for her dramatic changes, she replied:

> Our society does not teach nor understand nor accept forgiveness. Nor compassion. It's "Lock them up and throw away the key." That "compassionate conservatism" is a crock.
>
> You pull in front of me on the highway, man, I'm going to get around you. This is how we're raised in our world. And when you're taught all that—an eye-for-an-eye, a tooth-for-a-tooth—and what I know is an eye-for-an-eye makes both of you blind. But that was what was fed to me continually. So many people, and especially men, knowing I had worked for the police department and I knew how to handle a pistol, you're going through that trial. Do they search you for guns when you go in there? Go in there and blow him to Hell? My attorney told me, "You blow him to Hell and you'll never serve a day." And I said, "I'm a mother. He's got a mother." … But I thought his mother was like the mother that I am.

And we're not allowed to be compassionate, because you're weak. … And what that does—about the time you think you can let go a little bit of anger, somebody comes along and "should's" on you again, and shovel on some more. And because you are so raw, you are encompassed with what you should do. And you should hate him; he should never be free. So, you're fed this all the time. And that was part of who I was.

Coupled with this, and representative of her ongoing ambivalence, she was informed that Lester, who was, at this point, fourteen years into his sentence, would be up for parole. This created in her the same panicked feeling that she had to do something. What she was not aware of was that, due to Lester's dismal disciplinary record in the institution, there would be no chance that he would be considered for parole. At this point he had 148 major infractions, nevertheless, this was the beginning of her sense that she had to meet with him.

Anna Marie: … And I said, "Well, no, I gotta get a grip on this guy." So, my reason, first of all, was to get my questions answered, and, in the most lady-like way possible, to confront him with what he had done and I wanted to show him Bob's pictures. I wanted him to know who he killed. And he didn't know who he killed. Because I asked him, "Do you even remember what he looked like?" and he said "no, not really." I fell apart at that. You would think that when you murder somebody, you'd at least remember what they looked like. But the fact is, he didn't. That was terrible.
Interviewer: I'm always interested in that because that seems to be such a universal part of the process—the pictures. Was that something that just came to you in terms of the desire to do that, to bring pictures?
Anna Marie: Oh, yes. I took Bob's baby shoes, I took his baby pictures. I wanted him to get a grip on the person that he killed—not that kid, that guy. He. Him. The dude. This was a real person. This was my son. And he was alive and well until you pointed a loaded pistol at him and shot him. And I wanted him to know that. And the picture that I have of Bob is 14 × 18. It's no little, bitty snapshot. So, when I went, I didn't take little 3 × 5s; this was a life size picture of Bob, and I turned it this way, and if you watch, I was doing this—I was holding—like I was holding this child in my hands. So, it was pretty arresting, if you will.

This point is also made in my interview with Lester, who points out to me that the photograph was always in his visual field, and did, in fact, produce the result that Anna Marie had hoped it would.

Like some other victims interviewed, Anna Marie did not find the preparation all that helpful. At the time she was ready to meet with Lester, she just wanted to do it with minimum interference. However, she did find the initial meeting difficult.

Anna Marie: I'm really a loner. I need a lot of down time. I need a lot of time to process things … I didn't want to chit-chat; I didn't want to talk. I just wanted to go away. I felt very raw. Completely exhausted. As everybody does. But I didn't want to chit-chat; I didn't want anything to eat. I didn't eat for three days, or sleep for three days before. I was a mess. Just knowing I was going to be in the same room with him. It was not say as emotional as burying Bob but it was probably the next thing to it. Burying Bob was the hardest thing I've ever had to do in my life. And probably knowing I was going to be looking at him [Lester] was the second hardest thing. You can equate it to the same emotions as going through the burial because all those emotions were there. This is the guy that did it. It's that hand that held the pistol. And I don't know if other survivors articulate this to you or not, quite as adamantly, but I kept looking at his hand but that's the gun, in that hand right there. I thought of that. So, it's a pretty serious process.

Given Anna Marie's history, she also began to educate herself about the cultural black experience. She read a book by an author who grew up in the same projects as Lester did (*Out of the Madness*), along with *Black Rage* and pieces by Malcolm X. All this reading lent to the transformation that Anna Marie felt she went through: "but I believe that my soul path was to be who I am now. And bury Bob, and be able to reach out to Lester, which is why I'm here."

Anna Marie is clear, as one can see when reading the transcript of the meeting, of the important evolution for both participants. She tears up still when she tells me this story:

Anna Marie: When I started talking about how much Bob loved me. That was the clincher right there … And Lester leaned toward me, just a little bit, and he got this little wrinkle right here, and he'd say "well, how's the yard" and I'd say, "it needs mowing." And I wasn't even looking at him, and he'll say, "I'll come home this weekend and see about it." He dropped his head and I glanced up at him, and here are these two tears just cascading—he did this, and on that tape you can hear me pull a tissue from the box and I said, "Here." I swear to you that was really unconscious—my actions were as a mother to a child. And at that moment, I forgot that he was the child that murdered my child. At that moment, he was in great pain and I watched him—I felt his remorse. I watched him just crumble from this person to this person, for what he had done to Bob and to me. And I just don't have a hard heart, I guess. And I still didn't think I could touch him—I wasn't there, but I thought, he's sitting here with these tears—it was just so—the tears, and the tissue, and I just handed him a tissue. And it just escalated from there.

So, the night before, he had said, "She doesn't expect me to cry, does she? I've been in prison thirteen years and I'm tough." … But when I saw him begin to cry, it moved me, it touched me, it affected me. And although he was seventeen when I had seen him the last time, and he was thirty when I saw him this time, and he just didn't look that much older.

I took Bob's baby book. I showed him Bob's little feet and his little hands. And Bob weighed five and a half pounds. He was really tiny. The clincher was watching him, watching him. And you know what I say? I watched him grieve for what he had done to Bob, and almost—and he's the only one that could tell you this—but I felt that he was grieving for Bob. He didn't say that. He never said, "I'm sorry"—I never said, "I forgive you." Those words never passed our lips. He has said it since then, but he did not say it that day. I've got the whole eight hours, and he didn't say "I'm sorry." Now, what happened though, was his actions spoke louder than his words.

That was the epiphany—is that what you call it?

It was with this that Anna Marie began to also make a lasting connection with Lester, which she, in her inimitable way, concretized for Lester by making demands on him that he clean up his act. Stating that he had robbed Bob of the opportunity to finish school, she expected Lester to finish school. She also demanded that Lester stop his misbehavior in the institution: "If killing Bob and going to prison didn't turn you around .... Maybe looking at me, and looking inside my heart, knowing what you've done, maybe this will turn you around. Go by the rules. If they tell you to stand out there, you go stand out there."

In the years since this meeting, Lester has, in fact, turned himself around. He has received only one or two very minor infractions since meeting with Anna Marie. The educational promise, however, continues to be an issue.

While Anna Marie feels a significant change took place with Lester on that day, she is also realistic in terms of his history and his years of problems:

> And that day, that meeting, that time, that place, he's changed his life. That let me know he was sincere. Now he's still got some stinkin' thinkin', and he's still trying to con me and everybody else, but he's not being violent anymore.
>
> You know what I believe—because I'm spiritual—I believe I could just feel it .... But I believe our spirit knows things and can feel things. Not that I'm not conned. I'm so gullible.
>
> He really needs to go to school. And he wrote a letter and said, "They expect me to get up a three o'clock and go to school. This is ridiculous." And I'm going, "Where else are you going? You're in prison. Get your duff up and get to school." Because I worked to get him in school. They were never going to let him in school because of his disciplinary record, and being there for murder. And I talked to God and everybody, and I put a lot of time in it, and then he refused to go to school. I was furious with him. Needed to shake him. I confront him about these things. But he still has got criminal thinking.

Interviewer: So, in terms of the agreements that you made, he's not yet got his GED?
Anna Marie: No, he still does not have his GED, and it's been four years. And he had the opportunity and the option, and he chose not to do it. And he said, "Well, I take medication and it makes me sleepy." I said, "Well, you're not going to die from it—don't take the pills." So, I don't cut him any slack for that.

With all of this, Anna Marie remains realistic, if not somewhat pessimistic, regarding Lester's future opportunities.

Anna Marie: The thing is, he has no life skills, no job skills, no education, no people skills, no social skills. He is totally institutionalized by going in at seventeen and staying there for twenty years. Society has just gone past him for twenty years. And he will do at least twenty years. Because he's been there almost seventeen, and he's got three more. So, by the time he gets out, he will have done twenty years. No family support. Brothers in and out of prison, all of them.

And the truth is, I don't expect him ever to stay out. I won't tell him that. I always try to encourage him, but I don't expect him to stay out of trouble. He's going to be released with a bus ticket and fifty dollars. And go back to the hood and he'll go right back in. If he doesn't kill somebody else, he'll get caught doing something else. And I'm being honest. My expectations for him—if he makes it, I will be pleasantly, pleasantly pleased. But the letters that I get from him, "Lester, get with it!" Everything is always somebody else's fault. He never accepts responsibility. It's never his fault. So that's why I say—even though he has changed his action, and that he doesn't get in fights anymore, he hasn't been caught for stealing anymore, he hasn't been caught for being in riots anymore, it's in his head, that stinkin' thinkin' is still there. "Miss Jones, somebody stole my fan and I may go off and it won't be my fault." "Oh, yes, it will be. It will be your fault if you go off."

But he has changed his outward actions and he brags a lot about the good he did to meet with me. That was not good; you should have accepted responsibility for murdering the person that you did. But he said that, that he never really thought about it until then. And now, that he thinks about it all the time.

Anna Marie also feels that Lester's failure is a function of the institutional process in which he is living. At the time of my research interviews, Lester had been transferred from the institution he had been in, where he had made his most dramatic changes, to another. There was no apparent reason for this transfer, and when Anna Marie asked the warden about it, she was told that they "Needed to keep the bus drivers in a job."

> But maybe, I just want to cut somebody a little slack—I do think—that now this guy's quit fighting, he's quit being tacky—and then they ship him to the [new]

unit. I think they set them up to fail. I do. I swear I do. It's big business and it's the only business that it succeeds if it fails at what it's mission statement says. And they do not do anything to rehabilitate anybody. It is just zero. So, I have no use for the system. I guess you can tell that.

I asked Anna Marie what part she feels that "empathy" plays in the experience she has described to me.

Anna Marie: When you feel the other person's pain, to me that is empathy. You accept responsibility for the part you played in creating, or contributing, or causing that pain—to me, that's empathy. That's not sympathy. Sympathy is, "I'm so sorry that you hurt." "I'm so sorry that you're going through this, that you had to experience this." But empathy is "Oh, my God, look what I did!" It's awful what part I played in the pain of that mother, for the murder of that child, the rape of that lady. I don't know if that's the dictionary definition, but I think empathy is accepting responsibility for the part you played. Where when they say you empathize with somebody, I think it's more you sympathize. That to me is a feeling of really empathy.

I ask her if she feels that Lester achieved empathy, by her definition, in their meeting.

Anna Marie: He did that day. It took him a year to write me a letter where he mentioned Bob's name. "When I killed him …"—it was "him," "he"—And I was overwhelmed when I got a letter that he mentioned Bob. It was almost like Bob was a real person to him.
Interviewer: That's probably an important distinction.
Anna Marie: Yeah, but it took him a year, a little bit over a year. I think it was fourteen months before he ever wrote a letter—and he writes to me all the time—I get two letters a week. But he's got plenty of time—he doesn't go to school. Doesn't work. So, he's got plenty of time. But I was just overwhelmed when I got the letter that he mentions Bob, because it was almost like, "Yes!"

I asked Anna Marie about the place of "forgiveness" in the process for her.
Anna Marie: Well, Chad, what I say is that Lester and I made our peace. And forgiveness to me is letting go of the anger toward that person, not at what they've done, but letting go of the anger toward that person. And not saying, "It's OK," but ceasing to hate that so. I hated him … I would wake up every morning saying, "I hope he dies today." And I did that. Year and year and year. I would wake up, "Bob is dead; I hope he dies today." That was just like my "Good morning, world." And not that I still don't wake up and be aware that Bob is dead, but I feel that talking with Lester allowed me—forced and allowed—allowed me to release anger and pain that I'd not been able to do for thirteen years.

And did you see the ending of the film where I put my hand across the table, they turned the sound down a lot. I'm going to use the term—when I reached out and touched him, it was a blood-curdling scream that I'd held for thirteen years. I never allowed myself to let go that much. I'm such a lady, and I didn't want anybody to hear. I live in a townhouse. I didn't want anybody to experience the anguish inside, and I wouldn't even allow myself to. And in some way, reaching across, and what I say is, my soul, his soul, Bob's soul, they're entwined for eternity. This is a soul thing. And when I reached out and he took his hand, and he gripped it, and he put his other hand on mine, and he was just crying, and in some way, I was able—and I allowed myself—to release anguish and anger that I'd had for thirteen years. Thirteen and a half years. I never had done that before. Oh, I cried, and I got angry and I wrote journals and I tore them up, and I did all those things. But there was no one around. And here was [Mediator and two others in the room], but it didn't matter. The only two people in that room at that point were the mother and the murderer. That's the only two people that were present.

INTERVIEW WITH THE MEDIATOR

The mediator in this case (who worked with all three of these pilot study cases), is also a major figure in the restorative justice community. He was interviewed in the living room of his home, which is a lovely, warm place, representative of the nature of this individual. He came to the process from a history of theology and religious education, and had already been involved in corrections, having developed a program for violent sexual predators, before becoming involved in this work. He began the process in the state in which he lived, and he worked for many years with the Victim Services office, which was a division of the state's Criminal Justice Department.

In discussing the case of Lester and Anna Marie, he echoed their observations.

Mediator: Lester—Lester is one of those things where I genuinely believe this man was changed—every indication of that is he was as well behaviorally.
Interviewer: He's continued to have a free disciplinary …
Mediator: From what I've understood and yet here's the other side of that. This is not a panacea and it can't stand alone. Whether Lester can maintain that, I don't know. It'll be a shame because with the proper support, there's no doubt in my mind that he could maintain it. But God, you're talking about a whole life of—and whether he is able to—he's created an image of himself and so you know, he almost asks for trouble, just by being there. And so, if he does finally succumb to some temptation to go back to the old way, a lot of people will say,

"Well, see, that's just a failure." And I don't believe it for a moment. He'll definitely be a product of the system, if he can't maintain that.

This mediator has had great success in his state convincing somewhat hardened correctional staff that the program is worth supporting. He was even successful, one year, in having the department transport Lester to an annual symposium that the Victim Services office holds about their work. Correctional officers transported Lester, in handcuffs and shackles, to the table where he appeared with Anna Marie so the two could tell their story to the audience.

Mediator: And then the next year when I asked, they said, "No, we can't do that." Of course, they had had the escapes and everything, so they weren't buying it at all. I think any kind of interaction like that is critical. And that's the saddest thing. There's just so much that could be done, but they're just not letting you do it. So, you've just got to deal with the world that you can, with what you have at your arm's length.

He discussed his overall sense of the meeting, one of the early ones he had conducted.

Mediator: With Lester, just that overwhelming movement from hopelessness to hope. Just absolutely embodied in him. So, shame-based at the beginning, so emotive. That's what was so good about that. He didn't—even his talking, the little that he did, was quite profound at times. But it was that—it's the feeling that I had on the second visit with him when I showed him the video clip of Miguel and Gloria [the last of these three cases] and I just watched him out of the corner of my eye, and when it got to that point, he broke down, not just huge, but he said, "Oh, that kind of stuck on me" and he talked about his mother and was connecting on that level. So, I wasn't surprised, but I was overcome with the depth of the intensity of that particular mediation. It was long but I never experienced anything that intense, even since then.

DISCUSSION

Many significant factors in this case inform several related issues. The case exemplifies several important developmental themes in both the offender and the survivor.

Lester told me that he saw the preparation phase, which extended over many meetings with the mediator for a seven-month period, as being "like therapy." He mentioned to me, confirmed by the mediator, the significance of being able to view the video of the other meeting; this telling brought up an unexpected emotional response in him. He began, at some point in the preparation, to see the emotional risks he was embarking upon, and yet, remarkably, he proceeded. His statement, "She doesn't expect me to cry," seemed quite prophetic of what came in the meeting. He stated that he was also convinced that she would "go off on me," and vent her anger, given what he had seen in court and the video-taped statement that the students had shown him. Thus, coupled with his own inclination, the work done in the preparation and the relationship established with the mediator were vitally important transitions for Lester.

His comment that the thought of Anna Marie "completely took over my mind" is so important. This previously angry and violent young man became consumed with the image of this mother. His comment, "If this woman dies tonight in her sleep, she would have benefited from this, the questions that she has," is equally striking, given the parallel feelings that she had been having in hoping that Lester would die in his sleep.

The interview with Anna Marie was helpful to me in clarifying several issues that had come up during this research. Through the course of this meeting, she visibly created a profoundly close connection to Lester. I had observed this process in other mediations, and it almost appears that the mother is making a transferential relationship with the murderer, as the person who took the child's life, or the last person to see the child alive. Anna Marie speaks of this, overtly, in terms of her comment that Lester had prevented Bob from completing his college graduation, so she now expected Lester to fulfill this promise for him.

Anna Marie also had, against the desires of the program, maintained a correspondence with Lester, and had even visited him once or twice in prison since the meeting. This continuing relationship is unusual, and is most often discouraged by the mediation programs that I studied, since it is an unhealthy over-involvement. However, this admonishment was lost on Anna Marie. Because of her history with Lester, I began asking routinely what the mediators felt about the "bonding" that sometimes occurred because of these meetings and what their concerns about it were.

I went into this interview with Anna Marie expecting to be dealing with some form of unhealthy connection. However, she seemed to represent and give articulation to a position that has been voiced by some in the mediator community. This position is that of letting the individuals do what they need to do, and trusting their judgment to do both the work necessary, but also what is in their best interests. This stance is a variation on the "strengths-based model" that is seen in some social work training.

In my interview with Anna Marie, what seemed most compelling in her favor was the fact that she presented what she felt was a realistic appraisal of Lester's future, without a hint of romanticizing or an observable grandiose fantasy about her own involvement with him serving as a form of rescue. She saw that his history was a burden for his future goals, along with the reality of institutionalization. This seemed, in a way, both sad, but also realistic, giving her critics less to be concerned about. This rather pessimistic appraisal of Lester's future was also echoed by the mediator in terms of his evaluation of Lester's real choices.

The other significant observation that Anna Marie made, in our discussion, was the designation of Lester's real expression of empathy being when he arrived at the ability to call Bob by name. This step has been seen in other interviews with offenders as a key element related to their ability to develop an internal image of the victim, and see the victim as a real person.

Two very moving images remained with me about this case: in my interview with Lester, when I had finished and had run over my expected time with him, he asked me if he could hear some of his interview on the tape. I was confused at this request, but obliged him, rewinding the tape and stopping at a random section. What Lester was describing in this section was the murder of Bob. He listened to himself, enraptured, and when he heard his own words describe the shooting, he shook his head in seeming disbelief at what he was hearing. This incredible experience brought a couple of things to mind for me; one was the extent of dissociation that takes place in any of these acts; the second was a conversation that I had with Alan Sroufe regarding one of his research cases. In this case, a young, high-risk mother had a difficult time accepting verbal instructions regarding parenting skills, until she saw herself on videotape performing the questionable action.

The other image is of the videotaped mediation, where Anna Marie reached across the table and took into her hands the hands that murdered her son, exactly as Priam did with Achilles, and let out a wail that was, even with the sound down, otherworldly. As she stated, "The only two people in that room were the mother and the murderer. That's the only two people that were present."

CASE 2: LOUIS

In the winter of 1990, Louis raped and murdered Barbara, Gail's daughter and oldest child.

Barbara, just turned nineteen, was working at a convenience store, saving her money, and taking some classes. She was still living at home with Gail and her father and younger brother.

On the night of the murder, Louis had been drinking extensively, and had also ingested other chemicals. He thought they may have been amphetamines, but he really did not remember.

Louis had an extensive criminal history, which included violent acts toward his spouse and frequent physical altercations with others.

Louis had been raised in a household brimming with violence, chemical dependency, and mental health problems. In our meeting, while he downplayed this history, he admitted that he was often the subject of physical violence from his parents and others. He escaped from home by enlisting in the army, where he received an early discharge, with a report from an army psychiatrist saying that Louis was at high risk for later physical violence against others, especially if disinhibited by chemicals.

On the night of the murder, Louis, full of a variety of substances, went to the store where Barbara worked, filled his car up with gas, and then went inside, thinking he would rob the store. Barbara, working alone, put up no resistance, but, inexplicably, Louis put a knife to her throat and took her with him in his car, making her lie on the floor in the front seat.

Louis took Barbara to his home, as no one was there for the weekend, where he brutally beat and raped her. At one point, Barbara, in a desperate attempt to break free, cut Louis with his own knife. Louis recounts that this act must have enraged him to the point of strangling her. He then became aware that Barbara was dead.

Louis hastily dressed Barbara, even putting on her shoes and tying them. After putting her body in the trunk of his car, he drove aimlessly around the countryside, until he noticed that his car was almost out of gas. Then, he stopped, placed Barbara's body on the roadside, and drove away. He returned home, cleaned up the house, and went to sleep.

In the meantime, Gail, who worked for the State, got off work at about ten that night. She wanted to go by the store and check on Barbara, as she knew she was alone, but her husband suggested that Barbara would be mad if they did, since she would feel they were treating her like a baby.

Gail was getting ready for bed when she received a call from the police dispatcher saying that the store where Barbara worked had been found unattended. The dispatcher wanted to know if Gail knew where Barbara was. Gail said she thought she should be at work. The dispatcher said that a police car was on the way. Gail said it took a long time for the officer to get to their home, forty-five minutes, and her anxiety intensified. When the officer did arrive, he told them that someone had gone into the store to pay for gas and found the store empty and the cash register opened. The police thought that it had been about 10 p.m.

Early the next morning, a policeman, doing his rounds by car, found Barbara's body on the roadside.

In May of that year, four months following Barbara's murder, Louis and his wife got into an argument. Louis reported that, prior to this incident, he had no memory of that night, or of having kidnapped or killed Barbara. As the fight with his wife became more heated, and eventually physical, Louis stated that he grabbed his wife by the throat, and, at that moment, the entire incident with Barbara came back to him.

He stopped himself and slumped to the bed. He told his wife about his memory and what he was certain he had done. His wife did not believe him. She called the family priest, who came over to the house. He, too, did not believe Louis' story. Louis told the priest to call the police department, and inquire of them whether such a crime had been committed. Louis and the priest then went to the police, where Louis turned himself in for Barbara's murder. He was only relieved that he hadn't killed his wife as well, since he felt close to repeating the same actions.

While awaiting trial, Louis was confident that the state would seek the death penalty. He felt resigned to this fact. In any event, Louis was convinced that he would never see the outside world again, and that his days of freedom were over. Louis' attorney worked out a plea agreement with the county attorney that Louis would plead guilty, and give a full confession for a life sentence. That was arranged, and Gail, who had not been informed of this plan, was surprised to hear it when she went to Louis' arraignment. The family were also unaware that Barbara had been sexually assaulted. In fact, they were under the impression that Barbara had fought off her attacker, which led to her death. Once Louis had been arrested and charged, the police detective informed the parents of this fact, having held it back before. This new information gave the couple even more grief.

When Gail first saw Louis in the courtroom, she felt that he was a "smart-ass." She saw him as aloof and cynical. When the plea was agreed to, and Louis was found guilty and sentenced, Gail wanted to meet his mother and express her condolences, saying that she felt it would be, in ways, as hard for her as it was for Gail. However, in the courtroom that day, Gail heard Louis' father giving a statement to the press that she felt was somewhat indifferent, so she decided not to approach Louis' family. In fact, Gail reported to me that, because of this attitude, she "hated his father more than I hated Louis."

Beyond the disillusionment with Louis' family members, Gail was very disturbed at what she saw to be the insouciance of the entire system. She was upset by arriving at court one day, during these preliminary hearings, to find the county attorney and defense council with their feet up on their respective tables, discussing the benefits of various running shoes: "I was so angry, because how could he be so everyday about something. I mean, I wanted to jump the counter and get him more than I did Louis at that point."

For the next three years, following Louis' trial and sentencing, Gail basically did not leave the house. The couple had been very interested in seeing the conditions that Louis would be living in at prison. While he was still in the county jail awaiting transfer, Barbara's father went to see if he could meet with Louis. The jailer said that he was not on the visitor list, and asked his name. When the father told him, he simply laughed, and told him to go home. Basically, both simply desired to see a cell, to see what his life would be like. However, no one would even talk with them.

While watching TV, Gail happened upon a story compiled by HBO about mediations between non-violent offenders, charged with property crimes, and their victims. Gail called HBO and asked them if they would be interested in facilitating such a meeting between her and Louis. At the time, the state's program was just beginning to be organized, and Gail knew nothing about this. HBO was quite interested, and through a variety of means, received permission to film a meeting between Louis and Gail, which was to be chaired by the correspondent doing the story.

While Gail was excited to do this, as she had a burning desire to meet with Louis, she was also nervous. She was aware that it was somewhat of a miracle that the prison had agreed to allow it, having refused many times, but finally yielding to the tenacity of the HBO production staff. Gail was aware how every move she made would be scrutinized, and she felt the burden of responsibility for future meetings if she lost her temper or self-control.

The mediator was decided upon, and although Gail felt that he was a "nice person," there was not much support or preparation. In fact, the mediator stated that he did not want to talk with her about it much, as he wanted it to be "spontaneous" on her part. Gail was also aware of how "produced" the experience was, with the car being filmed driving in and out of the prison gates several times to get the shot just right.

The net result of this meeting was disappointing to her. When she got word of the beginnings of the state program, she contacted the director of that program, told her the story, and asked if they might work with her to have a second meeting with Louis that was more private and in-depth.

Her husband and son were not interested in meeting with Louis, and have been skeptical of the results of the meetings to date. They feel that Louis is only "telling me what I want to hear." They also have not had much desire to sit in a room and be civil to him. At the same time, Gail and her husband agreed to disagree about this, and, because it was important to Gail, the two agreed not to argue about the merits of the meetings if they was useful to her.

The first HBO mediation took place around four years following Louis' trial. The second took place a little over a year later, giving the mediator a chance to meet with and prepare both parties in the in-depth manner common to this state's program.

The two developed an agreement, as a part of the second mediation, that was multifaceted. Gail had become aware, during their first meeting, that Louis was artistically inclined, since he had spoken, at one point, about his painting and drawing interests. Because of this remark, Gail requested that

Louis do a drawing of Barbara. Louis, who claimed to have no visual memory of Barbara, agreed, and then researched, using primarily news photos from the time of the murder and the trial. Louis worked on this drawing intensively for the next year, and presented it to Gail in a brief meeting the two had.

Further, Gail requested that Louis write her an annual letter detailing his thoughts, progress, insights, and developments of that year. Louis has done this conscientiously since their meeting, which was some seven years before the time of my meeting them.

I met Louis during the pilot study, three years prior to my research interviews, at the same institution where I met with him a second time for the current project.

My first meeting with Louis was held in a lieutenant's office, deep within the prison walls. Louis had not been told that I was coming that day, and expressed consternation about this, as he stated that it took him several days of mental preparation to discuss Barbara's assault and murder.

Louis was brought in handcuffed, as he had been placed in administrative segregation some two years earlier, suspected of having gang affiliations with the Hispanic gang-world within the prison. While Louis disputed this claim, he presented at that time as resigned to his life in administrative segregation, saying that he would not be released to the general population anytime soon, if ever.

I asked the officer, who escorted Louis to the interview, to remove the handcuffs to allow Louis to sit down and be interviewed. The officer agreed only to place the handcuffs in the front, but then left us alone in the room and closed the door.

Louis presented as an introspective and pensive individual. Although he provided me, on our first meeting, with a sense of discomfort, I did not feel any sense of threat. However, while I did not ever feel personally threatened by Louis, at any point in either of our interviews, he did, in his affect and description of himself, give off an aura of menace that was both palpable and, at the same time, elusive. (While I was not able to engage Louis in a diagnostic formulation, he had been diagnosed with a variety of mental illnesses, which he reported had been confirmed by testing. He had been offered psychiatric medication, which he was refusing. I might well have been picking up a projective sense of this disorganization or anxiety in our meeting, as well as my own possible projective discomfort at his circumstances, since Louis was the first handcuffed offender I had interviewed during this pilot period.)

Louis is clearly a highly intelligent individual. He states that he has been largely self-taught, as he tells me extensively of his early history, which was, as described, filled with abuse and dysfunction. As a result of this chaotic home life, he left high school prior to graduation hoping to find a new life for himself in the military. Instead of providing Louis with the escape he had hoped for, the military only exposed him to the variety of chemicals that became even more dominant in his life.

He described himself as happy alone, so he did not feel that the segregation experience had been detrimental to him. (His day involved twenty-three hours in his cell and one hour for exercise and a shower.) He reported reading many books and was particularly interested in philosophy and the history of his own Yaqui heritage. He also continued to do his artwork and, although prolific, discounted his skills.

Even with his olive complexion, Louis showed a certain pallor that I have witnessed before in men who have been in isolation for long periods. At the same time, he affected a keen desire for dialogue, exchange, and relationship, showing a great desire to communicate his story.

What I left the pilot interview struck by was Louis' comments about his own assessment of his threat to others, contiguous with the profound meaning that meeting Gail had had on him.

Shortly into the first interview, Louis calmly told me the events of the crime and the meeting with Gail. When he was first approached, he had little hesitation about the meeting, although he was dubious about why she would want to meet with him or what good it would do her. At the same time, he was open to it, thinking that, given the pain he had caused her and her family, "it would be the least I could do for her."

After the HBO meeting, he told Gail, "If you have something to say to me, you know where I'm at. I told her, I'll be here, so I'll be here."

Louis stated to me that he had said to Gail, "After … everything that I've put her through—she told me it was not what I put her through, it was what I put Barbara through—I told her it was the least that I could do, give her the chance to say whatever she wanted to. Whatever she wanted to say."

In the first interview, I asked Louis if he thought there would be any benefit to him for participating in mediation with Gail.

> I think—don't get me wrong, it's not about forgiveness, I didn't do it for forgiveness, and I've told her that, I said, "I'm not asking you to forgive me, I don't even forgive myself, I don't expect anyone else to." I said, but I'd like the chance to tell her that I do regret what I did and that I am sorry. I may not show it, but I do, I do regret it. I wish I could bring her daughter back, but I can't. That's just … .
>
> I didn't expect it to go as well as it did; I expected her to be more angry, I guess. She was actually able to talk … So that was different—I was expecting more hostility, but it wasn't at all about that.
>
> I asked Louis what was the most helpful or memorable thing that the mediator did.
>
> *Louis*: "Talk. Talk. Mainly, that's the main thing—somebody to listen, I guess …"

The only thing that Louis could remember doing prior to meeting with Gail the first time was to go through all the news clippings that he had kept about the crime, his arrest, and trial. He wanted to be as clear as possible about the facts, at least as they were presented in the media, so he could be clear in case Gail were to ask him a question about something.

Louis: I told her regardless of everything that I've done in my past and everything—the only thing that I've been trying to stress that—whatever I do, I'm gonna be honest with her—I'm gonna tell her—if she asks me something, I'm gonna tell her. That's the way it is.

Louis immediately felt that there was a level of connection and communication between him and Gail that continues to surprise him, and is a quality that he has no explanation for.

Louis: It was pretty much, like the first time—I don't know what it was but there was a certain—we were really able to communicate, me and her.
… (It surprised me) that she laughed. Yeah, that really surprised me . . .
that we could laugh with each other, you know that's something that you know is beyond me, I couldn't understand that. But it was there … . That surprised the hell outta' me.

In both meetings, Louis was moved by the description that Gail gave of the impact of her loss.

Louis: … it bothers me. Regardless of the person people think I am—since I am all closed up, and it bothers me. I mean, I want it to bother me. I know that she's picked up the pieces, and she's doing real well now . … But I know that at that time, I really pretty much destroyed—I mean I destroyed her faith in religion at the time and all that, that's what she told me, she couldn't believe in a God that you know—she believed that her daughter was gonna call out for him and she couldn't believe that he wouldn't be there for her.

The effect of the meetings on him was profoundly draining. He would spend days in preparation and, then, days after thinking of nothing else. Part of the problem for him was the amnesia that he had around much of the event, coupled with a desire to remember more, to be able to answer Gail's questions.

Louis: It's pretty—each time I've talked with her its—even today, I was preparing myself to talk to you about it. … Pretty, it drains me pretty much. I think during all the court sessions and all that, I only saw her I think once, that I remember. She says she was always somewhere real close where I could see her,

but I never seen her. I didn't pay attention to nobody at that time. … She's a hell of a woman, she's a lot stronger than I woulda been, I know that much.
Interviewer: And your feelings about Barbara …?
Louis: That would kinda be the same thing. I didn't know her then—I didn't know her afterwards 'cause what I did was just what I did, there was no how do I put it, no feeling, no emotion involved in it. Hell, I couldn't even remember it at first. It was pretty much just … for the longest time I really couldn't remember what she looked like … but it comes back to you. Pretty much.

Beyond this, he felt the overall impact of the meetings to be generally positive for him. He did admit that he was into a dangerous lifestyle in prison, and had developed a reputation as a combative person. Just before he first met with Gail, he had been in the midst of an altercation, where an inmate had come up from behind and hit him.

Louis: … meeting with her kind of slowed me down again. It made me slow down, 'cause I was—the first time we met I was really getting into the violent side of prison life, ah, that's pretty much, I really get to a point where I don't care, I don't care—and I told her, meeting with her calmed me back down so it made me realize that. I already tore one family's life apart, and I don't wanna do it again. … But then you gotta look at where I am now, locked up [in segregation]. It's a contradiction, I think I am a contradiction—period. I'm always gonna be that way.

At this point in the first interview, we discussed the drawing that Gail asked Louis to do of Barbara, and how it related to his memory of her.

Louis: (I did) a picture of one of the newspaper clippings—she told me Barbara didn't look like that at the time. I said that I didn't remember what she looked like, I said I remember what she looks like, it's just that I can't draw anything outta my head. If I can see it, I can draw it, but I had to be able to see it … . It took a long time [to do the drawing]. I don't know how many times I started it and threw it away and started it again, and threw it away. I was trying to do the best I could—it's no substitute for her daughter but you know, I tried to do my best.
Louis: … she surprised me. She's nothin' like you can put it this way, me in her shoes, I would be a hell of a lot different. She's a pretty remarkable woman, she's, I don't know, I don't know how to say it, I don't know how to explain it, but she's pretty strong. I mean to actually be able to sit there and talk to me after knowing everything that I did to her, she was … that's something. Most people can't do that, I wouldn't be able to … . It's like I told her, from the very first time, if it had been my daughter, I know what I'd have done. I'd done everything possible to get rid of me, one way or another, and I think that's the difference between me being what I am and her being who she is.

In discussing his sense of Barbara and any internal image he had been able to develop of her, Louis was quick to dismiss any sense of similarity between them.

Louis: Not alike. Totally different. Different lifestyle, different—different everything, different goals. She was gonna be somebody. She was trying to make something of herself. I wasn't and I didn't.

At the time of the first interview, Louis was very clear about his potential for violence. He told me that he did not think he could or should be released from prison, and he was not confident that he would not be violent in the future: "I don't think they should ever let me out of here. I couldn't promise no one that I wouldn't do the same thing all over again."

Louis: I wasn't a very nice person. I don't think—I'm still not a very nice person. I don't know, but that night [of Barbara's murder], whoever was in that store that night, sad to say, but they were gonna die. Whoever it was. Once I got to that point it was—that's the truth of it.

INTERVIEW WITH GAIL

Almost three years later, I met Gail, and interviewed her at the school where she was substitute teaching. She had been very accessible, and more than willing to talk with me about the murder of her daughter, and her relationship with Louis.

As is the case with many of the victims that have engaged in this process, Gail has been active in the restorative justice and victim movements. She participated, for some time, in public presentations of her experience and consulted with other individuals who were deciding whether they wanted to go through mediation.

Gail told me that she was not as active as she had been in the past. She felt tired, and was feeling that it was time for others to take her place in the advocacy she had participated in for victims' rights, and work with the state's Restorative Justice office.

I met with Gail first thing in the morning, at a middle school, in the small, traditional community where she was working. She told me that she did not have a morning class, so we could find an office and have an hour or so to talk. While waiting for Gail in the school's main office, the principle came over the loud speaker to lead the children in the "Pledge of Allegiance." Everyone in the office stopped what they were involved in, stood, and saluted the flag.

Gail was likely in her late forties, and continued to be young-looking, for a woman who would have had two adult children. She was moderately overweight, which she referred to easily in our discussion. Since Barbara's murder, she had made slow progress in returning to some semblance of an outwardly "normal" life. Much of this progress had been facilitated by her original work with Louis and subsequent work she had done in the effort to deal with crime victims' needs. At the same time, she told me that she had had serious heart problems, including bypass surgery, and cannot seem to motivate herself to stop eating, which she was convinced was evidence of her ongoing chronic grief. Gail was convinced that she would soon, no doubt, die and seemed rather philosophical about this possibility. Some months after meeting Gail, I learned that she had also been diagnosed with cancer.

At the start of the interview, Gail's voice was extremely hoarse, and she apologized for this. By the midpoint of the interview, this quality had cleared, and her voice was quite bright.

Since Barbara's murder, Gail had been in contact with a psychiatrist and was taking antidepressant medication, and felt this was helpful. The psychotherapy she had received, she stated, had also been helpful, but she reports that it goes only so far in helping the ongoing deep wound she felt at the loss of her daughter. She was honest with me that she felt a grave responsibility for Barbara's death. Many people had made efforts to help Gail let go of this notion, to no avail.

Gail's marriage to Barbara's father continued and had grown stronger since their crisis, although Gail told me frankly of many problems the two had encountered in their relationship since the death of their daughter.

Their son, Barbara's younger brother, who also had several special needs, also had been profoundly and lastingly affected by Barbara's death. Not the least of these things, according to Gail, was the overwhelming overprotection given to him by his parents since the death of his sister.

In telling me about the crime itself, Gail recounted the progressive series of events that left Barbara vulnerable to attack, and which then determined the outcome. These included the return to school of a girl that she worked with, and the need for her brother, who had been going with her to her job at the convenience store, also returning to school. This left her, on this day, for the first time, alone at the store.

Gail also reported to me that, after Louis abducted Barbara, and when they got to his house, she briefly escaped from him and ran screaming down the alley. No one responded, and Louis recaptured her.

Gail proved to be an incredibly open, informative, and emotive interviewee, who told her narrative with almost no restraint or defensiveness. Given that Gail was my first interview in this series of interview meetings, it was a moving beginning to my journey.

Gail told me about the immediate influence on her after the police came to her home to tell her of Barbara's death.

Gail: It was my fault, for one thing. Total guilt. I was the one that said she needed to get a part-time job. I'm the mother; I taught her all of her—everything she wore, how she put her makeup on, so I felt a lot of guilt. I don't think I felt any anger at that point, because there was just still so much shock. And when they sent two police officers to the house, and I opened the door and there were two officers there, I knew at that point what they were going to tell me. Because when you see the TV, they always have two officers. So, I just knew. And I begged those two officers to let me go where she was. They wouldn't tell me where she was. I had no idea. And I was crying; my husband and I were crying, and holding each other. And the older officer put his arms around us, and the minute he touched me, that was it. It was just like, total awareness—OK, get ahold of yourself, you've got to follow through. And I think I just turned everything off at that point, and started doing things I had to do. Like call my mom. Things like that. My husband and I didn't have anybody, any family here, except for my sister. And my son is a real brittle diabetic so my brother-in-law went after [their son]. And I began calling the family. And things just went from there.

Their son came home around that same time, and Gail recounted how she broke the news to him, and also the beginning of what she now feels enormous guilt about regarding how he had dealt with the issues.

Gail: I think in the beginning we were all in so much shock still, and we were just going through the motions. I think that we were all thinking we had to stay very strong. I remember my son when he got there; he broke down into tears when he got into the house. He said, "I know something's wrong." And I took him in the bedroom and my husband and I told him what happened, and he was crying and crying and crying. They were really, really close. And I said, "[Son], we can't cry. We have to be very strong. There's lots of things we have to do. And we have to do this for Barbara. We have to get through this." I never saw my son cry again. And I knew that that was my mistake to him, because I never let him have that kind of release. But I just knew that whatever it took, we had to do. Whether it was right or wrong, we thought we were doing what was right.

Gail, as previously mentioned, was only aware of the extent of Barbara's experience after Louis had been arrested. Then, she was told the full details of Barbara's sexual assault and the extent of her injuries. This information, of course, predisposed her initial reaction to Louis, when she first saw him in the courtroom.

Gail: … And the first time I saw him, I thought, "He's so small." He's just a smart-ass. I thought, he's not bad looking. You didn't have to rape to get it. And he was quiet. He didn't seem—I mean, I thought he was a total smart-ass, but he didn't seem jokey or nothing … . The main thing I remember about Louis is his size. I just thought he was small.
Interviewer: How did you get the sense of him being a smart-ass?
Gail: Because of the way he held himself, his demeanor. Just how he came across to me. And then eventually whenever his family started coming, his family would sit in the back and they would talk back and forth like it was absolutely nothing. Just like—just something passing—something they were going through. And I just got the impression that that's what it was—it was just like—just party. It just was nothing—it meant nothing to any of them. Barbara was dead, but it didn't mean anything to anybody.

I remember when we pled on Louis, and I told my husband, I said, "You know, no matter what I think of Louis' family, this has got to be painful for his mom. And I'm going to tell her I'm sorry that she's having to hurt, because I know what you're feeling, some of it, and I'm sorry for you." And we was sitting out in the waiting area, by the courtroom, and it was all done so quickly that there really wasn't any media involved. I don't know how these guys got wind of it because it was just real quick. But they came and they asked [Husband] and I questions, and we wouldn't answer any questions. And they went over to Louis' dad, and they asked Louis' dad what he thought. And he just shrugged his shoulders and said, "Well, these things happen. When you do, you just gotta deal with it." And I hated that man more than I hated Louis. I just—and I still to this day cannot stand the family. They've made some really rude, crude remarks and I'm sick to death of people, his family, blaming me. It's point blank said that it's my fault he's in prison. I didn't do what he did. He did it. And I told Louis this when I talked to him and that it upset me. And he told me that he told his mom and dad not to say anything to anybody.

When the mediation was arranged, it was briefly unclear whether Gail's husband would be involved as well. There was apparently some ambivalence on everyone's part as to whether the husband should be involved, as one of the officer's claimed that he "saw something" in the husband's eye that made him uneasy as to Louis' safety. This information apparently also made its way to Louis, who then expressed concern, and it was decided that Gail would meet with Louis by herself.

Gail: And you know, really, my husband and my son wasn't—they weren't really interested in it anyway. I mean, all they wanted was five minutes with him. Period. But we had made an agreement that whatever I asked or whatever I thought I needed, that whenever it was through, it was over. We wouldn't go home and argue about it, we wouldn't do any of those things, and that's just how it went. He said, "If it helps you, that's good." But they both believe that Louis tells me what I want to hear, to pacify me. They don't believe that he's—but I do. I mean, I looked him straight in the eye and I believe he was as honest with me as he could be. I mean, I think that there's parts of it that he tries to shut out that he doesn't want to—but I believe he was as honest with me as he could be.

And I don't forgive Louis for what he did. I would never forgive Louis for what he did. I do know that I feel Louis has some serious problems. I think that the system let us all down. I mean, he was in and out of [a state facility], he was discharged from the military because of his behaviors. At one point in the documentation from the psychiatrist, he said if he didn't seek help, get help, and stay on medication, he would eventually kill somebody.

And in further discussing the issue of forgiveness, Gail states:

Gail: I personally could never forgive somebody for taking away from me what he did, and in the way he did. Over the time, though, it's got to be a lesser issue of forgiveness. It's happened. We've dealt with it. There's nothing we can do about it. And it takes too much energy and it keeps me too sick, dealing with the hatred. Even my husband—a couple months back, he asked me, he said, "Do you still have all that hate and anger inside you?" And I said, "No. I really don't." And he said, "You know, I don't either. It's just too much to deal with. Do you think that we're not being right by Barbara?" And I said, "No, I think it's just growth." But no, I could never forgive him for what he did. I can accept that he has mental problems. But there again, he could have stayed on the medication, and refused to. So, he still has to take responsibility for what he did.

Gail, in her narrative, discussed the events of the second meeting with Louis, and why this was important to her. She also made interesting observations about the preparation process, and her effort, as happens in each of these meetings, to make Barbara real to Louis.

Gail: And there were still answers that I wanted. And then, too, I wanted to give [the mediator] the experience. [This was one of the first mediations performed by this state office.] But there was still some impact that I wanted to make on Louis that I wanted to follow through with.

There are parts of the mediation program that I don't agree with now. I remember when I did it with [Mediator], and I asked Louis a question, he said, "Yeah, [Mediator] told me you was going to ask me that but … ." I was so angry at [Mediator], because I felt like he violated my trust. I didn't fill out those questionnaires, I didn't answer all those questions. We had talked personally and I remember how angry that made me. Just so angry. But that was just part of the learning. I believe that if people go through the program, that there's a great deal of healing that goes on whether you ever see your offender or not, by just answering that information.

And I believe that a lot of it has to be controlled, because there's just so much risk that the state was involved with, that they want to have that kind of control over it. And at times I feel like it's just like choreographed. Because he's got all of the questions and answers ahead of time, and you've put all of yourself into writing ahead of time. So, there's just no spontaneity in it. For me, it was important to look at the expression on Louis' face. He had told [HBO correspondent] that "I want you to tell her that I won't lie to her. I'll be honest with her as much as I can, but that there are things that I can't remember, or don't want to remember." So, I wanted to know if he'd remembered anything else, that was one of the reasons.

I took Barbara's clothes with me and the clothes she was wearing whenever she was killed, and I wanted him to feel those clothes because to me those clothes were just painful. Just nothing but pain. And I wanted him to feel them, and he didn't want to touch them. I said, "No," and I pushed them over in front of him and I said, "Feel these clothes. This is all you left me." I took a picture album, I put a picture album together from the time that Barbara was born, all the way up. I wanted him to know the life he had taken away. And so that was good for me.

And to see the changes in Louis. [Mediator] and they have a problem with the fact that I feel that no matter what, Louis is a part of me and will be a part of me from now on. He's just like glued to me. Because I can't ever think of Barbara that he doesn't come to my mind. And that's just a fact. But they don't think that that's healthy. Well, I don't see that it's not healthy, I just think it's factual.

Gail discussed with me the advent of asking Louis to draw a picture of Barbara. She was concerned that, given that the newspaper photos of Barbara were older, that the picture Louis drew would not look like Barbara at the point he killed her. Gail spoke with him about the changes she had made to her hair, and how she looked at the time of her death. I asked Gail what she had done with the picture that Louis drew for her.

Gail: I told him the next one he drew, he could give it to me. I wanted to see what they were. But Barbara had started letting her hair grow, and he did her hair exactly like the newspaper clippings. So, I knew he didn't remember Barbara other than what he had come to know. There were things like that that I just … .

… the picture is very good—he's very talented. I don't think he gives himself credit for it. And I'm not giving him an excuse, but … .

Interviewer: What did you do with the picture, Gail?

Gail: I put it in Barbara's chest. I put it in a frame and put it in her chest. But it was a good picture. And like I said, it was good for me to know that he didn't—which is another part of it—he didn't know her. He couldn't remember what she looked like.

Personalizing the experience (through the clothes and photo album), making Barbara a real person, and letting Louis know about the experience of the family, was very important to Gail. She felt that this was the point where Louis connected to this reality.

Gail: I remember during the mediation when I told him about Barbara's appearance and what I felt when I finally got to be with her, because we weren't allowed to see her. When we found out the cause of death, we found out over the TV. We were watching the news and they gave the cause of death over the TV. And that's how we found out the cause of death. But we hadn't been allowed to see her. Had no information. And I remember talking to him about that. And he leaned up on the table—the table wasn't any bigger than this—and he was kind of leaning on his elbows, and when I started talking to him, he kind of fell back in his chair. And I could see the expression on his face, and I knew that he was fighting back tears. And he told me, he said, "Nobody ever told me that." And I told him, "You know, nobody should have to tell you that. You did it."

But—there were things about it that made me realize he wasn't an animal, he wasn't a monster, and he was just a human being that Barbara just happened to take the brunt of his problem.

Gail shared with me the difficulty she had in initially meeting Louis, how she felt immediately before meeting with him, and what changed at the moment she saw him.

Gail: Oh, I threw up. I was sicker than a dog the night before. The first one, they told me, "Well, if you get in there and you see you can't do it, it's still OK." And they were great about it. I remember going into the prison and the warden that was there dealing with us on the first on, I asked him what he thought about the program, being able to do this. And he said, "Well, I'm like your husband. I don't think it means anything to him. But my wife is like you." And I remember they had that good-old-boy system. My husband didn't get you know the [search]. I had to go in the bathroom and be body searched. And that was very wrong. But the woman that did my search, she told me, she said, "I want you to know that I am so extremely proud of you. I'm a rape victim, and I could never do this. But you know, this really gives me hope." And I had a lot of that. And so, I knew that it had to go through, had to be done.
Interviewer: And once you sat down and looked at him in the eyes, as you said, and told him the impact on you of this, what was that like?
Gail: It just felt good. It was just like a relief. It was just a lot of pent-up—you sit there and you say, "boy, if I ever see him, I'm going to tell him—Boy, he's going to know this, and boy! he's going to know that." And then all of a sudden, you're doing it. And it's coming around. And it's just a lot of release afterwards. I know that I could never make him understand who Barbara was, because their encounter was just so brief. But I can help him understand what Barbara's life being cut short really was to us. I didn't want him to think that we had a life like

he had, and that it didn't matter. Because I don't think he thinks it ever really mattered to his mom and dad. He told me one time, he said, "when I was twelve years old, I was already an alcoholic. Been an alcoholic. I already had problems. My dad lifted his hand to me to slap me, and I shook my head at him and said, 'it's too late.'" Part of you thinks, why does God let this type of life go on? He's truly got problems.

And in discussing her view of Louis, Gail states:

> Well, you know, I knew he was mentally ill. When I did it, I knew that in order to find out anything from him, I couldn't treat him badly. I couldn't anger him or set him off, or I wouldn't get anywhere with him. So, I had decided that I would just treat him like a human being, the way I wanted to be treated. And I told [Husband], "If he smarts off to me, I'll probably just climb right over that table at him." And I meant it. I really thought I would. That's just like when I say—you know, if they let him out tomorrow, I'd have to wait for him at the gate. And I'd have to serve my time in prison. Because I could never live knowing that he could do that to another person. I couldn't do that. I couldn't get up every day. But whether I could really do it or not, but my gut feeling says, don't ever let him come out.
>
> But I think he had to put a face to the fact that he took the life of a human being, and that human being belonged to somebody. And I write to him, I answer his letter every year. In fact, I'm in the process now of writing another one.

Interviewer: This is part of your arrangement, that he would write every year?
Gail: Yeah. I know that there are lots of people that don't understand my letters to Louis. But to me they're therapeutic, plus that I feel like every time, I give him a little bit more insight to the effect he's had on the family. I don't think that he should ever become complacent in his feelings. But I'm angered at the system, that the system won't help him either. Because we both know that there's always a chance he'll walk out of there. And that the system doesn't give him some psychiatric help is very irritating.

… He has grandchildren—even though he's never seen them—he has grandchildren. I will never have a grandchild by Barbara. I will never be able to plan a wedding for Barbara. His two daughters got married in the last couple of years. And the only thing I have of Barbara is to go to the cemetery. Period. You have to—I don't know if everybody does—but I go through the guilt of the religious aspect. Where is she? What is she doing? Does she have memory? Is she with me? All those different things. It never goes away. It just gets a little easier. I mean, the acceptance of those stages you go through just get a little easier.

… I tell him about different changes in our lives [in her letters]. I just can't even think what I wrote. In this one, I'm in the process of—well, you know, you do a lot of reading and trying to figure things out. And one of the studies I did talked about religion, and Louis used to be a religious person. He told me. But he doesn't have any faith anymore. His priest said that he would stay in contact with him, and so forth and so on, he told me he never came. And he has no use for religion. Well, I read this one part and he talked about you can have a feeling that Christ is with you, but he's standing on the outside, he's not on the inside. If he's on the inside, you're not going to do anything bad, because he's there. Part to me, before something happens to Louis, I would like to—it used to bother me that if he said, "I'm sorry" that he would go to heaven, and then he could walk side by side with Barbara, after what he had done. So, I dealt with that and so that's why I started in with the trying to research some of this other stuff. And so, what I wanted was for him, if he really was sorry, to know within himself that he was really sorry. And that what he did was evil. And that evil does exist, and things like that.

And I talked to him in the last letter about how … let's see, I've had three heart attacks, I've had—last year I had open heart surgery. I've had two ablations, and they tell me I'm going to die of a massive stroke. I want him to know the effect that he's had on me. And this may be my last visit, if I get to go. I'm going, but whether they'll let me visit with him or not, I don't know. I haven't heard yet. But it would be my last one.

Interviewer: You said that because you're not sure of your health?

Gail: Right. I personally don't think anybody can tell you when, because it's not going to happen until then. But they keep giving me this crap. Last week I had a little mini-stroke and dropped in the classroom in front of everybody, that was pretty embarrassing, but anyway… it's just how life goes.

Later, I asked Gail if she felt that she had shared anything in common with Louis, if she saw herself being like him in any way.

Gail: Golly, I don't know if I want to share this or not, but I think some of it stems from my upbringing, my family life that I didn't have, that didn't exist. I had a stepdad that was a total alcoholic, very verbally abusive, mentally abusive. You were just so controlled—it was terrible. None of us could wait to get out of the house type of thing. And so, I think part of my upbringing—I think about him with—and I do know I have mental problems, but I deal with my mental problems. I want to be healthy; he doesn't. Things like that. And I think everybody knows that they could be violent, if you don't control it. That's just the whole thing: learning to control it.

Gail told me why she wanted to "step down" from her public speaking, and I asked her about the feeling of telling her story, and whether she felt this was helpful or not.

Gail: I think it's useful. I think it could go both ways. I honestly do. I'm never sure of it, to tell you the truth. But I think it can be very useful. I think the initial—when you first start talking about it and you work through, it's very healthy for you. But the more times you're asked to repeat it, I think you can learn to get a guilty feeling, like you're using the experience to be a crutch for what your feelings are at this point. And I think that can be unhealthy. And I always say, if you ever think that of me, tell me, and we'll stop. But I've come to the point—I used to get—I'd get sick and I'd throw up and have diarrhea before I would go and speak. And now I've got to where I can shut the one part of me off and just try and tell them what they want to hear.

... Well, you know, I guess a lot of it is my identity. It's changed my identity, not in the aspect of doing the mediation and helping, things like that. But I'm not Barbara's mother anymore. When people ask you, how many children do you have? What do you say? I have two? Do you say you have one? And I told you my son is very ill, and I mean, life/death, life/death all the time with him growing up. And I always knew that I'd have to bury him; it never, ever dawned on me that—and I always thought that when Barbara was older that we would have time for relationships and stuff, and I know now that there's never a right time for relationships. If you can have a relationship, you'd better jump on it, because there may not be a later. But now I don't—even with [Son]—I fought with him all the time, about taking care of himself and this and that. I don't anymore. I'm going to enjoy what I have. If it's going to be short-lived, then it's going to be short-lived. I'm not going to fight and argue with him for the rest of his life and mine, to get through this.

That's just like, for myself, the only thing that I really enjoy is eating. I'm home alone all the time, and I am not going to give up the only thing—what little bit makes me happy, to try and live a day or two longer. And they still can't tell you whether you're going to live or die. And I think it's made me more aware of other people and their needs. I've always been a giving person, I've always been a caregiver, so I mean a lot of that stuff hasn't changed. But I think before I did it because it was a routine. It was supposed to be. Now I do it because there's really the need there ... .

In her last statement to me, Gail summarized the significance to her of the process, the system, and her parenting.

Gail: Yeah. And you know, when we put Louis away, it was fifteen years was a life sentence, and now it's up to forty-five. But there's always technicalities. And those are the things that a victim's family always has to worry on. And these people, they go back for trial after trial after trial, I don't know how they do it. I swear to you, I don't know how they hold up to it. Or people that have their families where they've been dismembered, and—because—looking at Barbara was hard enough. I don't know how some people do it. And so that's just part of saying, like, mediation is good for you or not good for you. It's just whatever works for you.

It's hard enough that you had to lose somebody you love, without having to deal with the system. And people like to bury their head in the sand and not really think about it, because then they don't have to think about it could happen to them. And I'm just as guilty, but I just never—you figure if you tell your kids to stay away from certain people and you know they are, and they don't do this and they don't do that, that everything will be fine. And it's not.

SECOND INTERVIEW WITH LOUIS

I interviewed Louis the second time almost three years later. He remained in the same institution, and continued in administrative segregation. This time I met with Louis in a comfortable lawyer's interview office. The two young women officers who escorted Louis to the interview waited patiently outside the office, checking from time to time through the window in the door, and engaged in their own lively discussion.

I could not tell, when Louis saw who had come to visit him, if he was pleased to see me, or simply pleasantly surprised that I had, true to my word, returned to interview him again.

Louis looked older. As Gail told me in her interview, "Being in prison ages a person quickly."

The first thing that I said to Louis was that I was back to follow up with a few questions, since I had now seen the video of the mediation, and had interviewed Gail a few days earlier. The first thing Louis said to me was, "How's she doing?" He was interested, then, to know if she had said anything about his letter, which he had recently sent her.

I asked Louis to tell me what had happened in his life since we last met. Louis stated, "Nothing's changed here, it's still the same." He had reported to me, at the last visit, that he felt his stay in administrative segregation would be indefinite. This statement continued to surprise me, as, without being familiar with this state's institutional rules, it had been my impression that inmates did not stay in segregation indefinitely without severe provocation.

Louis: I'm going to be here, indefinitely, unless the system changes. I've pretty much accepted that.

I expressed surprise at this comment, but did not try to understand the reasoning or the rules behind this decision. I did state that I remembered that Louis had told me, when we last met, that he did not mind being alone that much.

Louis: I've always liked being by myself. Just, sometimes, it gets old, you know, you don't move around as much as you want to. Especially, now, with the shortage [of staff and funding] they have, we hardly go out anymore. I haven't been outside—I don't think I've been outside once this year. I'm kind of pale. But I like to keep busy. I read a lot. I read everything I can get my hands on to read. I draw a little bit.

Louis told me that he continues to work on his drawing skills and that he enjoys reading philosophically oriented material. Much of his reading tends toward spiritual themes, and he continues to struggle with his own relationship to spirituality, comfortable in the belief that he has no use for it.

Louis: I still read all that. I read whatever. I was talking about reading—I'm sure you've heard of Carlos Castaneda, right? I'm thinking about reading all his books again. I kind of like those … I read them all. Plus, having Yaqui blood, that's just something to read. Just to keep busy.

We speak of Louis' children, and, now, grandchildren. When we first met, his children and stepchildren were mostly adolescents. His younger children did not know him. His youngest daughter, now fourteen, was recently told about Louis as her father, and he was anticipating a visit from her, at some point. His son, now in college, had had a difficult time, dropped out for a year, and was now considering medicine. Louis states, "He says he wants to be a doctor, which would really be shocking, especially coming from me." I reminded Louis that he had told me that he was worried that his son would follow his path, and that he was hopeful that this would not happen. "He's definitely going to be different than me. He has a lot of my ways; he has my mannerisms, that's about the only thing." Louis said that his oldest daughter was also in college and doing something related to medicine. Basically, Louis reported, all his children were doing well.

We talk about how they remain connected, whether they visit or write. Louis stated that basically they write infrequently, and don't visit. Some maintain closer contact than others. Louis states, "That's to be expected. I've been gone so long."

I ask Louis if, since we last met, he has had any second thoughts about his meeting with Gail.

Louis: No, I don't regret talking to her at all. Actually, I think everyone should do it.

… You have a lot of people here, right, who didn't do things. Like there's one, in fact, I was talking to him and he says he's not a criminal. He doesn't consider himself a criminal. I said, "Well, what about all the things you done?" No, nothing wrong with that. Well, what if somebody does that to you? Well, then it's wrong. Don't make no sense. And that's the way they look at it. They don't look at it as hurting somebody else. That's the main thing. If you put a face to whatever you've done, it changes things. You look at it different.

Having seen the tape of the mediation (I viewed the one done by the state mediator, but have not seen the one produced by HBO.), I talk about a section that struck me in which Gail, tearfully, said to Louis that she felt that Barbara had been forgotten. Louis said to Gail that Barbara would never be forgotten. Gail became quite tearful, and said that people forget her all the time. Louis responded, "Well, I won't." I asked him if he remembered this interchange, and he said that he did.

Louis reported to me that he thought about Barbara every day, even though he had gotten rid of much of the data he was saving, such as newspaper clippings about the crime and material about the mediation.

We spoke about genuineness in these meetings, and how that is defined. Louis remains cynical about human nature, his included, but I suggested to him that in viewing the videotape, there was little question in my mind that he was genuinely engaged with Gail and honestly moved by the encounter.

Louis: Once that person's in front of you, it's going to be kind of hard not to realize you're talking to somebody about something—not just something that's happened that you never did. You put a face to it.

… I don't know—I look at it like this: in here, it's a different culture, right? And everything we do, you're never going to know anybody completely. Nobody's ever going to show you who they are. So, we're used to living that way. The person you talk to today is not the same person you talked to yesterday. So, you all come in here, you all just see us once every blue moon or so, I don't see how you all are going to figure it out. So even the officers, they're here all day long, and it's like with me. A bunch of officers will say, "It really don't seem like you should be here" and all this, and I tell him don't believe what you see. I told her, you just can't. Because the people here, they will think something about you. Like I tell them, I'm not a nice person. I'm here because I did something awful. Just because I'd do it [the meeting] doesn't mean that I've changed. To me, I'm still the same person.

I told Louis that I had struggled with this notion since we last met. I said to him that, in viewing the videotape, and in hearing his discussion of it, it was hard not to conclude that he had changed in some fundamental way from the person he was at the time of the murder.

Validating one of the key theories of change in the psychopathic personality, Louis stated to me simply, "I'm older." But Louis held to the two-persona theory.

Louis: It's just like my family. They don't know me. They know what they see in the visits, that's all. I'm not the same person to my family as I am to the people around here. I can't be. That's how I feel about this thing. It's totally different.

In another insightful comment, Louis extrapolated a common psychodynamic theory of juvenile delinquency, while telling me about his gang involvement.

Louis: ... that's why I'm not getting out [of segregation]. That's one of the major decisions I've made that I regret now, but I'm not going to go back. So even though I know it's wrong, I chose this life. I have to live with it now—matter of fact, being in a gang, there are certain things you're going to do. Certain things that you're not going to. We have rules. They have rules. Which really ... really doesn't make any sense. I said, we're here because we don't follow the rules. But still yet, we'll join something and put rules on ourselves. So, we *want* the rules. And we'll sit there and swear up and down, nobody's going to tell me what to do. But still yet, we sign our life away and somebody's always going to tell you what to do. And you're not going to argue about it, you're just going to do it. ... We're to the point where they're going to tell us when we're going to eat, when we're going to shower, when we do this. There's nothing you can do on your own.

Louis then told me the story of getting into a fight, in which he was taken by surprise. During a visit from his father and brother, he told them this, and told them that he was preparing to retaliate against his aggressor: "I'm not satisfied yet, I've got to take care of this when I get back out." Louis reported that his father asked him, for his sake and his mother's, not to retaliate. Louis reported to the father that he was asking a difficult thing of him, as he would surely be seen as weak if he did not carry out the expected retribution. But Louis agreed, did not retaliate, and took the expected grief: "Tell somebody something, you gotta' do it. If you don't do it, nobody's going to believe you. That's all we have here is our word. We ain't got nothing else."

I pursued with him, then, his theory of change in humans. He stated to me that he did feel that people can change.

Louis: The first part is you've got to accept everything that you've done and until they do that, you ain't never going to change. I know a lot of people here, they'll swear up and down that they've changed, but like I told Gail, we have these so-called Christians in here, but if you go to the wall, you'll find a lot of bibles, there's a lot of them, and they are the same people. That's the major change in here. When everybody gets tired of living life where you have to be stand-up, don't take nothing from nobody, don't ever let them get you, that's the main way out. You go the Christian route. So, the way it is now, in here, when somebody says they've become a Christian, nobody believes them. Because we've seen it happen so many times. Because we've seen them—they'll play Christian for two or three years, they'll get out, and within three months, they're back in prison. They were doing the same thing they were doing before. So, in here, it's easy to say you're going to do something, that you've changed, but until we see it—that's what I tell a lot of people, in here it's real easy to be a man because all you've got to do is fight. Don't take it. But to change, you've got to accept everything that you've done. You've got to learn to walk away from it.

I asked Louis to personalize this theory, to tell me where he thought he stood with this. He liked my question, found it provocative, and thought about it for a long time, with an introspective, "Hmmm."

Louis: There's a lot of things, now, that I don't let get to me. I don't let most of what happens here get to me, to the point where it's going to bother me. Because I know I'm going to be here. So, I've changed to that point. And I try to avoid things that in the past I wouldn't have. I've always been quiet anyways, so that helps. But now, things that are happening in the system now—the system's not the same as it was when I came in. So, whether or not you want to change, you're going to change. Because I wasn't—how would I say it?—not so much violent now, but there's—I know in me now that there's some things that if push comes to shove, I'm going to do what I need to do to exist. That's just being here. Whereas if I was on the outside, it wouldn't be that way, I hope.

I suggested to Louis that this sounded to me like the pessimistic view he had of himself when we last talked, and he asserted that he should never be released. However, his resolve had moved to a more ambivalent position.

Louis: I hope I'm changed. Seriously, I do not want to ever hurt anyone again. That's what I want. I want to help people now. That's why I talk to all the, listen, to the younger guys that's coming in here. Because they'll come in here with this big chip on their shoulder. And they think they have to do something, and it's like I told you earlier, it's real easy to be a man in here. It's not easy out there. They say, "Well, I don't take nothing from nobody." "No, you don't, but who's taking care of your kids? Are you there to help them?" But there's some guy out there working minimum wage and he may not have a new car, he may not have this, he may not have all that, but he's happy. It's different. Now me—everybody wants to get out. I want to get out. It's like I told Gail, would I ever do it again? I don't know. I didn't think I'd ever do it in the first place. That's what I told her. I can't tell you that no, I'll never do it. I can't tell you that. I'm not going to lie to you and I'm not going to lie to me.

I ask Louis how much of this had to do with his concept of accepting responsibility for his actions.

Louis: Accepting everything that I've done? I've accepted it. I don't remember all of it. I still don't remember all of it. And I don't think I'm ever going to remember all of it. I've accepted to the point where I know I did it. But there's still times where I don't feel it. I mean, I know what I've done, I should feel something, right? But there's times when I didn't. Because there's a lot of people will ask me, "Why did you do it?" I don't know. And I don't think I'll ever understand myself until I can understand that. Much less there's no way I'll ever forgive myself for the things that I've done. That won't happen.

Despite Gail's belief about Louis being mentally ill, he had told me about his psychiatric history when we last met, and that he had continued to refuse medications, and was not convinced that he had any diagnosable mental illness. He also minimized the role of his family history of abuse and violence in leading to his life situation. I continued to get the sense that his commitment to this belief was to not allow himself or others to see his family history or his psychiatric condition as "excuses" for his behavior.

Louis: I was the most violent person in our family. To me, the way I look at it, I was destined to be here, because of the way that I am, the things that I've always done. Like I say, I'm a real quiet person, but there comes a time when I get mad, and I'm going to do something. And I know what I'm doing, so I can't say that all that, when I get mad. A lot of people say that they'll get real mad to the point where they just do things, they ain't got no control. You do what you do, what you want to do. Like they say, alcohol or drugs, I don't use that either. Because whether you're drinking or whether you're doing drugs, whatever you do, it's inside of you. Now it's true that alcohol or drugs, it may lower your inhibitions, but still what you've done, that seed has been in you, so that's you. Because I know people that drank way more than I did, did way more drugs than I did, and they're not here, I'm here. So, all that blaming alcohol or the drug part, or because they didn't give me a good childhood, and I wanted this, and all that, I'll never believe that. Because that's the biggest crutch—every time you see something, anybody you see in the newspaper or magazines, everywhere, every time something goes wrong, well, "It's because of my childhood." Because of this, because of my parents, that's a crock, that's the way I look at it.

… I'm just that way. I don't understand it. I don't know why I'm that way. It's like nurture versus nature. And this is where I contradict myself, and I thought about it too. I'm this way. I was born this way. But still yet, I'll turn around and I'll say to you that my kids are not going to be like me because they weren't raised the way I was. So, I'm contradicting myself.

… And I look at it that I'm saying I'm this way because I was born this way. And my children aren't going to be this way because they were raised different. That's one thing I preach to my children—don't ever do anything that I did, nothing. And as long as that happens, I'll be satisfied. I'll never be happy in here. Some people say that they're happy—nobody's happy in here. But I'll live with it.

… I don't like me. So, I don't think I'll ever trust myself. I am my own worst enemy. That's true in my case. But I don't like me, because I know the life I'm living here, and I know it's wrong, but still, you know … because it's like I said, I gave my word to do a certain thing, and I'm not going to back out on that. It's like I tell everybody: I'm here for the duration. I'm going to be here. Chances of me getting out, they're slim. And if I do get out, I'm going to be very old. The decisions I've made so far, they weren't right. And even though I regret one of the major decisions I made, I'm not going to go back on it. Because that's all I have; I've got my word. Whatever changed, I think I've matured. I look at things differently now. I don't fly off—I don't lose my temper so quick. Which I never did lose very quick, it's just now, things that would have bothered me in the past, they don't bother me anymore. I just kind of grin and bear it. All right, whatever. It's basically here being in SEG, because I'm locked in the same cell. If somebody down the run is arguing with me, we're never going to touch each other. So what good is it going to do for him to be calling me all these names and me calling him all that. It's like we say here, as long as I'm here I'm going to be all that. And that's the truth. You can't change that. And a lot of that is just the fact that they're locked up and it gets to them. It gets to a lot of people. It gets to me. Even I, who like to be by myself all the time, I like being away from everybody. Everybody needs time alone, especially in here.

I asked Louis to reflect on any similarity he saw between himself and Barbara, or Gail.

Louis: I don't know much about Barbara. I know what little Gail's told me about her, but that's all. She hasn't really told me too much about her. She's showed me all of the pictures of her growing up and everything, and she told me what Barbara was like and what she wanted to be, so I know all of that. And I remember when Gail was talking about her alcoholism, about growing up like that, she was talking about that. And I said, "Well, I remember growing up like that, too." So, we had that in common. Which is—there has to be something, because like I keep telling her, I don't understand why you still want to talk to me. There's something—there's some kind of—I don't know what it is. I don't understand it. I don't think she understands it.

… Just now, like when you told me she tried to come again, and—my family, they say, "why does she do this? She needs to put it to rest." That's her daughter, she ain't never going to put it to rest. The least I can do is talk to her. Whatever she wants to say to me, she can say it. I'll keep that, I'll always be honest with her.

Louis then told me an extraordinary story of a memory that came to him:

Louis: There's only one thing that I've told [Mediator] that I'll never tell Gail. There's only one thing. And that's because a while back, I heard a sound, and it snapped inside my heart. I said, I've heard this before. Well, I've heard something similar to it. And I kept thinking about it for the rest of that day, and then I heard the sound again. And I finally figured out what it was—it was the sound of the air coming out of Barbara, when she was dead. So, I'll never tell her that. [Mediator] knows that. I've told [Mediator] when we were talking. He asked me if I remembered anything—I remembered that. Which is really strange, because what I heard has nothing to do with this and at the time I was in the middle of doing something else. And then all of a sudden, I stopped everything—why does that sound bother me? And then I remembered.

In discussing the connection between him and Gail, he suggested that this is simply due to Gail thinking about Barbara, and, naturally, then thinking about him.

Louis: … I'm never going to forget it. A day doesn't go by that I don't think about it. It's why I'm here. It's what I've done. So, it's always going to be there.

… I think it's just like my children, actually, or my family. Because I can be doing anything, I can be reading, I can be drawing, I can be talking to somebody, and all of a sudden, a thought comes into mind and I'll think about Barbara this, or Gail that. Just like I do with my children. I don't constantly think about it, but they're constantly on my mind. So, it's always there. It's always there.

I asked Louis if his thinking about the changes possible was related to his age, or to his developing philosophical position.

Louis: I think it's a little of both. I think it's a lot of about—like I said, being here and just to the point where I don't want to do anything. I'm getting older. I've seen what it's gotten me so far, it's a no-win situation. … The system is fixing to change. We've got a lot of people coming in with a lot of long times, and they ain't going nowhere. Well, the system's going to get a little bit rough. So, if you want to live that kind of life, chances are you're not going to make it in here. Nobody wants to die.

I think I could [make it if he were released]. I'd make it. I want to make it. I want to see my grandkids. Of everything that I miss the most, it's the fact that I have grandkids now and I'm not—that kills me. It's like I've told my daughters already, my grandkids, they're never going to know me, so there's no sense in you all even telling them who I am. I'll draw them whatever and I'll send it to them. As they get older, there's no sense in my trying to worry about it because then you're … .

Louis' comment trailed off here, he did not complete his sentence.

Excerpts from the videotaped meeting with Gail

Louis: I was real possessive and real jealous. The things you said about not being able to go to the store [about her own family history], I was like that. I don't know why I was that way, but I was. Probably still am. I don't think I've changed. People say that when they first met me here I was different. Quieter. Now they tell me I've changed. I don't think so.

In all honesty, regardless of what people say about me, some people who knew me before still can't believe that I did this. After we did the HBO thing, a lot of guards even said, they can't see me doing it.

Regardless of how people see me or what I'm doing, I'm a violent person. In all reality, I am. I mean I think I've got, I can be a good person, I'm not always violent. But when it comes right down to it there's violence and there's … . Maybe that's why I'm where I'm at now [in administrative segregation].

[Tells story of father asking him not to retaliate against the other inmate exactly as he recounted it to me]

That was the point when I got the letter from HBO. You remember when we first met I told you that you came at a time that kept me from getting involved in some things. You slowed me down because I was moving too fast.

As soon as that happened I knew if I kept on going they wouldn't let me talk to you. I let people say what they wanted to say.

Louis: I don't think I will ever forget [Barbara]. What do they say? As long as you remember somebody they're always there.

Gail: But everyone else forgets, Louis [very tearful].

Louis: I won't. I won't.

I can be sitting in the cell, and I can be reading a book, drawing (I draw) to working a crossword puzzle, listening to the radio, whatever. I'll hear a bird, whatever. And I think of her. The things that I think about when I do anything, and I think of Barbara.

So, it's there, every day, all the time.

INTERVIEW WITH THE MEDIATOR

The case of Louis and Gail was very important to this mediator, as it was the first case he had accomplished. He has maintained close contact with both Gail and Louis in subsequent years.

Mediator: Louis—Louis is one of those individuals that I hope—in fact with all of these—that I would like to keep in contact with the rest of my life. To think that here's a man that the greatest hope that he has is that maybe when he's seventy-five years old that he might get out. And yet, he continues to try to find some purpose and meaning in his life. There is no indication whatsoever that he is not trying to be as absolutely accountable as he possibly can be. And use the best of what he does have and understand about himself to help Gail. And now to help his children and his family. Every time I revisit with him, I have the same experience. I used him in an offender panel recently, a training we had of volunteer mediators that we brought down from [City]. And he just blew them away. He really—one can understand that when you look at his visage, how he doesn't emote drastically or whatever, and yet the sincerity I think has increased, at least in terms of being able to read that, than the opposite. And so, he's been consistent ever since I've known him. He's also shown some sensitivity toward just being brutally honest in that I think there's one thing that he does know that he's chosen not to share and that's part of the sexual assault that he did of Barbara, and has chosen just to not remember that, as far as informing Gail of it. He continues to struggle with nurture versus nature. And at first, he just totally disavowed any—but he was playing with himself and me on the part of the—but he genuinely tries to keep that intention, and where he'll catch himself in terms of saying that he was sort of born to do this, and then say, "Oh, maybe this is nurture."

These comments were a remarkable replication of my conversation with Louis and my own impression of him.

I asked him to tell me what images he holds onto from these individuals.

Mediator: … He really took on a position of just receiving what he could from Gail. There was not a lot of just profound film clips or sound bites out of Louis' and Gail's, but that didn't take anything away from it, it's just the process that they went through.

I recounted for the mediator my interview with Gail, and her interesting connection with Louis, and how moving her situation continued to be for me.

Mediator: Yeah—it's funny that you say that because I noted in a letter that I sent to the staff when I left—I go back to that first interview of Gail, that first meeting of Gail and Louis, and Gail taught the lesson of just the ongoing nature of this, that out of all the victims, even though she started it, in some ways it was the closest to the crime and she was less healed than many others at the time. She also had the greatest disdain of preparation, although since then, at least in one or two public opportunities, she said, and she'll still say, "I don't agree with all the preparation—it would seem intrusive in times" and whatever. And she did not do much writing at all but we talked through all of that. And so, she experienced the same level of preparation that others did. But she continues to try to grow, and she's facing I think, the cancer that's a part of her now is probably eventually going to take her. I don't know how fast that is moving. I would love

to have an opportunity to, because she is so ripe and ready in a lot of ways. Her family situation … [Husband] is not, [Husband] has always been supportive, but not believing Louis one bit. And yet vicariously, the way he talks, he has received so much from Gail. Anytime he would talk it would be a way to emote some of his anger, but you knew that some other things were going on inside.
Interviewer: She was intending on visiting Louis over the summer … .
Mediator: I was trying to set that up over the summer, but then this next phase of her illness kicked in. I was doing everything I could to make that happen. I don't know if it's going to happen now.

… Yeah, he's really tried to be very authentic and congruent. Yeah. And there again, there's so much we can learn from each other if we just take the time and opportunity.

DISCUSSION

This was another case that was very informative and stayed with me throughout the years following the pilot study. In many ways, Louis' presentation of his contradictions of what he called nature and nurture goes to the heart of my project. Clearly touched and greatly impacted, in the context of his meeting with Gail, he also told me that he had not changed and should never be released from prison: "I wasn't a nice person then, and I'm still not a very nice person."

What struck me about my first meeting with Louis was his commitment to having not changed, remaining dangerous, and not being safe to release from prison. Seemingly in opposition to this view was the genuinely moving reality connection he had made with Gail and, through her, with Barbara. These two individuals now clearly lived with him in a way that hadn't been the case prior to meeting with Gail. He had, with Gail and Barbara, achieved an ability to internalize and "mentalize" them as genuine object representations. Thus, my search for empathy in Louis was complicated by his seeming suggestion that he could compartmentalize his empathy, albeit after the fact in specific cases, but that he was not confident that it would have any prospective impact.

Like so many other offenders interviewed, one key component for Louis was his work, his preparation with the mediator. When asked what was helpful about what the mediator did, Louis simply responded, "Talking, just talking." This preparation process was likely the first time that anyone had shown an honest interest in Louis' story, or taken the time to elicit it from him.

In relation to the subject of empathy, Louis admired Gail for her treatment of him, and the respect she showed him. It was very important to him that she called him by name, and used his name in the meeting to address him. At the same time, he expressed confusion and wonder about this ability, saying that he, himself, could never do it.

He also showed an ability to create an internalized image of Barbara. Some of this ability was quite negative, in that he saw no connection between them, but some was clearly related to the fact that he took over a year to complete his drawing of Barbara for Gail.

In terms of his own genuineness, he also talked of the importance of being face-to-face with another individual: "With the person in front of you, it's hard not to realize that you're talking to another human being. You have to put a face to it."

The connection that Gail made with him in the discussion about his and her own family upbringing was not lost on Louis, as he recounted this to me by stating it may be one way the two might be similar.

Like others interviewed, Louis found it easy to characterize himself as two people, again replicating the true-and-false-self paradigm, or Kohut's vertical split concept.

Gail's comment, "It takes too much energy, and keeps me too sick dealing with the hatred …," summed up many responses related to the positives of these meetings for the victims. She also easily connected the question of "bonding" with Louis to a normative process for her, although she, too, was aware that this concept is viewed with some suspicion in her world. She stated that he is "part of me," and that he is "glued to me," and dismissed the controversy about this contradiction by blithely suggesting that it is "just factual."

Like others, her witnessing of Louis' emotion during the meeting was a turning-point experience for Gail. When she told him how she had heard of Barbara's death, it brought about an emotional reaction in him, and the sight of his tears allowed Gail to say that he, "wasn't an animal, he wasn't a monster, he was just a human being."

Perhaps the most poignant part of Gail's interview was the confidence she portrayed about her own death. She clearly saw her health history in recent years as being inexorably tied to Barbara's murder and she brought fatalism to this, to her own future, that was foreboding.

CASE 3: MIGUEL

Miguel was living the fast life. At seventeen, soon to be eighteen, he had quit school and was living with his brother or his friends. It was a time in which the image of a successful drug dealer carried a lot of panache in the culture, with the image of nice cars, pretty women, lots of money, and big, rich cartels. Miguel felt he was making headway in this regard. He had begun to develop a reputation among his peers, and was beginning to make a good living.

Consumed with their own lives, his family turned the other way, so he was left with little interference. He had some close associates, but mostly did not rely on anyone, feeling that he would do best if he counted only on himself.

Miguel had begun his rise to notoriety when he was just thirteen. He always hung around an older group, who initially treated him like a mascot, but eventually saw him as a sound dealer, giving him respect. At fifteen, he could afford his own car, and drove everywhere. This expanded his territory and he could meet a wider circle of people who continued to welcome Miguel, and educate him to the ways of the drug world.

At one point, at fifteen, Miguel got a job at a landscaping firm. The owner was impressed with Miguel's potential, and gave him a great deal of support and encouragement. Miguel eventually left this job, and made a clear commitment to the drug world, feeling that the "straight" life would not get him to his goals fast enough. In looking back on this time, Miguel clearly sees this as his choice between right and wrong. He also sees that his life, at that point, took a major turn, which then dictated his future.

One of the changes that happened to Miguel, during this time, was his exposure to violence. As he got deeper into the drug world, he and a friend were "kidnapped" by a rival, and were held, beaten, and threatened. Through a variety of intrigues, Miguel and his friend were able to outwit their captors, and get the drop on them through relatives of the friend. Thus, Miguel began his course toward violentization: "I already had it in my mind that I was going to go one step further [into the crime world] because it kinda' changed me that kinda' thing when someone is pointing a gun and slapping you around and everything it just—it was a turning point for me—it divided part of it, you know, and I said to him at that time, I said, 'Man, I'm not gonna let that happen to me again.'"

Miguel purchased and began to carry several guns. In a later fight, his assailant broke Miguel's nose, and Miguel retreated to his car, pulled out a .30–30 rifle, and shot at the offender. While he did not hit him, this shooting took his violentization to another level, and he continued to refine this reputation.

Miguel saw this all developing very fast, like stair steps, with each level bringing him some sense of fulfillment, but an inexorable feeling that there was no return. Miguel said to me, "Yeah, it was getting worse and worse you know, and with each incident it was something more aggravated."

One night, Miguel and his partner were at their favorite local hangout, and an associate approached the partner. Apparently, the partner owed this person money, and there was a brief hostile exchange between the two. In watching this exchange, several feelings rushed through Miguel. First, he was reminded of the power exerted on him by his rivals that night: "and it was the kinda' pressure that I seen him put on this dude was the kind of pressure

I had already experienced before with these other guys, and I said this other guy here might be a threat, you know? And from that point on, I was already on guard." Also important was the sense that he was being disrespected on his own territory.

Miguel had known of this person in the past, and they had "done deals" together, but by confronting Miguel's partner in public, and responding with a threat, Miguel felt that the situation had changed, and that this person had now become a threat.

Even with this, the two continued to deal with the associate, and the deals became bigger, moving from marijuana into cocaine, which was easier to transport and much more lucrative. Miguel, however, continued to feel nervous with this person, and the hostility between him and Miguel's partner regarding the money supposedly still owed continued to smolder each time the three of them were together.

In the last deal they engaged in together, Miguel decided that he had had enough of this "drama." The associate was due to come over to the house where they were staying to make a large purchase of drugs. Miguel ordered his partner to stay in the house when the associate got there, and Miguel would deal with him. Miguel would exchange the drugs for money, and send him on his way, so the partner would not have to deal with all the business about owed money.

When the associate arrived, the partner insisted on going out to talk with him and Miguel forced him to stay inside, physically pushing him back at one point. By the time Miguel came out to the driveway where the deal was to go down, the associate was pulling away in his car. This frustrated and angered Miguel even more, again making him feel discounted. He was aware that selling cocaine made him even more "big time'" and he had taken some grief from his supplier, who made fun of his age when he gave him the cocaine, as if he was not old enough to pull it off. Miguel was frustrated about having to deal with this person in the first place. In addition, he felt pressure from his supplier to close the deal since it was intended to be an $8,000 transaction.

When the associate came back, the two went into the garage to make the exchange. The associate was interested in talking with the partner, and Miguel became more frustrated, telling him to forget about the partner, that he was dealing with Miguel now. Miguel began to count the money, and it added up to only $5,000. He became angry and asked the associate what was up with that. The associate told him coldly that he had deducted $3,000 to pay the debt of Miguel's partner. Miguel remembers saying, "Look man, I don't need this stuff, and I don't need your shit. Like where do you think you are?" With this Miguel took the cocaine back, threw the associate his money and said, "Tell you what man, forget it. I don't need this. I'm leaving." As Miguel turned to leave, the associate grabbed his arm.

> *Miguel:* And he grabbed my arm and I had that gun with me and he grabbed me and I turned around and just the reaction … I wasn't ready for it, the reaction—and I went for the gun, and I knew the gun was there because I felt it there [in his waist band], and I'm not gonna let this dude hit me or whatever, you know, and I did first, one shot and, you know, and he fell down and then, I heard his girlfriend scream from the car, you know. And I just took the few steps to the car, walked down over there and stickin' my hand in the window and pulling the trigger two times, and it just happened just like that, in the time it took me to say it.

Miguel had only been vaguely aware that the associate's girlfriend, Caroline, was in the car when he arrived. In the heat of the transaction he had forgotten all about her. He had, in knowing the associate, known of Caroline and known that she was his girlfriend, but had never really spoken to her before. Now he had shot her twice in the head.

Miguel went back to the garage, picked up the money and the cocaine, and went into the house. His partner was excited, "What happened, what happened?" Miguel did not respond to him, rather he went into the kitchen and sat quietly at the kitchen table, just thinking. The partner went out to the car in the driveway, and came back quite agitated. The partner said, "What are you gonna do?" With this, Miguel said, "Shut the fuck up." And thought, then, that he would also shoot his partner.

He went out to the driveway, pulled the associate by his feet into the backseat of the car, took Caroline's body, and put it in the backseat. He then ordered the partner to follow him in his own car.

When Miguel went into the house to get the keys to his car, his brother had arrived entering through the front door. When the brother saw Miguel take his gun and put it in his waistband, he asked Miguel to leave the gun behind with him: "Man, I don't know what you did, but whatever you've done you've done enough for one night. Leave your gun here, man." Miguel, who respected his brother and felt close to him, was taken by this comment. So, he laid the gun on the table and left the house. This, Miguel told me later, spared the life of the partner, who Miguel was determined to kill that night.

Miguel drove the associate's car, with the two bodies in the backseat, to the bank of a small river close to their home. The partner pushed the car, headed toward the riverbank, into tall grass. The car went in only far enough so that it could still be seen. It was at this point, Miguel told me, that he would have killed his partner.

Later, after Miguel was arrested and was in the county jail, he asked his brother about that evening, and why he was so insistent that Miguel leave the gun at the house. His brother responded that he had seen "death in your eyes. I didn't see you, I saw death."

About a week later, Miguel was arrested. His first feelings while in jail were of disbelief. Everyone was asking if he really did it, and Miguel decided to deny the crime: "I had to make a decision, I guess, to build a wall, you know, and build a wall because I didn't want people to be—especially my family, to be hurt … if I had to lie to them I was gonna do that, because they would ask me, and I'd tell them no, because the shock that I seen in them."

Miguel: … it was a real experience in that I was—I had to deal with my own feelings you know, and my own thinking and try to balance it with somebody else's which is my family and everything and tryin' to be, so I can say to myself, I can make it—try to be strong try to show that everything is gonna be all right, not only for them but for myself you know, I had to be real—I just kept saying to myself man, I don't know if I kept saying it but you know, when I think about it now—what it was is that—at that point I went from being just a teenager dealing drugs to just being an adult, you know, in just a second and most people at my age at that time would take years to do and it was like—it had an effect where from being this one thing to being another and one extreme to the other … .

Miguel was found guilty and sentenced to life in prison. Approximately eleven years passed before the issue came up of meeting with Caroline's mother, Gloria. Miguel stated that it was coincidental since, at the point he was approached by the mediator to see if he would be open to a meeting with Gloria, he had been in a period of self-reflection, thinking about the past and the future. He had received a letter from an old girlfriend saying that he had been on her mind and talking about their past together. He stated that he was in a mood where he thought something important was about to happen to him.

When the mediator met with him, Miguel thought, "I guess this is it."

Miguel: … and [Mediator] came up here and told me what was going on and I guess it means what it is and you have to go one because I was at a point and I didn't know where I was gonna be and after ten years of doing nothing or am I gonna do another ten years of doin' nothin'? Twenty? You know, whatever, that's what I was thinking you know? I said, "Well, this is it." And that's what I said, you know, when he asked me I already knew I was gonna say "yes," that I was gonna do it. I had to and it was already inside of me, I had to say "yes," that I was gonna do this no matter what, that I had to do it if I was gonna be able to go on, you know?

In the first interview, it sounded to me like Miguel had already begun to make key philosophical shifts at the point he was approached by the mediator to meet with Gloria. He presented his decision at the time without even a trace of ambivalence, and when I asked him about this, he responded:

Miguel: Well, I didn't [have any hesitation]—when he started explaining things, I didn't think that, as far as terrible things about never getting out, it was more of something inside, because I always believe certain things happen for a reason and all that. I always had it in my heart that you know, you—in order to get something good, you have to do good and do right you know and that's not always the case, and you get sidetracked and a lot of times you don't really care. But I always had that, and I always knew that—that you had to do things to get something you know—you don't just get something because it's there or whatever or someone offered it to you, so when he did ask me, you know, and I felt like in order for me to move on, you know, I would have to give everything. I would just have to give up everything for me to go on, which is basically … that was my attitude that was my thinking you know, he was like, "You don't have to do this if you have a problem with that," and all this, and I was like, "Look, I don't," I made up my mind whatever's gotta be done I'm gonna do it.

… I was ready and you know like I said, I wasn't really concerned with what I got in return—I was more concerned with just doing it and getting it over with and getting it—taking that step.

The mediator met with Miguel and tried to prepare him. He was confused by Miguel's resolve at first, thinking that he was not taking seriously the potential for his own feelings being involved. Miguel felt that this was due to the mediator not being clear about the resolve he felt to meet with Gloria, and just do it. The mediator felt a need to tell him to "go slow, and be cautious," because of his own feelings.

On the day that Miguel met with Gloria, he was intensely nervous. He hadn't been prepared for this. To make matters worse, the meeting was put off for some time, and he had to wait for her to arrive.

Miguel: … I said, "I gotta calm down—somewhere." You know, I decided to just get up and walk, and start walking and I started walkin' back down the hallway and, I just turned off into the church and went into the church you know and during that time of day you have to have a pass to go into church and you gotta be—you know you get in trouble for … I didn't care—I walked in there and sat down real quiet and there were some people in there doing some things and people praying or whatever and just sat there and it was real quiet and that's what I needed, you know it was alright and I was thinking, thinking and things started to go slower and slower and a few minutes come by and here comes the chaplain and he comes in there and he says, "Can I help you with something?" I just looked down, "No I'm all right." He said, "Are you sure?" And I said, "Yeah." He said, "You have a pass?" And I said, "No." He said, "Well you know you're not supposed to be in here." And I said, "Yeah, I just want to be in here for a few minutes and then I'm leaving." And he goes, "Okay—are you sure you don't need anything, is there anything I can speak to you about or something?" And I said, "No it's okay. I'm all right." I just kind of smiled at him you know. But you know, what made me smile was that it kinda' calmed me down, he, you know sensed something, he sensed something that was going to do something or I was going to something you know and he wanted to be and just say something that he's there and I could talk to him and it would be alright so I smiled because he sensed that, you know… I didn't feel no kind of anxiety or whatever, everything was fine—walked back over here sat down you know. It was like the feeling I had before I didn't know it was different—what it was that you had to take a step back, you had to slow down and that's what I realized, you know.

Miguel resisted a lot of what the mediator attempted in preparation. He felt some instinct that he would know what to do and what to say. The writing exercises were of little use to him. He felt what he would need to do would come "from the heart," and nothing could prepare him for that.

Miguel had no memory of Gloria either from the trial or having seen her before. The initial meeting was uncomfortable, and the mediator attempted to calm them by asking benign questions. Then he had the two read the statements that they had prepared for each other.

Miguel had prepared himself for what he wanted to do in the meeting.

Miguel: … the first thing I really stuck to was that no matter what happens, not even in just the mediation but anything that you do—but be honest—that's the only way it's gonna come out and the only way anything's gonna be right and so that was my attitude going in there was to be honest about everything and to take it seriously and be accountable and show that you're accountable and remorse and be remorseful and all that—you know those three things and you have to do that even if you forgot just one of them it's not gonna work you know. So, I just really kinda stuck to that.

After my initial meeting with Miguel, I was able to watch the videotape of the meeting between Miguel and Gloria. One of the most powerful images of this for me was the point where Gloria showed Miguel the photo album of Caroline. What struck me about this sequence up to this point was how tentative and polite the two were being with each other, almost shy. Gloria, very tentatively, brought out the photo album: "Would you mind taking a look at a few of these pictures?" she asked. Miguel said that he would, and Gloria pushed the album over to him. He opened the front cover and began to page through the book. After looking at the first few photographs he broke down. He clearly was unprepared for what he saw, and the effect of it on him was palpable and profound.

In our first meeting, I asked Miguel, not knowing about this scene, if he had any surprises during the meeting.

Miguel: Yeah, I was surprised with the photo album—she brought a photo album of Caroline and growing up and that kinda had a real strong effect on me because it kinda broke the ice for me and that really surprised me—right there, because like I said, it broke the ice for me you know, to see those pictures because I told [Mediator]—you know you live all these years knowin' what you did and going through life tryin'—to close it off and not let it affect you and become kinda hard because you cannot show that in this environment. So the surprise for me was that—that you know being ten years in prison is hard—I was thinking that I would break down, I knew that—but I didn't know that would be the key, you know, and for me that was the beginning of the breakdown and, that's what you have to do—you have to break down—you have to come out with it and that was the, not the surprise [that it happened] but how it happened.

Miguel was also affected by a letter that Gloria had written to him prior to their meeting, explaining what she wanted to cover in their time together.

Miguel: … actually, it hit me pretty hard, but see—she wrote me a letter before I talked to her. [Mediator] showed it to me and, when I read it you know, I was like, numb you know? Because, you know—you just feel like some kind of—this power that you just know—then you knew—you don't feel that—in other words you just feel so small and when I read that letter—you feel so small, it makes you feel like you're—that's the way I felt, just small, you know, and like humiliating and that's good, you know, because here this lady went through so much and she wrote down and I read it and I didn't even think about it –somethin' you never even think about, something you knew never thought could have happened you know? And here you're reading it. Like I read it and felt my life's been nothing, you know—I [thought I] went through hell and I ain't been through nothing, and I had it easy, and that was the feeling … I had been humbled already, what could I possibly [say]—there was nothing that I could do to—or say to even comprehend or understand, you know, so why even try, just answer the questions she wants and be honest about it you know?

When I asked Miguel if there was anything he felt the mediator could have done to better prepare him, he only wished that he would have come to visit and talk with him more often. This was an interesting comment from him, given that he resisted the formal preparation the mediator attempted to engage him in. Eventually, it became clear that Miguel had never had an opportunity to sit down with anyone and tell them the story of his crime in all its detail, and the feelings he had about it. Either no one had been interested or just had not asked.

When I asked him what he felt immediately after the meeting, Miguel took a long pause to think, and said, "Probably a combination of relief and accomplishment … I don't want to say something lifted off my back, because it really was not like that, it was more like … you take a step and when you put your foot out there, you really see nothing and put it on and after it's over with, you find out it's all right … and I can bring my other foot over."

Regarding his feelings about Gloria, Miguel said:

> … the feelings I had toward her were like this a lot, a lot of respect, just you know you tell her you're sorry and you want to tell her so bad that you're sorry and wish you could take it back and so—because here's this lady, you know she's been through so much and you wish you could do something. And you feel that respect, you wanna show her that and feel that to her, and that's the way I felt and this lady here is something else you know?

I asked Miguel if he had developed any feelings for Caroline:

> Yeah, and like I said it really opened everything up … I thought about that and she … you know she [Gloria] never let us forget who was in there—not necessarily pictures but just … she was always there you know, those were the thoughts that I had—I was never gonna forget no matter what—even if that meant the mediation was gonna happen somewhere down the road that she was gonna have to pop up somewhere—that was the feeling that I had … . [The photo album stayed opened, with Caroline's high school graduation photograph in front of Miguel throughout the entire meeting.]

During the meeting, Miguel did not receive "forgiveness" from Gloria. He stated to me, "I never really expected her to forgive me, you know … . Just her decision, just whatever called her to come see me was enough, alone, for me."

Moreover, since the mediation took place, Miguel states that he has continued to benefit personally from the meeting:

> It's made me … I would say it's opened up a lot of things for me you know, it's gave me a lot more meaning that life is not just something that you do, that there's more to it and … experience what I've experienced [it] makes you—you had no choice but to realize that you know and I guess that everyone goes through their own little things in their life and comes to an understanding of that and I guess that would be that that means a great deal more than just livin' it. So, for me personally, I try to learn those things and just keep moving forward and try to understand more about what life is really about and what we're here to do.

In addition, regarding his sense that he may have been similar, in some way, to his victim, he stated:

Miguel: … I would like to probably say that I don't really know Gloria that well, but it seems to me that probably our families, or say our lives probably compare to each other with similar experiences you know, in life, you know? So, all, she went through a divorce and everything and a separation with her husband and Caroline had to go through that and I did too and so I could probably say that yes, there's similarities between the families you know? We happened to cross paths in that—it's just real sad that it had to happen this way and so I just—in that respect you know, I can relate to the type of person she is and the way—and probably the type of person Caroline was you know?

But whereas before this happened there was no way—Caroline was a girl who, you know, how can I say, was trying to live her life and trying to be happy, or whatever, but for me I was kinda the opposite I wanted to be happy, I wanted to do happy things but I was kinda being drawn in the opposite—what she was doing with [the drug dealing associate] I don't know man, what she was doing that night—just never understand it—I felt like had she been my sister or something I would not have let her do that and then I look back and I'd say, I got a sister and she's married to this dope dealer and I didn't step in so I felt like I [could understand with what happened to my sister].

In my first meeting with Miguel, we discuss an ongoing concern, expressed by the mediation community, that the changes experienced by many of the inmates who participate in this program make their return to the world of prison life more difficult. One mediator suggested that the participants should be, after the fact, transferred to a facility of their own, where they could continue their work in an environment of mutual support and continued growth. Interestingly, Miguel rejects this idea quickly and forcefully. He states that there should be no benefit to the offender for participating.

Miguel: … prison hardens you—you become conditioned to so many years to build up a defense and build up a, you know, to say to yourself to be strong because no matter what you've got to be prepared and strong and because if we don't people are gonna think you're weak and try to tear you up and so you build that up so when you do that you are very … courageous or you have a lot of courage and you're just—you start feeling that way and you're really not, you know, because most people come here scared and this place makes you build up that guard and a lot of the guys I talk to here they show me that and then I see that in myself that I did that too you know, but what the program has done for me was to make me realize that a lot of it was false, and that you built this wall around you and sometimes the more you never get the chance to climb that wall and see what's on the other side and that's one of the things I'd like to stress to other people is that they do have that wall around them and they need to find out what's on the other side and this program is the way to do it.

Like many of the offenders I have interviewed, one of the benefits that Miguel felt from the experience is a sense of being seen as a "human being." He said to me that the analogy of being behind bars, and sometimes in a "jungle," should not make people forget that the inmates are human: "I want the program to show people the human side of the whole thing, you know ... ."

> no matter what the situation, you're always gonna be around people, and you have to have respect for them. You have to show concern and have that realization that you have that responsibility as a human being to treat people as human beings, and that's what I want to come out of it."

In this first interview with Miguel, I saw him in a comfortable board-style meeting room in the prison where he was housed. There were interesting paintings on the wall that had been done by the prison population. This was also the room in which the meeting with Gloria took place. I had the distinct feeling of Miguel's near reverence for the space as we spoke that day. When we were done, and I thanked Miguel for meeting with me and being so frank, he said something along the lines of, "It's all right, it's not me." I was left pondering this statement, and, given his discussion with me, I was left with the sense that Miguel felt that he was now the embodiment of a larger reality, and was the vehicle for that. I also considered that there had been a radical change for Miguel of the definition of "me."

Close to three years later, I interviewed Miguel again in the same prison. This time, however, due to a fluke of communication, the warden's office was not expecting my visit. After some phone calls, I was allowed into the prison, and after a wait, I saw Miguel. However, this time we met in a visiting room where we were separated by a tightly meshed screen, which made it difficult to even see him. I decided not to make an issue of it, given the difficulties of the day, and decided that, since we could hear each other and the tape recorder was not impeded, I would cut my losses.

He, too, looked older. He continued to have a ready smile, and was, of course, more comfortable with the inconvenience of the interview situation than I was.

I asked how the experience of the mediation had lived with him since we last met.

Miguel: As far as the experience and the meeting with her, I think it's allowed me to touch base with some of the things that I was not aware of before, like, mainly remorse and feeling some of the feelings that go along with that. And realizing how—making me realize how—the enormity of what I've done and being aware of that. And then trying to come to grips with it, you know. So the past two or three years have been kind of like a, I'd say a trial—another trial.

… A lot of its emotional, you start experiencing a lot of mainly guilt and just—you start to see who you really are, and what you've become. You can see yourself, and it's kind of like you don't like what you see, and that's kind of what I've been going through right now. I didn't like what I saw. And then, too, the past two years, just trying to deal with that, to change it, to try to become a better person. And mainly, that's what's been going on for the past couple years. Working on that.

I asked Miguel how he was working on these issues:

Miguel: A lot of it's been through church activities, and spiritually. I've never been one to be close to God or anything like that. So I kinda went that way with it, because it's—sort of seeking out more meaning behind it. I went that way. It's given me a lot of answers. I'm not trying to say I'm holy or anything like that, I, just trying to find answers and deal with the questions I have in my mind, about what all that meant, and where my life is going from here. That aspect of it—that's more or less what I've been doing. As far as any other kind of activities, there's hardly anything to do here. There's really no other avenue that you can—like see a doctor, or anything like that—there's nothing there. There's nothing you can do. You just kind of have to go on, on your own. But not that there's been any type of illnesses or anything like that. Myself, I probably went through a couple of slight depressions, here and there. I'm pretty much sure of that. But overall, health-wise, I'm doing OK. Mentally, too.

Miguel feels that there is a great deal of depression in his family. He states that both his mother and one of his sisters have been treated for depression, and that his experience is much like theirs.

I discover on this visit, from a variety of sources, that members of Miguel's family have met with Gloria, in a meeting facilitated by the same mediator that worked with Gloria and Miguel. This had been something that members of Miguel's family had desired, and Gloria was more than happy to meet with them (more will be said about this meeting later).

Miguel: My family's met with Gloria. Her [Gloria] and her sister, they met—they got together and they watched the video. And I guess they did some talking amongst themselves, and it was a really good visit, from what I hear. There was a lot of feedback from both sides and a lot of good dialogue between the two sides.

… It went pretty good. And also, my sister and my brother and my dad, they went to a conference [an annual symposium on restorative justice, given by the state service] in [City] that they had … . Yeah, they do it every year or something like that. My family went to that. Participated in that. They had a—it was real meaningful for them. And then lately, right now, nothing's really been happening. I've kind of been out of touch with them as far as the program, but a couple of weeks ago, my sister and mom came up here and we talked about it, and my sister's talking about getting in touch with [Mediator] just to see how Gloria was doing and maybe touch base again. But I talked to them—I said, you know, it's an ongoing thing. It's not something where you just say hi one time and that's it. I think it would benefit them, that's what I was telling my sister and my mom, and they said, "yeah"—and they're going to try to get back involved in it a little bit more than they have been.

Miguel has increasingly been feeling the support and connection of his family. He says to me, "That's another thing that keeps me going too, in here."

In our meeting, I ask Miguel if there is anything, looking back on the experience, that he regrets now.

Miguel: I don't know about regretting, but I think there's some things that I probably would have liked to have said that I didn't say. But not because I held anything back. It just that, later on, when you look back, you say, man, I should have said this and I should have said that. But, yeah, there's some things that I wish I could have said, and I wish that I could say now even, but I said—that was meant to happen that way and that's the way it's going to stay. I'm not going to bring anything else out of it, and just leave it at that.

I asked Miguel how Gloria and Caroline stay with him in his current daily life. After a long pause, Miguel says:

Well, I guess you could say I think about them every day. Almost every day. Something I didn't use to do, and maybe that's through prayer. I ask God to help her and look out for her. And it keeps me aware of it. That's my way of keeping her on my mind. That's something that I didn't ever do. And I think that's one of the things that came out of it, was the realization of what they went through and just keeping that on my mind, not to kind of like—not as a negative way but as a positive way. Just to—it helps me to keep going, to keep pushing. From that aspect, yeah, that's where they're at.

I ask Miguel to talk more about how this has changed, and if in fact he doesn't think about this often:

No, not until she came up here. Like I told [Mediator], from the time that it all happened until the time she came here, everything was just like pushed back, out of the way. And you don't—you kind of harden yourself and you don't think

> about none of that anymore. You just try forget it really and that's basically kind of what happened. And ever since that day that she came up here, it's just like—before it never was a part of my life. Now it is, and it's not going to go away. And I don't push it away no more. It's there. Because I know what happened to me by pushing it away, in that ten-year period of time, whatever long it took, and I know the kind of person that I became. And if I'm truly trying to change and try to do something different, then I can't do that anymore. I can't push that back no more. I have to keep it in front of me and say, "Yeah, this is it." Just acknowledge it.

I ask Miguel to tell me about his theory of change in people, and whether he believes that people can change:

> Yes, I can say yeah because speaking from experience, my own experience. Like I said, there's many things that I've done and been through and many things that I've noticed in myself, I'm not doing anymore, or, just not, there's nothing there no more. Like I developed a whole bunch of habits over the years, and then all of a sudden you start saying, "Why am I doing this?" And just say, "I don't have to do it no more." And you change. A lot of it has to do with the way you think and the way you see life, the way you see people. And for me in here, that's pretty big because you're dealing with a lot of different people in here. There's a lot of negative influences in here, and it's easy to get involved with that. And unless you make a conscious decision to say, "I'm not going to do this"—you're going to be that way. At a point, you're going to have to say, like I did, "You know what? I can't do that no more." I can't be with—what they're doing—I can't do what they're doing anymore, and I had to change. So that's why, yeah, I'm speaking from experience, because I don't do the things I used to do. And I believe, yeah, I believe people can change, I believe that. I've seen it in other people, in other lives here.

Interviewer: How do you think you've changed?
Miguel: For me, I think it's more of an inner change, you know, more like a moral change. More like—having a better sense of right and wrong. And realizing that life is important, life is something that it's just not—every man for himself. And that's kind of the way I lived before all this happened. That was my whole attitude, just every man for himself. You just gotta do what you gotta do. And for me, that's kind of—based on what I went through and everything, I just look at it and I shake my head. It's unbelievable that I did the things that I did, thinking like that. And so I see myself not doing those things and trying to change, and thinking, that you know what? We don't live by ourselves. It's not every man for himself. There's other people around you you have to think about, and have responsibility for and stuff like that. You've got to think not only about yourself, but about other people. And it just opens up a whole new world. You gotta be responsible. You gotta say to yourself there's certain things you can do

and there's certain things you can say and you can't say. And you've got to go by that, and you've got to live by it. And one of the things for me is learning how to do that. Not just learning but doing it.

I reminded Miguel about our previous interview in which I had suggested, given my discussions with some of the mediators involved, that the changes in the individual offenders were so profound, it made it difficult to go back to the prison culture and survive. One mediator had suggested an idea that inmates that went through these experiences be transferred to a special unit where they could continue to provide each other with support, and continue to grow and change. Miguel had been quite opposed to this idea at that time.

Miguel: The reason why I said that was because in the beginning, when he first asked if I wanted to do it, and it's all about the motivation. Why do you want to do it? And all these thoughts come to your mind—why am I doing this? For me, he said—I remember him giving me this contract and saying, "there's not going to be this. No parole gain. None of this. You're not gonna get nothing out of this." So immediately I agreed to that. I was going to keep it that way. Simple. So, when you suggested that—when (you) brought up that it was good to have counsel, it was good to have people around that have been through it—and it is good that you do it. It would be a good idea. But to attach some kind of a sentence, where we're all going to be in one place, then it opens the door for someone to say, "I'd like to get out of this unit and do this." And that's the reason why I say that, no, that I don't think that would be a good idea. Because you're not going to get the same kind of person every time. In other words, you're not going to get people like—not to say that I'm anybody special, but—for me, I wanted to do it for nothing. And you're not going to get people like that all the time. Once word gets around and the program gets bigger, people are going to start thinking before they say "Yeah" and think, "What am I going to get out of this." "Well, you're going to get shipped to this unit." "Yeah, all right, I'll do it." So, the motivation becomes a factor.

… And that's why I told him, it's best that if it stays like this—and there might be some people who do need that, and maybe I did need it. I probably did need it. But I think it's made me a little stronger person as far as dealing with … . Maybe it's just me. You know, if you put people in that environment, there's no incentive to try and change, I think. Whereas if you pull them back in this environment, like I did, I went back into this environment. You have to make choices—that puts you in that decision-making mode, you know. When you have to start making decisions, start doing things. Whereas if you're not in that environment, you don't have to make decisions. And then, so, there's not going to be no change. You can say, well, I'm going to wait it out until it's time to go. That was my whole thinking behind it. And it's helped me. I don't know about anybody else. And I seen it—it has helped other people here. I know guys here on our unit who went to the program, and we've talked about the program, and what you do and everything, and they told me the same thing—it's helped them. They began to make their own decisions to change. To see other people and then see themselves, and say, "No, I can't do this. I've got to do this." Without that there, there's no possibility for that person to change.

Miguel discusses with me, along these lines, meeting and talking with other inmates that have either been through the program, or are considering it. He describes the struggles that some have:

Miguel: … because he [another inmate] came to me and asked, "Where do you go to? What do they ask you?" and all these things. And I just speak to him and said, this is what happened—this is what they want to know more than this, and this is why they come. And some of the guys that I spoke to that went through it, yeah, some of the basic things—yeah, we're all going to go through the same thing. And the victims, they want to know certain things. It would be different subjects, different ways of telling you, but it's basically all the same—that most—I couldn't say exactly, but along the same lines—why they come here, and what you go through, and what they want to put you through. They want you to see the pain and feel the pain, know the pain that they went through. And those three things, when you tell people that, they don't want to feel somebody else's pain. They don't want to know what somebody else went through. They don't want to see the things that they've done. So, they kind of shy away from it like this guy did: "I don't want to think about that—it's in my past now. I'm trying to forget it."

That was the attitude I had for ten years. I just want to forget about it and go on with my life. You can't really do that because it's going to haunt you for the rest of your life. I can see that in them—I see it in their eyes when they tell me, "No, I don't want to." Like this one guy, he just totally backed away. And then later when I'd see him around—I saw him around all the time, and he's like—I seen the way he was acting, and he's real comfortable. What I see in him, I see me. I see myself before. Comfortable, complacent. I like what I'm doing. Just trying to go on with my life and do my time. But I see the things that he's doing, and I see myself and it wasn't good. That's why I just looked at him and I said, "Well, it's not for everybody, I guess."

Miguel has strong feelings about personal gain and the changes he feels he has experienced, as he is not concerned with "scheming" and manipulating, as he saw himself in his past. We discuss the sense that some have that inmates, generally, are manipulative, and that is what drives their motivation to participate and meet with victims.

Miguel: Because the reason why I can do that is because when you live your life like I did for twelve years, and it's true about being manipulative, yes, we do become. This place makes you that. This place makes you do those things. And that's what I had become. I realize that now. I know that.

I suggest that Miguel, given his life as a drug dealer, must have developed a skill at manipulation.

Miguel: Yeah, and then at a very young age, here seventeen or eighteen years old, just think what I could be when I'm twenty-six, twenty-eight, and later ages. Especially in here where there's many more opportunities to practice it. So after about twelve years, you pretty much become an expert at it … I think for me, the way I look at it, is the old saying that actions speak louder than words. I can talk to you here or anybody until I'm blue in the face, and until that change starts to manifest itself and show itself not only to other people, but myself … . So, the difference from one who's probably doing it and one who isn't goes back to the motivation—why does that person say yes? That's the key, in the beginning. When you first come and ask the person, do they want to talk to you, do they want to talk to the victims, what is their answer? What is the questions they ask? And you've got to get it right then and there.

When [Mediator] came to see me, there was—not knowing what's going on—who is this person? And I said yeah even before I thought about it. Normally, I would think about it, like, that's my manipulative brain going—wait a minute—I didn't even do that; I just said yeah, and it wasn't until afterwards when I said, "What did I do?"

Interviewer: How do you account for that? Why do you think you did that?

Miguel: Just because of what I had become, my scheming nature that I had. I think we all have it, we just, most have it—a lot of people have control of it, some people don't. I didn't. Just that, being real cautious, like cornered. I didn't know what I'd do.

I review with Miguel his feelings before going in to the meeting, and his ambivalence, especially given that this was beginning to feel like a new and unfamiliar experience for him.

Miguel: … Was there times when I felt like backing out? Yes. I think some of the other guys that I've met, they went through the same thing. But they still did it. They went through with it. I think that's how he knows. There has to be doubt, but there has to be a persistent desire to go through with it.

Interviewer: We talked about that before, I think—about how you were feeling right before, and nervous and all that.

Miguel: Yeah, being torn between—I was really being pulled back by my—what I would almost say "my old self"—being pulled back to what was comfortable.

But yet being driven by a sense of some type of mission: this is what I have to do—I have to do this. I can't go back. So just being pulled between one and the other. And the ultimate, at the end, at the last moment, just taking that leap, saying to heck with it, here I go, just go. But once I did that it was like that was the beginning right there, of the end.
Interviewer: Would it be fair to say that it was the beginning of the end of your old self?
Miguel: Right.
Interviewer: Would it be easy for you today to get back into that life, or to plug all that kind of ability to wheel and deal and … ?
Miguel: I think it would be easy in the sense that to give up—if I didn't have the desire not to give up, I think I would. But the desire not to give up is unbelievable, man. I mean, some of the things that it gets me through, it just amazes me. Because there were many times I'd want to give up, and want to just say the heck with everything. But that desire has been there ever since. It's been pulling and pulling and pulling. But it's been pulling me for the better. And that's one of the things that I really hang onto. It's something that's really strong within me, is not to give up. Meaning, just to keep going. And things are going to take care of themselves; in other words, I just have the sense that I'm in the right place, doing the right thing, not only just because it's the right—it's something that's right to do—I'm doing the right thing because it's the right thing to do. And that's something that just drives me. It's pulling me. Other than that, it would be easy. Like I say, there's been times where I want to go do this and I want to go do that, and I have done it. But then automatically, I just say, "Nah, I'm coming back." I just keep going.

And I can pretty much say, too, a couple of guys that I know here, they done the same thing. And I seen them. They changed. Just totally different attitudes. And I've seen what they're doing and I say, "that's good." And I say "hi" to them all the time, and they're just like—they're just going, they're living their lives now, and you can tell the difference. You can see that they're real responsible now and they've got a purpose. They're on a mission. We just look at each other and it's like we're on a mission. We just know we're on a mission and we're serious. But it's between us, just ourselves. And you can tell the ones that are not. We can tell when we look at them, and say, "yeah, right." And when they start in to talk, it's like—because you know, you hear yourself saying the same things, and "yeah, right." And you don't see it—you don't see the actions. You hear the words but you don't see the actions. But I think it works. Personally, my own experience is: it works. You've got to add some things to it. You're not going to do it on—a program is just, like I always say, a starting point. You've got to build around it. You've got to do things. There are certain things you've got to start doing besides that.
Interviewer: And you feel like you've done that, you've carried that momentum?
Miguel: Yeah, I've built around it to keep it going and to build from it. And like I said, the goal for me is to become a better person, to become, I guess—when I

look back, say, OK, like it was a long time ago, and I've had some people write, some old friends, and they couldn't believe this happened, that I did this. They said, "You're not that type of person. I don't know what made him do that." They see me as some kind of inner nature within me—you know what, he's not that type of person. How could he have done that? And I think about what people have told me and I say, "Yeah, there was a person like." I know that I am that person, that's the person that I am. That's what I'm trying to become, and I just keep telling myself that, and gradually I'll be the person—I do want to be who I really am, not what I've become. Not something—like I said, the attitude that I have is every man for himself. So, going back to that, looking at it in that aspect, saying, "I'm not really this person."

Miguel felt that a significant turning point for him in childhood was his parents' divorce. He felt, at that time, that his mother, who was already depressed and overwhelmed, was left with five children and had little energy left over for him. He then began to see himself as largely independent and left to his own resources. He saw, fitting with Lonnie Athens' theory, his reliance shift from adults as models to other kids as models. He was twelve years old.

Miguel: And there was never any sense of knowing, deep down, right and wrong. And I just had lost it there, being the young one, you know. And then everything just happening. When it happened, I look back, and you know, a lot of it was just that—looking for approval, attention really. And I certainly did get it when I committed the murders. So, I can look back and say, yeah, that's what it was. But yeah, I did go back and try to piece it together, try to figure out what the motivating factor was, the root of the problem. And I think that's the way it was. And even throughout the years that I was here, that was my whole lifestyle, was to continue. And it didn't stop right there, after the murders. It continued, being—wanting attention, being approved by the other inmates here and stuff like that. Seeking affection, whatever. All that continued a long time. And what it did was it blinded me to some of the things I should have been aware of, some of the concrete things that people will do to live a normal life, I guess.

And so, when [Mediator] came, it was like talking to somebody and talking about feelings and wait a minute—I don't want to do that. And not only the feeling part but the thinking part. You know, you're blind to all that. You don't think about stuff like the pain that you caused other people, the destruction—you don't think about all that. You're not even aware of all that. It kind of just blew me away, is what it did. Opened everything up, opened a whole new world, a way of thinking. I said, "Wait a minute, something's wrong, something ain't right."

Miguel was very clear in differentiating the role of age, and the role of the inner voice, or phantom community and soliloquy that Athens describes:

Miguel: Right. I guess that other person, like I say, more just building up as something that you're not. I'm thirty-four years old now and I'm more able to think now. I'm more able to—so if you were to sit here eighteen years ago, there's no way I would be talking to you about what I'm talking to you now. I wouldn't have no idea, because I wouldn't even think about things like that. But now I do and I try to understand them and try to understand why they're important. As far as change, when people ask me: "Can people change?" Yeah, people can change.

I ask Miguel to talk about the relationship that is established between Gloria and him. Some of my interviewees have described this as a "bond" or ongoing connection. Miguel also makes an important connection in the following comment as to the meaning of the photographs that Gloria brought to him, which he was clear about in our first interview.

Miguel: Yeah, but not in a physical sense. It was more like a spiritual type or maybe even just a human sense. You start—you just—you're not as sensitive to any kind of reality or anything. You're not sensitive to it. You look at everything and it seems like it's an illusion, something—that's the way it is in here. And when Gloria—seeing her and then hearing her voice, and then all of a sudden it was like—I guess for me when I opened up the pictures, that was like the plug-in. If you want to say there was a connection, that was it. And it wasn't physical, it was just something deep down inside, something human that happens between people, between us.

… she [Gloria] wrote me a real long letter, and I think that was the starting point. And when I read that letter, it was like, man, I never thought about stuff like that. I never thought about the things that she wrote down. And when she started talking to me, telling me what—why I was here—it was like I was hearing that letter in her voice. And that's what I was thinking about, was that letter. And so, she asked me if she could show me some pictures, and I said yeah, OK. So, when I grabbed the pictures, it was like me grabbing the letter. It was like me reading the letter. And when I was looking through the pictures like that, I wasn't looking at the pictures—well, I was looking at them, but I was—what she was telling me in that letter was going through my mind. About how she was so close to those girls, the girl was her world, this girl was everything to her, and she wished she could do this. I can remember everything. I broke down—I was like—it became real, it became real. It wasn't a letter anymore. It wasn't somebody that—in other words, she became a human being, something that I wasn't even aware of. Because when I killed her, I didn't know her. It was like she was nothing. Nobody. And it was like she came back to life and she was a human being again, and her words in that letter did that. Her words in that letter to me brought that out and that's the reason why that happened like that. Because she became real again, she became real.

Prior to this, Miguel had a memory of a fleeting vision of Caroline before he shot her. "There for a brief instant, we made eye contact. She just looked at me and I looked at her and that was it … just a brief instant. She looked at me, I looked at her and that was it."

I asked Miguel what had been the hardest part of the experience for him.

Miguel: I don't really want to say it was the hardest part, but it was more being open. I don't want to say it was hard to be open—it was a struggle for me to put into words the things that she wanted to know. And to say it truthfully. For years, I would say—a lie—your life has been a lie, your life has been something that's not true. And it's real easy—it's real easy—it was hard in a sense for me to explain, try to talk in an honest way, not because I was trying to be honest … it was more like, when [Mediator] said, "try to keep it simple"—I went in there and said OK, that's what I'm going to do. The only thing I could think of was whatever happens, try to be truthful. In the back of my mind, I'm saying, "You been lying all your life. How you gonna do that?" So that right there was a conflict.

But then I just decided—before I went in there, I made up my mind that I was going to be calm and I was just going to go through it. Whatever happens happens. So, the struggle was that. The conflict was that. Something pulling me back, and at the same time, something driving me forward. Being able to express to her the events that happened that night, exactly as they happened, being open, not holding nothing back. I think that was probably, you could say, the hardest part. You want to sum it up, being focused, staying focused. There was a lot of internal stuff going on inside of me and it's like "whoa!"—trying to stay focused on that, that was hard. That was the hard part. That's really it right there.

In discussing the future, Miguel is clear as to his goal, and his struggle.

Miguel: … As far as the future, basically right now I'm just trying to get my life in order, develop sort of some guidelines to live by here, sort of a foundation, so when I get out, I can build on that. As far as long-term future, I think one of the things that I set out to do from the very beginning was to be open, to listen, and to be prepared, and just prepare myself to change. Because I know that that's going to be a lifelong thing. That's not going to be something that's just going to happen for the short-term, or just maybe even while I'm here. That's going to be long-term throughout my life.

… I'll carry this with me for the rest of my life, and I think that knowing that requires that I keep that in mind. Requires that I keep the change in mind. Because there's going to be obstacles, there's going to be things that are going to go on.

… And basically, what I've been through, I've been doing that all my life. I'm tired of it; I don't want that no more. It has to be a higher standard; it has to be something more to live up to. To me that's what it is. Striving to be better; striving not to fail. Yeah, that might happen, but if you don't strive, you strive not to make it happen, you do the thing that needs to be done. And don't use it as a copout. That's my attitude now. That's my whole attitude in everything that I do. It's not going to happen overnight; it's going to be ongoing. It's going to be with me for the rest of my life. Being responsible. Like [Mediator] talks about accountability, and being open to change. Listen to people. Sometimes you can't listen if you're not open. So those are some of the things for me, to continue to do. And that's something that I told [Mediator] from the very beginning: I'm not going to give up. I'm not going to stop. This is something that's going to happen all the time. And so far, so good. It's been good for me.

… I think if you have any say ghosts in the closet, you'd have something to be worried about. I don't have any ghosts in my closet. That's one of the things, for me, probably the biggest thing personally internally, is the ghost, the things you have hidden. We all have them, and we all somewhere or other got to deal with them. It's the ones that don't that will worry about getting out. I've done all I can in the past years to deal with them, here, and I deal with them all the time. And I'm always searching for that little hidden thing. And they come out—believe me—they come out.

… you're just going to be out there, you're going to go find something—so that'll be something to motivate me more. To try to be more, I guess, successful. A part of society.

A friend of mine, I told one time, I said, "Why do you keep coming back?" He was back five times. And I don't know, just out of the blue, I talked about—I said, "You know what your problem is, man? You get out there, man, and instead of becoming society, you get out there and you're just a part of society." In other words, you go out there and you're just a part of society. You're just a little—you're just doing your own thing. When you get out there, you've got to *become* society. You've got to become your environment. You've got to be who they are. And that requires change. And he looked at me, like, "What?" It's true. That's why you keep coming back. Until you start assimilating what's going on out there, you're always going to come back in here, because you've assimilated what you've been doing in here. And you take it out there, and it don't work. He just looked at me … .

INTERVIEW WITH GLORIA

The day after meeting with Miguel, I met with Gloria in a diner close to her office.

Gloria looked more coifed and professional than I had remembered her from the video meeting with Miguel. Gloria has remained an active part of the victim's community, and continues to lobby the state legislature on a variety of issues of interest to herself and her associates. She participates in the annual Restorative Justice Symposium, sponsored by the state's Victim Services office.

Gloria began our discussion by recounting the events of learning of Caroline's death. The story, strikingly like many I was told, was fraught with insensitivity and shock. (The funeral director, serving as the county coroner, said, "Lady, your kid is dead.") At that point, Gloria did not know the details of Caroline's death, whether she had been killed in an accident or what had been the cause. It was on the local TV news that the family discovered the details of Caroline's death.

This began a contentious relationship for Gloria with the news media, which, following the murders, set up shop across from her home, looking for footage.

Gloria told me that the case was initially broken by the homicide investigators who told her that it was likely the murderer would come to Caroline's funeral. In fact, Miguel's partner did come to the funeral, along with some relatives, and when no link could be found between him and Caroline, the police, who had videotaped the attendees of the funeral, had their first break in the case.

Gloria was enthusiastic about the role of the police in the case, and felt that they performed a very professional investigation, kept her informed, and were thoughtful. She had less praise for the county attorney's investigation, and for what she felt was their bumbling job. She and Caroline's boyfriend's mother began their own investigation, traveling to parts of town that were unsafe and greatly concerning to the police department. This, however, is very characteristic of Gloria.

At the same time, Gloria's independence and strong will were respected and admired by the police detectives, and she has remained friends with them. Gloria reported that during the trial, they were very protective of her, and that some were not in favor of her developing interest in restorative justice and in meeting with Miguel, for fear that she would soften in her feelings for him.

Gloria stated that when he was arrested, Miguel was a large and "husky" kid, who appeared menacing. This is borne out by his arrest photo, which I saw. She stated that he looked meaner to her than when she met with him later: "Because one of my biggest surprises in the mediation is how he had not aged a day… . And he did look real mean [at the time of the trial]. He looked, as my mother called him, 'like a hoodlum.'"

At the time of the trial, Miguel had lost a lot of weight, and had begun to lift weights, preparing, apparently, to go to prison.

Gloria: … And I think even when I went to trial, the one thing I did notice was that Miguel would never look at me. Even when I was on the witness stand, he

never looked. He never would look up at me. I did notice that.
But I still was in such anger. I was still so angry at him that I think that's what I was looking for, as opposed to really looking at it rationally. He could have had a halo, and I'd have still thought he looked like Satan.

At the time of the trial, Miguel had just turned eighteen, and was looking more his age. He had, what Gloria called, a "baby face," and she felt that the purpose of his losing weight was to look younger, as an effort to elicit sympathy.

I asked Gloria how her feeling that meeting with him or talking with him would help her had developed.

Gloria: Yes, I wanted to talk to him. At first, you know, it was that I couldn't understand why this happened. And of course, there's all kinds of rumors. When anything like this happens, there's rumors going all around… I was afraid that if I did meet with him, I would try to hurt him. And even for a long time after I was approached about the mediation, that's what I was scared of. That was one of my biggest fears is that I will try to hurt him. Because at the time of the murder, I would say up to five or six years, I would have hurt anything that belonged to those two [Miguel and his partner]. So after—it's kind of like a period in there that no, I didn't want to meet with him and have anything to do with him.

Gloria continued to be concerned that she would not be able to restrain her desire to strike out at Miguel if she met him. She began to have discussions with Gail (who had met with Louis) after seeing the spot on HBO. The restorative justice movement was in its fledgling stages now, and Gloria was an articulate person, who was in favor of the movement in principle. Nevertheless, she continued to refuse the thought of doing a meeting with Miguel herself, for fear that she could not restrain her physical anger. She did agree to write articles for popular magazines, and this began a new direction for her.

She was intrigued by the thought of meeting with Miguel, however, and continued doing research on the process and thinking about it herself.

Gloria: And so, as I started doing the research, I thought, well, maybe I can do this. So, I called [Mediator] up and I said, "You know, maybe I can do this." And he said, "Well, I think you can." And you know, that was kind of how it got started. It was like, [Mediator] said yeah, I think I can—I'll be down there … And so that was kind of how it—and even up until he walked in that room, I was scared that I would try to hurt him. And I told [Mediator], if he would have walked in with what I call the inmate smirk, or the inmate stroll, I think I would have. But he didn't. You'll notice in the tape that he doesn't look at me. He doesn't look at me for I guess a good—the guard told me it was about five minutes. He sat over there and timed it. And it was really funny because the guard was big. I said, [Mediator] make sure I got a big guard. But that's what I was scared of. I wasn't scared that Miguel would do something to me. I wasn't scared of that.

Gloria felt, as soon as she got in the room and saw Miguel, that "I think he was really a lot more apprehensive than what I was. I think he was very, very nervous. I think that he … thought it was going to be more like a screaming match [with my yelling], 'This is what you did.' And when I was sitting there talking to him rationally, I think that's when he got over a lot of that."

Gloria continues to struggle with the fact that Miguel looked young and fit when she met with him. She was wanting "prison to be so bad. I wanted him to be wrinkled and gray-headed." Gloria, who was advocating for capital punishment at the time of the trial, felt that it was because of this appearance that one of the jurors voted against the death penalty.

She reports to me that the changes that have been precipitated in Gloria since her daughter's death have been interesting to her. She reported herself to be very fearful of many things prior to the murder: "I don't have any fear now. Because what can they do to me that's any worse than what's happened to me, except take my other child. So, for my safety, I've gotten to where I don't even care about it anymore."

Gloria: Well, I think one of the things … but I have no fear now. Another thing is that I'm very, very vocal about—it's like murder has gotten pushed to the back. And I'm not saying there's anything wrong with—I'm not saying that child abuse is okay, and domestic abuse, and the thing that we go round and round about is, I'm not saying you should drive while you're drunk. But why is the bond for DWI more than for murder? I'm very vocal about that. It changed me drastically in the fact that out of my mother's four children, I was kind of the one that just went with the flow. I was, as my brother tells me, the good child. I never really gave my parents—and I now I am very vocal—I'm very protective, very combative, if I think you're going to hurt my son or my grandson. As a matter of fact, I think that's one of the things that scared my brother the most is the fact that I turned around to him right after Caroline was killed, and I said, "I could kill him, and have no remorse whatsoever." And now him, he knew he could have done that, but that was even before. But it really scared him, that here was his sister that never did anything like this, and that changed a lot, that I knew that I could hurt someone and never bat an eye about it.

… Another thing is I do a lot of public speaking, and matter of fact, one of the ladies that taught English when I was in high school called me and she had been in an audience where I was speaking and she told me, "I did not come up and speak to you afterwards, but I did want to tell you …"—because in her class I took a zero—and she said, "I would have never dreamed …" And I said, "It's because now I have a cause." I don't want this to happen to any other family. But I think another thing … is that I realize that I have a talent of writing. I have written poems and like a lot of people are intrigued on how I wrote for the mediation is I took each feeling separately… and that's something that I do now a lot of is writing. Of course, I don't send it off to sell it, you understand. But—well, I did send one to "Good Housekeeping" and it was about what victims go through, and she called me and she said—one of the editors—and she said, "You know, we do not print this kind of article but I'm going to tell you what to do. Do it in a novel, because people will buy it in a novel." And I told her, "I want people to see what victims go through—not what the defendant goes through. We get this all the time … But, I want people to know what the victim goes through." And so, she said, do it as a novel. So, I've started it.

I ask Gloria to tell me about her initial reactions to Miguel in the meeting, and ask as well about the photo album. Gloria tells me of a poem that Caroline wrote, which forecasts her death. Gloria included this poem in the album.

> Well, my—the reason I wanted to meet with Miguel was that I wanted Miguel to know that Caroline was a real person. That she was not something that was pretend and that this is what he took away from not just me, but all of Caroline's friends, all of Caroline's family; I wanted him to know that this is what you did. "You're not going to shuffle this to the back of your mind and act like she was never anything." And I really think that if nothing else comes out of that meeting, I think I got that across to him. Is that Caroline was a real person.

Interviewer: Was it your idea to bring the album?
Gloria: Yes. And the reason I even had that album is Caroline's brother wouldn't deal with it. I mean, he dealt with her death per se but he would talk about Caroline up until the murder happened, and then that was it. And he never went back to the cemetery. So, Parents of Murdered Children said—it's kind of like AA or Al-Anon—put this album together and start with when she was a baby and go up to when she was killed, and then just lay it around and leave it. And [Son], like two weeks before she was killed, she wrote this poem called "Remember Me." And so that was all in the album. And sure enough, they were right. My son, you'd see him, when he didn't think anybody was looking, pick it up and look at it. So that's why the album was even made. And so that's why I want him to look at it, because it starts when she was a baby. Well, it starts with a poem …

In the poem, Caroline discusses a feeling that she is going to die. When Gloria first saw the poem, and confronted her about it, she said:

"Caroline, why would you write something like this?" And she said, "Mother, I'm not going to be with you much longer." And so, I started with—that's how I started the album. And went all the way through … . And I didn't want to find out what happened that night. I don't want to know that. And I think I know it the best that I'm going to know it. And I think I accomplished that. Of course, when I look at the video, some of the looks that I was giving him, I'm going, "Oh, whoa … ." I certainly looked awful mean.

On the day that the two met, it was Caroline's boyfriend's birthday. Gloria says at one point during the meeting that she is sorry that it is that date, and that this was not planned. This moved Miguel's family, when they viewed the video, given that Gloria shows such consideration for Miguel's feelings.

I tell Gloria that what has stayed with me in the years since I first saw the video of the mediation was Gloria's courtesy with Miguel around the issue of looking at the album. As mentioned, she appeared tentative, and was clearly giving him a choice to view it or not.

Gloria: … And I know his family thought that that was awfully nice. That I do apologize. And I didn't—it was not a setup. Probably because I hadn't thought about it! But it wasn't. And I did—I did want it to be his choice that he look at that album. And if he's really remorseful and he really means what he's saying, then he's going to look at it. And he did.

… Well, to me the most important was that, for me was that I got across to him that Caroline was real. I think that was important. Another part that really stands out for me is when I asked him—and when I was asking the question—I have read and met people that have been parents or family of the defendant and apparently they go through the same grief process we do. I mean, not as severely as we do, but they have a lot of the grief process that we do. And so that's what I was asking about, and he apparently misunderstood that and he started crying. And he tells me that his parents tried to raise him right, that even after he started getting in trouble, that his folks really tried to get him to straighten up. And he cried from that part. So, even if he's never remorseful for what he did to my family, he is remorseful for what he did to his family. He is very remorseful.

Another thing is I felt like Caroline was there. I felt like Caroline was there. And that's what I told [Mediator] at the end. He goes, "Are you OK?" Oh, yeah, I'm perfectly fine. And then I burst into tears. And [Mediator's] going "Oh, whoa … ." But I did—I felt like—because Caroline was the type that she's forgiven him. She's forgiven him. I haven't. And [Mediator] says that he uses what I say at the very end. Maybe somehow, some day, some way, Caroline's brother and I can forgive him … .

This brings up the issue of forgiveness and the process of that. I ask Gloria what she thinks of this, both for herself and for the movement in general.

Gloria: Well, I don't think I have to forgive him. And I tell him that. That's between him and his God. It isn't between him and I. If he wants forgiveness, he needs to talk to his God. Don't talk to me. Because I'm not going to forgive him. And of course [Mediator] and I—I call it a debate—he thinks in my own way I have forgiven him. That I have forgiven him, according to [Mediator], in my own way. And I tell [Mediator]—and he said, "You have not let it eat you up and destroy your life." And I said, "No, because I made the choice that he got my daughter's life. He wasn't getting my son and I." And I don't mean I was scared of him killing me. I don't mean that. I mean I was not going to let that destroy my life. Don't get me wrong—it was hard. But I don't think anyone should be told they have to forgive. I really don't. Because I think that my God is a very forgiving God. And I don't think he's going to just zap me to hell for not forgiving this guy for murdering my daughter. I just don't think he is. He may, but I don't think so. I think he understands.

… I think people—and this is just my opinion—I think they dwell on that too much. And I'm not just talking about victims and survivors. I'm thinking about the whole nine yards. I think a lot of times if you just leave people alone, they're going to come to their own conclusion. … And I think that if you'll just leave them alone, they can come to their own conclusion if they have to forgive or not. And that's just how I feel. It's just like I said—I don't think that God's going to zap me to hell. He may, but I don't think so. And maybe I have forgiven him—maybe [Mediator's] right. But I don't think so.

The new relationship with Miguel's family feels quite easy to Gloria. Given my previous experience with an offender's parents, I am interested in this, and in her sense of their process being like hers. The question of Miguel's sincerity, no doubt related to the process of forgiveness, seems to be a constant question. One of the agreements that were made between Gloria and Miguel was that they would, together, speak with juvenile offenders. This has been difficult to do, with Miguel in a maximum-security institution, but the plan might go forward if he is released.

Gloria: You know, if he's willing to really do the stuff that we agreed to. Now his sister and I went to the cemetery Saturday and we sat there about two hours. But one of the things—she turned around and she said, "I'm going to go and see if he will come to the cemetery." And she said, "If he is really remorseful, he will do it when he gets out." And she said, "How did you feel?" I said, "Well, I feel the same way you do." But yes, if he's really remorseful, then he's going to do it. So I think that's how I'll really know. And to me, I didn't care if he was manipulative or not. I wanted him to know what Caroline—I wanted him to know that she was a model. I wanted him to know that even her priest could hardly do the funeral because he had watched her grow up. That was like one of his own kids. I wanted him to know that. And even if he didn't want to listen, some of it had to sink in. So that's how I thought—I don't care if he's manipulative. I don't care if he thinks he's getting something. And if he does get something, who cares? He still had to sit there and listen to me. And they may go in there with "The Attitude," as I call it, but you can't tell me that they can tune us out the whole—what did we meet? Like six or seven hours … . But see, that's how I felt, was that who cares? They still have to sit there and look us in the face.

Gloria is frank with herself and me about the progression of her feelings in this process:

> Well, you think maybe subconsciously is: "I don't want to trust him." [She says this with a quality of rye humor.] I have to be honest with myself. I think that I just don't want to like him. I don't want him to be a nice person. So subconsciously I think maybe I do want him to mess up so I can say, "well, see, Miguel, you're not the nice guy you try …" But you're right, the jury's still out. He's got to show me that he really—and maybe it's—subconsciously, when he was telling me "I'm doing this for you," maybe subconsciously I was just looking for something to say. No, [Mediator], he doesn't mean this. But I'm very honest in the fact that I think he's remorseful for what he did to his family. If not for my family, he is remorseful for what he did to his family. What he has put his mom and daddy through. He is remorseful for that.

I then ask Gloria for her theory of change in people, and whether she feels this is possible.

Gloria: Yeah, I think people change. I think it's like with anything. None of us can change you. When people talk to me about rehabilitation, and having all these drug programs, and all these alcohol—my thing is these guys—we can sit them in it all day long, and if they don't want to quit doing drugs and they don't want to quit doing alcohol, they aren't going to stop it. I don't care what we do. And I think that's the same thing with Miguel or any person. He has got to want to do that change. Don't do it for me. Don't do it for Caroline. Do it because you want to change. And yes, I think if he really wants to change, and I think—you know, like he told me when I was talking about juveniles, he said, "where we need to go get them is not once they get into trouble. We need to get out on the streets and get them, when they're out there just fix them. When they really think they're the macho, the really bad kids, that's when we need to get them." So, he does have some good ideas, but—and I can believe anybody that wants to can change. But he has to want to, for himself. Not for his mom and daddy, and not for any of us … .

Gloria describes her process in meeting with Miguel's family. It was during this discussion with me that she began to show emotion. Apparently, one of Miguel's brothers initially asked if Gloria would be willing to meet with the family early in the process, during the trial. At that point, Gloria was unwilling. She was aware of Miguel's mother, and felt her connection and desire to talk with Gloria: "(She) would just look at me and cry."

> … And at that point, it's like—I was very honest with the [family], if they'd have had a bird, I'd have hurt it. I wanted them to hurt as much as I hurt. And so, as the years—and I don't want you to think it was right overnight, because it was five, six, seven years down the road when I got over the anger and realized it wasn't the family that did this. And so that's one of the things I told [Mediator]. I said, "You can tell Miguel to tell his family that we will meet with him—or with his family." And [Mediator] said OK. And Miguel did ask me about that. And he also asked—his father wanted to go to the cemetery this Saturday—an emergency came up. And he also—his father wanted a picture of Caroline. And then when I met with the family, they actually have like—they wanted to put the picture on the wall with the brothers and sisters because they feel like that Caroline has become a part of their family now.

Apparently, Miguel's family expressed this desire to Gloria, and she offered them a variety of photographs of Caroline. They were very particular regarding the one they wanted, and they do, now, have her photograph hanging with other family photographs in their home.

Gloria met with the family with her sister, who was the only one of her family members interested in participating in this meeting.

Gloria: And it was really funny, because only my sister would go. None of the rest of my family would go, only my sister would go. And on the way over there, we kept looking at one another, and I think if either one of us would have said, "We're out of here," we wouldn't have showed up. And we learned quite a bit. I was surprised when they talked about the anger and the hatred that they felt toward Miguel. It was real—I don't know what I would—if I was the mother of the defendant. And one of the things Mrs. [Mother] does bring out—in the video with him, I don't think—because she's crying a whole lot and sometimes you can't understand—but she did—she was talking about her feelings and stuff and then she made one of the most pertinent statements: "But he was my son. I couldn't turn away from him."

Gloria breaks down here.

> And I thought, that brings it home for me. That no matter what, you love them. You might not like what they've done. And it's amazing … So, there were a lot of parallels in our families that really amaze you. And it was really interesting, and we didn't do—we kind of sat in a circle and [Mediator] would ask us these questions, and then he—he separated my sister and

me. Then we would start and go around that way. And he had gotten this rock, and I think he told me it was from the museum about the Holocaust, but it was like—I believe he said the Indians, when they do I guess it's a powwow but it's like a speaking stick. And so that's what this rock was. And it was really amazing because when it was all over with, that rock was red hot. Really amazing. [Second mediator] put it in her hand and she said, "My God! There was something in this room. Feel this rock." And it was—it was really hot to the touch. And it was—we talked about—it was like the brother said, he still is embarrassed, because people still come up to him and say, "Isn't your brother the one that murdered that girl?" And he said he still has the anger. But I think that was one of the big surprises for me is how angry they were with him.

... Well, it surprised me when Miguel asked me if his father could go to the grave. I never thought that they would think about going to the grave. And Miguel said his dad had wanted to go since the murder happened, but that he, out of respect for us, he didn't go. And I thought, that's just something I would have never thought they wanted to do. But I also think—because [Miguel's sister] had a difficult time Saturday—oh, she had a difficult time. She was really mad at her daddy too, and I said, "Well, do you think it's kind of like a man thing?" That because there's going to be females here, he didn't want to break down in front of us? And she said, "You know, I didn't think about that." And I said, well, I bet that's what it was, is that ... . But I told [Sister], I'll bet it's because us girls were going to be here. And she said that now she could tell him where it was at, and he could go by himself. But she was really angry and she did have a hard time. She said, "This is like the funeral for me." And see, I never thought about that.

Gloria seems determined to present a picture that would satisfy her police detective friends, and not appear to be soft on the offender, or forgiving of him. She maintains an image of herself, which is often echoed among her friends and family, of being strong and resolute. I ask her to tell me about the issue of any bond or attachment developing between her and Miguel.

Gloria: No, ain't no bond. It's like I tell everybody—they sit there and say, well, you go and talk to these inmates. Because my thing is that we're going to have to face reality. The majority of these people are coming out of prison. I don't care what rules you make, what laws you make, they're coming out of there. OK, we know up to this point the kind of rehabilitation that we have tried does not work. OK, so if we want this restorative justice, we're all going to have to sit down together. And I mean, I'm talking about police officers, I'm talking about people like you and [Mediator] and me, defendants, John Doe Average Citizen, and we need to come together and have these ideas. And I think one of the things is like a lot of the experts say now, when these defendants look us in the face and really

know what this crime does, it's going to make a big impact. So, I think that's one of the things that we're going to have to worry about is—I forgot your question. Ask your question again, I'm sorry.
Interviewer: The bond, attachment issue?
Gloria: Oh, yeah. What I tell—and they go, "You go into the prison and you went and talked to this guy" and I said, "It doesn't mean I'm going to ask him home for dinner." And it doesn't mean that I'm going to become his best buddy. It means that he now knows what he took away from me and what he did to my family. And if he goes to talk to—it's like I spoke to these inmates—and the inmates get madder than anybody when I tell them—they don't think I should have talked to him, I mean, you know. But when I told them that he wants to go around and speak to juveniles, they say, "Well, he's going to get real food." Who cares? That's not my concern. If we save lives, that's what we have to worry about. But that doesn't mean I want him out of prison. And that doesn't mean I'm going to fight for his not to get paroled. And I'm very honest with him. And he tells me—he knows, so no, between me and Miguel, I don't see a bond forming. Maybe between other people. And I have seen some victims that I worry about.

… I told Miguel that. I told Miguel in our mediation, I said, "we will always be joined at the hip … I know where you're at and what you're doing, who you're doing it with. We'll always be connected at the hip." But that doesn't mean I'm his friend. And that doesn't mean I'm going to go places with him and do—other than to talk to juveniles and that kind of stuff. But like entertainment or recreation, no. But there always will be some kind of connection, yeah.

INTERVIEW WITH THE MEDIATOR

In discussing this case with the mediator, I find he has remained in close contact with all the parties, and, as seen, facilitated the meeting between the two families. The significance of this meeting seems profound to me, and the meeting itself remains very close to the mediator's consciousness when we meet.

Mediator: … and this is what just kills me in this, is the lack of contact. And I have not had a lot of contact with Miguel over the last two years and yet what was consistent with that is every time I returned to him and thought, "Surely, you're somewhere else," he again confirmed some real depth for me. And what happened between Gloria and his family was really remarkable. That's an instance with Gloria, in terms of—she keeps thinking that I challenge her in terms of forgiveness, but I never have. But she's just locked in on that. What I've always told her is that I don't care what you call it, what I do know is that what you have done in the face of what you have said that you will never, ever forgive him, you have done forgiving things. And she agrees to that. And other people have called what she's done forgiving. But it doesn't matter. In fact, it's horrible to even deal with that word, because just her behavior speaks for itself. And she has been one again that her—a wonderful example of [the] process. Now she continues to grow and identify some things in herself and how, almost in spite of herself, what she did with that family at every turn was so perceptive on some stuff.

Interviewer: Yeah, her description of the meeting was quite moving. The interview with her was interesting because that issue came up, and she did represent this as an ongoing battle that the two of you were having. But on two occasions, she just throws in this line, "Well, maybe I have." But then she's got a self-definition about that that's very important for her to hold onto.

Mediator: And what other people think. And what her daughter—although if she goes back to—that's where that power of the video was so strong, to be able to go back and show her that point where she says, three or four times through the session, "I will never, ever forgive him." And then when she goes out and I interview Miguel separately and then she comes in and we talk and debrief. And then the last thing, "Well, is there anything else?" And she says, "Well, no, not really. But as I was out there, I felt that Caroline was really with me and that knowing Caroline, she's forgiven him and I know I can't do it now, but some day, I believe I might be about doing that." And she's just so powerful, which you don't need to corner her, you don't need to do anything with that but just experience it.

And Miguel is one that, I don't know if we have all the truth, and certainly, she doesn't believe that. And yet what I also know—and I don't have that need to push on that, because I just see where she's going with it—she had such a strong relationship with the detectives and there is that element of what the police and the detectives determined as the truth, and what was absolutely the truth from Miguel's perspective, and then what's become her truth. The truth is somewhere in that; God only knows. But I've learned not definitely to accept the police's version as the truth, that's for sure. Although it creates that tension that needs to be there. And is that important anyway? To some element it is. And so, there are things—I would love to see how Miguel continues to grow. He has been restricted by opportunity. As all of them have, really. Lester got a chance to fulfill some of that opportunity which was really, in fact, enacted by Gloria and Miguel. They're the ones that had initially wanted to present together. Miguel was not allowed that because of the warden. And yet he has tried to do many, many things and yet, not because he didn't want to, and not because he wouldn't have grown from it, but because he was just denied the opportunity [by the prison officials].

In discussing the changes that are observed in Miguel, the mediator discusses the sadness he feels at the potential of a loss of opportunity. He describes the changes seen by other inmates:

Mediator: And so, I'm not sure whether—so again, it's just so sad. I have real sad feelings toward him, and I want to write him very soon, just to continue encouraging him because I think he's the one that they had sort of that relational evangelism that took place, that came back and saw that Miguel was different. And finally, it was other offenders that came up to him and said sort of like … "I want what you've got." Well, that's kind of what I'm thinking about Miguel—because other offenders said, "You changed—something happened." And so, they began their own group, and then, we were going to take off on that but weren't able to. So that's all sorts of areas that I would love to see developed.

I ask him to discuss his experience with the meeting of the two families:

Mediator: Yeah, that was remarkable—first of all, I did minimal preparation. The more preparation, the better it would have been. I know it, but we did some mental preparation and one of the—the first circle in using what I call or renamed "a listening piece" instead of a "talking piece"—they just introduce themselves. The second is what were they feeling when they first heard what Miguel had done. And the sister was the first one and she said, "I just hated him. I couldn't believe …" and then it went to the parents and the son, and that first circle, there was so much bonding, just on that level.

And you had asked a question earlier about bonding between offender and victim, and I don't know if we got to that—well, I guess we did.

There's always some dangers with that, but I think it depends on your hearing change, of what you feel happens there. And you know, what I keep holding up, or wanting to hold up to people, is that we want to disavow the validity of that, and so, what has worked before that has been so much better that you want to hold onto? So, the separation has created what? And so, you really need to hold people to task there on what is your purpose in trying to detract from what happened here? Why do you stress that so much?

I ask him about the remarkable request of a photograph of Caroline to put on the wall with the other pictures of the family members.

Mediator: Yeah, and in fact, just considering the father alone, the father and the mother were—the fact that they were together in the same room, because they had divorced, and there was some strong feelings between them, and yet you could tell the stuff that happened between them even then, but they still couldn't communicate directly to each other, even when they were in the room. But he was not a very verbal person, not eloquent at all, similar to what you've heard from me this morning! Just stumbling over himself, and, yet, the more he talked, the more powerful it became, because he got into his feelings, and you could tell how sincere he was regardless of what he was saying, and that really moved so many of the things that he said and did, or "be-d," that sense of being really moved Gloria. And so, that one of his requests was for the letter, which just blew everybody away—I didn't know that was coming—but one of his requests also was that they go to the cemetery. Well, that has never happened at this point. And Gloria's assessment I think is right on. Her sensitivity to that was so profound of saying that that was just his—as a man, from his vantage point, he could only show so much. And our last conversation, she said, "Maybe you can help with—he didn't have to go there with me, but maybe just you and he could go." And I thought, "God, that's great." And so, there's just some great power there.

DISCUSSION

Having come to this, the last case, I again see it as a remarkable example of both Athens' theory of the concept of the violentization process, and the incorporation of the phantom community of voices that support the building lifestyle.

Miguel is also a good example of my concept in this process, of the evolving series of crises that serve as step-by-step epiphanies, which eventually result in the mediation and its effect.

For Miguel, this process started by building up to the shooting, which was almost predictable, as the issues developed between these three players. The actuality of the murders "happened as fast as [I'm] just now telling you." The realization, which was impacted by his encounter with his brother, who "saw death in his eyes," and the arrest and his reaction, picked up by Gloria, of not wanting to hurt his family. He said, "In that second, I went from being just a teenager dealing drugs to an adult."

Important to note, also, is Miguel's description of time, and the use of time while in prison. He spent "ten years doing nothing." Then, because of a girlfriend from the past reminding him of what he used to be, he begins a course of self-evaluation when, with a certain quality of serendipity, the request came to meet with Gloria. He knew he would say "yes" to this request, and did it without thinking.

In the evolving series of epiphanies that Miguel experienced, the two that were most important to him were the letter that Gloria wrote to him prior to their meeting, and, as has been seen almost universally in this study sample, the photograph album that she had him look at. He describes the impact of the letter on him as, "feeling so small," "humiliating," "my life's been nothing. I thought I went through hell, but I ain't been through nothing." And then he nicely describes the meaning of these events to him.

Miguel: … And so, she asked me if she could show me some pictures, and I said, "Yeah, OK." So, when I grabbed the pictures, it was like me grabbing the letter. It was like me reading the letter. And when I was looking through the pictures like that, I wasn't looking at the pictures—well, I was looking at them, but I was—what she was telling me in that letter was going through my mind … the girl was her world, this girl was everything to her, and she wished she could do this. I can remember everything. I broke down—I was like—it became real, it became real. It wasn't a letter anymore. It wasn't somebody that—in other words, she became a human being, something that I wasn't even aware of. Because when I killed her, I didn't know her. It was like she was nothing. Nobody. And it was like she came back to life, and she was a human being again, and her words in that letter did that. Her words in that letter to me brought that out, and that's the reason why that happened like that. Because she became real again. She became real.

The meeting with the mediator and the opportunity, for the first time, to tell his story in its entirety to someone who cared about the story and its meaning again supports this entire process.

Again, as part of this evolution, Miguel can develop an internalized image of Caroline, who he felt, as did Gloria, was in the room with them, and who he now reports is in his thoughts daily.

He reports that the meeting also "opened up a lot of things," especially that there was a new "meaning that life is not just something that you do," along with a sense of responsibility for and to others. This change has been apparently striking enough to be noticed by his colleagues.

As has been discussed in other cases, Miguel also developed a conception of his "old and new self." In discussing how firm he is in these changes, he does allow that the old self is still available to him, and might even return, but he sees the option of this return as "giving up." This realization is significant in that he does have a history of depression, which is evidenced, and the role this depression plays in his behavior and choices is no doubt profound. It also speaks to the question raised in other interviews about the future of the change seen, and whether, given the realities of the social situation, along with the lack of supportive experiences in the prison environment ("There's nothing available, like talking to someone. Nothing you can do, you have to go on on your own."), these changes can be sustained. It does, as was discussed in Lester's situation, leave an open question as to a return to society since there would be such an inclination to "give up."

However, Miguel gives a hopeful and optimistic response related to his own self-evaluation on this matter:

> … And basically, what I've been through, I've been doing that all my life. I'm tired of it; I don't want that no more. It has to be a higher standard; it has to be

> something more to live up to. To me that's what it is. Striving to be better; striving not to fail. Yeah, that might happen, but if you don't strive, you strive not to make it happen, you do the thing that needs to be done. And don't use it as a copout. That's my attitude now. That's my whole attitude in everything that I do. It's not going to happen overnight; it's going to be ongoing. It's going to be with me for the rest of my life. Being responsible. Like [Mediator] talks about accountability, and being open to change. Listen to people. Sometimes you can't listen if you're not open. So those are some of the things for me, to continue to do. And that's something that I told [Mediator] from the very beginning: I'm not going to give up. I'm not going to stop. This is something that's going to happen all the time. And so far, so good. It's been good for me.

And, as he told his friend, who was a constant recidivist, you need to "become society," and be who *they* are, not simply a "part of society." Moreover, as he states, "that requires change."

In discussing the mediation with Gloria, the most important thing she felt about it was that she could make Caroline "real" to him. I doubt that anyone who saw this moment in their meeting would question its veracity and its incredible power.

Her struggles with the concept of forgiveness are of note, but it is also important that she, like many others, ultimately see this as unimportant. She is not being eaten up by her anger, and she states, "If you just leave people alone, they're going to come to their own conclusions."

Her comment summing up the future is very important:

> Because my thing is that we're going to have to face reality. The majority of these people are coming out of prison. I don't care what rules you make, what laws you make, they're coming out of there. OK, we know up to this point the kind of rehabilitation that we have tried does not work. OK, so if we want this restorative justice, we're all going to have to sit down together. And I mean, I'm talking about police officers, I'm talking about people like you and [Mediator] and me, defendants, John Doe Average Citizen, and we need to come together and have these ideas. And I think one of the things is like a lot of the experts say now, when these defendants look us in the face and really know what this crime does, it's going to make a big impact.

Especially striking in this comment is her belief in the need for the defendant to "look us in the face and really know what this crime does," which replicates the face-to-face meaning and importance that has been cited by so many of these respondents. She also supports the connection that is made, but, like Miguel, does not want to relegate this to a personal relationship, but a connection that has been made because of the crime that means they will always be "joined at the hip."

Not unlike the mediator, I was left, following both of my meetings with Miguel, with a profound sadness. The change in him is palpable, but his new and profound realization and responsibility for his actions temper this. He is left with his remorse, and a sense of guilt and depression that he had previously been able to deny and rationalize. He was able to bury and hide from these feelings for the first ten years following his actions. The process he used to do this speaks to the inadequacy of our current system of justice. It speaks to what becomes of "time," when one has no options. The notion of prison time, when first conceived of, was for meditation and then penance based on one's actions. Clearly, the internalization of these actions goes beyond simply being given time to think about one's crime, or even time as punishment.

Conclusion

My original question was whether violent individuals can achieve empathy. If so, how is that achievement possible and what is the ultimate meaning to the individuals involved?

CAN EMPATHY BE ACHIEVED?

There is clear evidence of empathy, by means of the definition I am using here, demonstrated in all of the offenders I studied because of these encounters. Empathy is attained as part of the process described in the findings, centering on a series of epiphanies that are internalized and, therefore, are life-changing events. In even those offenders where the process of empathic development is questionable (given their degree of personality disorder), some strong and notable reactions could be determined (gauged by their self-reports to corrections staff or their general course in the prison population).

How I gauged the acquisition of empathy relates to the developmental research I find compelling, and is then supported by the observations and interviews of the participants:

Empathy is realized, both in child development and in these encounters, in dyadic relationships. The disruption of the development of empathy in early childhood is, through the lived experience of the individual, because of mutual dysregulation in the parenting relationship. These individuals are left with the difficult, if not impossible, task of self-regulation and attunement to the other.

With the men I studied, as a function of the entire experience (commission of the crime, arrest and trial, incarceration, approach by the mediator, telling the story, and ultimate mediation) and the epiphanies that result throughout this developing set of shocks, the individuals acquire a sense of agency for their situation, and a concept of the theory of mind of the other, which leads to a previously undeveloped reflective self-function.

This mentalizing ability (vs. their previous tendency toward impulse and action) allows these individuals to accept responsibility for their actions, engage in the ultimate ownership of the action, and then seek reconciliation. This evolving process takes place within the relationship between victims, offenders, and mediators, and is one in which the participants are encouraged to engage in a narrative process.

WHAT WAS THE MEANING MADE BY THE PARTICIPANTS?

The dual (the experience of both parties) experience of psychic trauma seems to be a form of connection between victims and perpetrators that facilitates their connection. This recognition of each other creates what appears to be at times an odd bonding between the two, and is often spoken about, sometimes uncomfortably, by those observing or participating in these meetings.

The acquisition of empathy is enhanced by the movement toward the declaration of this trauma through its naming and recognition. This serves to moderate or decrease the experience of trauma in both parties.

One of the most significant affects in observing the relationship that is established during these encounters on both individuals is the facilitation of the process of mourning, which will be discussed later.

These encounters clearly lead to change in the individuals, and ultimately, their larger social structures and ways of relating to others. These changes result from victims and offenders coming face-to-face, or "eye-to-eye," and they together incorporate elements of developing empathy for both parties, which is likely recognized intersubjectively. This process is analogous to the ethic of care process, which will also be discussed later.

Finally, therefore, empathy seems to exist as a function of a community and is found by all participants and the wider social system through the process of restorative justice.

THE SOCIAL MOVEMENT OF RESTORATIVE JUSTICE

The practice of restorative justice also incorporates a secondary effect on the larger social system, providing a "ripple effect" on the communities inhabited by the participants. Restorative justice, as a method of facilitating a uniquely human process, is highly effective and leads to a profound outcome for the participants.

The restorative justice criticisms of our current form of justice are well founded. Our current form of justice apparently leads to perpetrators who are not encouraged to take responsibility for their actions, and, therefore, conceive of themselves, ultimately, as the victims of their crimes. This is, at the very least, ironic, unless you are of the mind that incarceration is, in and of itself, a sufficient form of retribution for crime and that the ultimate acceptance of responsibility by the perpetrator is unimportant to this end, or does not affect the likelihood of future crimes being committed by this same individual.

In this same vein, the current system of penal system incarceration, designed to punish offenders, serves to exacerbate and reinforce the very qualities that it is charged with eradicating. This observation is one that I quickly came to in my work at San Quentin, and is supported by many of the men I interviewed for this work, along with more casual conversations held with a variety of inmates I came to know in my travels in each of these prisons.

One of the findings that I really didn't expect, but one that ultimately began as a question during my years at San Quentin, was that the long-standing belief of the ineffectiveness of relationship-oriented therapeutic approaches in dealing with offenders, ("psychopaths" or "sociopaths") and the possibility that these approaches would have any power in affecting their development, is brought into question by the findings of this study. This is supported by the clear evidence that the period of preparation of the participants is a significant and vital part of the process, in which the concept of relationship is introduced as a vehicle for healing and change. The vehicle for this is simply talking and eliciting history, stories, and the associated feelings.

Let me return for a moment to my definition of empathy and how this evolved in my understanding because of this research.

In viewing the results of this research through my lens of empathy, the experience of these participants clearly falls more closely into the original definition of the word, *Einfühlung*. I suggest that as the term is commonly used and conceived of in the treatment community, this gives the term and concept a more active rather than passive connotation.

The original term *Einfühlung*, you may remember, coined by Theodore Lipps in the nineteenth century, was meant to define the emotive experience we have while viewing art or while engaged in other aesthetic contemplation. Lipps characterized this experience as a process of involuntary, inner imitation where the subject identifies through feeling the movement of a dancer, or the illusory upward lift of an architectural column, or a work of art in a museum. Lipps saw this response as an involuntary process and defined complete empathy as aesthetic, providing nonrepresentational access to beauty.

The meaning of this to the participants in these dialogues fits this description in that it becomes closer to the nonverbal and noncognitive experience embodied in metaphor or the experience of profound feeling.

Later, it was Husserl who made a phenomenologically purified concept of *Einfühlung* to account for the way the self directly recognizes the other. Thus, *Einfühlung* is not to be equated with human understanding (as pointed out by Dilthey); it is rather meant to represent a feeling state. Whereas understanding is reflective, empathy is prereflective (Makkreel 1975).

I further stress that this process can occur in a system or dyad, which has significant implications on the sense of self and self-agency for all involved. Harter suggests that mutual empathy is characterized by a flow of empathic attunement between the parties involved. She suggests that this attunement, ultimately, has the power to alter or shift the boundaries between subject and object, thereby profoundly altering the sense of separateness: "In true empathic exchange, each is both object and subject, mutually engaged in affecting and being affected, knowing and being known" (Harter 1999, p. 292). It is important to note that, in such an exchange, the individuals do not lose their sense of self, but that the relatedness with the other brings focus and clarity to the sense of self, enhancing the experience of reality. The emphasis here is that this sense of reality and the enhancement of the sense of self happens through an experience of *connectedness* and *mutuality*.

In phenomenological research, the *verstehen* doctrine is a uniquely human process and way of seeing the world. Translated as "understanding," it is the underpinning of naturalistic inquiry. This underpinning holds that human beings need to be understood and studied in a different fashion than other objects, since humans are so complex (embodying purpose, emotion, planfulness, culture, and values). As Patton describes, and significant to my project here, the *verstehen* tradition in phenomenological methodology "stresses understanding that focuses on the meaning of human behavior, the context of social interaction, an empathic understanding based on personal experience, and the connections between mental states and behavior" (Patton 1990, p. 57).

As seen in the findings, all parties, including the researcher, were impacted by the *verstehen* doctrine, as all were influenced by an emphasis "on the human capacity to know and understand others through empathic introspection and reflection based on direct observation of and interaction with people" (Patton 1990, p. 57).

I have delineated, from a developmental perspective, the journey that the offenders in this study took that led to their eventual crime and incarceration. I would suggest that the concept of trauma is central to each of their experiences. Significantly, the concept of trauma is eventually what connects them to the victim or survivor. One of the outcomes of the process of meeting appears to be the addressing of this trauma, through its recognition and naming, and the aftermath of mourning. If there is any "closure" to be identified in the process, this outcome seems to be the most essential.

For the offender, there is a cumulative experience of trauma, which leads eventually to the experience of the meeting and its consequence. Most of these offenders come to their crime already conversant with trauma. This accounts for their ready ability to dissociate, which most experience at the time they commit the crime. However, I will suggest that the commission of violence, for these individuals, was a further traumatic experience. Their arrest, criminal investigation, charge, and trial follow this experience, and also accumulate trauma. As they recount this period, they often continue to dissociate; however, they all recount strong emotional and visual memories of the experience, which often include the victims and survivors, at their trial.

I would suggest that one of the consequences of this trauma is the reduction of the capacity to "reflect" on the experience, which leads to nonreflective internal working models. This internal process is a defensive posture, which leads to the inability to depict the mental states of themselves or others. The ability to reflect on the situation they find themselves in appears to be the first step in transforming the experience from one of repetition and accumulation of prior trauma, to the possibility of epiphany, insight, and change.

The approach by the mediator, following a request by the victim or survivor for a meeting, provides the next stage in comprehension, preparation, and anticipation, which occurs within an intensive dyadic relationship. For most offenders, this is the first relationship in which they have given a narrative account of their lives leading up to the crime. This process concludes with the meeting with the survivor, the coming eye-to-eye. As stated by Eric, "There is so much gained by just that first minute or two, just by sitting down in front of each other … there is so much said without saying anything."

The meaning of this process could not be any more clearly understood than by the number of times metaphors such as, "It was like stepping off a cliff" are used by the offenders to describe it.

"THE VILLAGE"

The case of this young boy and offender coming together in their meeting represents a true depiction of the systemic meaning of this process.

The case highlights a process whose influence goes well beyond the significant individual meaning to the offender and his young victim. It represents a profound example of the term "interactive," as it is a true depiction of an interactive experience.

All the actors who came together in this journey formed an interactive and interpretive community. It is a community of people who came together to not only make meaning of the experience, but to support and facilitate the process of mourning.

The focus for the young victim is that of remembering, telling the story to an eager and empathic listener, and allowing for his own experience to be defined, which facilitated his own process of mourning. While the concept of "closure" is not even necessary to the case, he did clearly resolve the inner conflicts that were causing his disruption both internally and socially.

Much the same could be said for the offender and his family, who came together too as a supportive group, to understand and make meaning of their history and experience. Many of the offenders, who continued to work with their own families, said that their father's, especially, were felt to become more open and emotive.

"THE EXCEPTION AND THE RULE"

This case is presented as an example that is unlike other cases prepared for restorative justice dialogues in a variety of ways. As was suggested in this case, while it presented in ways as anomalistic to the other cases seen here (or like many occurring universally), it was also, nevertheless, quite profound to those involved.

For Harry, who clearly represents the extreme end of the psychopathic continuum previously outlined, his stated objective was to do something positive for Lucy, to atone for the murders he admitted to. While his motivation was clearly complex, there is no reason not to think that his objective was a form of empathy, and the only form of empathy available to him. In fact, it could well be argued that, within the context of his "relationship" with Lucy, this degree of empathic ability both spared her life in the first instance, and allowed her to face him in the second.

In his complexity, Harry cannot avoid attempting to exert sadistic power over Lucy, even in the meeting. However, his inappropriate behavior gave Lucy the opportunity to stop him, with a single gesture and word, which was the most important moment in the mediation for her. In fact, this seemingly small and inconsequential gesture contributed to an ultimate healing in her psychic struggles that proved a major change in her inner-psychic structure.

"THE UNIVERSE"

Athens' definition of the process of violentization makes the process dependent on the support of a community. He proposes that initially the process is made up of a community of real actors, parents, peers, and neighbors, that eventually becomes internalized as a phantom community which becomes supportive of violent solutions to life situations. Violence, thus, supported as a value, is reinforced by the internal soliloquies of the phantom community. I am proposing that this community is analogous to the process of internal working models discussed in earlier chapters.

Thus, through the mediation experiences discussed, these internal working models become open to alteration and modification, with the opportunity of a new community. It is in this manner that Achilles finds his "pity," which I propose is related both to his developing a capacity for empathy as well as his own humanity.

As Emde has stated, "Once we are in touch with another's emotional life, we are in touch with his or her humanity" (Emde 1983).

While Danny mostly attributes his hallucinations to his extensive history of psychedelic usage, his case file indicates a long history of psychotic disorders and treatment. Currently, Danny is without medication. He is not hallucinating, and he is proceeding with his goal of writing, all the while he is socializing more in the institution and working in a fulfilling job.

Danny underscores, also, the nature of the experience in his discussion of being face-to-face: "I feel that I owe her that, owe her to sit in front of her and just say things … saying the unspeakable is very difficult." And later, he states, "It [the meeting] had to be done. If I had backed out then, there would never be anything resolved or any kind of reconciliation." And in speaking to the "ripple effect" commented on by mediators, Danny tells us, "I've got this idea that not only is it about the victim, it's about other victims too, and other offenders."

Eric's interview provided me with his narrative basis for the meaning of the experience. His statement was (I am paraphrasing):

> It is easy to let people become statistics or numbers or get mad at the system or whatever, and a lot of guys have animosity toward the system. I could be angry at the sentence I got, and blame the system for that. But with the mediation it wasn't the system that I was being held accountable to, it was the human being whose daughter I killed. It's one thing to be mad at the state for the sentence I got. It's altogether another thing to be sitting across the table from the parent whose child you killed and try to explain to them the reason.

PILOT STUDY CASES

Several cases powerfully indicate the endurance of the mediation experience and its depth of consequence for them. Miguel and Louis' interviews testify to this depth.

Miguel's experience with depression is clearly an ongoing life function for him, related as it is to his family history. While awaiting sentencing in jail, he made a "bargain" with God that if he didn't receive the death penalty for having killed Caroline, he would never again deny the crime.

Miguel was described, after the meeting with Gloria, as having a kind of "evangelism" for his experience with her. While Gloria refuses to "forgive" Miguel, their experience together suggests that what is most significant about the restorative justice process is that, at its most central point, it facilitates mourning. This achievement may, ultimately, be more important to the participants than forgiveness.

At the same time, when forgiveness takes place it is a significant event. For the offender, the act of apology and the taking of responsibility is "an act of giving that can be as powerful and transforming as forgiveness" (Karen 2001). Apology and forgiveness may be indistinguishable, releasing us from our worst feelings about ourselves and making us feel cared about and connected again.

Miguel stated to me that Caroline was nothing to him when he killed her, a "nobody." He described the act as impulsive, "and it just happened just like that, in the time it took me to say it." He described his experience prior to meeting with Gloria as a film he watched, repeatedly, but without emotion. Not until the meeting with Gloria was he able to attach the emotion. This accomplishment is movingly clear during the videotaped meeting as he looked at Caroline's baby picture. He reported, "she came back to life and she was a human being again. She became real."

> And when I was looking through the pictures like that, I wasn't looking at the pictures—well, I was looking at them, but I was—what she was telling me in that letter was going through my mind. About she was so close to that girl, the girl was her world, this girl was everything to her,
>
> … I can remember everything. I broke down—I was like—it became real, it became real. It wasn't a letter any more … in other words, she became a human being, something that I wasn't even aware of. Because when I killed her, I didn't know her. It was like she was nothing. Nobody. And it was like she came back to life and she was a human being again, and her words in that letter did that. Her words in that letter to me brought that out and that's the reason why that happened like that. Because she became real again, she became real.

Because of the process, he states that he assumed an important responsibility, that "you have that reaction that you have the responsibility as a human being to treat people as human beings."

> For me I think it's more of an inner change, you know, more like a moral change. More like—having a better sense of right and wrong. And realizing that life is important, life is something that it's just not—every man for himself. And

> that's kind of the way I lived before all this happened. … And for me, that's kind of—based on what I went through and everything, I just look at it and I shake my head. It's unbelievable that I did the things that I did, thinking like that … . We don't live by ourselves. It's not every man for himself. There's other people around you have to think about, and have responsibility for and stuff like that. You've got to think not only about yourself, but about other people. And it just opens up a whole new world. You gotta be responsible. … And you've got to go by that, and you've got to live by it. And one of the things for me is learning how to do that. Not just learning but doing it.

Louis also discusses the importance of "putting a face" on what you've done, which enhances the ability to take responsibility for it.

THE OPPORTUNITY FOR CHANGE AND THE ROLE OF EPIPHANY

The concept of personal change is at the heart of this work, and it is implied in the research focus. There is little question, for most people, that change is possible in human beings and yet it is a concept that many people feel cynical or pessimistic about.

Furthermore, there are a variety of ways individuals achieve a profound personal change: some experiences happen in a moment; some last over many years. Saint Augustine, of course, achieved a major life change without the benefit of psychoanalysis. I would suggest that there are far more similarities in the connotation of change than differences.

Many of the participants in this study credited as the basis for their change either a discovery, or a reunification with their spirituality. Winnicott suggests that the religious experience, in adult development, bears the closest similarity to childhood's transitional experiences (Winnicott 1953, Lear 1993).

In a recent session with a schizophrenic patient, who has a history in theology, he suggested to me (unbidden) that, "epiphany opens the door to the Holy Spirit."

There are a variety of methods by which a process of change can be described. Denzin (1987) has tried to look at the process of chemical dependency treatment, which many participants see as a life-saving process. Individuals who are recovering from serious chemical dependency, whose lives have been virtually destroyed by chemical use, undergo a dramatic change as individuals following treatment related to their addictions, which affects their personal relationships and relationship to self.

Cohler (1993) suggests that one of the changes that occur because of a successful psychoanalysis relates to the creation of a more coherent narrative. He suggests that previous narratives are incorporated into the life story, which is coherent to the narrator (related to personal history, development, and reasons for the outcome of events). During a change process (e.g., psychoanalytic process), there is also a change in the personal narrative. This development, in psychoanalysis, occurs in the context of the relationship:

> ... one of the major accomplishments of the psychoanalytic process is the collaborative revisions of the analysand's narrative of development into one which is more readily followed, providing for a less rigidly maintained portrayal of the past than was possible prior to that point. (Cohler and Freeman 1993, p. 146)

In describing a change process, which is reminiscent of epiphanies, Cohler suggests the experience of past events becomes less important than the way these events become experienced in the present in the internal narrative. He suggests that the course of life is better seen as a "series of abrupt transformations, in which the past is successively refashioned in terms of present understandings of self, others, and expectable problems and challenges" (Cohler and Freeman 1993, p. 153). Thus, there is a continuity of change in the life course over time that is more related to "epigenesis" than to a linear or continuous course of past relationships into present experience.

GRIEF AND MOURNING

> To mourn is to love again, even if it only happens in pieces. I think it is one of the primary goals of psychotherapy, to help us get past our defenses and reexperience the world of feeling we have left behind. But to reexperience the love is also to reexperience the agony of hurt and loss. These threads of feeling are bound together. (Karen 2001, p. 264)

As has been noted in the work of Main (1990), the issue of grief and unresolved mourning is often a function of attachment failure. This attachment failure can either be a result of the actual loss of the parenting figure, or the loss of the emotional connection with the parenting figure, suffered through neglect or abuse. The result of this loss, as defined by any number of theoreticians, is developmental arrest and depression.

In offenders, it is likely that they are dealing with both issues of mourning as well as clinical depression. In studies reported by Solomon, it is well established that adolescent offender populations studied show evidence of clinical depression (Solomon 2001, pp. 187–89). The concept of depression as the underlying psychic issue in adolescents who become violent or self-destructive has long been established as the underpinning of behavior disorder or acting out in developmental theories (Blos 1979).

Mourning and loss are present, I would suggest, in both offender and victim/survivor participants in the dialogues. The issues of mourning also exist in the larger social system inhabited by both parties.

As I have proposed, the facilitation of mourning is perhaps the most significant impact of the mediation dialogues. I would suggest that the result of a process of mourning (as opposed to an arrest) is the facilitation of individuation and a sense of self and self-definition. Through the process of mourning, the individual engages in the creation of meaning. This meaning making is "at once a work of personal growth and a work of culture," where, "the self both appropriates from the past what has been lost, and, at the same time, actually creates for itself in a fresh way these meanings" (Homans 1989).

The facilitation of mourning is a meaning-making enterprise. Meaning making has both a logical and an emotional component: "Associated with the requirements for coherence, continuity, and integrity is a tremendous human intolerance for meaninglessness .... What is emotionally relevant is likely to be particularly significant for the maintenance of selfhood. If meaning is not provided by the conventions of language or habit, it will be provided out of one's imagination" (Klein 1976).

Depression and mourning are related, as I would propose in these findings, but Cavell also suggests a significant connection related to the split self that is so often described by the offenders:

> We might infer, then, that whereas melancholia is mourning forestalled, producing a split self in the process, the healthy conscience, evolving from mourning undergone, is whole. (Cavell 1993, p. 225)

This sense that unresolved or unfelt mourning leads to two unrelated parts of the self is meaningful for the joint experience between victims and offenders as well.

> Mourning requires ... a recognition that persons, both the mourned and oneself as the mourner, are "whole" persons in the sense defined earlier. (I am the same person whether I am feeling anger or love toward you, as you are the same "object" of my different passions.) This true belief about the nature of persons is then among the conditions of mourning. (Cavell 1993, pp. 228–229)

Related to my findings, and well stated by Hassoun, "the melancholic is tormented not by a loss, but by the lack of possibility for naming and designating this loss" (Hassoun 1997, p. 29). The naming of the loss, and its designation, bears considerable importance for these participants.

In putting this process in the therapeutic frame, Hassoun states:

> The knowledge constituted in the transference tends to allow the subject to mourn, and from this mourning reconstitute the (previously ever-absent) internal object that should have been his support.
>
> To replace naked, enigmatic pain by the work of mourning, mourning, that is, for an object or an abstraction set up in its place—that is our task. (Hassoun 1997, p. 23)

In a profoundly important statement, Burch suggests that an important shift must occur, even in mourning the loss of a childhood full of abuse and neglect, where the failure finally is more "tragic than willful," and the individual can let go of good/bad distinctions characteristic of more primitive mental states.

> Mourning is a kind of final act of love. When love has been choked off by the nature of the loss, however, attachment remains but is denied … .
>
> What is required for recovery is not retribution and triumph, not just the relief of rage, not even simply forgiveness, but a rediscovery of the original attachment, genuinely experienced, however betrayed it was. This means acceptance of one's perpetual vulnerability to betrayal. (Burch 1989)

FORGIVENESS

The concept of forgiveness (referred to by one of my mediator subjects as "the F word") has been controversial in the restorative justice movement. The victim's community has been largely wary of forgiveness as a goal of the dialogues, believing, in some instances, that forgiveness should not be given to the perpetrator, and, especially, not coerced. One of the mediator's interviewed suggested that it is better to simply leave the concept alone and deal with it only if the victim or survivor states it as an inherent goal.

The interviews showed that when it occurred in the meeting, it became a highly significant event for both parties. (It, at times, was also described as significant by its absence or refusal.) In any event, when discussed in its aftermath, the subject of forgiveness was always an emotional one for the participants.

Hillman suggests that, "Forgiveness, like humility, is only a term unless one has been fully humiliated or fully wronged" (Hillman 1975).

Only when the degree of wrong is extremely vital does the question of forgiveness take on any meaning whatsoever.

Important to my observations of when forgiveness becomes a factor in these meetings, Hillman states:

> But forgiveness is so difficult that it probably needs some help from the other person. I mean by this that the wrong, if not remembered by both parties—and

> remembered as a wrong—falls on the betrayed. The wider context within which the tragedy occurred would seem to call for parallel feelings from both parties. They are still both in a relationship, now as betrayer and betrayed. If only the betrayed senses a wrong, while the other passes it over with rationalizations, then the betrayal is still going on—even increased. This dodging of what has really happened is, of all the sores, the most galling to the betrayed. Forgiveness comes harder; resentments grow because the betrayer is not carrying his guilt and the act is not honestly conscious .... To carry one's sins, one has first to recognize them, and recognize their brutality. (Hillman, 1975, p. 79)

The concern about forgiveness is well founded, however, if, as a concept, it is an end rather than a product of a viable process that is likely an ongoing phenomenon.

> I am opposed to the forgiveness of the unrepentant; I believe it facilitates malignant dissociative contagion and evil's reproduction.
>
> ... To embrace the unrepentant perpetrator in the soft envelope of forgiveness is to abandon the perpetrator to the loneliness of his own depravity. And, in its failure of intersubjective recognition, such forgiveness/acceptance also represents a failure of historical inscription: the perpetrator is never seen in execution's moment—not in the moment when he himself was annihilated, nor in the moment when he annihilates another. (Grand 2000, pp. 156–157)

Whatever this process of feeling is, and it has been described in these interviews in a variety of ways, for the offender the experience might be defined best in Cavell's statement:

> A constitutive feature of guilt as it regards our actions and intentions toward other persons is, I suggest, a certain kind of love, namely love for the other as a separate person from oneself, with values of his own that one values just because they are his. Such love has to be distinguished from valuing another as means to one's own ends, because of some service he performs for the self, or because in his reflected light one can love one's self better. (Cavell 1993, p. 217)

THE TALIONIC IMPULSE

The talionic law demands that a wrong is set right only by an act of the same kind or identical with the original wrong. It is the basis of "an-eye-for-an-eye" belief systems that are the foundation of our system of punishment.

The talionic law is also rooted in archaic systems of belief related to proprietary rights relative to gain and loss, as well as retribution to "save face," by way of expiating guilt and shame:

> revenge possesses a basic knee-jerk quality which reflects the most primitive efforts to cope with insult and loss. Similarly, it reflects a sensorimotor, preoperational cognitive style (Masterson 1980, p. 495).

Through the facilitation of grief and mourning, restorative justice confronts the need for retaliation in real terms, providing the participants a sense of actual accomplishment. In interviews with those who desire simply vengeance, you sense the presence of a never-ending cycle, where retaliation perpetuates the violent cycle and becomes a shrine, inscribed by vengeance through a continuation of disrespect and dehumanization.

The talionic impulse derives from the experience of the small and powerless child, who determines never to undergo, passively, the experience of pain, and is an effort to "pay back" the perpetrators, either real or imagined. In those determined to seek revenge, Masterson states that, "As long as their aggression is channeled into revenge, it is not available to build psychic structure" (Masterson 1980, p. 495).

It is the need for revenge which is also characteristic of primitive emotional organization, which is reminiscent of primitive pathology.

> For whether it is disguised behind the autoplastic symptomatology of neurotic suffering, bizarrely portrayed in the behavior of the psychotic, or acted out characterologically, the persistence of talionic morality reflects persistent infantilism with its attendant failure to attain the personal wholeness inherent in true selfhood. (Masterson, 1980, p. 496)

Clinicians have long been familiar with the tendency to blame, recognizing it as a function of the attempt to defend against shame. To ward off the sense of shame, someone else must be blamed as the problem, and the blaming that takes place is often rancorous.

This developmental evolution, however, is a process with many pitfalls. It leaves the individual without any easy answers to the complex problems of human suffering and behavior.

Hanna Arendt's premise of the banality of evil comes to mind as the lesson of these events. Arendt, in discussing Adolf Eichmann, states, "and a more specific, and also more decisive, flaw in Eichmann's character was his almost total inability ever to look at anything from the other fellow's point of view" (Arendt 1963). The controversy in Arendt's report, however, is her implication that the system of justice attempting to hold one individual accountable for actions is far too simple-minded and convenient, given the complex nature of Nazi atrocities, and the broad-based complicity of virtually all aspects of society, even the victims themselves.

In the psychological system, this concept is represented by Sullivan's fundamental one-genus postulate, in which he states:

> We shall assume that everyone is much more simply human than otherwise, and that anomalous interpersonal situations, insofar as they do not arise from differences in language or custom, are a function of differences in relative maturity of the persons concerned. (Sullivan 1953)

This assumes that it is not possible to set apart from ourselves actors and their behaviors that are abhorrent to us.

AGENCY AND THEORY OF MIND

Evident in the process is that the offender experiences a new sense of agency, sometimes the first such experience. Self-agency implies the awareness that they have control over their actions, thoughts, and emotional experiences. Further, they experience a sense of volition and control over their behavior. Each one assumes the role of "the architect of one's intentions and plans" (Harter 1999).

Early trauma has been associated with the lack of ability to form a sense of self, especially as a "causal agent." It is universally seen that these offenders did not perceive themselves as causal agents at the time of the crime, and showed little evidence of a sense of agency, often blaming the victim or other outside sources.

Harter has suggested, quoting a study by Howe and Courage (Howe 1993), that the ability to even create autobiographical memory relates to the unimpeded early ability of a sense of agency and of self-recognition (Harter 1999).

Developmentally, it seems clear from the current research that an infant acquires a theory of mind during the second year of life, if not interfered with by the environment:

> Although this emergent ability onsets in the preverbal toddler, it is later in the third year that the child begins to acquire the verbal mental state terms of his language.... These data suggest that the intra- and interpersonally adaptive theory of mind is essentially nonverbal and that empathy involves not so much an awareness of another's cognitions as another's feeling state. (Schore 1994, p. 496)

The basis of my foundation in attachment theory supports the belief that all early forming psychopathology constitutes disorders of attachment and manifests itself as failures of self and/or interactional regulation (Grotstein 1986). This theory has major implications on people's ability to self-regulate, receive, encode, and process the data of emotional experience they are subjected to.

Grotstein discusses an experience that he describes as a "covenant" between children and parents in which the infants/children need to invest in people they feel are "willing to suffer their pain," which happens through identification and empathy. This covenant remains until the developing children can tolerate it themselves.

In child development, Grotstein sees the normal developmental course eventuating in an ability to engage in "reflective" intersubjectivity (relating to object permanency and object constancy, e.g., the depressive position), thus allowing the child to know that another world exists and "is occupied by external *subjects* who are separate from the infant and who existed before the infant" (Grotstein 2000, p. 157).

The resulting personality organization struggles to attain a "psychic organization that can generate complex symbolic representations that contain information about transitioning out of stress-induced negative states. Instead they frequently access pathological internal representations that encode a dysregulated self-in-interaction-with-a-misattuning-other" (Schore 1997).

The powerful interlocking sets of dramas, seen in this project, are examples of how therapy progresses in the context of a community or system. This is true for both the therapist and the clients, who both represent and are held by communities. In this, I use "therapy" as a broadly defined interactive and interpretive process. In fact, restorative justice seems to be the quintessential social work intervention, as it takes place in a relationship-focused activity that enhances reflection and introspection, while having considerable social network ramifications.

This process also confirms Kohut's original notion of empathy as an action or tool. The value of dialogue, either "therapeutic" or "restorative" in motive, has a connection to any dynamic interaction between two individuals. Thus, the impact is significant for inner-psychic, interpersonal, structural, and community domains, with the opportunity of making change possible.

Kohut, himself, seemed to be moving in the direction of the intersubjectivity defined by Atwood and Stolorow (Atwood 1984). Their argument is that any two persons in a relationship psychologically structure the relationship in "accordance with the separate but interrelated subjectivities of the two participants" (Ulman and Brothers 1988).

> ... the two participants in any relationship are often psychologically organized at different developmental levels and in accordance with different central organizing fantasies. However, despite these differences, the respective subjectivities of each participant must always be taken into account in understanding the nature and explaining the meaning of psychological phenomena arising within the intersubjective context of that relationship. (Ulman and Brothers, 1988, p. 218)

Fonagy quotes Akhtar (1992) in an effort to differentiate the philosophical basis for differing object relations schools. As psychoanalysis has moved more toward experiential models, that stress phenomenological beliefs (such as the individual's experience of the self, and the structure of relationships), the role of attachment theory has become more significant to the overall model. Akhtar breaks the theory base into the "classic" schools, epitomized by Kant's belief that the individual strives toward autonomy and reason, and believes this to be the essence of humanity. The "romantic" school, on the other hand, based in Rousseau and Goethe, stresses authenticity and spontaneity more than reason and logic.

Several authors localize the function of the emotions, specifically empathy, to the prefrontal orbital cortex. This structure is in the prefrontal lobe of the right hemisphere, is usually activated under stress, and is essential to the perception of communication, especially of nonverbal cues, and the perceptions of the emotional states of others: "the self-system is more localized in the right, rather than the left brain" (Schore 1994). This data gives Modell and Levin's concepts even more significance related to the activation, through metaphor, of a variety of brain centers, not just the right hemisphere.

An important example of this interaction is seen in the work of Modell (1997), who suggests that the use of metaphor in treatment serves the function of recontextualizing affects and generating new meanings:

> Inchoate feelings, that is, affects that are cognitively unspecified, require metaphors. We know that intense affects, both positive and negative, may be experienced as if they arise from a source outside of the self and hence are believed to be uncontrollable. Metaphor provides a schema through which such disorganizing affective experiences can be brought within the agency of the self. (Modell 1997, p. 210)

This concept is reminiscent of the experience of transference (which I am using in its broadest and most ubiquitous definition here). The experience of transference is important because it activates working memory and readies the individual for structural change.

The experience of transference and the use of metaphor in treatment enhance opportunities for learning, and, as a result, change. This change takes place, in part, due to the involvement of the various parts of the brain activated in the process. This process activates a number of brain centers, and, ascribing to a "split brain" theory, it particularly involves an integrated function of the right and left hemispheres (Pally 2000).

In a more philosophical vein, the use of metaphor, and its emotional sequelae, is reminiscent of the participants' descriptions to me:

> When we speak metaphorically, we use words and concepts in an unfamiliar way, one which trades for its effect on established meanings, on a relatively fixed way of classifying things.... A metaphoric use of language depends on

> there being prior meanings, and so inspires us to see one thing in new ways, which we can do only if we have articulated them differently to begin with. (Cavell 1993, p. 171)

Several authors localize the function of the emotions, specifically empathy, to the prefrontal orbital cortex. This structure is in the prefrontal lobe of the right hemisphere, usually activated under stress and essential to the perception of communication, especially of nonverbal cues, and the perceptions of the emotional states of others. "...the self-system is more localized in the right, rather than the left brain" (Schore 1994). This data gives Modell and Levin's concepts even more significance related to the activation, through metaphor, of a variety of brain centers, not just the right hemisphere.

I suggest that the experience of these face-to-face encounters, and the preparation for them, approximates the experience of the use of metaphor, as well as the experience of transference, which takes place between the actors involved. This relates to the definition of empathy, defined as *Einfühlung*, as the emotion experienced when the self directly recognizes the other and is recognized by the other. This is as much a "felt" experience as it is a cognitive experience.

My offender group, because of this compilation of experience, showed that an important internal shift occurs, which allows them to internalize the other's perspective, because of the emotional impact of seeing the other.

> The ability to take on the perspective of a distressed other also requires the ability to shift from a neutral or positive into a negative state and to tolerate distress within the self in order to be aware of and thereby read one's own internal emotional experience. In order to offer comfort to another the self must have access to an internal self-comforting mechanism that can regulate negative affect and shift it back into a positive state. (Schore 1994, p. 496)

Finally, it has been suggested by Masters' that a significant overarching concept to account for the meaning of restorative justice is the feminist ethic of care (Masters, 1997). This was first delineated by numerous feminist theoreticians in the 1980s as an answer to Kohlberg's model of the development of moral reasoning (Kohlberg and Diessner 1991) based on the sense that his model was gender-biased toward males, and saw females as being less morally developed. The ethic of care suggested that men see moral dilemmas as a conflict of rights to be solved by abstract formulaic reasoning, whereas women see moral dilemmas in more concrete and contextualized terms. Thus, men work from an ethic of justice, women from an ethic of care. The ethic of care defines the self as embedded in relationship, where the ethic of justice sees the self as ideally autonomous. When conflicts arise, men tend to compete, form hierarchies, rank, or take turns. Women attempt to deal with conflict in inclusive ways.

The original concept came under increasing attack as a model that attempted to put forth a wholly different developmental and moral course for men and women, a suggestion that was tenuous at best. As the concept has evolved, the ethic of care is now seen as less gendered and more related to values or culture.

Tronto best defines the concept in a way most relevant to my study participants, as a "contextual meta-ethical theory." This pushes the concept into moral development in its actual practice in which "one's moral imagination, character, and actions must respond to the complexity of a given situation" (Toronto 1993, p. 248). She further expands this to say:

> As a fully developed moral theory, the ethic of care will take the form of a contextual moral theory. Perhaps the most important characteristic of an ethic of care is that, within it, moral situations are defined not in terms of rights and responsibilities but in terms of relationships of care. The morally mature person understands the balance between caring for the self and caring for others. The perspective of care requires that conflict be worked out without damage to the continuing relationships. Moral problems can be expressed in terms of accommodating the needs of the self and of others, of balancing competition and cooperation, and of maintaining the social web of relations in which one finds oneself. (Toronto 1993, p. 249)

THE ILIAD OF HOMER

In *The Iliad*, Homer's rhapsodies serve the function of mediating the personal experience of those involved.

Not unlike many of my research subjects, who experienced "disrespect" from outside of themselves, Achilles was shamed by Agamemnon, who first deprived him of his honor by stealing his love, and then, after he abandoned the war, caused the death of his friend Patroclus who he had left to fight in his place.

I see Achilles as an epic hero, who has suffered a narcissistic injury compounded by trauma, who returns to the war in a "berserk state," having lost his humanity.

> So, the illustrious son of Priam begged for life but only heard a merciless voice in answer: Fool, don't talk to me of ransom. No more speeches. Before Patroclus met his day of destiny, true, it warmed my heart a bit to spare some Trojans: droves I took alive and auctioned off as slaves. But now not a single

Trojan flees his death … sons of Priam least of all! Come friend, you too must die. Why moan about it so? Even Patroclus died, a far, far better man than you. (Homer *Iliad* 21.110–20)

Because of his eagerness to kill Hector, Achilles, in his rage, kills so many Trojans that even the river, choked by the corpses, rises and asks Achilles to stop. He refuses. He is intent on his revenge.

And old king Priam was first to see him coming, surging over the plain, blazing like the star that rears at harvest, flaming up in its brilliance … and the old man moaned, flinging both hands high, beating his head and groaning deep he called, begging his dear son who stood before the gates, unshakable, furious to fight Achilles to the death. The old man cried, pitifully, hands reaching out to him, "Oh Hector! Don't just stand there, don't, dear child, waiting that man's attack …. You'll meet your doom at once …." (Homer *Iliad* 22.31–45)

Despite both Priam and his mother's pleas, Hector continued to wait for Achilles to come and fight him.

After killing Hector, and scoffing at his dying plea to not defile his body, Achilles lashed the body to his chariot:

… and now he was bent on outrage, on shaming noble Hector … lashed them to his chariot, left the head to drag and mounting the car, hoisting the famous arms aboard, he whipped his team to a run and breakneck on they flew, holding nothing back. (Homer *Iliad* 22.465–472)

This sight threw both Priam and his wife into fits of grief, along with most of the other Trojans witnessing the spectacle from behind the city walls.

But even the culmination of these violent acts didn't help Achilles' grief for his friend:

"Farewell, Patroclus, even there in the House of Death! Look—all that I promised once I am performing now: I've dragged Hector here for the dogs to rip him raw—and here in front of your flaming pyre I'll cut the throats of a dozen sons of Troy in all their shining glory, venting my rage on them for your destruction!" (Homer *Iliad* 23.22–27)

But Achilles kept on grieving for his friend, the memory burning on … and all subduing sleep could not take him, he turned and twisted side to side …. (Homer *Iliad* 24.4–6)

The gods, alarmed by Achilles' behavior, protect Hector's body from harm, so, as much as Achilles drags it about the walls of the city, no harm comes to it.

Apollo continued to be angry at Achilles' acts, admonishing the gods:

> But murderous Achilles—you gods, you choose to help Achilles, that man without a shred of decency in his heart … his temper can never bend and change—like some lion going his own barbaric way, giving in to his power, his brute force and wild pride, as down he swoops on the flocks of men to seize his savage feast. Achilles has lost all pity! No shame in the man … (Homer *Iliad* 24.45–52)

Eventually, Achilles' own mother, Thetis, a god herself, comes down from Mt. Olympus to try to help Achilles regain his humanity:

> My child—how long will you eat your heart out here in tears and torment? All wiped from your mind, all thought of food and bed? It's a welcome thing to make love to a woman …. You don't have long to live now …. I bring you a message from Zeus: he says the gods are angry with you now and he is rising over them all in deathless wrath that you in heartsick fury still hold Hector's body, here by your beaked ships, and will not give him back. O give him back at once—take ransom for the dead! (Homer *Iliad* 24.155–167)

With this, Achilles agrees to ransom Hector's body. The gods go to Priam and tell him to prepare for the trip to Achilles' camp, but not to be concerned, as he will be escorted and protected by Hermes. Hermes, in the role of the mediator in a restorative justice dialogue, prepares Priam to meet with Achilles in his camp. He promises that he will transport him safely into the camp, much as the mediator secures entrance of the victim into the prison.

It is in this meeting that the two come together and it is here the strength of the mediation process is felt. Given Achilles' softening to his mother's pleas, he begins to regain his capacity for pity, and thus his humanity.

Both Achilles and Priam are perpetrators, and survivors, as they are both racked with grief regarding the losses they have experienced throughout this long war.

When Hermes is successful in sneaking Priam past the others in Achilles' camp, and the two come face-to-face, eye-to-eye at last, Priam invokes the name of Achilles' father. Their almost immediate effort to find common ground through dialogue is reminiscent of many of the meetings I witnessed.

Priam pleads:

> Remember your own father, great godlike Achilles—as old as I am, past the threshold of deadly old age! No doubt the countrymen round about him plague him now, with no one there to defend him, beat away disaster. No one—but at least he hears you're still alive and his old heart rejoices, hopes rising, day by day, to see his beloved son come sailing home from Troy. But I—dear god, my life so cursed by fate …. I fathered hero sons in the wide realm of Troy and now not a single one is left, I tell you.

> … But one, one was left to me, to guard my walls, my people—the one you killed the other day, defending his fatherland, my Hector! (Homer *Iliad* 24.559–580)

And Priam's plea invokes in Achilles a great feeling, which overwhelms him. The two cry together, and experience deep grief and mourning.

> Those words stirred within Achilles a deep desire to grieve for his own father. Taking the old man's hand he gently moved him back. And overpowered by memory both men gave way to grief. Priam wept freely for man-killing Hector, throbbing, crouching before Achilles' feet as Achilles wept himself, now for his father, now for Patroclus once again, and their sobbing rose and fell throughout the house. (Homer *Iliad* 24.592–600)

This mourning then stirs empathy in Achilles, and he gives voice to it to Priam. At the same time, he also indicates that he accepts responsibility for his acts and the meaning of these acts to the father:

> Then, when brilliant Achilles had had his fill of tears and the longing for it had left his mind and body, he rose from his seat, raised the old man by the hand and filled with pity now for his gray head and gray beard, he spoke out winging words, flying straight to the heart: "Poor man, how much you've borne—pain to break the spirit! What daring brought you down to the ships, all alone, to face the glance of the man who killed your sons, so many fine brave boys? You have a heart of iron." (Homer *Iliad* 24.605–609)

The respect he shows Priam for simply coming to meet with him is also expressed by many of the offenders in this study, who respect the bravery of the victims.

Eventually, after Achilles asks his servants to prepare Hector's body, Hermes is successful in transporting Priam, with his son, out of the enemy camp. Priam returns the body to his family, and Achilles, true to his promise, calls off the war until the Trojans can have their customary period of mourning and burial. It is with the burial of Hector that Homer ends *The Iliad.*

The meanings that emerge strikingly through the words in this epoch are remorse and reconciliation. Gustafson suggests that it was left to the Apostle Paul to coin the word "reconciliation," related to the Iliad, as, apparently, Homer had no Greek equivalent. The mutual enactment of mourning, as is present in the dialogues, leads to a remarkably similar outcome.

Most momentous is the connection made between two people, engaged in a life-changing moment, and, I remind the reader of Lester and Anna Marie. In my interview with Anna Marie, she spoke of a portion of the videotaped meeting in which she, at the end of the encounter, reached out and took Lester's hand:

> He dropped his head and I glanced up at him, and here are these two tears just cascading—he did this, and on that tape, you can hear me pull a tissue from the box and I said, "Here." I swear to you that was really unconscious—my actions were as a mother to a child. And at that moment, I forgot that he was the child that murdered my child. At that moment, he was in great pain and I watched him—I felt his remorse. I watched him just crumble from this person to this person, for what he had done to Bob and to me. And I just don't have a hard heart, I guess. And I still didn't think I could touch him—I wasn't there, but I thought, he's sitting here with these tears—it was just so—the tears, and the tissue, and I just handed him a tissue.
>
> … And did you see the ending of the film where I put my hand across the table, they turned the sound down a lot … when I reached out and touched him, it was a blood-curdling scream that I'd held for thirteen years. I never allowed myself to let go that much. I'm such a lady, and I didn't want anybody to hear … . I didn't want anybody to experience the anguish inside, and I wouldn't even allow myself to. And in some way, reaching across, and what I say is, my soul, his soul, Bob's soul, they're entwined for eternity. This is a soul thing. And when I reached out and I took his hand, and I gripped it, and he put his other hand on mine, and he was just crying, and in some way, I was able—and I allowed myself—to release anguish and anger that I'd had for thirteen years. Thirteen and a half years. I never had done that before … . The only two people in that room at that point was the mother and the murderer. That's the only people that were there.

Compare Anna Marie's narrative about the reconciliation with Homer's:

> The majestic king of Troy slipped past the rest and kneeling down beside Achilles, clasped his knees and kissed his hands, those terrible, man-killing hands that had slaughtered Priam's many sons … so Achilles marveled, beholding majestic Priam. His men marveled too, trading startled glances. But Priam prayed his heart out to Achilles. … "Pity me in my own right, remember your own father! I deserve more pity … I have endured what no one on earth has ever done before—I put to my lips the hands of the man who killed my son." (Homer *Iliad* 24.559–591)

Bibliography

(1994). *Diagnositc and statistical manual of mental disorders*. Washington, DC, American Psychiatric Association.

Aitken, K. J. and C. Trevarthen. (1997). "Self/other organization in human psychological development." *Development and Psychopathology* 9: 653–677.

Akhtar, S. (1992). *Broken structures: Severe personality disorders and their treatment*. Northvale, NJ, Jason Aronson.

Allen, D. S. (2000). *The world of Prometheus: The politics of punishing in democratic Athens*. Princeton, NJ, Princeton University Press.

Arendt, H. (1963). *Eichmann in Jerusalem: A report on the banality of evil*. New York, Penguin Books.

Athens, L. H. (1992). *The creation of dangerous violent criminals*. Chicago, University of Illinois Press.

Athens, L. H. (1994). "The self as a soliloquy." *The Sociological Quarterly* 35(3): 521–532.

Athens, L. H. (1995). "Dramatic self change." *The Sociological Quarterly* 36(3): 571–586.

Athens, L. H. (1997). *Violent criminal acts and actors revisited*. Chicago, Univeristy of Illinois Press.

Atwood, G. E. and R. D. Stolorow. (1984). *Structures of subjectivity*. Hillsdale, NJ, Analytic Press.

Bard, M. and D. Sangrey. (1979). *The crime victim's book*. New York, Basic Books.

Blos, P. (1979). *The adolescent passage*. New York, International Universities Press.

Blumer, H. (1969). *Symbolic interactionism: Perspective and method*. Berkeley, University of California Press.

Bowlby, J. (1944). "Forty-four juvinile thieves: Their characters and home-life." *International Journal of Psychoanalysis* 25: 19–53.

Bowlby, J. (1980). *Attachment and loss: Vol. 3. Loss: Sadness and depression*. New York, Basic Books.

Breckenridge, C. C. and C. T. Anderson. (1981). The special care program: Exploring a future of prevention. *Treating families in the home*. M. Bryce and J. C. Lloyd (eds.). Springfield, Charles C. Thomas.

Bretherton, I. and K. A. Munholland. (1999). Internal working models in attachment relationships. *Handbook of attachment: Theory, research, and clinical applications*. J. Cassidy and P. R. Shaver (eds.). New York, The Guilford Press: 89–114.

Bretherton, I., et al. (1990). Assessing internal working models of the attachment relationship: An attachment story completion task for 3-year-olds. *Attachment in the preschool years: Theory, research, and intervention*. M. T. Greenberg, D. Cicchetti and E. M. Cummings (eds.). Chicago, University of Chicago Press.

Brooks, P. (1994). *Psychoanalysis and storytelling*. Oxford, Blackwell.

Burch, B. (1989). "Mourning and failure to mourn—an object relations view." *Contemporary Psychoanalysis* 25: 608–623.

Cavell, M. (1993). *The psychoanalytic mind: From freud to philosophy*. Cambridge, MA, Harvard University Press.

Cohler, B. J. and M. Freeman. (1993). Psychoanalysis and the developmental narrative. *The course of life: Early adulthood*. G. H. Pollock and S. I. Greenspan (eds.). Madison, International Universities Press, Inc. 5.

Denzin, N. K. (1989). *Interpretive interactionism*. Newbury Park, Sage Publications.

Denzin, N. K. (2001). *Interpretive interactionism*. Thousand Oaks, CA, Sage Publications.

Dietz, M. G. (1988). *Between the human and the divine: The political thought of Simone Weil*. Totowa, NJ, Rowman & Littlefield.

Eissler, K. R. (1947). *Searchlights on delinquency*. New York, International Universities Press, Inc.

Emde, R. N. (1983). "The prerepresentational self and its affective core." *The Psychoanalytic Study of the Child* 38: 165–192.

Emde, R. N. (1989). The infant's relationship experience: Developmental and affective aspects. *Relationship disturbances in early childhood*. A. J. E. Sameroff, R.N. New York, Basic Books.

Fagles, R., Ed. (1990). *Homer: The Iliad*. New York, Penguin Books.

Feldman Barrett, L. (2017). *How Emotions Are Made*. Boston, Houghton Mifflin Harcourt.

Fonagy, P. (1993). "Psychoanalytic and empirical approaches to developmental psychopathology: An object-relations perspective." *Journal of American Psychoanalytic Association* 41: 245–260.

Fonagy, P. (2001). *Attachment theory and psychoanalysis*. New York, The Other Press.

Fonagy, P. and M. Target. (1995). "Understanding the violent patient: The use of the body and the role of the father." *International Journal of Psychoanalysis* 76: 487–501.

Fonagy, P., et al. (1997). The development of violence and crime as it relates to security of attachment. *Children in a violent society*. J. D. Osofsky (ed.). New York, The Guildord Press: 150–177.

Foucault, M. (1991). *Discipline and punish*. London, Penguin Books.

Fraiberg, S. (1980). *Clinical studies in infant mental health: The first year of life.* London, Tavistock.

Geertz, C. (2000). *Available light: Anthropological reflections on philosophical topics.* Princeton, NJ, Princeton University Press.

Gilligan, J. (1996). *Violence: Our deadly epidemic and its causes.* New York, G.P. Putnam's Sons.

Goldberg, A. (1999). *Being of two minds: The vertical split in psychoanalysis and psychotherapy.* Hillsdale, The Analytic Press.

Grand, S. (2000). *The reproduction of evil: A clinical and cultural perspective.* Hillsdale, NJ, Analytic Press.

Greenberg, M. T., et al. (1993). "The role of attachment in the early development of disruptive behavior problems." *Development and Psychopathology* 5: 191–213.

Grotstein, J. S. (1986). "The psychology of powerlessness: Disorders of self-regulation and interactional regulation as a newer paradigm for psychopathology." *Psychoanalytic Inaquiry* 6: 93–118.

Grotstein, J. S. (2000). *Who is the dreamer who dreams the dream? A study of psychic presences.* Hillsdale, NJ, The Analytic Press.

Gustafson, D. L. (2001). *Encountering the other: Vision and values for the victim/offender peacemaking process.* Wichita, KS.

Halleck, S. L. (1971). *Psychiatry and the dilemmas of crime.* Berkeley, University of California Press.

Hallinan, J. T. (2001). *Going up the river: Travels in a prison nation.* New York, Random House.

Harter, S. (1999). *The construction of the self: A developmental perspective.* New York, The Guilford Press.

Hassoun, J. (1997). *The cruelty of depression: On melancholy.* Reading, MA, Addison-Wesley.

Hauser, M. D. (2006). *Moral Minds: How nature designed our universal sense of right and wrong.* New York, Hrper Collins.

Heider, F. (1958). *The psychology of interpersonal relations.* New York, Wiley.

Herman, J. L. (1992). *Trauma and recovery.* New York, Basic Books.

Hesse, E. and M. Main (2000). "Disorganized infant, child, and adult attachment: Collapse in behavioral and attentional strategies." *Journal of American Psychoanalytic Association* 48(4): 1097–1127.

Hickey, E. (1991). *Serial murderers and their victims.* Belmont, CA, Wadsworth.

Hillman, J. (1975). *Loose ends: Primary papers in archetypal psychology.* Dallas, TX, Spring Publications.

Homans, P. (1989). *The ability to mourn: Disillusionment and the social origins of psychoanalysis.* Chicago, The University of Chicago Press.

Howe, M. L. and M. L. Courage. (1993). "On resolving the enigma of infantile amnesia." *Psychological Bulletin* 113: 305–326.

James, B. (1994). *Handbook for the treatment of attachment-trauma problems in Children.* New York, Lexington Books.

Janoff-Bulman, R. (1992). *Shattered assumptions: Towards a new psychology of trauma.* New York, The Free Press.

Johnson, A. (1947). Sanctions for superego lacunae of adolescents. *Searchlights on Delinquency*. K. R. Eissler (ed.). New York, International Universities Press, Inc. Seminal paper on superego lacunae, parental projection.

Johnson, A. M. and M. D. Szurek. (1952). "The genesis of antisocial acting out in children and adults." *Psychoanalytic Quarterly* 21: 323–343.

Karen, R. (2001). *The forgiving self: The road from resentment to connection*. New York, Doubleday.

Karr-Morse, R. and M. S. Wiley. (1997). *Ghosts from the nursery: Tracing the roots of violence*. New York, The Atlantic Monthly Press.

Klein, G. S. (1976). *Psychoanalytic theory: An exploration of essentials*. New York, International Universities Press, Inc.

Kohlberg, L. and R. Diessner. (1991). A cognitive-developmental approach to moral attachment. *Intersections with attachment*. J. L. Gewirtz and W. M. Kurtines (eds.). Hillsdale, NJ, Lawrence Erlbaum Associates.

Kohut, H. (1971). *The analysis of the self*. New York, International Universities Press, Inc.

Kuhn, T. S. (1962). *The structure of scientific revolutions*. Chicago, The University of Chicago Press.

Lange, D. (1995). *Dorothea lange: Photographs of a lifetime*. New York, Aperture Monograph.

Lattimore, R., Ed. (1951). *The Iliad of Homer*. Chicago, University of Chicago Press.

Lear, J. (1993). "An interpretation of transference." *International Journal of Psychoanalysis* 74: 739–755.

Lewin, K. (1933). Environmental forces. *A handbook of child psychology*. C. Murchison. Worchester, Clark University Press: 590–625.

Lewis, D. O. (1997). "Objective documentation of child abuse and dissociation in twelve murderers with dissociative identity disorder." *American Journal of Psychiatry* 154(12): 1703–1710.

Lewis, D. O. (1998). *Guilty by reason of insanity: A psychiatrist explores the minds of killers*. New York, Fawcett Columbine.

Lewis, D. O. and D. Balla. (1976). *Delinquency and psychopathology*. New York, Grune & Stratton.

Lewis, D. O., et al. (1989). Child abuse, delinquency, and violent criminality. *Child maltreatment: Theory and research on the causes and consequences of child abuse and neglect*. D. Chiccetti and V. Carlson (eds.). Cambridge, Cambridge University Press.

Lewis, D. O., et al. (1979). "Violent juvenile delinquents: Psychiatric, neurological, psychological and abuse factors." *Journal of the American Academy of Child and Adolescent Psychiatry* 18: 307–319.

Lewis, T., et al. (2000). *A general theory of love*. New York, Random House, Inc.

Main, M. (2000). "The organized categories of infant, child, and adult attachment: Flexible vs. inflexible attention under attachment-related stress." *J.Amer. Psychoanal.Assn* 48(4): 1055–1096.

Main, M. and R. Goldwyn. (1984). "Predicting rejection of her infant from mother's representation of her own experiences: Implications for the abused-abusing intergenerational cycle." *Child Abuse and Neglect* 8: 203–217.

Main, M. and E. Hesse. (1990). Parents' unresolved traumatic experiences are related to infant disorganized attachment status: Is frightened and/or frightening parental behavior the linking mechanism? *Attachment in the preschool years: Theory, research, and intervention.* M. T. Greenberg, D. Cicchetti and E. M. Cummings (eds.). Chicago, University of Chicago Press.

Main, M., et al. (1985). Security in infancy, childhood, and adulthood: A move to the level of representation. *Growing points of attachment: Theory and research.* I. Bretherton and E. Waters (eds.). 50: 66–104.

Makkreel, R. A. (1975). *Dilthey: Philosopher of the human studies*. Princeton, Princeton University Press.

Masterson, J. F. (1980). "The role of the talionic impulse in the development of morality." *Bulletin of the Menninger Clinic* 45(5): 482–497.

Masters, Guy (1997). "Reintegrative shaming in theory and practice. thinking about feeling in criminology." Lancaster University. Unpublished doctoral dissertation.

Mayes, L. C. (1999). Clocks, engines, and quarks—love, dreams and genes: What makes development happen? *The psychoanalytic study of the child.* A. J. Solnit (ed.). New Haven, Yale University Press. 34: 169–192.

Mead, G. H. (1934). *Mind, self, and society*. Chicago, University of Chicago Press.

Meyers, W. C., et al. (1995). "Psychopathology, biopsychosocial factors, crime characteristics and classification of 25 homicidal youths." *Journal of the American Academy of Child and Adolescent Psychiatry* 34(11): 1483–1489.

Modell, A. H. (1997). Reflections on metaphor and affects. *The Annual of Psychoanalysis*. J. A. Winer. Hillsdale, NJ, Analytic Press. 25: 210–241.

Pally, R. (2000). *The mind-brain relationship*. London, Karknac Books.

Perry, B. (1997). Memories of fear: How the brain stores and retrieves physiologic states, feelings, behaviors and thoughts from traumatic events. *Images of the body in trauma*. J. Goodwin and R. Attias (eds.). New York, Basic Books.

Perry, B. D. (1994). Neurobiological sequelae of childhood trauma: Post-traumatic stress disorders in children. *Catecholamine Function in Post Traumatic Stress Disorder: Emerging Concepts*. M. Murberg (ed.). Washington, American Psychiatric Press, Inc.: 233–255.

Perry, B. D. (1995). Incubated in terror: Neurodevelopmental factors in the 'cycle of violence'. *Children, Youth and Violence: Searching for Solutions*. J. D. Osofsky (ed.). New York, Guilford Press.

Perry, B. D. (1996). Neurodevelopmental adaptations to violence: How children survive the intragenerational vortex of violence. Cleveland Ohio, Urban Child Research Center, Cleveland State University.

Perry, B. D., et al. (1995). "Childhood trauma, the neurobiology of adaptation and use-dependent development of the brain: How states become traits." *Infant Mental Health Journal* 16(4): 256–333.

Peterson, M. R. (2000). The search for meaning in the aftermath of homicide: A hermeneutic phenomenological study of families of homicide victims. *School of Social Work*. Minneapolis, University of Minnesota: 254.

Popper, K. R. (1963). *Conjectures and reflections: The growth of scientific knowledge*. New York, Harper & Row.

Post, S. L. (1980). Origins, elements, and functions of therapeutic empathy. *International Journal of Psychoanalysis, 61,* 277–294.

Radke-Yarrow, M., et al. (1985). "Patterns of attachment in two and three-year-olds in normal families and families with parental depression." *Child Development* 56: 884–893.

Rhodes, R. (1999). *Why they kill: The discoveries of a maverick criminoloogist.* New York, Alfred A. Knopf.

Rosenthal, R. (1966). *Experimenter effects in behavioral research.* New York, Appleton.

Rosenthal, R. (1989). "Definition and interpretation of interaction effects." *Psychological Bulletin* 105(1): 143–146.

Rosenthal, R. (1989). "Statistical procedures and the justification of knowledge in psychological science." *American Psychologist* 44(10): 1276–1284.

Rosenthal, R. and L. Jacobson. (1968). *Pygmalion in the classroom.* New York, Holt, Rinehart and Winston, Inc.

Rosenthal, R. and R. Lawson. (1964). "A longitudinal study of the effects of experimenter bias on the operant learning of laboratory rats." *Journal of Psychiatric Research* 2: 61–72.

Sameroff, A. J. and R. N. Emde (1989). Relationship disturbances in context. ks. *Relationship disturbances in early childhood: A developmental approach.* A. J. Sameroff and R. N. Emde (eds.). New York, Basic Boo.

Schore, A. (1994). *Affect regulation and the origin of the self: The neurobiology of emotional development.* Hillsdale, Lawrence Erlbaum Associates.

Schore, A. (1997). Interdisciplinary developmental research as a source of clinical models. *The neurobiological and developmental basis for psychotherapeutic intervention.* M. Moskowitz, C. Monk, C. Kaye and S. J. Ellman (eds.). Northvale, NJ, Jason Aronson, Inc.: 1–72.

Schore, A. N. (1994). *Affect regulation and the origin of the self: The neurobiology of emotional development.* Hillsdale, Lawrence Erlbaum Associates.

Schore, A. N. (2000). "Attachment and the regulation of the right brain." *Attachment & Human Development* 2(1): 23–47.

Schwartz, J. M., et al. (1996). "Systematic cerebral glucose metabolic rate changes after successful behavior modification treatment of obsessive-compulsive disorder." *Archives of General Psychiatry* 53: 109–113.

Shabad, P. (1993). "Repetition and incomplete mourning: The intergenerational transmission of traumatic themes." *Psychoanalytic Psychology* 10(1): 61–75.

Shane, M., et al. (1997). *Intimate attachments: Toward a new self psychology.* New York, The Guilford Press.

Siegel, D. J. (1999). *The developing mind: Toward a neurobiology of interpersonal experience.* New York, The Guilford Press.

Solomon, A. (2001). *The noonday demon: An atlas of depression.* New York, Scribner.

Spitz, R. A. (1945). Hospitalism. *The Psychoanalytic Study of the Child.* New York, International Universities Press. 1: 53.

Spitz, R. A. and K. M. Wolf. (1946). Anaclitic depression. *Psychoanalytic Study of the Child.* New York, International Universities Press, Inc. 2: 313.

Sroufe, L. A. (1989). Relationships, self, and individual adaptation. *Relationship disturbances in early childhood.* A. J. Sameroff and R. N. Emde (eds.). New York, Basic Books.

Stern, D. (1989). The representation of relational patterns: Developmental considerations. *Relationship disturbances in early childhood: A developmental approach*. A. J. Sameroff and R. N. Emde (eds.). New York, Basic Books.

Stern, D. N. (1985). *The interpersonal world of the infant*. New York, Basic Books.

Sullivan, H. S. (1953). *The interpersonal theory of psychiatry*. New York, W.W. Norton & Co.

Terr, L. (1983). "Chowchilla revisited: The effects of psychic trauma four years after a school-bus kidnapping." *American Journal of Psychiatry* 140: 1543–1550.

Terr, L. (1991). "Childhood traumas: An outline and overview." *American Journal of Psychiatry* 148: 1–20.

Toronto, J. (1993). Beyond gender difference to a theory of care. *An ethic of care: Feminist and interdisciplinary perspectives*. M. J. Larrabee (ed.). New York, Routledge: 240–257.

Trevarthen, C. and K. J. Aitken. (1994). "Brain development, infant communication, and empathy disorders: Intrinsic factors in child mental health." *Development and Psychopathology* 6(4): 597–633.

Ulman, R. B. and D. Brothers. (1988). *The shattered self: A psychoanalytic study of trauma*. Hillsdale, The Analytic Press.

Umbreit, M. S. (2001). *The handbook of victim offender mediation: An essential guide to practice and research*. San Francisco, Jossey-Bass.

van der Kolk, B. A. (1996). The complexity of adaptation to trauma: Self-regulation, stimulus discrimination, and characterological development. *Traumatic stress: The effects of overwhelming experience on mind, body, and society*. B. A. van der Kolk, A. C. McFarlane and L. Weisaeth (eds.). New York, The Guilford Press.

van der Kolk, B. A. (2014). *The Body Keeps the Score*. New York, Viking.

van der Kolk, B. A. and R. Fisler (1994). "Childhood abuse and neglect and loss of self-regulation." *Bulletin of the Menninger Clinic* 58: 145–168.

van der Kolk, B. A., et al. (1996). Dissociation and information processing in post-traumatic stress disorder. *Traumatic stress: The effects of overwhelming experience on mind, body, and society*. B. A. van der Kolk, A. C. McFarlane and L. Weisaeth (eds.). New York, The Guilford Press: 303–327.

Van Ness, D. W. and K. Strong. (1997). *Restoring justice*. Cincinnati, Anderson Publishing Co.

Weil, S. (1977). The Iliad, poem of might. *Simone Weil Reader*. G. A. Panichas (ed.). Wakefield, Rhode Island, Moyer Bell.

Widom, C. S. (1987). "The cycle of violence." *Science* 244: 160–165.

Winnicott, D. W. (1953). "Transitional objects and transitional phenomena." *International Journal of Psychoanalysis* 34: 89–97.

Winnicott, D. W. (1956). Primary maternal preoccupation. *Collected Papers*. New York, Basic Books: 300–305.

Index

About the Author

Chad C. Breckenridge received his MSW at the University of Minnesota and his PhD at the Institute for Clinical Social Work in Chicago.

He was president of the National Federation of Societies for Clinical Social Work from 1994 to 1996, and was elected as a Distinguished Practitioner in Clinical Social Work in the National Academy of Practice in 1997.

He lives in Minneapolis, Minnesota, with his wife, the artist Sally Brown, and continues to teach at the graduate level and maintain a private practice in psychotherapy.

www.ingramcontent.com/pod-product-compliance
Ingram Content Group UK Ltd.
Pitfield, Milton Keynes, MK11 3LW, UK
UKHW040154091026
15587UKWH00018B/269

9 781498 558518